Learning C#

A Practical Approach

- Volume 1 -

Bruce Schurter

Learning C#: A Practical Approach - Volume 1

Infinite Root Software Inc.
663 South Rancho Santa Fe Road #282
San Marcos, CA 92078
http://www.infiniteroot.com

Ordering Information:
Quantity sales. Special discounts are available on quantity purchases by corporations, associations, and others. For details, contact the publisher at the address above.

ISBN-13: 978-0-9967888-0-9
ISBN-10: 0996788808

First Edition

Cover photo: Sawyer Glacier, Tracy Arm fjord, Alaska © Bruce Schurter

This book is dedicated to my family, without whom this would not have been possible.

To Caroline, my dearest wife, who supported me through long, sleepless nights and endless weekends sitting in front of the computer.

To Caitlyn and Brianna who were very patient with daddy while he slipped away to quickly write a paragraph or two. I promise, we'll get the dollhouse done now!

Contents at a Glance

Table of Contents

About the Author

Bruce Schurter has been a software engineer since Commodore 64s were considered cutting edge. Currently, he works for Intrusion Inc., a company specializing in network secutiry, as a Principal Software Engineer. Bruce is also founder and Chief Software Architect of Infinite Root Software Inc. where he develops software solutions for a wide variety of customers, mostly using the .NET Framework and the Windows environment. Bruce has also been an instructor at UC San Diego Extension since 1999, teaching all levels of C# and Visual Basic, software architecture and distributed programming. Besides programming, he also enjoys martial arts, woodworking, sketching, Lego and spending as much time with his family as humanly possible.

Introduction

Welcome to the exciting world of programming with curly braces and semicolons!

Who Should Read This Book

This book is for people new to the world of programming with C# and .NET. Even if you have experience programming in another language, this text will describe features specific to C# and the .NET Framework and help you make the transition to this language.

System Requirements

As this is a programming book you will be required to enter programs into a computer. Clearly, you can read the book without performing any of the exercises, however there is no substitute for actually slamming keys and seeing the results of your labors. Here are the recommended minimum requirements:

- Intel Core x86/x64 compatible PC with 1GB RAM
    - Preferred i3 or better processor with 4GB RAM
- Windows 7 or newer operating system
- Visual Studio 2015 (or newer) Community Edition
    - Preferred Professional Edition or better

Formatting Conventions

Naming Conventions

Due to the necessity of displaying special terms directly within the text of the book, special formatting is used to help call those items out.

Naming Conventions

Type	Description	Examples

Keyword	Keywords are special, reserved words used by C#, such as "for", "int" and "do". They are presented in a fixed-width font and blue (for color editions of the book).	`for`
		`int`
		`do`

Type names	Types are special constructs, such as classes, structs and enums, that encapsulate some distinct data and functionality. They are shown as a turquoise color (for color editions of the book).	Console DateTime ConsoleColor
Methods	Methods are named blocks of code that can be called by other code. Methods are indicated with a trailing set of parenthesis.	Console.ReadLine()
Variables	Variables are named memory locations that contain a value. Variables are shown in italics.	*x* *name* *today*

Keyboard Actions

When special key presses are required the key names are displayed in a special font that looks like a key on a keyboard. For instance, if you are requested to press the "F5" key, it will displayed as such: [F5]

Occasionally, several keys must be pressed simultaneously (or as close to it as humanly possible), known as a chord. The keys of a chord are joined with a "+" symbol between them. An example of this would be bringing up the "Run" window of the operating system which requires holding down the Windows key then pressing the "R" key. This would be displayed as: [Win]+[R]

Some keyboard commands require multiple successive chords or keystrokes where each chord is separated by a comma ",": [Ctrl]+[E], [C]

Many of the keyboard shortcuts described in this book are based on the C# programing environment settings of Visual Studio. If some shortcuts are not working for you it is possible you have a different environment setting.

Code Samples

As this book focuses on programming in the C# language there will be many code samples throughout its pages. For examples that only require one line of text the code will be displayed as an indented line with a monospace typeface as such:

```
Console.WriteLine("Hello World!");
```

However, for longer and more complex code samples a code block with line numbers will be used instead of a single line.

```
1 static void Main(string[] args)
2 {
3   Console.WriteLine("This is a number: {0} and a string: {1}", 123456,
      "Hello World!");
4   Console.ReadLine();
5 }
```

Note that the line numbers do not indicate the actual line numbers as they would appear in Visual Studio, rather they are relative to first line of code in the sample. Also, if a line of text is longer than the format allowed by the book it is continued on the next line and the line number will not increase until the next complete statement, as shown between lines 3 & 4.

Electronic copies of the code samples in this book can be downloaded at:

```
http://www.infiniteroot.com/learningcsharp
```

My Two Cents

Although programming falls under the discipline of computer science, it frequently feels more like computer ***art***. This is primarily due to the fact that individual problems can be solved in many distinct ways. Some of these ways are "better" than others. "Better" is in quotes because good coding is subjective and one person's elegant code could be another's bowl of spaghetti. This book attempts to present information as factually as possible; however, sometimes I like to chime in with my opinion on the subject. These sections will be clearly identified as follows:

In these blocks I will voice my opinion about certain topics and how I dealt with them in my professional career. By no means should you take what I say in here as gospel, rather use it to help form your own opinions.

I wish you the best of luck in your learning endeavors and hope you find this book a useful stepping stone on your way to programming excellence!

Now, on with the show…

1

1. Introducing C# and the .NET Framework

C♯, pronounced "See Sharp" is one of Microsoft's primary programmng languages designed to work with the .NET Framework. The name is typically written as C# since not all fonts support the "sharp" character (Unicode 0x266F) but all have the similar looking number symbol. Before learning the technical details of programming with C# it is important to investigate the language's history and its ties to the .NET Framework.

1.1 History of C#

In 1995, Sun Microsystems released a revolutionary new programming language called Java. Based on the popular C and C++ syntax, this language was designed to work with virtually all contemporary operating systems, promising a "write-once, run anywhere" environment. Java is able to be compiled once on a single machine and run on any operating system due to the use of byte code in conjunction with a runtime specifically designed for the target operating system. Byte code, which is the result of Java program compilation, is unlike native machine code as it does not utilize native commands available to operating systems running on various CPUs. Instead, the runtime, which is designed specifically for a given operating system and CPU, takes the byte code and converts it to native machine code just prior to execution. This is known as "just-in-time" compilation. Although this provides optimzations over a strictly interpreted language, or a language that is evaluated and compiled as it is executed like many scripting languages, it typically does not reach the same performance levels of a program comiled natively for a specific environment like C and C++. However, the performance shortcomings are typically acceptable as they are offset by the speed of development, especially for business-class applications.

Microsoft saw great potential in the Java environment and created their own proprietary version of Java called Visual J++. Unfortunately, Microsoft did not adhere completely to the Java language specification by adding optimizations designed to make Java programs run faster under Windows. This led to litigation between Sun and Microsoft and ultimately resulted in the abandonment of Visual J++. However, Microsoft was not deterred and still believed in the concept of managed programs, or code that runs in conjunction with a runtime environment like Java.

The C# programing language was developed in the early 2000's and formally released as C# 1.0 in 2002 with Visual Studio .NET 2002. The primary developer of the language, Anders

Hejlsberg, was also responsible for other popular languages such as Turbo Pascal and Delphi prior to coming to Microsoft. In fact, Anders was the lead architect of the Visual J++ project so he had first-hand knowledge of the benefits and limitations of the Java language and runtime. Like Java, the goal of C# was to marry the popular C and C++ syntax with the rapid application development benefits of Microsoft's Visual Basic and Visual C++. Since Java had been around for several years prior to C#'s implementation, the development team was able to design a language that included the best features of Java and provided features desired by Java programmers that could not easily be retrofitted into the Java language.

The one drawback to Microsoft's implementation of the .NET Framework, the runtime for C# and the other .NET languages, is that they solely focused on Windows and no other operating systems. This decision, while controversial, makes sense since as of 2015 over 90% of traditional desktop and laptop computers still run some flavor of Windows. This number is actually a *decrease* from previous years as Mac OS X and Linux are growing at a small but steady rate. However, a group called Xamarin, completely independent from Microsoft, developed a compatible framework called Mono that allows C# programmers to target Linux and Mac OS X. In 2015, Microsoft released .NET Core, which is an open-source implementation of the .NET Framework. Although it does not contain the entire framework, it does include the core pieces of the CLR (Common Language Runtime) and BCL (Base Class Libraries) so it can be freely implemented on other operating systems. In fact, Mono 4 was re-written to utilize the .NET Core source code bringing it closer to the Windows native implementation.

1.2 C# Basics

C# and the .NET Framework can be used to create applications on a wide variety of hardware and operating systems. Currently, C#, in conjunction with some flavor of the .NET Framework, is supported on all versions of Windows desktop and server since 2000, Windows Mobile/Phone, Linux and Mac OS X. C# can be used to create applications of almost every variety, from business application to games. The following is a brief list of application types supported by C#:

- Console applications – Text-based programs that run within the context of a command console (think traditional DOS applications).
- Windows GUI applications – Graphical, window-based applications with buttons, text boxes, dropdown lists, etc., typically interfaced with a mouse, touch screen or keyboard.
- Web-based applications – Applications that are run through a browser like Internet Explorer, Edge, Chrome or Firefox.
- Mobile applications – Programs that can be run on tablets, PDAs or smart phones.
- Modern applications – Programs designed to take advantage of Windows 8 (and newer) modern tile-based interface.
- Services – Programs that run on a server providing data or other functionality for clients.

C# is a multi-paradign langauage that owes its syntax to traditional C and C++. C# is considered multi-paradigm because it is comprised of features of the following paradigms:

- Structured

- Imperative
- Object-oriented (OOP)
- Event-driven
- Functional
- Generic
- Reflective
- Concurrent

Structured Programming

The structured programming paradigm is a paradigm with the goal of making code easier to read and to reduce development time, and therefore costs. Structured programs are combination of three different control structrues, subroutines and blocks. The control sturcutes are identified as:

- Sequence – statements executed in a specified order
- Selection – statements executed based on the state of a program, such as `if` and `switch` statements
- Iteration – statements that are executed a number of times until a specified state is achieved, such as `for` and `while` loops

Subroutines, or methods in C#, are a mechanism for grouping a sequence together that can be executed or called via a single statement. Blocks, like subroutines, are a mechanism to group a sequence together as if they are a single statement.

One of the common beliefs among structured programming proponents is that the `goto` command is evil as it can lead to "spaghetti code". This sentiment is also frequenelty expressed by C# programmers as well.

Imperative Programming

In simplest terms, imperative programming involves the changing of state, or memory contents, to achieve desired results. With most imperative languages, variables represent the state that is manipulated to calculate results and dictate the flow of execution.

Object-Oriented Programming

Object-oriented programming (OOP) deals with objects (data structures) that are composed of data variables and methods that manipulate that data. With procedural programming, a subset of imperative programming, methods are the focus of the code. OOP, however, takes an object-first approach. Therefore, with procedural programming, more emphasis is placed on the "how" aspect of coding while with OOP the emphasis is placed on the "what".

Event-Driven Programming

Event-driven programming is a paradigm where the flow of execution of a program is determined by events, or actions taken by a user or some other signal generated by code. Most program user interfaces function based on this premise, where the user interacts with the code by clicking buttons, swiping screens or typing on a keyboard. Basically, event-driven programming is all about responding to input in a non-sequntial manner.

Functional Programming

Functional programming is almost the opposite of imperative programming in that computation is the execution of mathematical functions and avoids changing state. Functional programming is useful for solving complex problems without the side-effects that may occur with mutable, or changing, data.

Generic Programming

Generic programming is paradigm where classes and algorithms are written using types that have yet to be defined. Known as template programming in other languages, generics provides a mechanism to program in a general manner regardless of the data type that will be utilized in the code.

Reflective Programming

Reflection in programming is the ability for a program to examine itself, possibly making changes to its own code at runtime.

Concurrent Programming

The concurrent programming paradigm is one of the most complicated yet one of the most useful styles of programming. The idea is to allow multiple, simultaneous paths of execution, potentially speeding up the processing of certain algorithms. Virtually all computers sold today employ CPUs that contain at least two cores, or essentially two CPUs joined together into a single unit. The more cores a CPU contains the more concurrent code can be executed.

1.3 Structure of a C# Program

A C# program is comprised of at least one ".cs" file that contains the code to compile and execute. Typically, a C# program file contains the following sections:

- `using` directives

- `namespace` declaration
    - `class` or `struct`
        - Methods, like Main(), that are to be executed

The simplest executable program type is a console application which will be discussed in detail in Chapter 3. Essentially a console application opens a command prompt window which contains only text. Text can be output to the console window or input via the keyboard. The following code snippet shows the basic structure of a C# console application:

Listing 1-1. Sample C# Application Code

```
1  using System;
2
3  namespace HelloWorld
4  {
5    class Program
6    {
7      static void Main(string[] args)
8      {
9        // All code goes here...
10     }
11   }
12 }
```

For many C# application types, the Main() method represents the entire life of the program. In other words, when the program is run, the code contained with the curly braces of Main() is executed. Once the last line of code before the end curly brace is executed the program terminates. In the above example the only code between the curly braces is a single comment so this program will essentially do nothing. However, once you learn new commands and replace that comment with functional code, the program will become much more interesting.

On line 3 you will notice the `namespace` declaration. By default, this is the same name as the project and it is used for organizational purposes only and doesn't really affect how your code behaves. Try not to worry about it now – just don't delete it from your code!

1.4 The .NET Framework

Although C# is a language that can technically have a compiler written for it independent of any runtime it is most commonly associated with the .NET Framework. All of the memory management, library access and operating system interfacing is actually handled by different parts of the .NET Framework, essentially making C# dependent on the framework. In reality, C# can work in conjunction with any runtime as long as that runtime implements specific functionality defined by the Common Language Infrastructure. The .NET Framework is actually a set of many interoperating subsystems that together provide the runtime environment that languages like C#, F# and Visual Basic depend upon.

CLI – Common Language Infrastructure

The Common Language Infrastructure, or CLI, is the specification that defines how programs written to target the .NET Framework will interface with its runtime components. In general, the CLI encompasses four areas:

1. The Common Type System (CTS)

The CTS describes data types, their sizes and how they are interfaced in memory. As the word "common" implies, all of the languages that target this specification must work with these data types in a common manner. This is essential to accomplish one of the main goals of the .NET Framework which is language interoperability.

2. Metadata

Metadata is used to describe the contents of a program in a language-agnostic manner. This metadata can be used by tools like Visual Studio's IntelliSense to display additional help to the programmer. Metadata can also be used by multiple tools to provide a conventient interchange mechanism between them.

3. The Common Language Specification (CLS)

The CLS defines a set of conventions that a programming language and a runtime must both agree to for proper operation. In the case of C# and the .NET Framework, the CLS specifies how the two must communicate with each other. Since the same rules also apply to other languages, such as Visual Basic, the CLS guarantees that programs written in different langauges to accomplish the same task will work almost identically.

4. The Virtual Execution System (VES)

The virtual execution system implements and enforces the CTS equirements. It is responsible for loading and executing programs targeting the CLI. The VES, as implemented by the .NET Framework, is called the Common Language Runtime, or CLR.

CLR – Common Language Runtime

You may have heard that C# is a "managed" language. What exactly does that mean? Let's look at unmanaged languages to help answer this question. C and C++ are unmanaged langauges which means that there is no runtime governing how programs compiled using those languages operate. For instance, to create a new data in memory in C or C++ requires a memory allocation call. Likewise, when the data is no longer needed the memory must be returned so it can be reused somewhere else. Failure to do so results in memory leaks. C and C++ also allow direct access to memory using pointers. This feature can greatly enhance the speed of an application but it can also lead to massive headaches if memory is changed at an invalid location. As you may have guessed, manged languages, for the most part, don't allow direct memory allocation or access. Instead, a runtime engine is responsible for allocating, deallocating and accessing memory. In the .NET Framework, the CLR is responsible for all of these tasks.

Just-in-Time Compilation

The CLR is the Virtual Execution System component of the .NET Framework and manages the execution of .NET programs. One of the key components of the CLR is the Just-in-Time (JIT) compiler. When a C# or Visual Basic (or any CLI language) program is compiled the result is not native code that can be executed directly on a computer. Instead, the result is CIL (Common Intermediate Language) byte code. This CIL code is a series of assembler-like instructions that describe the low-level operations that correspond to the original source language instructions. The output CIL is packaged into a file, or group of files, called an assembly. CIL assemblies are then deployed to a destination computer or device where they await execution. When a .NET assembly is run, the appropriate version of the CLR is loaded and uses JIT compilation to optimize the CIL into native machine instructions. If the .NET Framework is not installed on the target machine then the CLR is not found and the program will not execute.

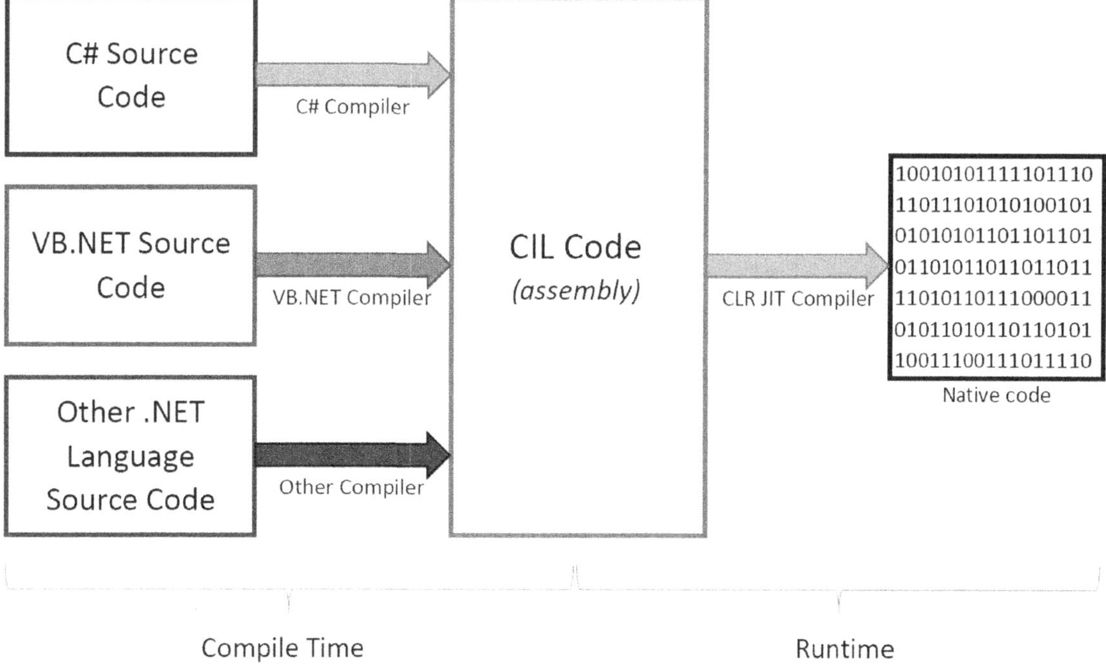

Figure 1-1. CLR JIT Compilation

It is possible to pre-compile to native code thus avoiding the use of the CLR JIT compiler. A tool called the Native Image Generator (`ngen.exe`) is supplied with every version of the .NET Framework. It is a command line executable and it is not directly available from within Visual Studio; therefore, understanding its command line arguments is critical to ensure a successful compilation. Two of the benefits of pre-compilation are improved memory use in a shared application environment and faster startup times due to the elminiation of JIT compilation. Just be aware that using pre-compilation requires more effort at build-time and can complicate some deployment scenarios. The specifics of these issues are not important at this juncture but they are well documented on MSDN and other .NET-centric web sites.

Common Intermediate Language

The following C# project is pretty much as simple as it gets. It is a console application that outputs the text "Hello World!" to the console window and then terminates.

Listing 1-2. Hello World Example C# Project

```
using System;

namespace HelloWorld
{
  class Program
  {
    static void Main(string[] args)
    {
      Console.WriteLine("Hello world!");
    }
  }
}
```

When this code is compiled in Visual Studio, a process that will be discussed in greater detail in Chapter 2, an assembly called "HelloWorld.exe" is generated. This assembly is composed of CIL code that looks like:

Listing 1-3. Example CIL

```
.method private hidebysig static void  Main(string[] args) cil managed
{
  .entrypoint
  // Code size       13 (0xd)
  .maxstack  8
  .language '{3F5162F8-07C6-11D3-9053-00C04FA302A1}', '{994B45C4-E6E9-11D2-903F-00C04FA302A1}', '{5A869D0B-6611-11D3-BD2A-0000F80849BD}'
// Source File 'C:\Users\Bruce\SkyDrive\Learning C Sharp\Samples\Chapter01\HelloWorld\Program.cs'
//000008:    {
  IL_0000:  nop
//000009:      Console.WriteLine("Hello world!");
  IL_0001:  ldstr      "Hello world!"
  IL_0006:  call       void [mscorlib]System.Console::WriteLine(string)
  IL_000b:  nop
//000010:    }
  IL_000c:  ret
} // end of method Program::Main
```

The above CIL represents the compiled form of the C# code in Listing 1-2. The comments with the line numbers show the original source code followed by the corresponding CIL instructions. It is this code that is further compiled to native machine code when executed by the CLR.

To view the CIL code of an assembly, Visual Studio contains a tool called the Intermediate Language Disassembler ("ildasm.exe") which can be executed from the "Developer Command Prompt for VS2015". From the main dialog's "File" menu, the assembly executable file can be opened. Then, the entire assembly can be inspected, including its manifest and compiled CIL code.

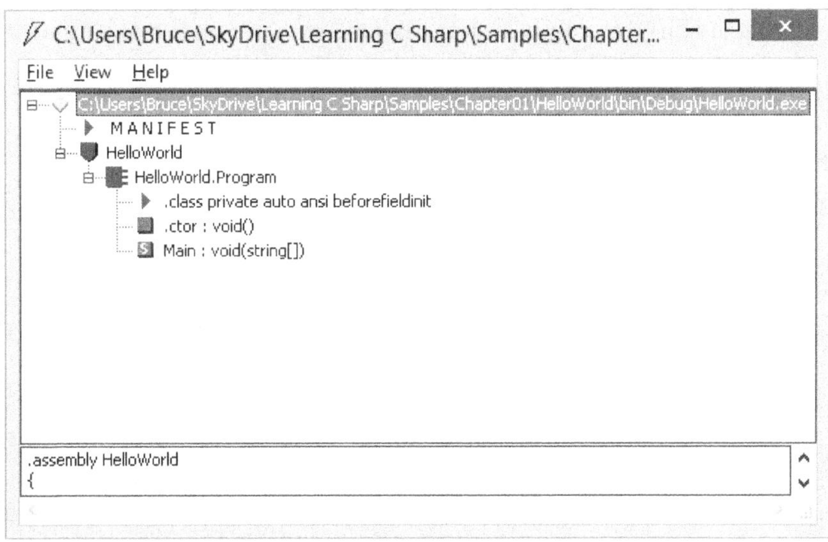

Figure 1-2. Main Dialog

HelloWorld.Program::Main : void(string[])

Find Find Next

```
.method private hidebysig static void  Main(string[] args) cil managed
{
  .entrypoint
  // Code size       13 (0xd)
  .maxstack  8
  .language '{3F5162F8-07C6-11D3-9053-00C04FA302A1}', '{994B45C4-E6E9-
// Source File 'C:\Users\Bruce\SkyDrive\Learning C Sharp\Samples\Chapt
//000008:         {
  IL_0000:  nop
//000009:              Console.WriteLine("Hello world!");
  IL_0001:  ldstr      "Hello world!"
  IL_0006:  call       void [mscorlib]System.Console::WriteLine(string
  IL_000b:  nop
//000010:         }
  IL_000c:  ret
} // end of method Program::Main
```

Figure 1-3. Main() CIL

ILDASM has limited functionality but is sufficient for most tasks requiring inspection of CIL. There are third party tools, such as Redgate's .NET Reflector, which provide more robust CIL disassemblers, but most are not free.

Garbage Collection

One of the key features of manged runtime environments is memory management. Typically, a program managed by a runtime must utilize that runtime's services to allocate and access memory. The .NET CLR in particular is responsible for allocating and deallocating memory in the heap, a location in memory to store large amounts of data. Whenever a program makes a request for heap memory the CLR finds a location that can accommodate the size of memory requested and assigns that memory chunk for use by the requester. When the CLR detects that this memory is no longer in use it will reclaim the memory and make it available to other requesters. This process is known as garbage collection. In addition to allocating and deallocating memory, the garbage collector also defragments and compresses the memory to avoid running out of places to store new data. This defragmentation process is why C# generally doesn't allow direct access to memory contents using pointers since the location of data can change dramatically over the course of a program's execution.

.NET Framework Versions

As of July, 2015, there have been 10 releases of the .NET Framework, starting with version 1.0 and culminating in version 4.6. Some of the frameworks have been released in lock-step with Visual Studio; however, several versions have been deployed without an explicit version of Visual Studio to support changes. The following chart shows the releases of the .NET Framework and the version of C# supported with each release.

Table 1-1. .NET Framework, C# and Visual Studio Versions

.NET Version	CLR	Released	C# Version	Visual Studio
1.0	1.0	2002	1.0	2002
1.1	1.1	2003	1.2	2003
2.0	2.0	2005	2.0	2005
3.0	2.0	2006		
3.5	2.0	2007	3.0	2008
4.0	4	2010	4.0	2010
4.5	4	2012	5.0	2012
4.5.1	4	2013		2013
4.5.2	4	2014		
4.6	4	2015	6.0	2015

As you can see, a new .NET Framework is released almost every calendar year. However, you will also notice that the CLR is not always updated with each new framework. For instance, the 3.0 and 3.5 frameworks actually depend on the 2.0 version of the CLR deployed with the .NET Framework version 2.0. The C# language version is also quite different from the framework version as it is also developed on a different schedule from the framework. Complicating matters is the version of Visual Studio used to build .NET applications. Newer versions of Visual Studio can target versions of the .NET Framework released after that particular Visual Studio was released. So, an application built using Visual Studio 2013 can target the 4.6 framework. Just be aware that any new language changes, such as those specific to C# 6.0, may not be valid within the code editor of Visual Studio 2013. As a rule of thumb, try to use the version of Visual Studio released at about the same time as the target framework or newer.

Class Library

Included with the .NET Framework is a set of class libraries that provide additional functionality to C# programs such as access to the underlying operating system, the file system and network resources. The majority of the types witin the class library belong to the System.* and Microsoft.* namespaces. The class library is composed of two parts, the Foundation Class Library (FCL) and the Base Class Library (BCL).

FCL

The Foundation Class Library (FCL) contains the basic classes and types required by the .NET CLR. The FCL is a smaller subset of the class library than the BCL and is present within the .NET Compact Framework, Silverlight and Mono (open source CLI implementation). Most of the underlying code of the FCL is contained within `mscorlib.dll`, `System.dll` and `System.core.dll`.

BCL

The Base Class Library (BCL) includes the classes and types necessary to work with Windows Forms, ADO.NET, ASP.NET, Language Independent Query (LINQ), Windows Presentation Foundation (WPF), and the Workflow Foundation (WF). The BCL actually encompasses the FCL in addition to these other items. Whereas the FCL provides the basic types and functionality for programming, the BCL includes many utilities and helpers to interact with the operating system and users.

The .NET Framework Stack

The .NET Framework Stack is a representation of the individual components in each version of the framework. Typically, each major release of the framework incorporates new technology that is added to the technology stack. Like a stack of coins, the .NET Framework Stack is typically depicted as a vertical stack of modules with the oldest technology at the bottom of the stack and the newest at the top. The following diagram and descriptions illustrate the .NET Framework as it currently exists. Any new technology added to the framework in future versions would be added to the top of the stack.

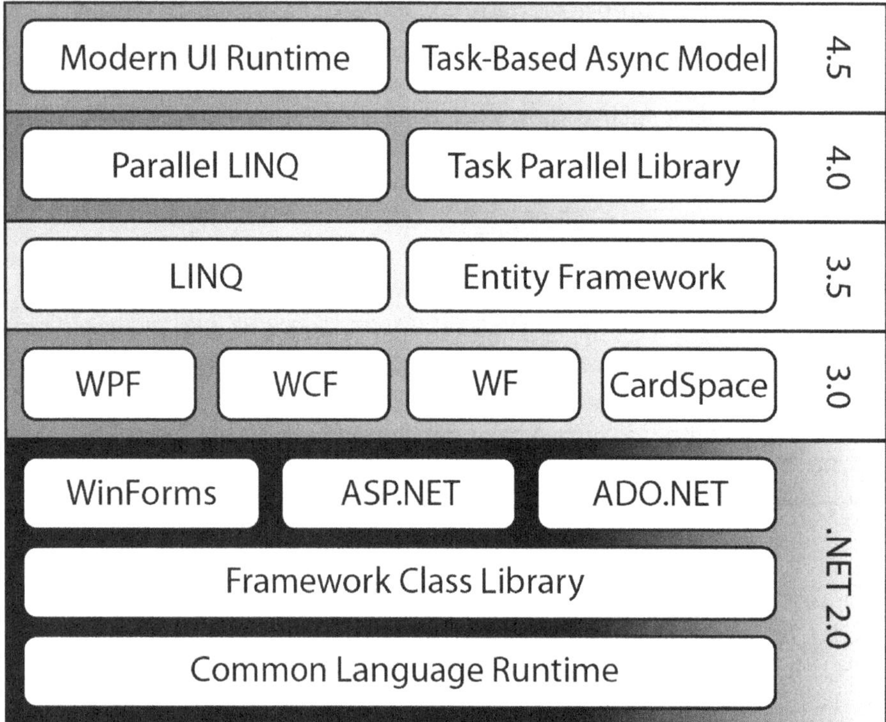

Figure 1-4. The .NET Framework Stack

WinForms (Windows Forms)

The WinForms libraries provide a mechanism for designing native Windows user interface applications. This technology uses GDI+ (Graphics Device Interface Plus) to draw windows, controls, images and text to the screen. GDI+ is predominantly a two-dimensional drawing engine and has a simple learning curve. WinForms is sometimes considered "old-style" Windows programming having been superceded by WPF. However, the simplicity of the programming model makes it ideal for rapid business-style application development.

ASP.NET

ASP.NET (Active Server Pages) actually encompasses several different technologies for programming web-based interfaces. Traditional ASP.NET WebForms uses a WYSIWYG (What You See Is What You Get) interface similar to WinForms but designed to produce HTML. ASP.NET MVC (Model View Controller) uses a more modern, REST-like approach to deliver web resources. REST stands for Representational State Transfer and is a very popular programming architecture for modern applications. Finally, ASP.NET Web API provides client-server programming interfaces to deliver resources other than web pages. Many parts of ASP.NET are developed out of sequence from the .NET Framework and can be updated using the NuGet package management system.

ADO.NET

ADO.NET (ActiveX Data Objects) is the primary technology in .NET for accessing relational databases like SQL Server and Oracle. ADO.NET allows the programmer to work with data in the .NET language of their choice using CTS types rather than raw binary or text. Much of the focus on ADO.NET has been shifted to LINQ-to-SQL and Entity Framework.

WPF

WPF (Windows Presentation Foundation) is a UI technology that delivers better resolution and performance than traditional WinForms. WinForms is primarily raster-based (bitmaps/pixels) while WPF is vector-based (lines/shapes). WPF is fantastic at scaling due to its vector-based nature and includes storyboarding and animation. While WinForms is designed using the language of your choice (C#, VB, etc.), WPF also utilizes a language called XAML (eXtensible Application Markup Language) for layout. WPF has a much higher learning curve than WinForms so it is not always preferred for business applications.

WCF

WCF (Windows Communication Foundation) is .NET's primary distributed programming technology. WCF allows programmers to define services that can execute code remotely from clients, either on the local network or on the other side of the world.

WF

WF (Windows Workflow Foundation) provides a graphical flowchart-like interface for designing workflows. Main functionality is accomplished using activites that can be linked together to accomplish complex tasks. Activities can be scheduled to run at specific intervals or as data is passed to an activity.

CardSpace

CardSpace was an identity management system released alongside .NET Framework 3.0 but has since been abandoned.

LINQ

LINQ (Language Independent Query) makes it possible to perform complex SQL-like queries directly in C# or Visual Basic. LINQ works with many providers such as database engines, XML and POCOs (Plain Old CLR Objects).

Entity Framework

Entity Framework (EF) is Microsoft's open source object-relational mapping (ORM) technology. EF uses .NET class objects (models) to represent data tables and properties to connect the models together. Originally released as part of .NET 3.5, EF is now developed out-of-band from the framework and can be updated using NuGet.

Parallel LINQ

Parallel LINQ (PLINQ) allows LINQ queries to run parallelized, utilizing tasks (threads) to increase performance.

Task Parallel Library

The Task Parallel Library (TPL) enhances and simplifies the threading model provided by the .NET Framework BCL making multi-threaded programming much simpler.

Modern UI Runtime

The Modern UI Runtime is the set of .NET libraries that provide access to the Windows Runtime (WinRT). This runtime exposes features of the Windows 8 (and above) tile-based app interface.

Task-Based Async Model

The Task-Based Async Model added improvements to the TPL by providing new constructs to simplify the execution and synchronization of tasks.

1.5 Silverlight

Silverlight is not actually part of the .NET Framework; instead it is an independent framework that contains a subset of its functionality. Silverlight is a "portable" framework designed to be used as a browser plug-in, much like Adobe's Flash. Its UI components are very similar to WPF and code can be easily ported from one to the other. Microsoft is no longer planning future releases of this technology but it can still be found in use, especially for video streaming sites.

1.6 .NET Core

Simultaneous with the release of the .NET Framework 4.6, Microsoft released .NET Core which is an open-source, partial implementation of the .NET Framework. Unlike the full .NET Framework which only runs on Windows operating systems, .NET Core has been developed with compatibility for Windows, Linux and Mac OS X. The general purpose of .NET Core is to make the runtime modular, allowing the programmer to pick and choose the individual components needed for an application rather than depending on the entire BCL. Initially, .NET

Core targets Windows Store applications and ASP.NET 5 applications but other application types can be developed using the new framework.

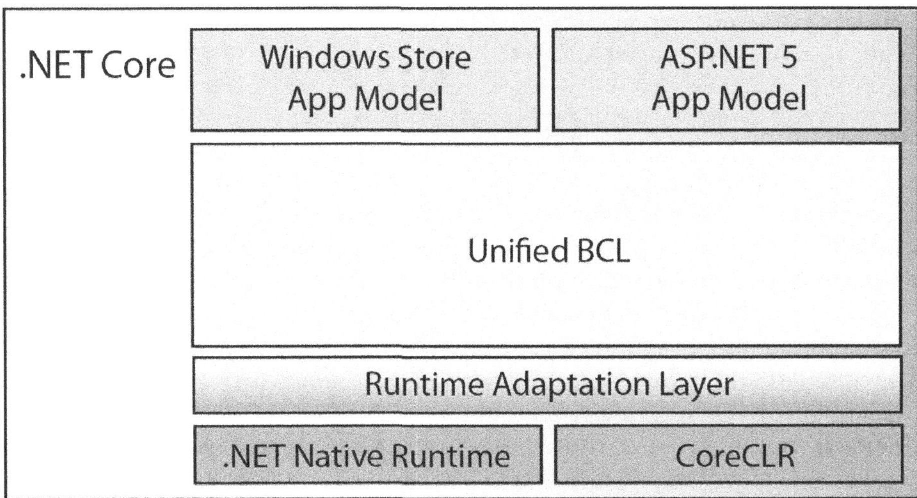

Figure 1-5. .NET Core

Architecturally, applications that utilize .NET Core are more agile and stable than those that target the full .NET Framework. Agility comes from the fact that individual components of .NET Core can be updated as they are released. When an application is deployed, the .NET Core components it was built against are installed side-by-side with the application, locking them together until the next release of the application. This adds stability to the application as a machine-wide .NET Framework update will not impact its functionality. Consider an application built using .NET 4.0 is deployed to a customer's computer. Sometime in the following year, .NET 4.5 is released, replacing all of the .NET Framework 4.0 binaries on the system. If one of the changes in the new framework causes the application to no longer function correctly a new build would have to be created, fixing the problem while targeting the new framework version. An application targeting .NET Core would not have this issue as the .NET components are installed together with the application and not impacted by system-wide modifications.

The full .NET Framework is still the platform of choice for rich Windows desktop applications, such as WinForms and WPF, but .NET Core will likely be the runtime of choice for other application types in the future. The reason the UI components will likely never be migrated to .NET Core is fairly straight-forward - implementing WinForms and WPF on other operating systems is a very costly proposition since they are tied so closely to Windows. After all, a Windows application running on OS X or Linux would look positively out of place. Web-based UI's, such as those generated by ASP.NET, render HTML and are not tied to any operating system or design language (like Modern UI) since the output is consumed by web browsers.

.NET Core will be updated more frequently than the full framework so most new features will be available in .NET Core prior to implementation in the full .NET Framework. It is estimated that the full framework will be updated on an annual basis with service packs released on an as-needed basis. .NET Core has no pre-defined release schedule and components are likely to change at random intervals. So, if you want the latest-and-greatest, .NET Core is the best way to go.

In Visual Studio, applications based off of .NET Core utilize different project templates than the traditional .NET Framework projects. Additional components and updates to .NET Core can be loaded using the NuGet Package Manager.

1.7 WinRT and Universal Apps

WinRT (Windows Runtime) is a runtime built for Windows 8 and above that provides access to functionality specific to the modern desktop and Windows Store app interface. WinRT is actually based on COM (Component Object Model) which predates the .NET Framework. Any Windows Store app that is written using a managed language like C# or Visual Basic must interface with WinRT using a language projection. Put simply, a projection is the way for C# to interface with WinRT utilizing the same syntax and libraries as found in the .NET Framework. In reality, working with WinRT simply feels like working with a subset of .NET rather than working with a completely new technology. Yes, there are key differences that in all likelihood wouldn't make much sense to you right now, but just keep in mind working with WinRT is not much different than working with the .NET Framework or .NET Core.

Windows 8.1 introduced a new type of application called Universal Apps. The Universal App Platform is actually a superset of WinRT and, starting with Windows 10, is designed to be compatible across all Windows platforms, including Windows Mobile and XBox. Each platform targeted by an app requires different UIs due to the varying hardware and user exprerience of each device, but their underlying logic can be identical, hence the "universal" name. Be aware that developing Windows 10 Universal Apps requires Windows 10 for desktop applications but can utilize emulators for devices like Windows Mobile.

1.8 Summary

C# is a robust language that can be used in the generation of aplications ranging from simple console applications to multi-tiered web solutions. Since C# supports many different programming paradigms, programmers from very different backgrounds can typically find familiar bits to help them acclimate to the new environment.

C# goes hand-in-hand with the .NET Framework; however the .NET Framework is an ever changing product meaning that what you can do with C# changes all the time. .NET Core is the first major step toward making the framework modular and officially supported on operating systems other than Windows. In the future it is entirely possible that large .NET Framework distributions will be replaced by smaller, statically linked .NET Core compoenents. Regardless of the CLI implementation used, C# is Microsoft's premiere language for developing world-class applications and will likely remain the first choice for Windows (and possibly Linux and OS X) developers for years to come.

2

2. Visual Studio

Visual Studio is Microsoft's leading Integrated Development Environment (IDE) for developing applications using C#, C++, Visual Basic, F# and JavaScript. Visual Studio is arguably the best IDE on the market today as it comes complete with a rich toolset with the following features:

- Developing applications for various platforms, including:
  - Windows/Windows Mobile
  - Android
  - iOS
- Working with multiple langauges. Out of the box, Visual Studio supports context highlighting and IntelliSense with the following languages:
  - C#/C/C++
  - CoffeeScript
  - CSS/SCSS/LESS
  - F#
  - HTML
  - JavaScript/TypeScript
  - JSON/XML
  - T-SQL
  - Visual Basic
  - XAML
- Local and remote debugging including devices and emulators for various platforms
- Developing databases using relational database designers and tools
- WYSIWYG designers for WinForms, WPF, Silverlight, mobile devices and the web
- Integrated source control and team management tools
- Sophisticated testing tools
- Code analysis
- Plug-in capabilities allow Viusal Studio to be customized by 3rd party tools, enhancing the Visual Studio expreience

There are many versions of Visual Studio from the free Express and Community editions up to the Ultimate or Enterprise Editions. Microsoft has always placed a great deal of importance on the developers of its ecosystem, and the Community edition of Visual Studio demonstrates that commitment by providing superior tools at no cost to the developer. Interestingly enough, it is possible to create full C# applications using nothing more than Notepad and the command line compiler (CSC.exe) that comes with the .NET Framework; however, since the Community edition of Viusal Studio is free there is no reason to put yourself through that pain. Check with Microsoft online if the paid editions of Visual Studio provide enough of an advantage to you to justify their expense. Nothing in this book will require more than the free, Community edition of Viusal Studio, although some of the advanced features in the paid editions will be demonstrated for information purposes only.

Visual Studio is a very complex and customizable program. In reality, describing all of its features would require a book several times this size. So, rather than wasting your time discussing every nook and cranny of the IDE, this chapter will highlight the most important features to get you up and running as quickly as possible. I strongly suggest supplementing this material with other resources if you require more detail on a specific feature of Visual Studio. MSDN Online (http://msdn.microsoft.com) is always a great starting place.

2.1 Installing and Configuring the Visual Studio IDE

Visual Studio is a fairly large product, consuming over 20GB in some configurations. Some of the largest files in Visual Studio relate to the virtual hard disk images for the various emulators that can be used to test deployments to different systems like Windows Mobile and Android. Once you have determined the appropriate version of Visual Studio for your needs, expect the full install to take up to an hour to download and configure your system. It is also possible that your system may require several reboots depending on the configuration. For your information, the majority of the examples in this book were generated using Visual Studio 2015 Community Edition.

Something new to the latest versions of Visual Studio is the ability to sign into Visual Studio Online so you can sync your environment settings between computers. When you run Visual Studio 2015 for the first time you will be prompted to enter your Microsoft ID (such as a Hotmail, Live or Outlook account):

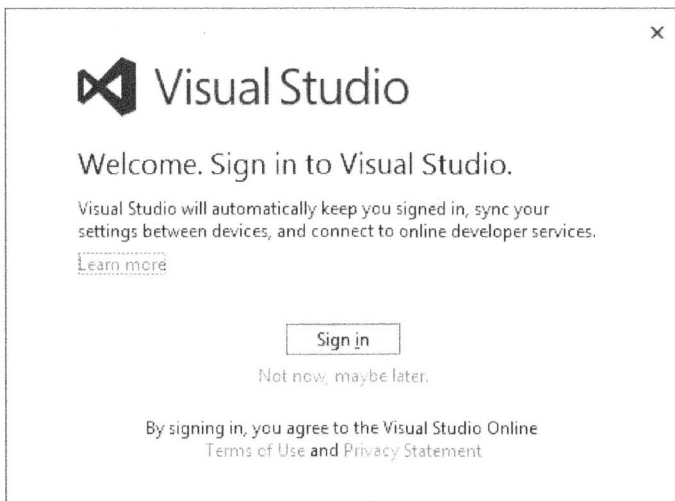

Figure 2-1. Signing Into Visual Studio Online

If you choose to skip this step you can always sign in at a later time by clicking on the "Sign in" link in the top-right corner of the menu bar:

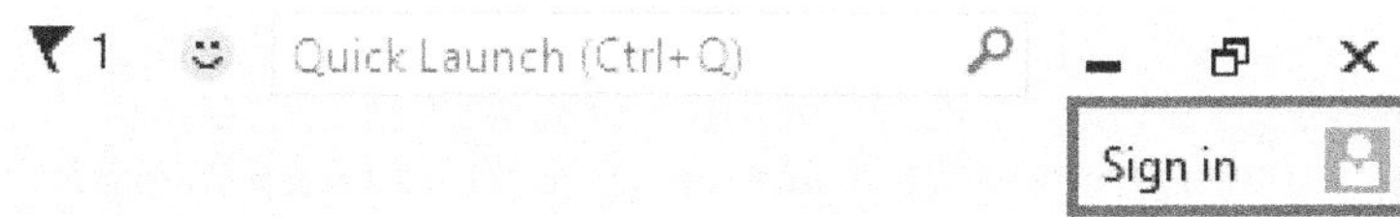

Figure 2-2. Signing Into Visual Studio Online from the IDE

Next, you will be promopted to select a development environment. Since this book is focused on C# development, the recommendation is to select "Visual C#".

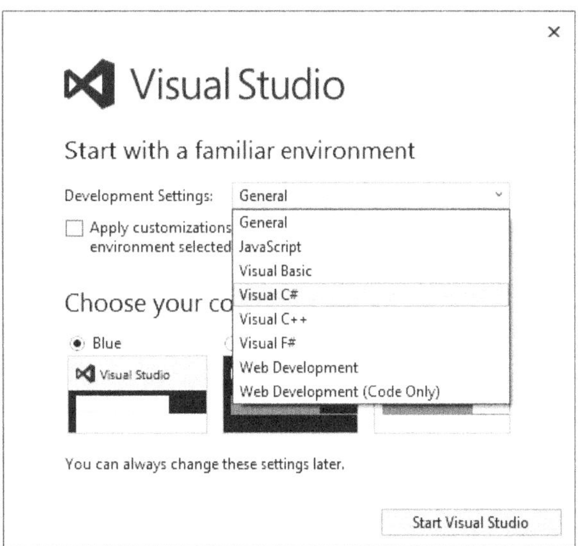

Figure 2-3. Initial Development Environment Settings

The biggest difference between the environments is the initial layout of the tool windows and the keyboard mappings to various shortcuts. It is common for developers to rely on keyboard shortcuts while coding as it can increase productivity by removing the need to move their hands from their keyboard to a mouse or touchscreen and back. When appropriate, useful keyboard shortcuts will be presented in this text based on the "Visual C#" environment theme. If you decide to change to another language environment at a later time, or if you simply wish to reset your settings, this can be done via the "Tools" → "Import and Export Settings…" menu.

Initial Screen Layout

Once Visual Studio is done asking for initial configuration information, the IDE (Integrated Development Environment) is displayed. By default, the initial view will be that of the "Start Page" as displayed below. The Start Page is a launching point to create new projects, load an existing one as well as reading current news about Visual Studio and the programming community.

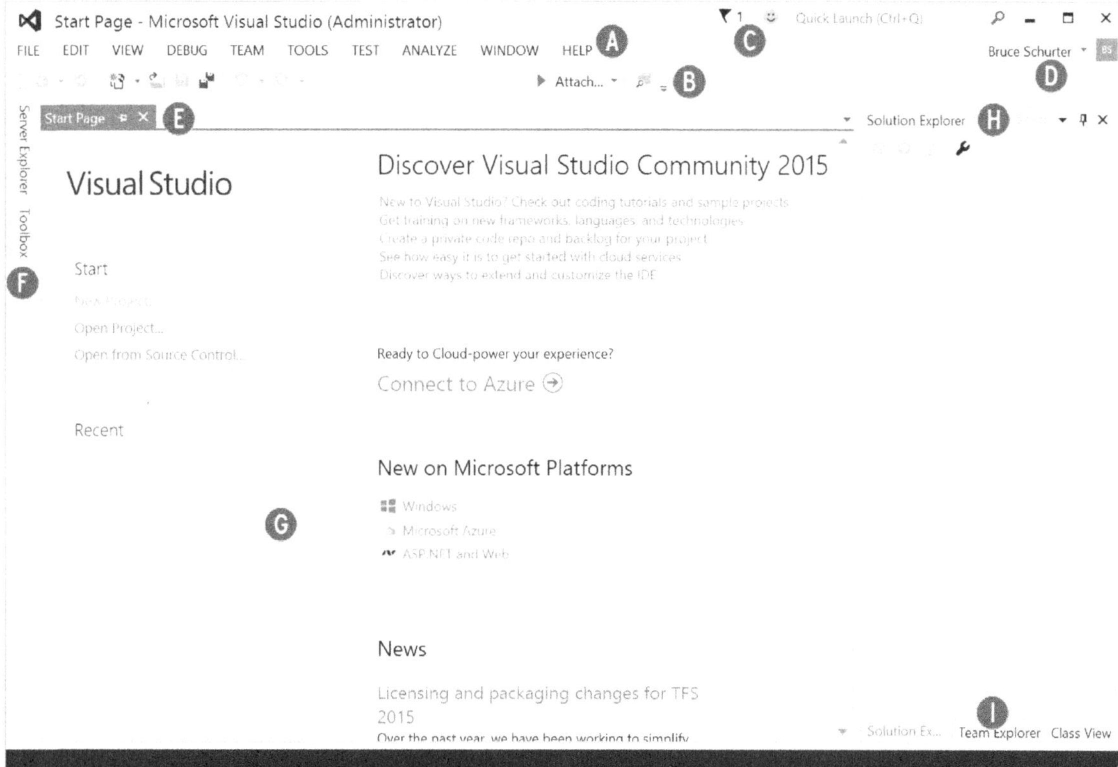

Figure 2-4. Visual Studio IDE (Start Page Shown)

The tags in the above image correspond to the following features:

A. Standard menu bar – The menus displayed are context sensitive and will change based on your current activity.
B. Menu toolbars – The toolbars provide quick access to common tasks. In this initial configuration, only the "Standard" toolbar is displayed. Additional toolbars are available from the "View" → "Toolbars" menu.
C. Notifications – Visual Studio occasionally receives updates or other items that require your attention and will be presented here.
D. Visual Studio Online menu – Actions related to your Visual Studio Online account are displayed here.
E. Document bar – The tabs here represent the documents currently open for viewing and editing. Documents displayed here include C# source files, web pages and any other file resource that you wish to view or edit.
F. Left toolbar snap area – Toolbars can be "snapped" to this area for quick access. In the default configuration the toolbars are hidden, showing only tabs with the toolbar names. Clicking on a tab displays the toolbar temporarily. In its default configuration the Server Explorer and Toolbox toolbars are docked in this area.

G. Document display area - The document selected in the document bar is displayed here. This is where you will do the majority of your coding.
H. Right toolbar snap area - Toolbars can be snapped to this side of the editor as well. The Solution Explorer toolbar is displayed in this location by default. Also notice that the toolbar is expanded unlike the left-side toolbars. We'll look at configuring toolbars a bit later.
I. Right toolbar tabs - The right toolbar also has multiple toolbars docked by default. By clicking on one of the other tabs the Solution Explorer toolbar is replaced by the corresponding toolbar.

Toolbar and Tool Window Docking

The Visual Studio IDE is extremely configurable. Almost every toolbar and tool window (we'll just call them toolbars, collectively) can be docked in virtually any of the four cardinal directions. Additionally, the toolbars can be configured to always be visible or stay hidden until its tab is clicked on.

Figure 2-5. Toolbar Titlebar

The above image displays three buttons on the right edge of the Solution Explorer toolbar titlebar. The first button is a dropdown menu that contains the following options:

- Float - Changes the toolbar to a floating toolbar that hovers above the IDE.
- Dock - Docks the toolbar to a specific location.
- Dock as Tabbed Document - Docks the toolbar with other toolbars much like the initial layout where Solution Explorer, Team Explorer and Class View share the same space.
- Auto Hide - Automatically hides the toolbar when it is no longer being used.
- Hide - Hides the toolbar. To redisplay a hidden toolbar it must be selected from the "View" → "Toolbars" menu or from wherever the toolbar was initially displayed.

The second button "pins" the toolbar to its current position. This toggle duplicates the "Dock" and "Auto Hide" features in the dropdown menu above. The "X" button is the same as the "Hide" menu option - it closes and hides the current toolbar.

In addition to the actions available in the toolbar titlebar, individual toolbars can be "dragged and dropped" to other locations in the IDE. When the toolbar is dragged, positional icons are displayed in various locations throughout the IDE. By moving the mouse onto one of these icons, and then releasing the mouse button, the toolbar will be docked into the location indicated by the icon. If the mouse button is released while not hovering over one of the positional icons the toolbar will revert to a floating toolbar.

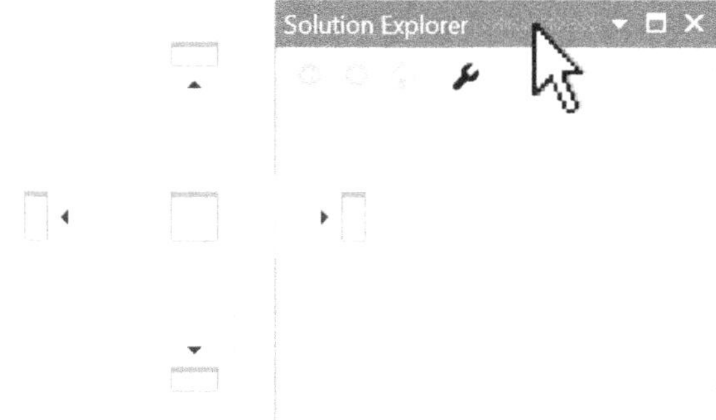

Figure 2-6. Moving Toolbars

My preferred layout for Visual Studio is very similar to the default configuration. The major difference is that I like to have the Properties toolbar positioned just under the Solution Explorer.

2.2 Visual Studio Toolbars Detailed

This section will discuss the important toolbars available in Visual Studio. For practical reasons, the toolbars specific to debugging will be discussed in the debugging section later.

Solution Explorer

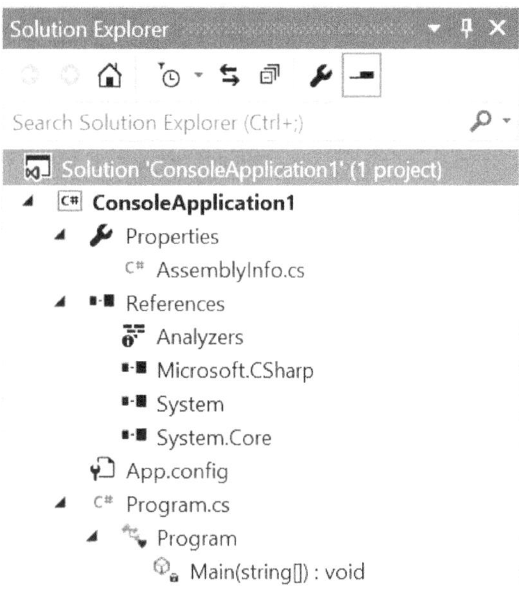

Figure 2-7. Solution Explorer

To display: "View" → "Solution Explorer" or Ctrl+W, S
Typical Location: Docked on right side of IDE

The Solution Explorer represents the physical layout of solutions and projects as a "tree" where each branch represents a category of items in the solution. Each branch can also have additional child branches and other items. The button bar at the top of the Solution Explorer window is context sensitive and will display tools specific to the selected item in the tree.

Table 2-1. Solution Explorer Buttons

Button	Description
	Standard document navigation buttons, similar to a web browser's navigation buttons.
	Filters the view to show only the documents with pending changes.
	Filters the view to show only the documents that are currently open for editing.
	Synchronizes the Solution Explorer with the active document.
	Refreshes the Solution Explorer.
	Collapses all branches in the Solution Explorer.
	Toggles whether hidden and non-included files are displayed.

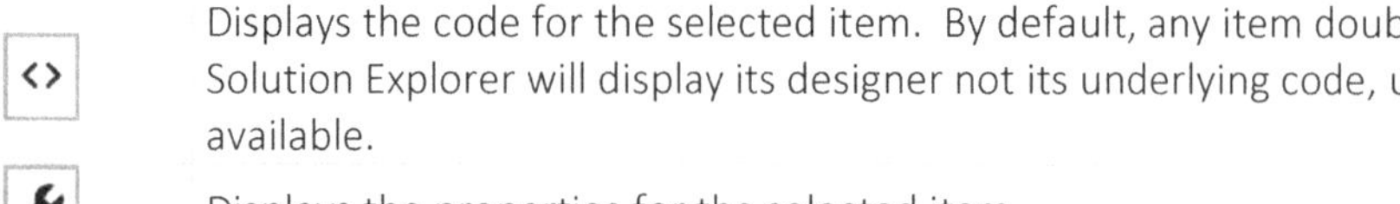

<>	Displays the code for the selected item. By default, any item double-clicked in the Solution Explorer will display its designer not its underlying code, unless no designer is available.
	Displays the properties for the selected item.
	Toggles whether or not the selected item is previewed in the editor without the need to double-click on it.

Immediately under the button bar is a search bar that allows you to search the entire solution for specific files, classes or methods.

The solution tree is the main component of the Solution Explorer. Depending on your configuration settings, the top branch of the tree will either be the current solution or current project. To change whether the solution is always displayed as the top-level item in the tree, go to the "Tools" menu, select "Options..." and navigate to "Projects and Solutions" in the category list on the left side of the dialog. On the right side of the screen there will be a checkbox called "Always show solution".

The typical layout for the Solution Explorer tree has the following appearance:

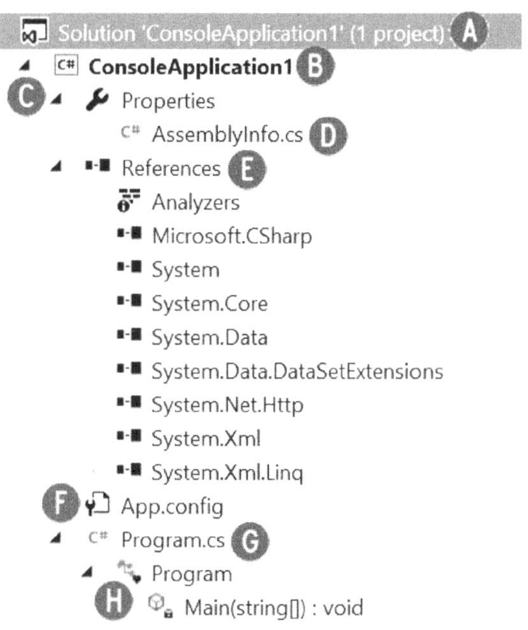

Figure 2-8. Solution Explorer Details

A. This tree item represents the current solution, and there can only be one solution loaded at any time. A Visual Studio solution configuration is stored within a file with the ".sln" extension. Right-clicking on this item exposes the tools specific to a solution, such as "Build Solution", "Properties", "Open Folder in File Explorer" and "Add". The first three aforementioned menu options are relatively self-explanitory. The "Add" menu, however, provides a mechanism for adding new projects and web sites to the solution. You can also add solution folders to organize the projects into categories. These solution folders don't actually represent folders on the file system. Rather they are "virtual" folders managed by the solution.

B. Immediately under the current solution is a list of projects that comprise the solution. By default, each project will reside in its own folder in the file system and its configuration is saved in a ".csproj" file for C# projects. Typically, there is at least one project associated with a solution. The first project added to a solution normally has the same name as the solution. Right-clicking also exposes project-specific menus, such as "Build", "Debug", "Set as StartUp Project", "Properties" and "Add". Most of these context menus are duplicated in the "Project" menu in Visual Studio's main menu bar. The "Add" menu will be frequently used to add new files to your projects.

C. The "Properties" item represents an actual folder within a project called "Properties". Double-clicking on this item brings up the project's property window.

D. Stored within the Properties folder is a file called "AssemblyInfo.cs" which maintains some of the metadata associated with the project, such as version numbers and copyright information. The information contained within this file can be edited directly or manipulated via the project's property window under the "Application" tab and clicking on the "Assembly Information..." button. Removing this file is not recommended.

E. References are links to the libraries of classes and functions that the project has access to. Right-clicking this item exposes the "Add Reference..." menu item so you can add additional libraries, and therefore functionality, to your projects.

F. The "app.config" file (known as "web.config" for web-based projects) contains the declarative configuration information that governs how your project runs.

G. At this level, the code files contained within your project are listed. The initial content of this list is governed by the project type. In this image, the project type represented is a console application.

H. Expanding a code file by clicking on the triangle to its immediate left will show the logical contents of the file. The details shown here are very similar to what is displayed within the Class View toolbar.

Class View

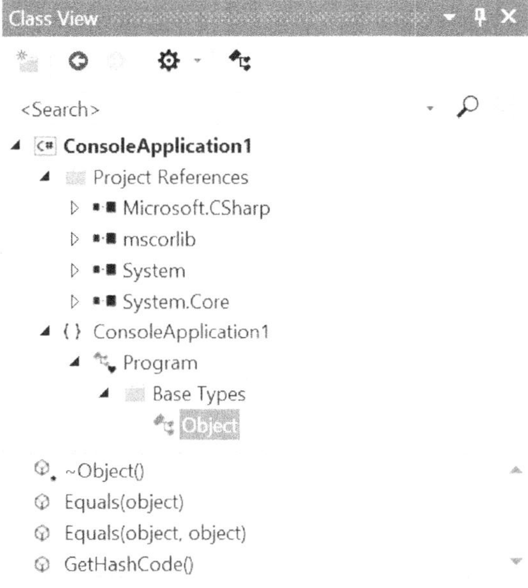

Figure 2-9. Class View

To display: "View" → "Class View" or Ctrl+W,C
Typical Location: Docked on right side of IDE

The Class View is a logical view of the current solution and its projects. Unlike the Solution Explorer which is file-based, the Class View, as you may have guessed, is class-based. Since C# classes can be spread across multiple files, this view is useful if you wish to organize your projects based on logical constructs rather than the files that comprise those constructs.

Table 2-2. Class View Buttons

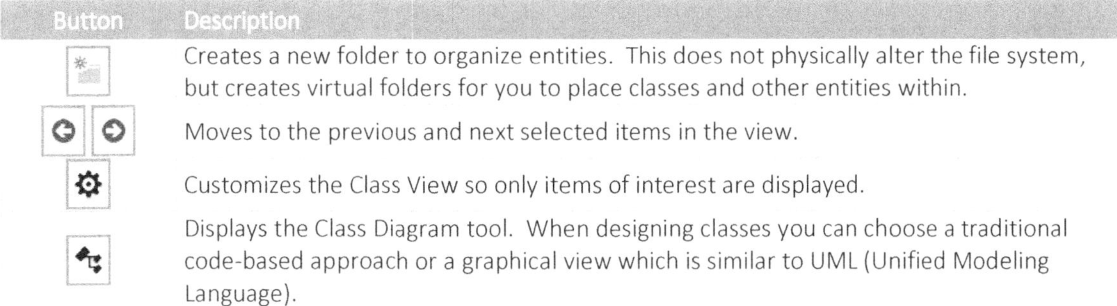

Button	Description
	Creates a new folder to organize entities. This does not physically alter the file system, but creates virtual folders for you to place classes and other entities within.
	Moves to the previous and next selected items in the view.
	Customizes the Class View so only items of interest are displayed.
	Displays the Class Diagram tool. When designing classes you can choose a traditional code-based approach or a graphical view which is similar to UML (Unified Modeling Language).

Immediately under the button bar is a search tool that allows you to search for items within the current solution.

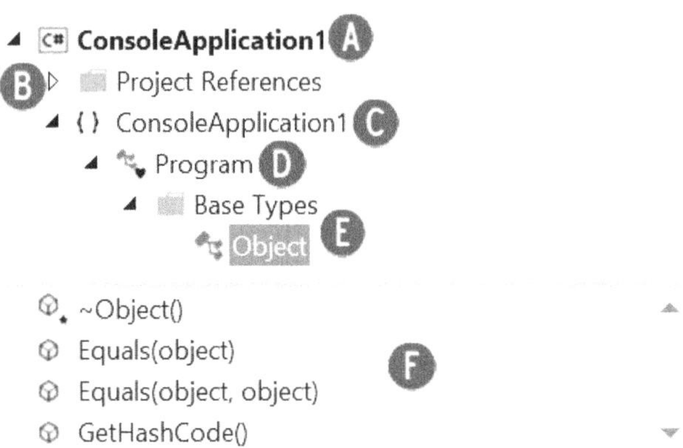

Figure 2-10. Class View Details

A. The top-level items are the projects within the solution. Just like the Solution Explorer, right-clicking on a project will display a context menu, from which you can add new classes or references or display the project's properties.
B. The project's library references are listed here.
C. This level of the tree displays namespaces contained within the project. A namespace is similar to a folder and is used to organize classes into uniquely-named containers.
D. The classes and other types (structs and enums) are displayed within the namespace nodes.
E. Since C# is an object-oriented language that supports inheritance, the base types of the classes are shown underneath the class nodes. Inheritance is an advanced topic so you don't have to worry about the details right now.
F. The bottom portion of the Class View is an information area that will display content-sensitive details of the item selected in the Class View's tree. Double-clicking on an item in this area will display the Object Browser detailing the item selected.

I actually prefer the Solution Explorer over the Class View. Since the Solution Explorer includes details also displayed in the Class View it seems like a more well-rounded view for programming. However, this does not mean I do not use the Class View as well, just not as much as the Solution Explorer. Since screen real estate can be at a premium, I very rarely have both tools open simultaneously.

Object Browser

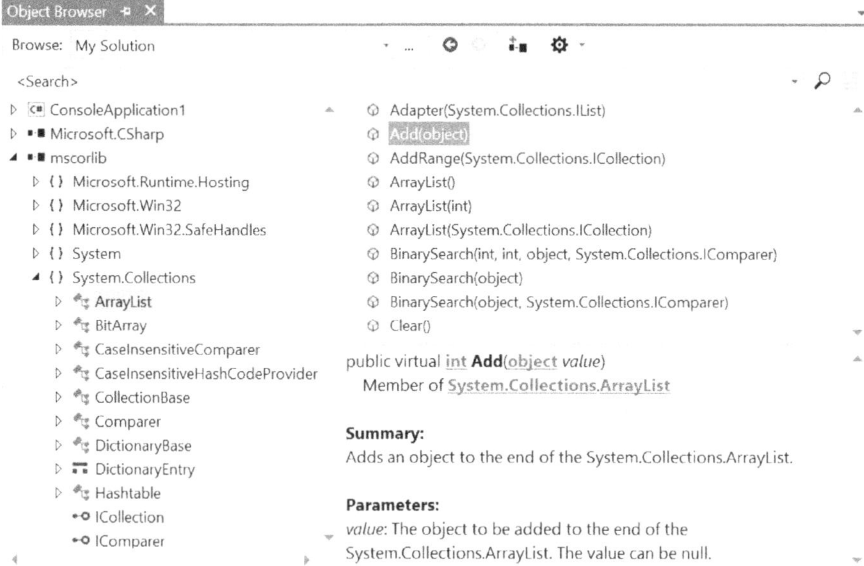

Figure 2-11. Object Browser

To display: "View" → "Object Browser" or Ctrl+W, J
Typical Location: Document editor area

The Object Browser is used to investigate the contents of the current solution as well as libraries referenced by the projects contained within it. Due to its use of metadata stored in the libraries, the Object Browser also behaves like a help rerference for programmers. The Object Browser can be docked like any other toolbar, but it really should be displayed in the main display area since it has a larger footprint than most toolbars.

Table 2-3. Object Broswer Buttons

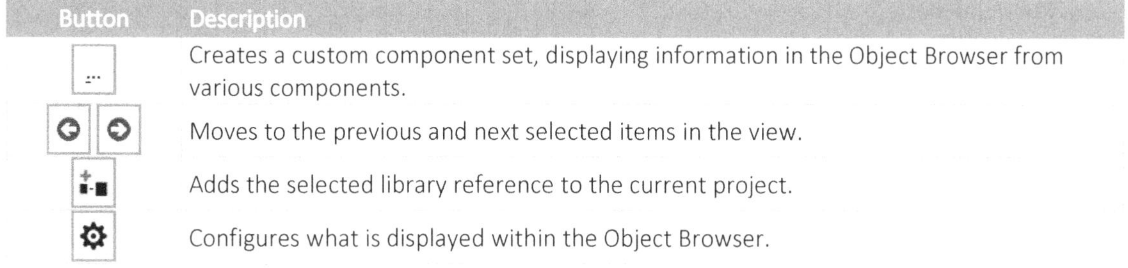

Button	Description
...	Creates a custom component set, displaying information in the Object Browser from various components.
← →	Moves to the previous and next selected items in the view.
(add reference)	Adds the selected library reference to the current project.
(settings)	Configures what is displayed within the Object Browser.

Properties Window

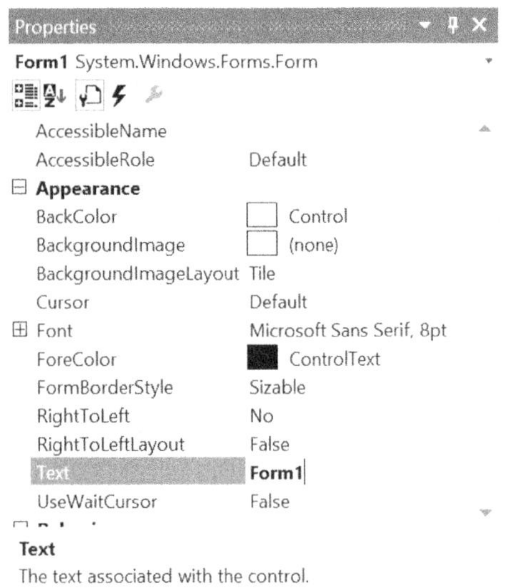

Figure 2-12. Properties Window

To display: "View" → "Properties Window" or Ctrl+W,P
Typical Location: Docked on right side of IDE, below Solution Explorer

The Properties Window is a context-sensitive window that displays the properties of the currently selected item in one of the other toolbars or editor/designer window. These properties are key/value pairs where the key represents the property name and the value represents the value for that particular property. Some of the properties are plain text while others are graphical and may display a popup window to modify the property value. Property values that cannot be modified are displayed in gray. Properties that have been modified from their default values are displayed in bold text. In addition, some properties are comprised of multiple values and will include a "+" button to the left of the property name to expand the tree showing the individual values.

Table 2-4. Properties Window Buttons

Button	Description
	Organizes the properties by category.
	Organizes the properties alphabetically.
	Displays the properties for the selected item in the editor or other toolbar.
	Displays the events for the selected item in the editor or other toolbar.
	Displays the property pages for the selected item if supported.

The Properties Window button bar and contents are customized based on the project type and the type of item that is selected. Therefore, the options you see may be very different from what is displayed here.

Server Explorer

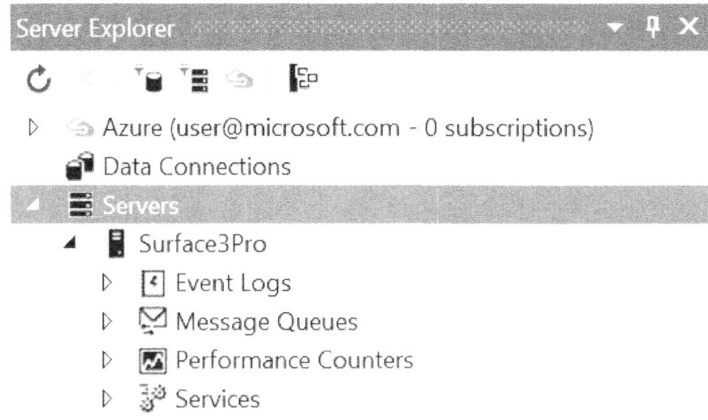

Figure 2-13. Server Explorer

To display: "View" → "Server Explorer" or Ctrl+W,L
Typical Location: Docked on left side of IDE

The Server Explorer tool window provides access to a variety of server-specific items, such as Azure (cloud server) subscriptions, database connections and computer-specific services. By default, the local machine is included in the "Servers" list but additional machines can be added as long as you possess the appropriate credentials to access them.

Table 2-5. Server Explorer Toolbar Buttons

Button	Description
	Refreshes the items in the Server Explorer.
	Stops the reresh operation. Since many servers and services can be connected simultaneously, a full refresh can take a long time.
	Makes a new database connection.
	Makes a new server connection.
	Connects to a Microsoft Azure subscription.
	Launches the SQL Server Object Explorer tool window.

Toolbox

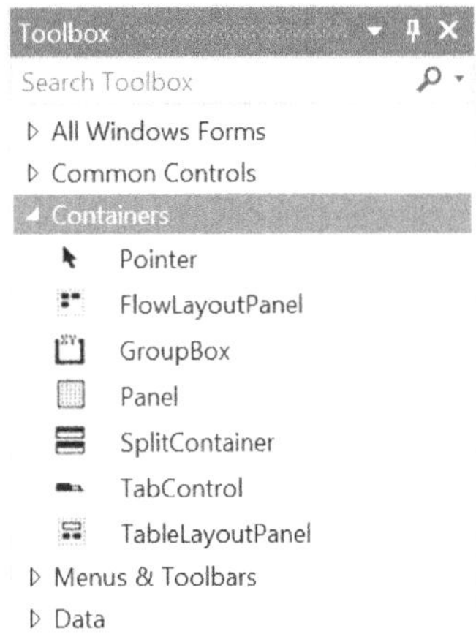

Figure 2-14. Toolbox

To display: "View" → "Server Explorer" or Ctrl+W,X
Typical Location: Docked on left side of IDE

The Toolbox is most commonly used with visual designers, such as WinForms, WPF, XAML and WebForms. The Toolbox initially contains the controls and components most commonly used for a particular editor environment. A search bar can be used to find components by name or you can expand the categories and find the appropriate control. Right-clicking anywhere in the Toolbox provides a context menu from which the "Choose Items…" option is used to add components and controls not ordinarily in the list, such as 3rd-party compoenents or custom controls. Items from the Toolbox are added to a designer using the click-and-drag technique.

Output

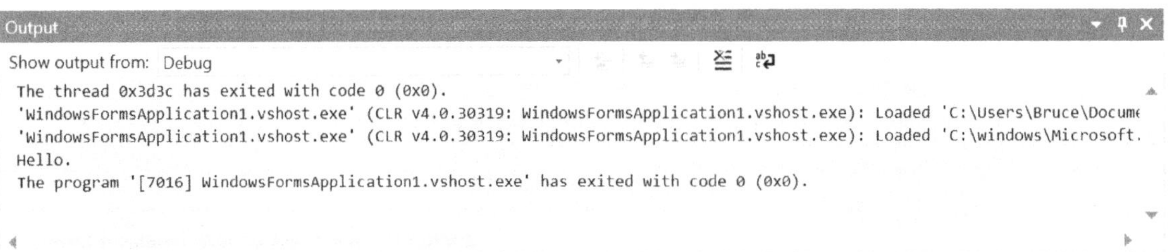

Figure 2-15. Output Window

To display: "View" → "Server Explorer" or Ctrl+W,O
Typical Location: Docked on bottom of IDE

The Output tool window is a console-like terminal display that contains output from various streams such as Debug and Build. As this window is used exclusively for displaying output, not user input is allowed in this window.

Text can be manually added to the Debug stream from code using the following methods:

- `System.Diagnostics.Debug.Write();`
- `System.Diagnostics.Debug.WriteIf();`
- `System.Diagnostics.Debug.WriteLine();`
- `System.Diagnostics.Debug.WriteLineIf();`

Alternatively, the Console.Write() and Console.WriteLine() methods also redirect their output here if an application does not feature a dedicated console window.

Task List

Description	Project	File	Line
TODO: This needs to be fixed	ConsoleApplication1	Program.cs	14

Figure 2-16. Task List

To display: "View" → "Task List" or Ctrl+W,T
Typical Location: Docked on bottom of IDE

The task list scans the solution for comments with specific text and aggregates them into this view. This tool is useful for developers so they can keep track of known problems in the code and other issues they wish to follow. Initially, Visual Studio scans for the following text at the beginning of all comments:

- `HACK`
- `TODO`
- `UNDONE`
- `!UnresolvedMergeConflict`

You can modify this list via the "Tools" → "Options" menu, under "Environment", "Task List".

Double-clicking on an entry in the Task List will immediately load the file where the comment is located and set the cursor to that line.

Error List

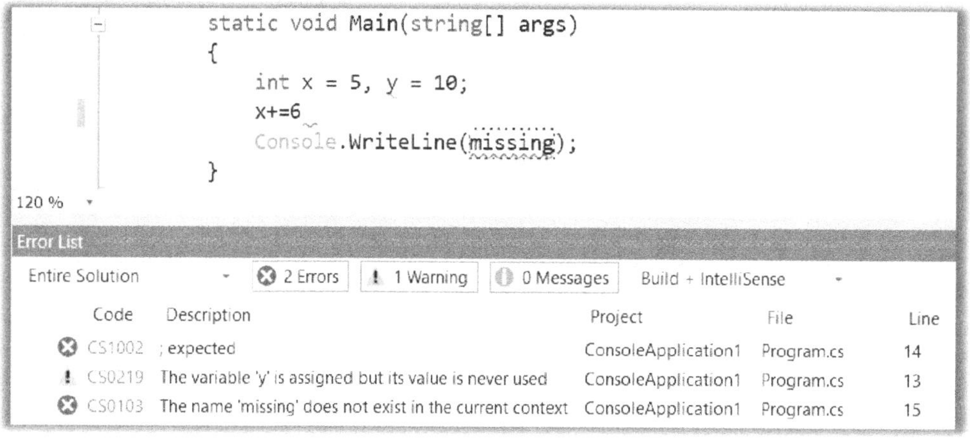

```
static void Main(string[] args)
{
    int x = 5, y = 10;
    x+=6
    Console.WriteLine(missing);
}
```

120 %

Error List

Entire Solution | 2 Errors | 1 Warning | 0 Messages | Build + IntelliSense

	Code	Description	Project	File	Line
✖	CS1002	; expected	ConsoleApplication1	Program.cs	14
!	CS0219	The variable 'y' is assigned but its value is never used	ConsoleApplication1	Program.cs	13
✖	CS0103	The name 'missing' does not exist in the current context	ConsoleApplication1	Program.cs	15

Figure 2-17. Error List

To display: "View" → "Error List" or Ctrl+W,E
Typical Location: Docked on bottom of IDE

The Error List window displays all known syntax and compiler errors and warnings. When you are typing in code it is very common to accidentally omit important symbols, like ";", or misspell a variable name. The Error List utilizes real-time code checking to detect these issues as well as compilation to detect more complex problems. The Error List can be configured to display three different priorities of issues:

- Errors – Problems with the syntax of the code that will prevent the code from running
- Warnings – Items that are identified as something that the programmer should address but should not keep the code from compiling and running
- Messages – These are the lowest priority issues that may be of interest to the programmer

Unselecting an issue priority button will hide issues of that type. It does not solve the problem but it will hide the issue from sight. Errors must be fixed prior to running the code, and warnings should be fixed, but is not always necessary.

Each row in the Error List is composed of six columns:

- Error Priority – An icon that indicates the severity of the issue
- Code – Compiler-specific code that indicates the classification of the error. Clicking on the code number will launch the help viewer providing more details about the problem.
- Description – Brief description identifying the problem encountered
- Project – Project where the error is located
- File – File where the error is located
- Line – The line number in the file where the error is located

Double-clicking on a row will load the file where the problem is located and move the cursor to that spot. If the error is not code related (possibly a configuration issue) then double-clicking may have no effect. Once the offending code has been fixed the row is removed from the Error List. Sometimes, a recompile is required to remove error notifications from the list.

2.3 Application Templates and New Projects

Visual Studio 2015 comes pre-installed with several dozen application templates. These templates are designed to make developing software of a specific type and platform simpler than starting from a blank solution. When a project is created, references necessary for the requested application type are added automatically to the References folder of the project. Frequently, sample code files are also added demonstrating the basic functionality of that project type. To view the available project template types, create a new project from the "File" → "New" → "Project…" menu or from the Start Page's "New Project…" link. Note that some templates require an additional download step the first time they are used.

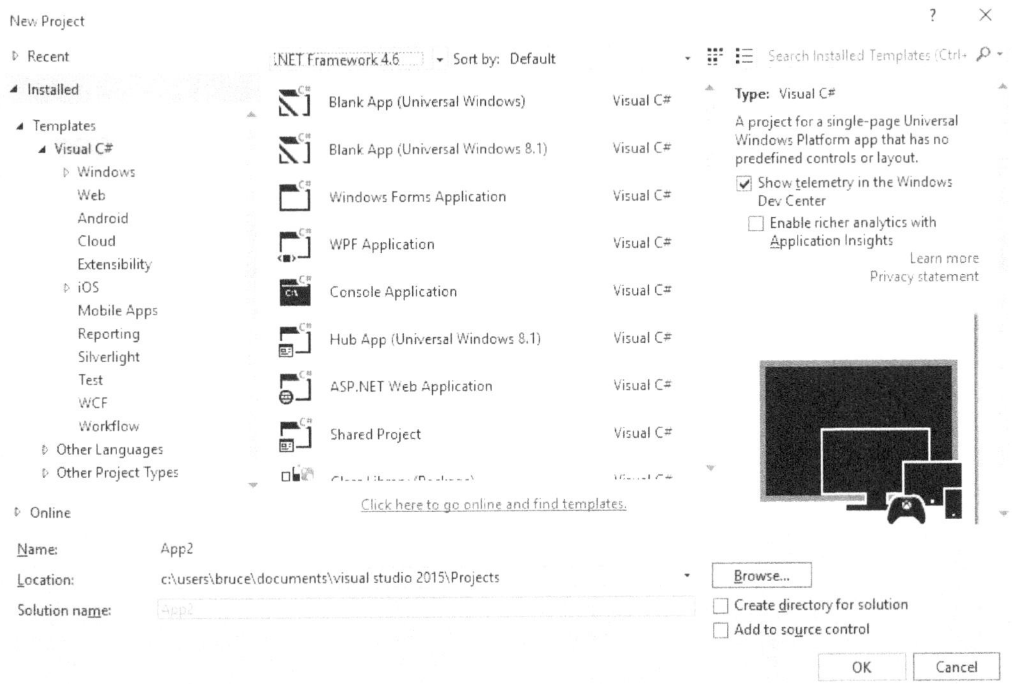

Figure 2-18. New Project

The "New Project" window lists the available project templates by category on the left. This list is grouped first by language, then application type. Clicking on one of these categories narrows down the list of available projects shown in the center of the screen. Additionally, not all projects are available in every version of the .NET Framework. The dropdown box at the top of the screen selects the version of the framework to target and will also filter the list of available templates. For Windows 10 Universal Apps, .NET Framework 4.6 or newer must be selected.

Once the desired template is selected an appropriate name must be entered in the "Name" textbox to identify the project. This name will also be used for the solution unless it is overridden in the "Solution name" textbox. The solution name setting is only available if the "Create directory for solution" checkbox is enabled.

Clearly, all of the available project types will not be covered in detail within this text, but there are some you should be aware of to make the most of your learning experience. Also, keep in mind that these template names may change with new releases of Visual Studio.

Console Application

The Console Application project type is one of the simplest project types you can create in C# and, as a result, will be the primary project type focused on in this book. Console applictions are text-based applications that don't require a mouse or fancy graphics, just a keyboard and a command prompt.

After creation, the project will contain a file called Program.cs that contains a class called Program. Within this class is a method called Main() which represents the boundary of the program's code.

Chapter 3 will discuss this project type in detail.

Windows Forms Application

The Windows Forms Application (WinForms for short) project template creates basic desktop Windows applications which can contain buttons, textboxes, dropdowns and simple, 2D graphics. This project type is considered the simplest way to develop programs that contain a graphical user interface. The most common form of user interaction with an application of this type is with a mouse and keyboard.

A WinForm application also contains a Program.cs file with a Main() method inside, but its entire responsibility is to launch the form, or window, contained in Form1.cs. Form1 is the name of the class contained in Form1.cs, plus there is an additional file associated with Form1.cs called Form1.Designer.cs that contains the visual layout for the form. As you progress through this material you will learn that the default names chosen by Visual Studio are rarely ideal.

WPF Application

WPF, which stands for Windows Presentation Foundation, is also a graphical application type but is more advanced than WinForms. Many of the same controls that are available in WinForms programs are also available in WPF, but the engine responsible for drawing the screen elements is generally superior in performance and quality.

WPF applications have a very different program structure than WinForms applications. The primary window of the WPF application is called MainWindow.xaml. There is also a different file extension of type ".xaml" for the window. This represents a completely different langauge from C# that is also used in Silverlight and as one of the design langauges for Universal apps.

ASP.NET Web Application

The ASP.NET Web Application project template is the gateway template for designing web applications of many types. Creating a project of this type involves a wizard to select the style of web project to create, such as traditional ASP.NET, MVC and Web API.

Class Library

A Class Library is a special type of project used to create a sharable resource. These libraries contain classes and methods that can be utilized by many different C# programs.

Blank App (Universal Windows)

Universal Windows Apps come in two flavors, those that support Windows 8.1 and those for Windows 10. Windows 10 Universal apps can be designed to work with all Windows devices such as the traditional Windows desktop operating system, Windows Phone and XBox One.

2.4 Editors and Designers

Editor and designer windows are where programmers spend the majority of their time when creating applications. Visual Studio's code editors are designed to interpret the code as it is being entered, providing color-based syntax highlighting making reading and analyzing the code easier for the programmer. IntelliSense, which will be discussed later, also provides instantaneous help while typing code, making your life that much simpler.

The C# Code Editor

Anytime a file with the ".cs" extension is loaded into Visual Studio, the editor window is configured to interpret the file as C# code and provide feedback to the programmer regarding syntax and errors. Many of the built-in tools to process C# code are configurable through the Options dialog found in the "Tools" → "Options" menu. You'll look at this later. As the programmer types code in this window, Visual Studio tests the text for validity, making sure variables are spelled correctly, functions are called with the correct arguments and that the structure of the code is sound. Any syntactic issues are flagged with red underlines and entries are added to the Error List window.

C# does not utilize line numbers like some older langauges; however, line numbers are still used by Visual Studio to call a programmer's attention to a specific problem or syntax error. As such you may wish to turn on line numbering in the Options menu so you can quickly identify the offending line(s) of code. Alternatively, the code editor displays the line number and column where the cursor is located in the bottom status bar.

At the very top of the code editor window is a series of dropdown boxes used to quickly navigate to other parts of the code. The first dropdown box displays the project name that the code belongs to. This dropdown is typically informational only. The second dropdown displays the class or struct the code under the cursor belongs to. Since a file can contain many classes this list can be manipulated. However, most programmers recommend that only one class should be contained in a single file; therefore, the majority of time this box will also have only one item in it. The final dropdown displays the member of the class where the cursor is located. Typically this will be a method/function name or a field variable declaration. Since classes typically contain multiple items, this list is useful for quickly navigating to a specific member.

The bottom-left of the status bar provides a control to adjust the zoom setting of the editor window. This setting applies to all files open in the editor window. Alternatively, using the mouse scroll wheel in conjunction with the [Ctrl] key will also adjust the zoom percentage.

Keyboard Shortcuts

Most of the tools provided to enhance the programming experience can be reached using toolbars and menus but most programmers learn keyboard shortcuts to provide quicker access to these features. Like other shortcuts we've already discussed, most of the code editor shortcuts are also environment specific. If you choose an environment other than C# then you will need to determine the shortcuts on your own. Most of the Windows standard keyboard shortcuts for text editing are also the same in Visual Studio, like [Ctrl]+[C] and [Ctrl]+[V] for copy and paste, respectively.

Table 2-6. Text Editing Keyboard Shortcuts

Shortcut	Description
[Ctrl]+[L]	Delete the entire line of text where the cursor is located.
[Ctrl]+[←]	Moves the cursor one word to the left.
[Ctrl]+[→]	Moves the cursor one word to the right.
[Ctrl]+[Shift]+[←]	Selects the word to the left.
[Ctrl]+[Shift]+[→]	Selects the word to the right.
[Ctrl]+[]]	When the cursor is on a delimiter character, like "(" or "}" this key combination jumps the cursor to its matching partner.
[Tab]	Increases the indent of the selected code to the right.
[Shift]+[Tab]	Decreases the indent of the selected code to the left.
[Ctrl]+[U]	Converts the highlighted text to lowercase.
[Ctrl]+[Shift]+[U]	Converts the highlighted text to uppercase.
[Alt]+[↑]	Moves the selected line(s) up.
[Alt]+[↓]	Moves the selected line(s) down.
[F2]	Renames the selected item.

Table 2-7. Commenting Keyboard Shortcuts

Shortcut	Description
Ctrl+E, C	Comments the line(s) where the cursor is located.
Ctrl+E, U	Uncomments the line(s) where the cursor is located.

Table 2-8. Building and Debugging Keyboard Shortcuts

Shortcut	Description
F6	Builds the entire solution.
Shift+F6	Builds the current project.
F5	Starts or continues debugging.
Ctrl+F5	Starts the program without debugging.
F10	Steps over the current line.
F11	Steps into the method or property under the execution pointer.
Shift+F11	Steps out of the current method.
Shift+F5	Stops execution of the running program.

Table 2-9. Search and Replace

Shortcut	Description
Ctrl+F	Searches for text in the current file, project or solution.
Ctrl+Shift+F	Searches for text in all files of the solution.
Ctrl+H	Searches for and replaces text in the current file, project or solution.
Ctrl+Shift+H	Searches for and replaces text in the files of the solution.

Table 2-10. Miscellaneous Keyboard Shortcuts

Shortcut	Description
F1	Displays the help viewer with information about the item under the cursor.
Ctrl+G	Moves the cursor to the given line number.
Ctrl+,	Moves the cursor to a given search term.
F12	Goes to the definition of the element that is selected.

Other Editor Tips

Block Selection

Standard text selection using the mouse to click-and-drag a selection is standard among text editors. For programmers, however, a continuous selection is not always appropriate. Instead, it may be desirable to select text as a block, ignoring standard text flow and line feeds. Consider the code in the next figure:

```
using System;

namespace HelloWorld
{
    class Program
    {
        static void Main(string[] args)
        {
            Console.WriteLine("Hello world!");
            Console.WriteLine("A test");
            Console.WriteLine("Another test");
        }
    }
}
```

Figure 2-19. Before Block Select

If we wanted to select all of the "Console" text in this code we could hold down the Alt key and then click-and-drag which would yield:

```
using System;

namespace HelloWorld
{
    class Program
    {
        static void Main(string[] args)
        {
            Console.WriteLine("Hello world!");
            Console.WriteLine("A test");
            Console.WriteLine("Another test");
        }
    }
}
```

Figure 2-20. After Block Select

Now, if any typing is done, or if text is pasted, the entire block of text would be replaced by the new text.

Renaming Classes, Methods and Variables

When you need to rename an item, you can simply double-click on the item and start typing the replacement text. When you are done typing you will notice a lightbulb in the left margin that represents "Quick Actions" that can be performed as a result of the change. If you click on the icon, a dropdown list will appear with a selection called "Rename 'XXX' to 'YYY'". If you choose this option, anywhere this item is referenced in the code will automatically be changed to the new name. If you do not choose the Quick Action item then only the text that was changed is modified. Alternatively, you can type F2 to activate the rename action.

The "Quick Actions" menu is new to Visual Studio 2015. Previously, a similar action menu would be represented by a small rectangle button under the text in question. However, many programmers, myself included, had trouble consistently activating this button and ended up relying on right-click context menus instead. These Quick Action menus will appear all the time when editing code, not just for renaming items, so just be on the lookout for them. Typically, "Quick Actions" will be the first item in the right-click context menus as well.

Refactoring

Sometimes when you are adding code to a method that method grows larger than what is desirable. Typically, this happens because the method is doing more than a single operation. A common technique is to extract part of the large method into another method and then replace that block of extracted code with a single method call to the new method. Visual Studio provides a very useful technique called method extraction that can be invoked using the Quick Actions context menu called "Extract Method". The new method will have the name "NewMethod" which can be changed by typing over the name. If the extracted block of code referenced variables declared outside of that block they will become parameters to the new method. Since method creation is a technique that you may not be familiar with at this point you can file this information away for later use.

2.5 Options Window

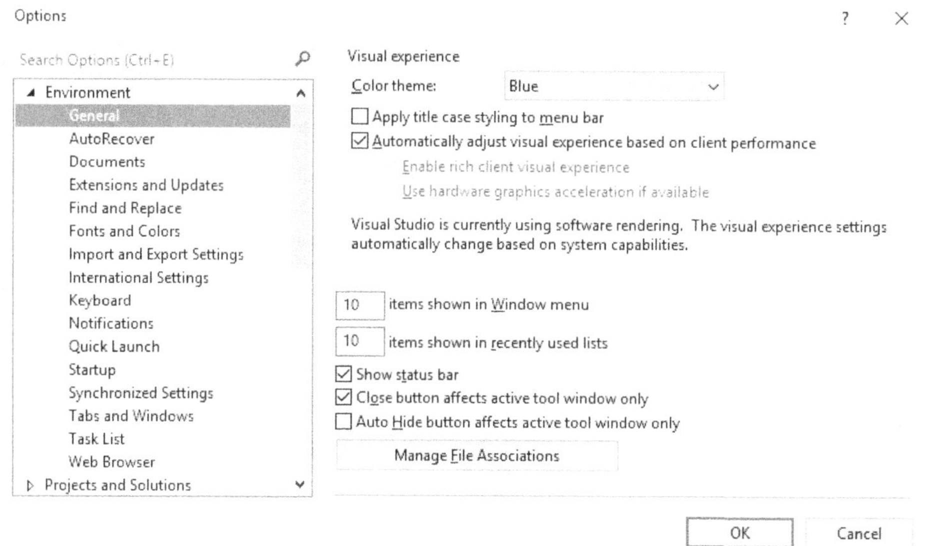

Figure 2-21. Options Window

The Options window, found by selecting "Tools" then "Options" is the master repository for Visual Studio's myriad of settings. Rather than cover every individual setting, only the most crucial properties for getting you up and running will be examined. A word of caution - there are settings available in this dialog that can result in abnormal behavior of Visual Studio. Do not make random changes without first consulting help online at MSDN or other resource.

Environment

General

In this view, you can change the color theme of Visual Studio. Many programmers prefer a darker background due to eye strain when constantly viewing a white desktop. Additionally, the MRU (Most Recently Used) file and project list settings are found here.

Fonts and Colors

On this page you can adjust the fonts and colors used in all aspects of Visual Studio. By default, Consolas 10 point is used for all code editors.

Startup

The Startup settings page contains settings for configuring Visual Studio's behavior at start up.

Projects and Solutions

General

The primary settings for projects and solutions can be found on this window. Of particular interest are the following settings:

- Projects location - default directory to store new projects and solutions
- Always show Error List if build finishes with errors - self explanitory
- Track Active Item in Solution Explorer - This synchronizes the Solution Explorer view with whatever document is currently being edited
- Always Show Solution - This setting forces the solution to be displayed in the Solution Explorer even if it has only one project

Build and Run

This page configures how builds are processed by Visual Studio. The first setting indicates how many projects can be built simultaneously. Automatically, this will be set to the number of CPU cores on your system. Other settings on this page control how often to rebuild projects and how verbose the build process should be.

Text Editor

Each language supported by Visual Studio has its own language settings under the "Text Editor" heading. Since this book's focus is C#, those are the only settings that are discussed here. However, once you start working more with .NET and Visual Studio you will likely branch into different langauges so you may want to research those settings when that time comes.

C# → General

Of note in this window are settings to utilize IntelliSense, hide or show advanced members and displaying line numbers in the left margin. You can also enable automatic brace completion and word wrap.

C# → Tabs

Strangely enough, something as simple as using tabs or spaces in your C# code, and how many spaces are used for indentation, can lead to massive arguments among programmers. There is no "right" answer, but it is common to use a tab size of 4 and keep tabs instead of spaces. Also, Visual Studio's "Smart" indenting is failry sophisticated and matches many C-style programmers' formatting standards.

C# → Formatting

There are several pages of settings related to C# code formatting related to indentation, new lines, spacing and wrapping. The default settings are usually sufficient; however, feel free to fine tune the settings based on your personal preferences.

2.6 IntelliSense

IntelliSense is a tool built into Visual Studio to assist the programmer as they are typing code or working with a designer. Typically, IntelliSense presents itself as a small popup window where either the mouse or keyboard cursor is located. Sometimes the IntelliSense popup is informational only; however, most popups are interactive, meaning the programmer can make a selection in the popup to complete a task.

List Members

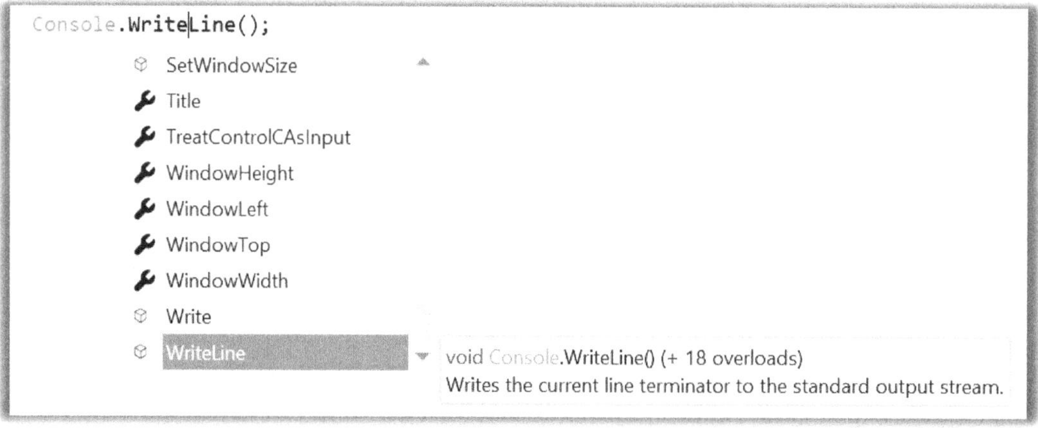

Figure 2-22. List Members

The most encountered IntelliSense popup is the List Members window. This popup is displayed when the [.] key is pressed after a class or variable name is typed in the code editor. The list displays the items that may legally follow the "." and an item can be selected from the list either by mouse click or by hitting Tab or Space on the keyboard. The list can also be narrowed down by typing the first few letters of the item you wish to select. You can also manually display the List Members popup by typing Ctrl+J on the keyboard or from the "Edit" → "IntelliSense" → "List Members" menu.

Parameter Info

```
Console.WriteLine( );
▲ 2 of 19 ▼ void Console.WriteLine(bool value)
    Writes the text representation of the specified Boolean value, followed by the current line terminator, to the standard output stream.
    value: The value to write.
```

Figure 2-23. Parameter Info

The Parameter Info popup is similar to the List Members popup except it is displayed while arguments are being typed in a method call. As arguments are filled in and commas are typed to separate them, the information displayed changes accordingly. This window may also be invoked manually using the Ctrl+Shift+Space chord or from the "Edit" → "IntelliSense" → "Parameter Info" menu.

Quick Info

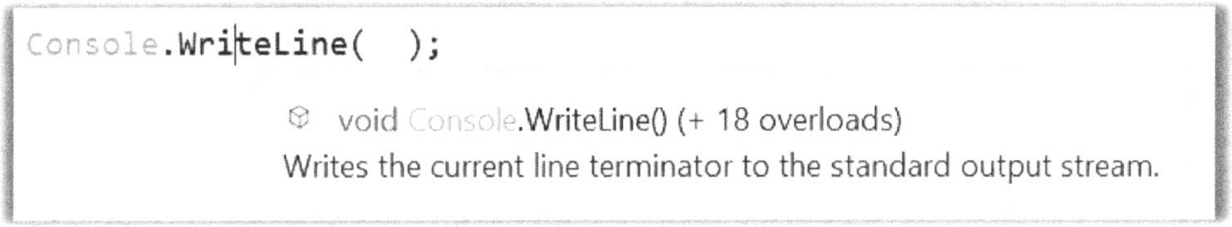

```
Console.WriteLine( );
    void Console.WriteLine() (+ 18 overloads)
    Writes the current line terminator to the standard output stream.
```

Figure 2-24. Quick Info

The Quick Info popup is displayed when the mouse is hovered over an item in the editor window. The IntelliSense Quick Info window displays a summary about the identifier directly under the cursor. This window may be invoked manually by typing Ctrl+K, I or from the "Edit" → "IntelliSense" → "Quick Info" menu.

Complete Word

The Complete Word function of IntelliSense completes the rest of a variable or function name once it has enough characters to uniquely identify an item. Essentially, once the List Members popup has been narrowed down to a single item, typing Ctrl+Space will select that item and complete the typing for you.

2.7 Building Projects

Building a project is the process of compiling all of the code contained within the project and emitting the resulting IL (Intermediate Language) as an assembly. An assembly is simply a file or group of files that represent the compiled code. This process is automatically done any time the project is "run" by using the start button or pressing F5. If the build fails then the IL code cannot be executed. To build a project without running the resulting assembly, press Shift+F6. If there is more than one project in the solution, pressing F6 will build all projects.

Build Configurations

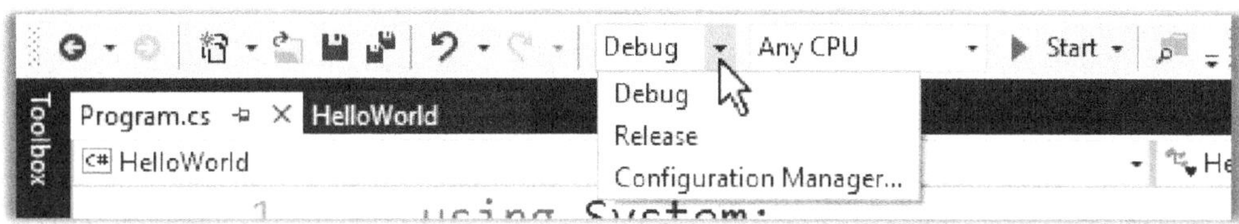

Figure 2-25. Build Configuration

By default, Visual Studio provides two build configurations: Debug and Release. The current configuration is selected via a dropdown box in the Standard toolbar.

The Debug configuration adds metadata and other information to the built assembly providing links that Visual Studio requires to debug projects. Debug assemblies do not run as optimally as Release assemblies because they are designed for testing and debugging, not production. Additionally, some methods in the System.Diagnostics.Debug class only work when compiled and executed using the Debug configuration. The resulting assembly and supporting files are output to the following subdirectory under the project directory:

```
<Project>/bin/Debug
```

The typical files generated for a console application include the following:

- `<Project>.exe` — Compiled assembly
- `<Project>.exe.config` — Assembly configuration file (from app.config)
- `<Project>.pdb` — Program debug metadata file
- `<Project>.vshost.exe` — Visual Studio debugger assembly
- `<Project>.vshost.exe.config` — Debugger assembly config file
- `<Project>.vshost.pdb` — Debugger debug metadata file

As long as the correct .NET Framework is installed on the target machine only the first two files in the list are required to run the program there. If debugging information is desired on the target machine (not typical) then the third file (*.pdb) is also required. The final three files are used by Visual Studio when running the program in debug mode.

The Release configuration is very similar to the Debug configuration. In fact, they emit the same output files, except Release builds output their files to:

```
<Project>/bin/Release
```

Again, the biggest difference between the configurations is that the Release-mode files are optimized for deployment to a target machine but Debug builds are optimized for Visual Studio debugger integration.

Additional build configuration information is located in the "Project" → "Properties..." window under the "Build" tab.

2.8 Debugging

Let's face it, nobody writes perfect programs on the first attempt, especially for non-trivial programs. As a result it is useful to be able to see what is actually going on in the code as it is executing. Visual Studio has a robust debugging system that allows programmers to temporarily stop code execution, interrogate or change the values of variables and then continue execution either one line at a time or without further interruption. This is generally considered far superior to emitting text in the output windows, although that can be a very useful technique as well.

Breakpoints

```
class Program
{
    static void Main(string[] args)
    {
        Console.WriteLine("Hello");
    }
}
```

Figure 2-26. Breakpoint

Breakpoints are like stop signs that are placed in code to pause execution of a program. A standard breakpoint is placed in the code by either left-clicking in the left margin next to the code to pause or by clicking F9 while the cursor is in the desired line of code. A breakpoint is removed by performing the same action. Whenever execution reaches this breakpoint, the code is immediately paused allowing the programmer to evaluate the contents (state) of variables.

Not all code lines are legal candidates for breakpoints. For instance, it is possible to put a breakpoint anywhere within a method (function) except on the method name. If you try to put a breakpoint on a line of code that doesn't support breakpoints Visual Studio will either ignore the request or place the breakpoint at the next legal position.

Since hitting a breakpoint requires the code to be executing, typically the programmer will either click the "Play" button in the Standard toolbar or press F5 to get the code running. When a breakpoint is reached, a yellow arrow will appear at the position where code execution stopped. This arrow is known as the execution pointer.

```
class Program
{
    static void Main(string[] args)
    {
        Console.WriteLine("Hello");
    }
}
```

Figure 2-27. Breakpoint Hit

It is important to note that the line of code where the execution pointer appears has not yet been executed. It actually indicates the next line of code that will execute. In fact, the arrow can be dragged to a new location, completely changing the pre-defined execution order of your code. Be aware that performing such operations can result in unwanted side-effects in the code's execution.

Conditional Breakpoints

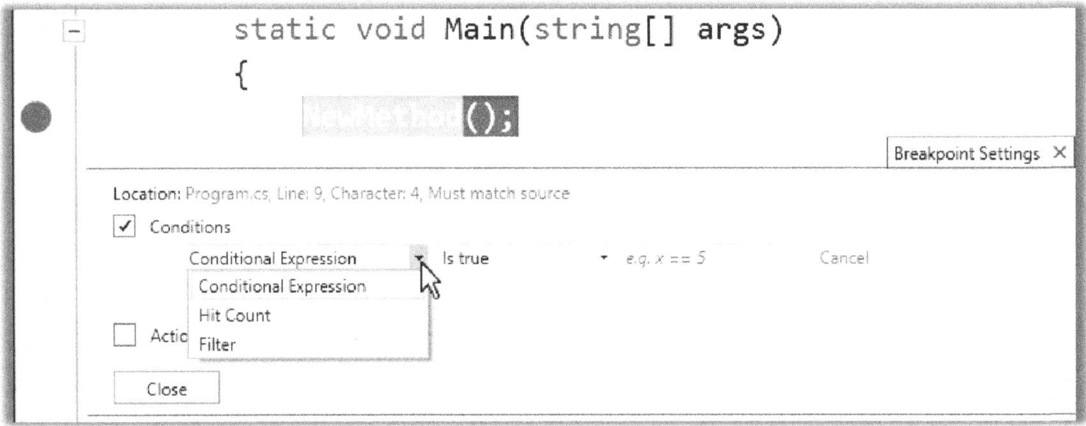

Figure 2-28. Conditional Breakpoints

Breakpoints can be configured to support more states than simply on or off. Right-clicking on a breakpoint brings up a context menu and one of the entries in the menu is "Conditions". Selecting this menu option pops up the "Breakpoint Settings" window. Breakpoint conditions can be configured to trigger the breakpoint when:

- a conditional expression evaluates to a given value
- the line that contains the breakpoint executes a given number (or multiple) of times
- the machine name, process or thread matches a given value

The first option, "Conditional Expression", is useful when you only want the code to pause when a variable equals a specific value. Since problems in code may occur only when varaibles reach certain values a conditional breakpoint like this can save many presses of the F5 key. Likewise, the second option "Hit Count" can be useful when you need to pause the code after the line with the breakpoint has executed a certain number of times. For instance, you may know the code runs just fine the first 100 times a line of code executes, but fails on the 101st iteration. Again, it is helpful to not have to hit F5 100 times just to get to that state. The last option, "Filter" is mostly useful when debugging multithreaded code.

A second checkbox exists on the Breakpoint Settings popup window called "Action". This setting allows you to write a value to the Output window. Alternatively, you could also add System.Diagnostics.Debug.WriteLine() statements directly in the code, but then you would have to rememebr to either remove them or comment them out.

You can view all breakpoints in the Breakpoints window using the "Debug" → "Windows" → "Breakpoints" menu or the Ctrl+D,B shortcut.

Code Stepping

Once program execution is paused due to a breakpoint, the programmer controls how execution proceeds by using step commands which are located in the "Debug" toolbar found in the "View" → "Toolbars" menu.

Figure 2-29. Debug Toolbar

The following table describes the functionality of the buttons in the toolbar.

Table 2-11. Debug Toolbar Buttons

Button	Shortcut	Description
	Ctrl+Alt+Break	Pauses the executing program.
	Shift+F5	Terminates the executing program.
	Ctrl+Shift+F5	Terminates the executing program and then restarts it.
	Ctrl+Shift+R	Refreshes a Windows app.
	Alt+* (Num*)	Shows the next statement.
	F11	Steps into the method or property that the execution pointer (yellow arrow) is on.
	F10	Steps over the method or property that the execution pointer is on.
	Shift+F11	Steps out of the executing method or property back to the statement that called this method.

Button	Shortcut	Description
		Shows the thread that code statements are executing within when paused in the debugger.
Continue	F5	This button continues execution of the program until another breakpoint is encountered or the program ends. *This button is actually in the Standard toolbar and is the "Start" button when code is not running.*

When your program is in break mode, you may wish to continue execution immediately which is done by clicking the "Continue" button (F5). However, if you wish to execute one line at a time that is accomplished with the "Step Over" (F10) and "Step Into" (F11) buttons. If the execution pointer is on a function call, using "Step Into" will cause the execution pointer to step into that function. The "Step Over" button, on the other hand, executes that function as a single statement anddoes not evaluate each line of that function individually. When inside a function, the "Step Out" button will finish executing the function in a single step and return control back to the calling code. If you wish to terminate the code immediately, the "Stop" button will cancel all execution and return Visual Studio to edit mode.

Watch Windows

Stepping through the code after a breakpoint is only useful if you can see what is going on with the state of your program's variables. There are many ways to accomplish this. The simplest technique is to hover the mouse over a variable you wish to see the value of:

```
static void Main(string[] args)
{
    int x = 5;
    x++;    x 5
    Console.WriteLine(x);
}
```

Figure 2-30. Showing Value of a Variable

However, this technique is only good for showing one value at a time. Instead, consider using one of the "watch" windows. A watch window is a table that either automatically displays the types and values of variables or can allow the programmer to type in variables or simple expressions to evaluate.

Autos

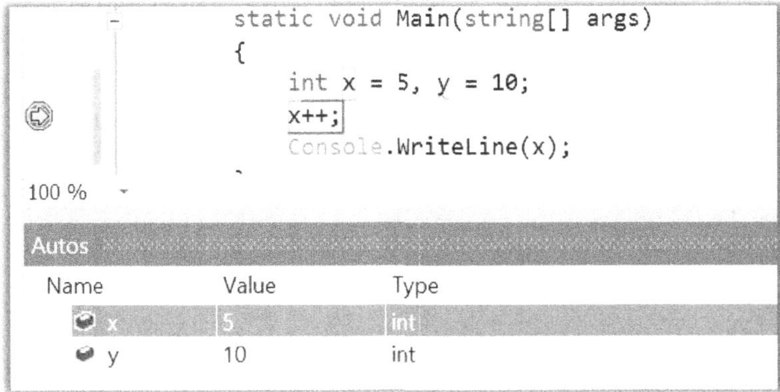

Figure 2-31. Autos Window

The Autos watch window displays the variables contained on the current line of execution and the previous line. By clicking on the value of one of the variables you can manually edit its value. This feature is especially useful if you need to reproduce execution of the code with a specific set of values and you don't wish to "hardcode" those values in the code itself. To show this window, Visual Studio must be in "run" mode and then select "Debug" → "Windows" → "Autos", or Ctrl+D,A.

Locals

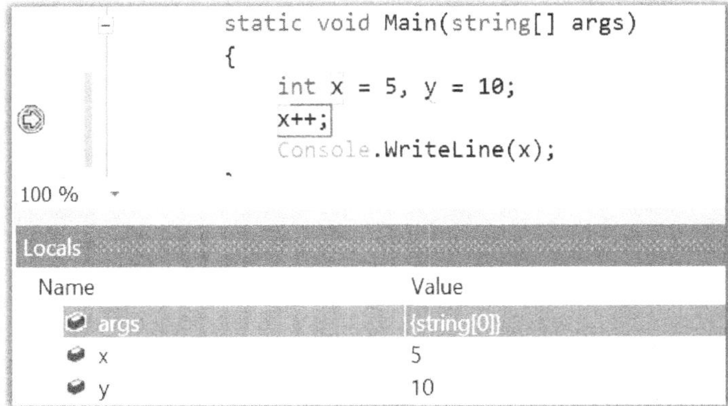

Figure 2-32. Locals Window

The Locals window provides almost the same functionality as the Autos window except it displays all of the varaibles defined within the local scope. In other words, it shows the variables declared within the function that the execution pointer is in. If there are a lot of variables defined within the local scope, this view can be very "noisy". Switching between the Autos and Locals windows is a common technique employed by programmers. Just like the Autos window, the values can be changed by clicking on them with the mouse and typing in a new value. This window is found under "Debug" → "Windows" → "Locals", or Ctrl+D,L.

Watch

The Watch windows are very much like the Locals and Autos windows; however, instead of only monitoring the value of variables, simple expressions can be analyzed. There are four Watch windows that can contain their own item and they are located under "Debug" → "Windows" → "Watch". Alternatively, you can right-click on a value and select "Add Watch" while the code is in break mode.

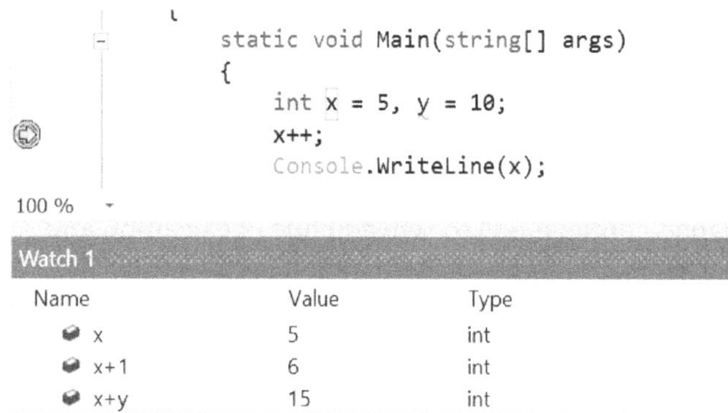

Figure 2-33. Watch Window

The row below the last entry in the Watch window is editable which allows you to add new entries. In the example above, the last two rows were added manually using this technique. If the Name entry in the grid is invalid, or the variable indicated does not exist, an error is displayed in the Value column. Note that in this example the value of *x* is not actually modified. "*x* + 1" is evaluated without altering the current value of *x* since it is used as an rvalue in the expression. Just be aware that expressions like "++*x*" can affect the value of variables from the watch window.

Edit and Continue

Another useful feature of programmingin C# is the ability to change the code while debugging. When the program is in break mode code can be modified by the programmer without having to completely stop the program, modify the code and restart the program and attempt to return to the state where a problem was detected. Essentially, when Visual Studio detects a change has been made to the underlying code it will recompile the program on-the-fly and then return to normal execution. Be aware, certain changes should be avoided that would leave the program in an unstable state, such as completely removing variables that have dependencies in other parts of the code, such as loop variables or other critical data. Clearly, this is a powerful tool, but it can also lead to other issues so care should be taken when employing it. "Edit and Continue" is managed via the "Tools" → "Options" window under "Debugging" → "General".

2.9 Code Snippets

Code snippets provide a way to insert pre-defined snippets of code within your programs. Each language has its own set of snippets packaged with Visual Studio that can be inserted via the "Insert Snippet" context menu or by typing a snippet's shortcut. For instance, a common command in C# is Console.WriteLine(). Instead of typing this entire command you could enter: [C][W][Tab][Tab], that is "cw" followed by two tabs.

Other snippets are intended to wrap, or surround, existing code like a `try` block. These snippets can be added to the code by selecting the code you wish to wrap then picking the appropriate snippet from the "Surround With…" context menu, in this case "try".

Customization of code snippets is possible by editing the existing snippets shown in the "Tools" → "Code Snippets Manager" window. Most snippets are stored in the following directory and require administrative privileges to modify them using Visual Studio, Notepad or some other text editor:

```
%VSINSTALLDIR%\VC#\Snippets\1033\Visual C#
```

Any changes to snippets may require a restart of Visual Studio to take effect.

Snippet syntax utilizes XML (Extensible Markup Language) which is beyond the scope of this book. There are many online resources discussing the modification and creation of snippets which you can find doing a simple web search.

2.10 NuGet Package Manager

Rather than come up with a new description of what NuGet is, here is what is stated on the www.NuGet.org site itself:

> "NuGet is the package manager for the Microsoft development platform including .NET. The NuGet client tools provide the ability to produce and consume packages. The NuGet Gallery is the central package repository used by all package authors and consumers."

In a nutshell, NuGet is the place to get new and updated components to enrich your .NET-based applications. Moving forward, many of the core components of .NET will be deployed via NuGet update packages at a faster rate than full .NET Framework releases. In addition, some components that are useful for creating robust applications are available only from NuGet, especially new ones.

NuGet Package Manager UI

The NuGet Package Manager provides a convenient interface to browse for packages and install them in your solutions and projects. To display: "Tools" → "NuGet Package Manager" → "Manage NuGet Packages for Solution…"

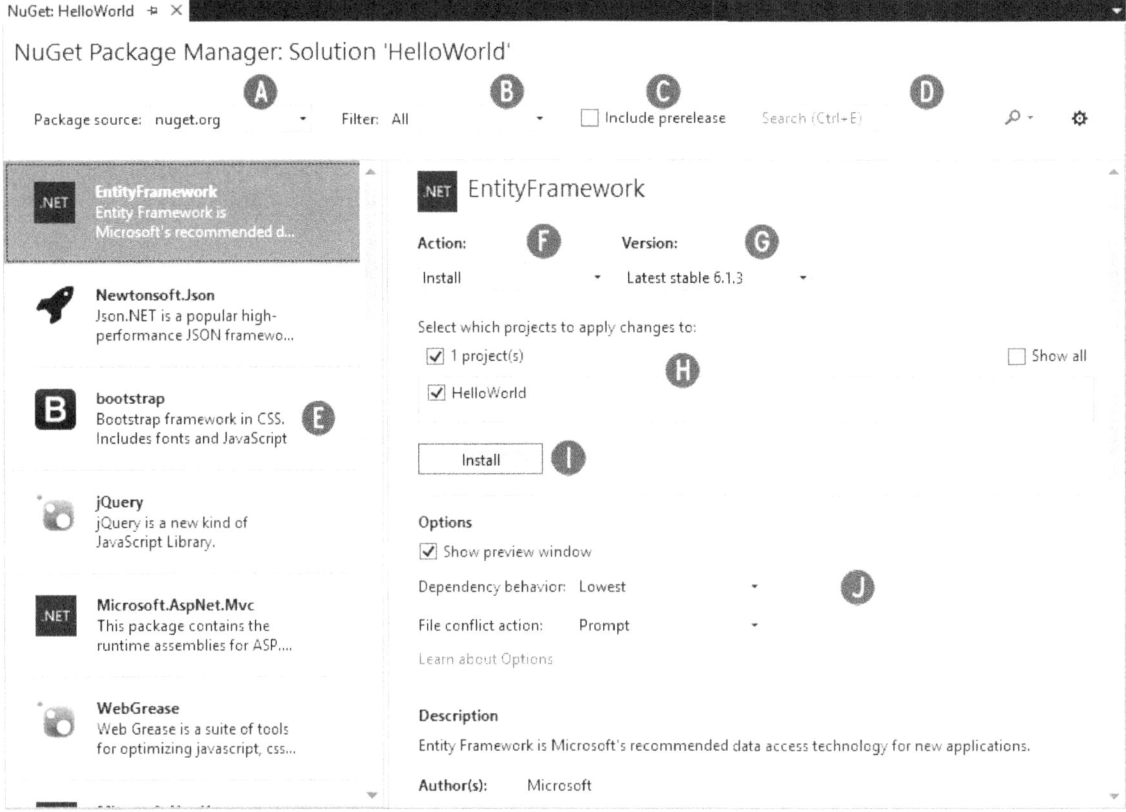

Figure 2-34. NuGet Package Manager User Interface

A. The "Package source" dropdown selects the source of the NuGet packages. The choices are "nuget.org" and "Microsoft and .NET". The "nuget.org" source is a superset of all packages in the NuGet repository. The "Microsoft and .NET" source contains only official .NET packages developed by Microsoft and the .NET team.
B. The "Filter" dropdown has three selections: "All", "Installed" and "Upgrade available".
C. "Include prerelease" indicates if you want to see "beta" packages, or packages not released for production. Use these with caution.
D. Text to search for within the available packages based on the criteria selected in the first three selections.
E. List of components that match the given search criteria.
F. Indicates the action to perform regarding the selected component. The choices are: "Install", "Update" and "Uninstall". These choices are filtered based on the current status of the selected component within your project.
G. The specific version of the component you wish to target can be selected here.
H. This list contains the projects to install/update/uninstall the component to.
I. This button performs the component update.
J. This section contains the configurations for dealing with conflicts and installation options.

Once the desired component is installed or updated, the References folder in the Solution Explorer will reflect the change. In addition, the downloaded component assemblies will be placed in a "packages" folder inside the solution directory. If this folder is deleted or damaged it will be repaired the next time the solution is built.

Package Manager Console

The Package Manager Console is an alternative mechanism for maintaining NuGet packages. Instead of a UI to install and manage packages, a console tool window is displayed that allows allows text input. To display: "Tools" → "NuGet Package Manager" → "Package Manager Console".

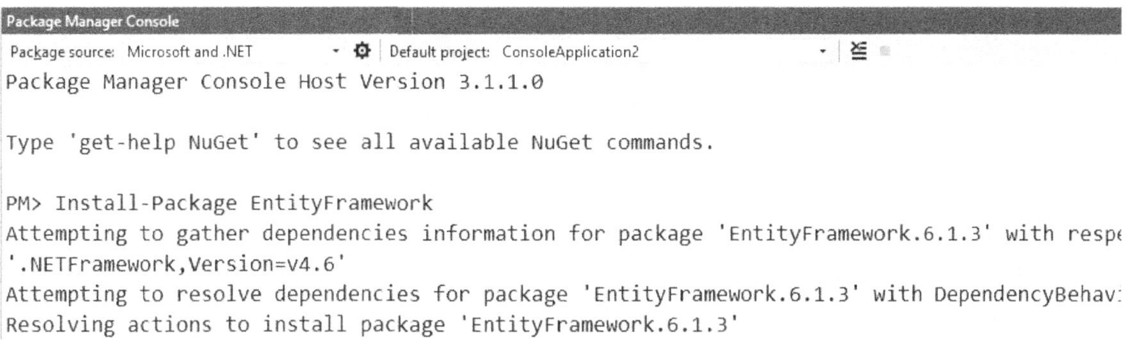

Figure 2-35. NuGet Package Manager Console

There is no real benefit for using the NuGet console instead of the UI, but it can be quicker to install items that you know the package names for. The most common commands are:

- Install-Package <package name>
- Update-Package <package name>
- Uninstall-Package <package name>

Each of these commands has optional parameters to select the specific project to modify and what version of the package to install or update. For detailed information about each of these and other commands enter the following command:

- get-help NuGet

If the NuGet help packages are out of date this command will prompt you to update them. Alternatively, go to http://docs.nuget.org for up-to-the-minute documentation on NuGet.

2.11 Summary

Visual Studio is one of the best programming tools available on any platform. The IDE supports dozens of built-in tool windows and third-party plug-ins. Additionally, different versions of Visual Studio also support team environments for superior code collaboration. With the release of Visual Studio 2015 most key platforms such as Windows, iOS and Android can be targeted directly from this single environment. Most importantly, Visual Studio provides an interface to perform all of the code examples within this text. Now it's time to get your feet wet and start programming in C#...

3

3. Console Applications

3.1 Console Applications

A console application is one of the simplest program types available to C# programmers. Unlike more sophisticated Windows Forms or XAML-based applications, console applications are not graphical. They consist only of a window that allows simple input and output of text. In many ways, the console window is a holdover from the days of MS-DOS (Microsoft Disk Operating System), the operating system that preceded Windows. Actually, Windows used to run on top of DOS, but that is another conversation entirely. In fact, many of the familiar commands from DOS are still available, such as "CD", "DIR" and "XCOPY". Console applications can be run by double-clicking on their program icon like any other Windows program or they can be run within the context of an already running "Command Prompt" shell by navigating to their directory and typing in the app name. You can bring up a console window by searching for the "Command Prompt" program from the Windows Start Screen/Menu (Windows 8+) or by pressing [⊞]+[R] then typing in "cmd.exe". Figure 3-1 demonstrates a console window.

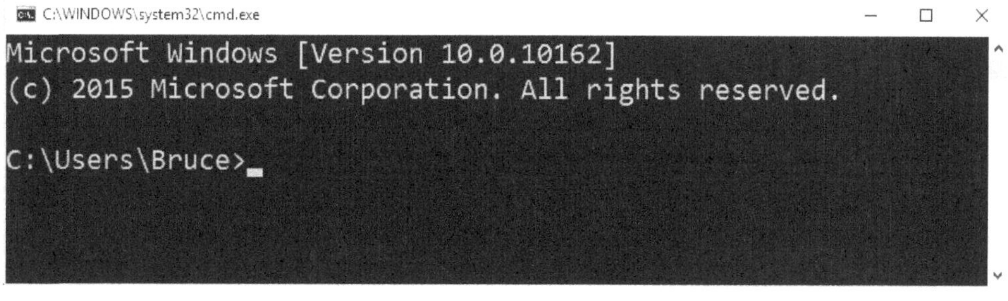

```
C:\WINDOWS\system32\cmd.exe
Microsoft Windows [Version 10.0.10162]
(c) 2015 Microsoft Corporation. All rights reserved.

C:\Users\Bruce>_
```

Figure 3-1. Sample Console Window

By default the console window can display 25 lines of 80 characters. This can be altered by selecting the control box icon in the top-left of the window and clicking on "Properties". Additionally, you can change the font and size of the text which can be helpful based on your monitor's resolution. However, you should always maintain a minimum of 80 characters in width to maintain compatibility with most console applications.

Because of their simplicity, most of the exercises in this book will utilize console applications. This way you can focus on learning the C# language first, then apply what you've learned to more interesting program types.

Creating Console Applications

To create a console application, first launch Visual Studio. Then, under the "File" menu, click "New", then "Project" (You can also select "New Project" directly from the Start Page if it is displayed). You should then be greeted with the New Project dialog, as displayed in Figure 3-2.

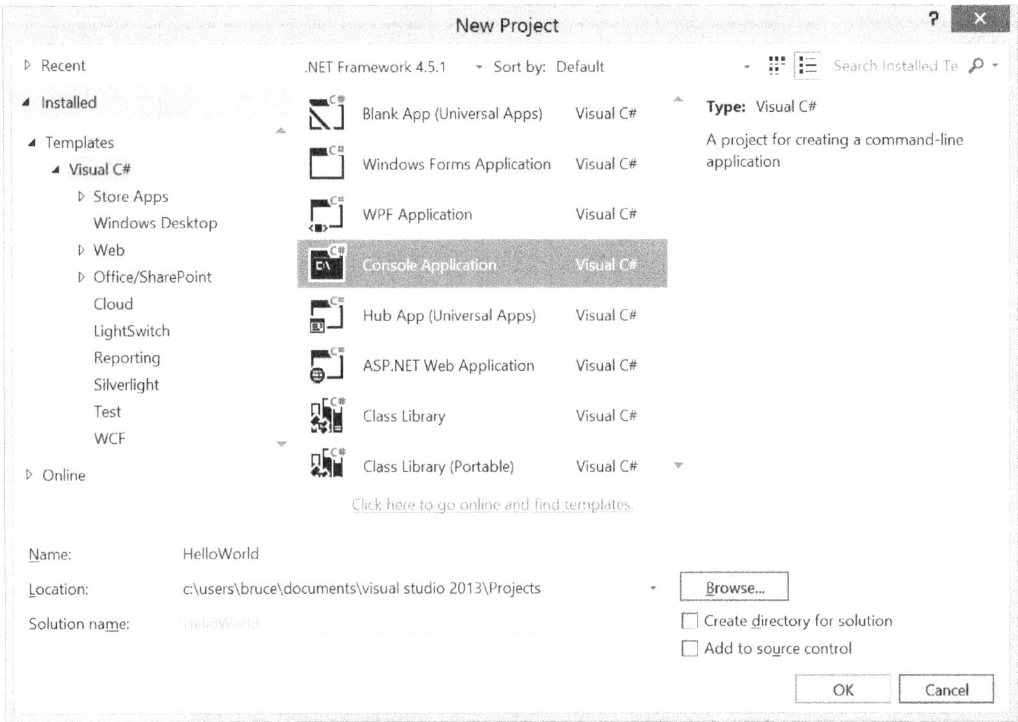

Figure 3-2. New Project - Console Application

Typically, you will want the most recent .NET Framework selected in the dropdown list at the top of the dialog. On the left side of the dialog, ensure you have "Visual C#" selected under the "Templates" heading. Then, select the "Console Application" template in the center of the dialog. Depending on the version of Visual Studio you are using, the list of templates may not match the example shown, so it may require a bit of scrolling to find it. Alternatively, you can search for a template using the text box in the top-right corner of the dialog.

It is not necessary, at this stage, to create a separate directory for the solution since there will typically only be one project in the solution, so leave that option unchecked. Later on, when you create more advanced solutions with multiple projects, then it makes sense to have a separate solution directory.

Set the name and location of the project to something appropriate - by default it will place the project in your documents folder under "Visual Studio XXXX/Projects", where XXXX matches your version of Visual Studio. For this example, the project name is "HelloWorld". Click "OK" to create the project and begin editing the C# program. In the next section we'll look at how we can modify the program to do something interesting.

3.2 Program.Main()

The life of a console application exists between the curly braces "{ }" of the "Main()" method of the Program class. Any text you wish to read from the console window or write to it must occur inside this method. Later on, we'll discuss creating other methods that you can call from Main(), but for now we'll keep our code constrained to this one method. FYI, method is another word for function, and the term method is more commonly encountered in the C# world. Also note the Main method belongs to a class called Program, part of a namespace called "HelloWorld", but that conversation is also best left for a later time. The basic structure of a console app is illustrated in Listing 3-1.

Listing 3-1. The Main Method

```
1  using System;
2  using System.Collections.Generic;
3  using System.Linq;
4  using System.Text;
5  using System.Threading.Tasks;
6
7  namespace HelloWorld
8  {
9    class Program
10   {
11     static void Main(string[] args)
12     {
13       // All code goes here...
14     }
15   }
16 }
```

In the above example, all of your custom code would replace the comment in between the braces immediately under the Main() method definition at line 13. For the rest of this chapter we will only look at the Main() method, however the other code must remain intact for the program to run, **so don't delete it!**

3.3 The Console Class

Now that we have the basic structure of the console application in place we need a mechanism to interact with the console window that is created when the program runs. Fortunately, there is a Console class that provides this functionality right out of the box. Without getting into the details about what a class is, we can still utilize Console to process our inputs and outputs. The Console class is essentially a container that holds methods that allow us to print text data, known as strings, to the console screen or read strings in from the keyboard.

Console.Write()

First, let's look at how we can write text to the console. The Console class contains a method called Write() that does precisely what we need to output text to the console. So, if we were to follow programming tradition, out first program would simply display "Hello World!" and then exit. To do this, we will pass that text to the Console.Write() method as shown in Listing 3-2. Notice that the text to be printed is surrounded by quotes which are the delimiters for string data. Any text that does not fit on a single line in the console window is automatically wrapped to the next line.

Listing 3-2. Hello World! in C#

```
static void Main(string[] args)
{
  Console.Write("Hello World!");
}
```

We could then compile and run the application by pressing F5, or clicking the play button in the standard toolbar. However, if you do this you may notice that the console window simply flashes on your screen without giving you enough time to read what was printed. There are several ways we can deal with this problem. The first method would be to execute the program directly from the command prompt in an already open console window. This, however, requires you to open a console window (⊞+R, cmd.exe), then using the "CD" command to navigate to the "bin/debug" directory under the project folder wherever it was created. Let's consider that approach an academic exercise that we will use only when absolutely necessary. The next option is to programmatically pause the program after our output has been displayed but prior to the closing curly brace of "Main". We will use the Console.ReadLine() method to force the application to pause until the user presses the Enter key.

Console.ReadLine()

The ReadLine method of Console behaves similarly to the Write() method except instead of passing a string of text that needs to be displayed to the method, any text entered from the keyboard is returned as the result of the ReadLine() call. Since we have not discussed variables and method return values yet, this information may be a little harder to understand than the Write method. However, at this juncture, we don't really care what the user may type on the keyboard, so all we need to do is execute the ReadLine() command and ignore any return value. Later, when we need to store any input the user may type prior to the Enter key, we will assign the result of the ReadLine() method to a string variable.

Listing 3-3. Pausing Execution with Console.ReadLine

```
static void Main(string[] args)
{
  Console.Write("Hello World!");
  Console.ReadLine();
}
```

Now, when we run the program with F5 we will see the "Hello World!" text displayed in the console window that pops up. The program will terminate when we hit the Enter key.

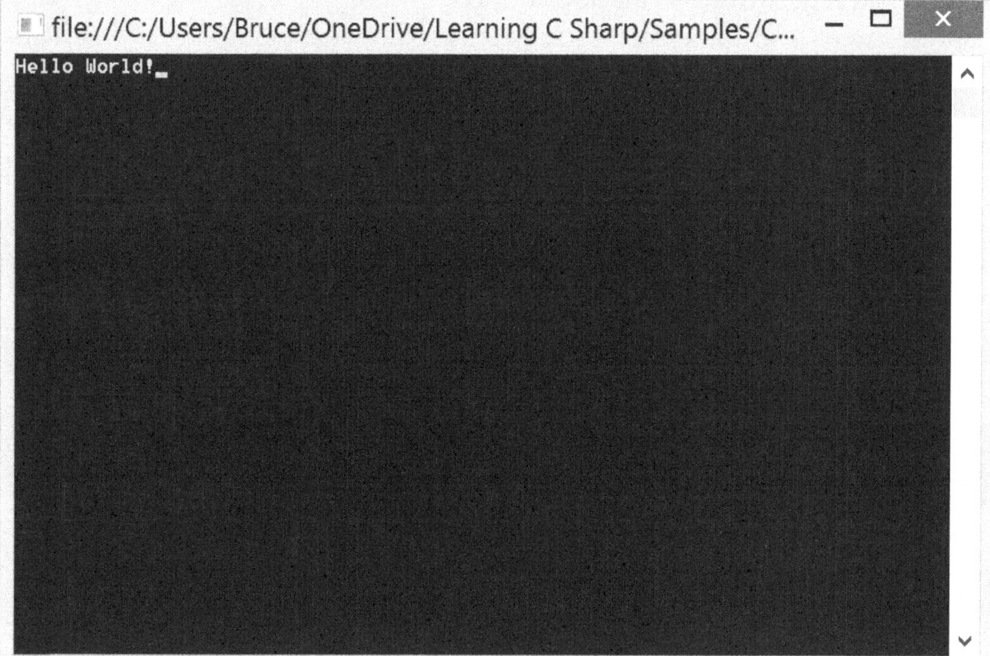

Figure 3-3. Hello World! Output

Notice that we made one huge assumption with this program – we assume the user knows to hit the Enter key to terminate the program. It is obvious to us since we wrote the code, but it is a very important lesson to learn: don't assume the user knows how to use your applications! To alleviate this problem it would be helpful to provide a prompt to inform the user what is expected of them.

It is important to emphasize that all user input from the console is always text, whether it is string data using ReadLine() or characters (char) using one of the other read methods. This being the case, it is the responsibility of the programmer to take these text-based values and convert them to other data types when necessary. This topic, parsing, is covered in detail later in the book.

Console.WriteLine()

If we were to add another Console.Write() statement immediately after the existing one, any text we output would be jammed right up against the "Hello World!" text. This is because the Console.Write() method places the caret, or the text cursor, immediately after the last character printed – the "!" in our case. So, any additional text that is output to the console will start at that position. Fortunately, the Console class also has a WriteLine() method which outputs text in the same manner as Write(), with the addition of a carriage return after the last character printed. This means that the cursor will be placed on the first character positon of the next line. So, with a few modifications to our code, we can get the desired effect.

Listing 3-4. Hello World! with Prompt

```
static void Main(string[] args)
{
  Console.WriteLine("Hello World!");
  Console.Write("Press <ENTER> to quit...");
  Console.ReadLine();
}
```

Now the output from running the code should look like:

Figure 3-4. Hello World! with Prompt Output

As you can see, the output now matches our expectations.

3.4 Adding Color to the Console

By default, the color of the console window is black with gray text. While this is sufficient for most console apps, you may desire more bling for your interface. For instance, changing the color of the console text may be desirable if you wish to differentiate prompts from user input. The Console class has two properties that allow you to change the background and text color: BackgroundColor and ForegroundColor, respectively. These color properties apply to both input and output. All color settings retain their values until they are changed again. The example in Listing 3-5 demonstrates how to manipulate the text color depending on whether the text is being output to the console or input from the keyboard.

Listing 3-5. Console Colors

```
static void Main(string[] args)
{
  Console.ForegroundColor = ConsoleColor.White;
  Console.Write("Please enter your name: ");
  Console.ForegroundColor = ConsoleColor.Yellow;
  string name = Console.ReadLine();
  Console.ForegroundColor = ConsoleColor.Cyan;
  Console.WriteLine("Hello, " + name);
  Console.ResetColor();
  Console.ReadLine();
}
```

Notice that the color "`White`" in the first assignment has the prefix "`ConsoleColor.`" All 16 possible colors are defined in a data structure known as an `enum` called ConsoleColor. It is not important at this time to fully understand what an `enum` is, just how to use it. Visual Studio's IntelliSense feature makes using enums easy. After the "." is typed following ConsoleColor, the complete list of possible colors is displayed, which can be selected by mouse or keyboard (Tab or Enter). The above example first changes the foreground to white to prompt the user for information. The text color is then changed to yellow for the text the user types in using the keyboard. The value the user types in is stored in a `string` variable called "name" which is used again when the name it is output back to the console in a salutation. That greeting is set to cyan (turquoise). Finally, a call is made to reset the color to its default value: Console.ResetColor(). Figure 3-5 shows what this output looks like.

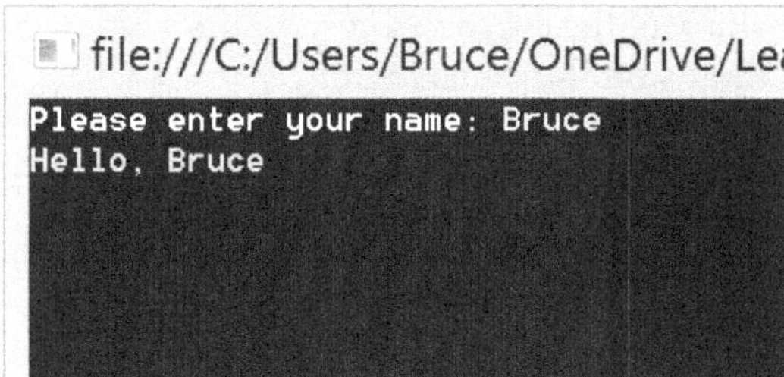

Figure 3-5. Console Color Output

3.5 Resizing the Console and Repositioning the Cursor

Another customization available to console applications is changing its size. Sometimes 80 columns is not sufficient for the information you wish to display. In those instances you can set the property Console.WindowWidth to the desired number of columns. You can similarly set the height using Console.WindowHeight. If you wish to change both values at the same time you can also do that using the Console.SetWindowSize() method, where the two required parameters represent the desired width and height, respectively. Just be sure to check the

LargestWindowWidth and LargestWindowHeight properties of Console before changing the size, otherwise you may try to make the window bigger that what is allowed causing an exception to be thrown. Listing 3-6 demonstrates how to adjust the console window size.

Listing 3-6. Console Window Size

```
// Get the maximum extent for the console window width and height
int maxWidth = Console.LargestWindowWidth;
int maxHeight = Console.LargestWindowHeight;
Console.WriteLine("The largest window is " + maxWidth + " by " + maxHeight);
// Set the size using the individual properties
Console.WindowWidth = maxWidth;
Console.WindowHeight = maxHeight;
// Or, set them both with one command
Console.SetWindowSize(maxWidth, maxHeight);
```

Another thing to note is that the console window size is based on the font selected. A larger font will shrink the allowable window size, whereas a smaller font will increase the maximum size of the window. Unfortunately, it is not possible to change the font using the Console class; it must be done manually from the console window itself.

Not only can you change the size of the console window, you can also change where the cursor is located. This is a very useful feature if you need to jump the cursor to a location other than where the default position would be. For instance, let's assume your program requires a number to be input from the console and the user types in "ABC". Since this is invalid data you may want to have them retype a new value in the exact same place.

Setting the cursor position is very similar to how you change the window size. There are two properties that allow you to set the left and top position of the cursor, Console.CursorLeft and Console.CursorTop. Similarly, you can set both values simultaneously with Console.SetCursorPosition(). Both methods are shown in Listing 3-7.

Listing 3-7. Changing Cursor Position

```
// Set the cursor to the top-left position using properties
Console.CursorLeft = 0;
Console.CursorTop = 0;
// Set the cursor position using a single method call
Console.SetCursorPosition(0, 0);
```

3.6 Command Line Arguments

A common feature for Windows applications is the ability to pass arguments to the application. For instance, if you run Notepad.exe using the command line (or ⊞+R) you can actually tell it what document to initially load by specifying it after the program name, such as:

```
C:\>Notepad.exe "sample.txt"
```

Figure 3-6. Sample Command Line Argument

In this example, the filename "sample.txt" is an argument passed to the Notepad application. There is no restriction as to what text can be passed as an argument to an application; however, there is a functional limit to the maximum size of a command issued from the command line (it is quite large for most modern version of the Windows OS, approximately 32,000 characters). Also, programs can specify any number of arguments that can be accepted, once again subject to the command line length limit. Multiple arguments are automatically separated into individually values using whitespace as the delimiter. In the following example, we are calling the "DIR" program telling it which directory to display files from, and that it should use "wide format":

```
C:\>DIR "C:\Program Files" /W
```

Figure 3-7. Multiple Command Line Arguments

Notice that the directory "Program Files" contains a space. To keep that from becoming two separate arguments, "C:\Program" and "Files", the entire argument is surrounded by quotes. There is a second argument with the "/W" value, which for this program means "wide format". For the "DIR" program, the order of these two arguments is irrelevant. However, some programs require the arguments to be in a very specific order. Additionally, some programs prefer "switches", like the "/W" above, to use hyphens instead of slashes, like "-W". Each program's documentation should list what arguments are valid and what format they must be in.

Most executable style applications you can create using C# also support command line arguments. You may have noticed in previous examples that the Main method of the Program class, where we've written all our custom code, accepts a parameter. Here's a refresher of what that looks like:

Listing 3-8. Command Line Arguments in Main()

```
static void Main(string[] args)
```

This parameter, called "`args`", is a `string` array. An array is a variable that contains zero or many items of the given type, in this case strings. Arrays in C# are 0-based so the first item is at index 0, the second at index 1, the third at index 2, etc. So, if we write a program that accepts command line arguments, and the arguments passed in are the same as in the DIR sample in Figure 3-7, we could read and display those values with the following code:

Listing 3-9. Processing Command Line Arguments

```
if (args.Length >= 2)
{
  Console.WriteLine("First: " + args[0]);
  Console.WriteLine("Second: " + args[1]);
}
```

The corresponding output would be:

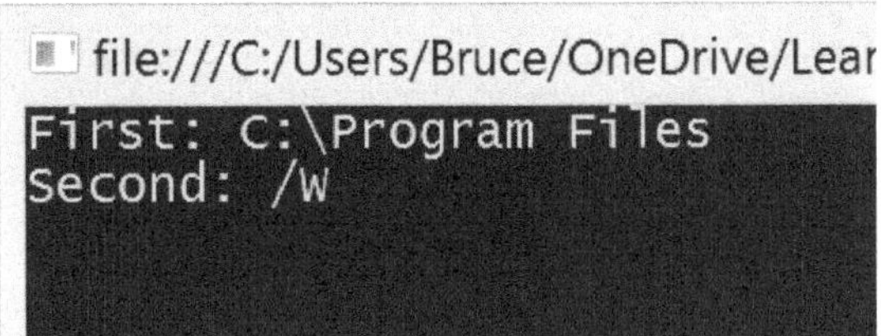

Figure 3-8. Command Line Arguments Output

It is very important to ensure you do not access an index of an array that does not exist, which is why the code is wrapped with an "`if`" statement. Accessing *args*`[2]`, for instance, would yield an exception. Likewise, it is never acceptable to access an array with a negative index. However, this section is not about arrays, so please refer to Chapter 5 for more details.

Accessing Command Line Arguments via Environment

It is also possible to access the command line arguments from methods other than Main(), without having to pass the arguments to those methods. The Environment class, which is part of the System namespace, contains a method and property to access the command line arguments.

The Environment.CommandLine property returns the entire command line (including the path and executable name) as a single string. This can be useful if you need the full context of how the application was launched.

The second method is to call Environment.GetCommandLineArgs() which returns an array identical to the *args* parameter of Main(). If you do all of your command line parameter processing in Main there is seldom any reason to call this method.

Debugging Command Line Arguments

There are several ways to pass arguments to an executable, some of which are not very conducive to debugging in Visual Studio. Since testing code is a vitally important step to developing robust programs, it is helpful to know how best to deal with command line arguments when testing in debug mode.

The first way to pass arguments to a program is to type in the executable name and arguments on the command line or the Windows Run prompt. However, the only way to debug an application in this manner would be to either put many debugging output statements in your code or to attach the Visual Studio debugger to the command line process. Neither of these approaches are ideal as the debugging output would clutter your console window and attaching to a process can be tricky.

The second way of passing arguments to an application is to drag and drop a file onto an executable. Clearly, this approach is only useful if your program expects a filename (or several if many are dropped). Also, you are left with the same debugging limitations as presented in the first method.

The third way is to use Visual Studio itself to pass command line parameters to your program's Main method. From the menu, select "Project" followed by "XXX Properties…", where XXX is the name of your project. Alternatively, double-click on the "Properties" node in the Solution Explorer. In the properties window that is displayed, select the "Debug" tab on the left. Look for the "Start Options" section in the property page. In there you will find the text box titled "Command line arguments". Type in this box whatever arguments you wish, as demonstrated in Figure 3-9.

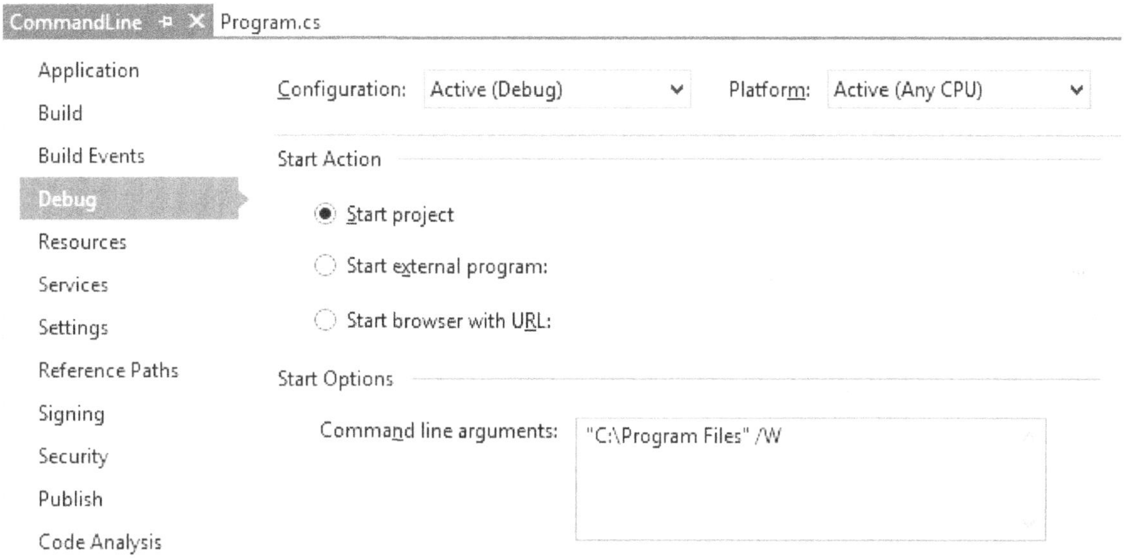

Figure 3-9. Command Line Arguments Debugging

Now, when you run your application in debug mode with F5, the values typed in that debug text box will be parsed into the *args* parameter of Main(). When you no longer wish to have debug command line arguments, simply clear that text box.

Note: The values in that are typed in the "Command line arguments" debug textbox are persisted in the project's "user" file which is stored alongside the ".csproj" file. If you delete this file the text box will also be cleared.

3.7 Other Useful Console Features

The Console class contains many other methods and properties which we have not discussed, some of which are far too advanced to be meaningful here. However, it is still important to know what other features are available even if you are not able to appreciate them at this time. The following chart lists some of the additional members of the Console class that we have not yet covered.

Table 3-1. Console Members

Console Member	Description
BufferHeight	The height (lines) of the memory buffer that stores console output
BufferWidth	The width (columns) of the memory buffer that stores console output
CapsLock/NumberLock	Gets a bool value that indicates if the Caps Lock/Number Lock key is pressed
CursorSize	An int value (0 – 100) that indicates the size of the cursor
CursorVisible	Indicates if the cursor is visible
Error/In/Out	Gets the standard error/input/output stream
KeyAvailable	Indicates if a key press is available in the input stream
Title	Title displayed in the console title bar
Beep()	Plays a beep sound
Clear()	Clears the console window
Read()	Reads the next character from the input stream
ReadKey()	Reads the next character or special key from the input stream

3.8 Summary

Console applications are text-based applications that allow for simple text interaction between the user and the program. The console can be resized to suit the program's needs and the text color can be changed to emphasize certain text or to simply provide a more pleasing UI. The data read from the console is always text based and additional steps must be taken to convert any input data into other types.

Console applications can accept command line arguments to customize how the program should be run. These arguments are application defined and are processed using the "`string[] args`" parameter of the Main() method.

4

4. Basic C# Constructs

This chapter will lay the foundation for your understanding of the C# language. Unfortunately, many of the features of C# are intertwined so you will learn some parts in this chapter while other parts will be addressed later in the book. Feel free to jump ahead to take a sneak peak but don't let the sheer volume of information overwhelm you.

We'll start by looking at some constructs for annotating your code with comments. It may seem like a secondary concern, but comments will help you write both understandable and maintainable code.

Later we'll look at the various data types built into the .NET Framework and C# and how to create, assign values to and modify variables of these types. We'll also briefly look at some advanced topics such as value and reference types and how to use them appropriately.

Finally we'll look at data conversion, or how to convert data from one type to another.

4.1 Comments

Comments are specialized statements that allow you to annotate your code but are not functional in terms of program execution. Comments help clarify your code by describing the functionality or purpose of that code. There are three flavors of comments in C#:

- Single-line comments
- Delimited Comments
- XML Comments

Single-Line Comments

Single line comments can be used on a line of code all by themselves or after the semicolon of a complete statement. The character sequence used to initiate a single-line comment is a double slash "//". No other statements can occur after a single-line comment, and the comment ends at the carriage return at the end of a line. Example single-line comments:

Listing 4-1. Single-line Comments

```
const double pi = 3.14159265359;  // Math π constant
double radius = 10;
// The next line calculates the area of a circle using the formula: A = π·r²
double area = pi * radius * radius;
```

Delimited Comments

Delimited comments, also known as comment blocks, are similar to single-line comments except they are intended for longer comments that span multiple lines of text. This is a technique commonly used to keep long comments from expanding beyond the right side of the editor window. The starting delimiter of this type of comment is "/*" and it ends with "*/". No functional code may exist between the delimiters. Also, carriage returns are treated like any other whitespace characters between the delimiters.

Listing 4-2. Delimited Comments

```
/*
The following code calculates the first 100 Fibonacci numbers.
The sequence starts with two 1's.  The next number in the series is
the sum of the previous two numbers in the sequence.
Ex: 1 1 2 3 5 8 13 21 34 55 ...
*/
```

XML Comments

XML comments are a special type of comment that is used to annotate entities in C#. These entities can be classes, structs, enums, variables, methods and events. XML stands for e**X**tensible **M**arkup **L**anguage and is a common data format used to represent hierarchical data. Data is stored as key-value pairs (tags) where the key tag is identified within angle brackets "<" and ">" and the closing tag includes a slash after the left angle bracket "</". The value for a key is stored between the key's open and closing tags. The following is a sample XML key-value pair where the key is "name" and the value is "John":

```
<name>John</name>
```

XML can also have nested elements, but that level of complexity is not necessary at this particular time.

Unlike other comment types, XML comments have the benefit of becoming embedded within compiled assemblies. This "metadata" is then used by IntelliSense and the Object Browser to display this information when contextually relevant. XML comments follow a specific template which is constructed when you type "///" on the line prior to the element you wish to annotate. For instance, when you type three slashes on the line prior to the Main() method, the following is displayed:

Listing 4-3. XML Comments Template

```
/// <summary>
///
/// </summary>
/// <param name="args"></param>
static void Main(string[] args)
{
```

The template that is created is tailored to the entity that is being annotated. In Listing 4-3 there are two areas that can be annotated, the first between the "`<summary>`" and "`</summary>`" tags, and the second between the "`<param name="args">`" and "`</param>`" tags. The first tag represents the summary, or description, of the method. The second tag is the description of the "args" parameter. Assume these fields are populated with data in Listing 4-4.

Listing 4-4. XML Comments Template Complete

```
/// <summary>
/// This is the main method of the program
/// </summary>
/// <param name="args">Command line arguments passed to the program</param>
static void Main(string[] args)
{
```

Then, once the program is compiled, these comments will be embedded in the application metadata and are visible from the Object Browser, as such:

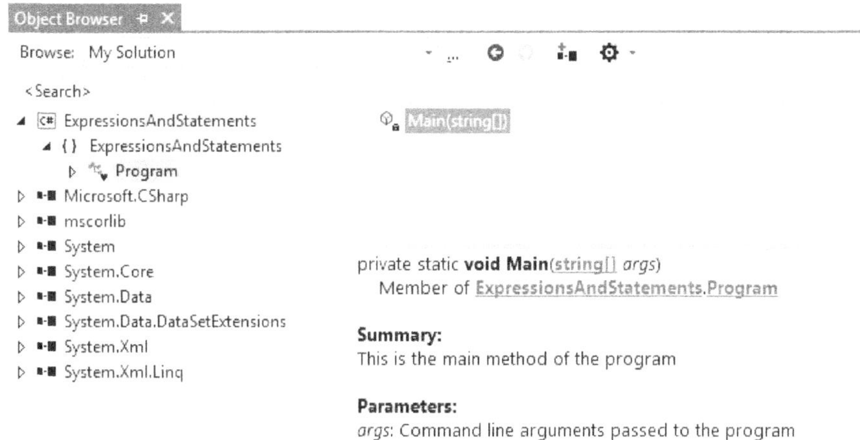

Figure 4-1. Object Browser Showing XML Comments

In the case of a method that you can call from Main(), adding XML comments to that method will display help to the programmer as they are typing in the method call. Even though creating methods is probably beyond your current expertise level, the results should be relatively self-explanatory based on the following examples.

Listing 4-5. XML Comments on a Method

```
/// <summary>
/// Calculates the area of a cricle with the given radius
/// </summary>
/// <param name="radius">Radius of circle</param>
/// <returns>Area of a circle with the given radius</returns>
static double CircleArea(double radius)
{
  return Math.PI * radius * radius;
}
```

Then, in code, when the programmer starts typing in a call to CircleArea(), IntelliSense will provide a popup tooltip with context-sensitive help, including the XML comments.

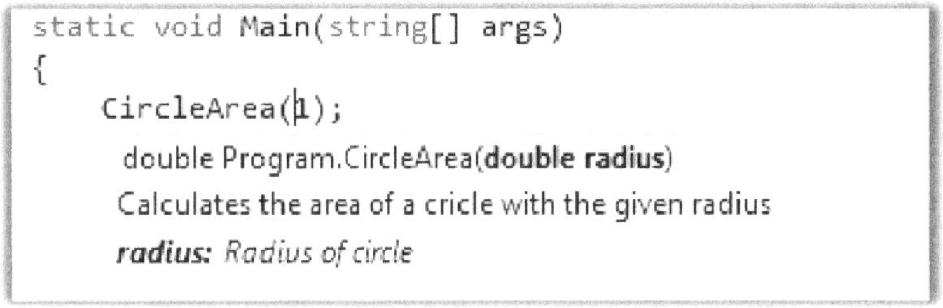

```
static void Main(string[] args)
{
    CircleArea(1);
     double Program.CircleArea(double radius)
     Calculates the area of a cricle with the given radius
     radius: Radius of circle
```

Figure 4-2. XML Comments and IntelliSense

It is also possible to emit the XML comments into a separate file when a program is compiled. This allows you to use a help file generating tool to create documentation for your application based on the embedded XML comments. To turn this feature on, go to the project's property page (Menu: Project → Properties...) and select the "Build" tab. On this tab you will find the Output section and there is a checkbox to turn on the XML documentation output file and a textbox to identify the filename.

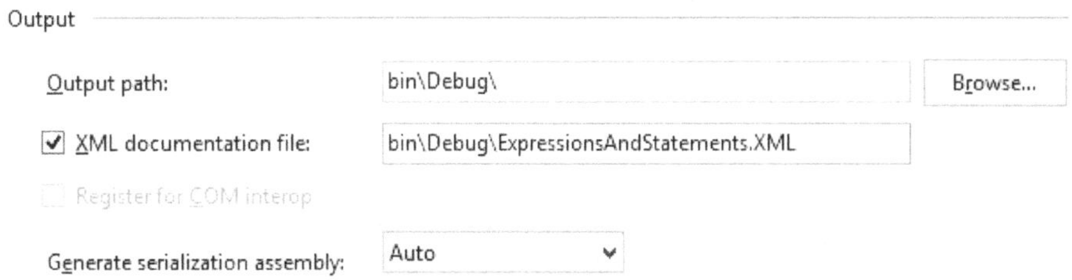

Output

Output path: bin\Debug\ Browse...

☑ XML documentation file: bin\Debug\ExpressionsAndStatements.XML

☐ Register for COM interop

Generate serialization assembly: Auto

Figure 4-3. Emitting XML Comments

4.2 Code Regions

Code regions are a feature in the C# used by the code editor that allows you to group code into named regions and collapse or expand their text as desired. Code regions have no effect on the code at compile or runtime – it is strictly a text-editing feature for organization. The start of a region uses the "`#region`" directive followed by some text to identify that region (the text is actually optional but it make the code easier to read). To end a region the "`#endregion`" directive is used, also with optional descriptive text. It is a common technique to use the same text for both directives which makes the code easier to follow. Some rules regarding regions:

- Regions should not overlap other constructs. In other words, it is bad practice to start a region within a method and end it outside that method.
- Regions should not overlap. In other words, you should not start "`#region A`" followed by "`#region B`" then close the first region with "`#endregion A`" followed by "`#endregion B`". In this case, the "`#region A`" directive would be paired with the "`#endregion B`" directive which is probably not what you would want.
- Regions can be nested.
- Regions cannot overlap other pre-compiler directives such as `#if`.

The most common use of code regions is grouping similar code together by category, such as methods, properties, events, etc. Since we have not covered any of these topics yet it the use of regions may seem limited right now.

```
 9    class Program
10    {
11        #region Main()
          0 references
12        static void Main(string[] args)
13        {
14            string name = "John Smith";
15            Console.WriteLine("Hello, " + name);
16        }
17        #endregion Main()
18    }
```

Figure 4-4. Region Expanded

```
 9    class Program
10    {
11        Main()
18    }
```

Figure 4-5. Region Collapsed

As you can see in Figure 4-4, there is a `#region`/`#endregion` pair surrounding Main(). When the "-" button to the left of the `#region` directive is clicked, all of the code between `#region` and `#endregion` is collapsed to one line with the region label displayed. Notice that line numbers 12

- 17, to the left of the code in Figure 4-5, are skipped. Those lines are still in the code, they are just being hidden until the region is once again expanded.

4.3 C# Data Types

A common feature of virtually every programming language is the ability to store and manipulate data of various types. For the most part, the basic data types can be grouped into three categories: numeric, text and complex types. Numeric data types can be further subdivided into integral-style and floating point-style values. Textual data types consist of single characters or groups of characters known as strings. Complex types are special types that are composed of multiple values. We'll primarily be looking at numeric and text types for now.

All .NET languages support the Common Type System (CTS) which requires certain intrinsic types to be treated the same no matter which language they are used in. The CTS type names are frequently different from the names C# adopted to represent them, mostly due to C#'s roots in C and C++. You are allowed to use either the CTS names or the C# aliases in your code but it is generally preferred that the language-specific aliases be used.

The following table enumerates the fundamental data types of the .NET Common Type System, their aliases in C#, range of legal values, storage requirements in Bytes, default values and whether they are CLS compliant.

Table 4-1. Built-in Data Types

C# Name	CTS Name	Range	Size	Default	CLS	Purpose
bool	Boolean	`true` or `false`	1	`false`	✓	Represents a true/false, yes/no or on/off flag
byte	Byte	0 to 255	1	0	✓	An unsigned value representing 8 bits
sbyte	SByte	-128 to 127	1	0		A signed version of the `byte` type
int	Int32	-2,147,483,648 to 2,147,483,647	4	0	✓	Stores and manipulates whole numbers between -2 and +2 billion
short	Int16	-32,768 to 32,767	2	0	✓	Similar to `int` but allows a smaller range of values
long	Int64	-9,223,372,036,854,775,808 to 9,223,372,036,854,775,807	8	0	✓	Similar to `int` but allows a far greater range of legal values
uint	UInt32	0 to 4,294,967,295	4	0		Similar to `int` but only non-negative (unsigned) values are allowed
ushort	UInt16	0 to 65,535	2	0		Similar to `short` but only non-negative values allowed
ulong	UInt64	0 to 18,446,744,073,709,551,615	8	0		Similar to `long` but only non-negative values allowed
float	Single	$\approx -3.4028 \times 10^{38}$ to 3.4028×10^{38}	4	0	✓	A single-precision floating point number
double	Double	$\approx -1.79769 \times 10^{-308}$ to 1.79769×10^{308}	8	0	✓	A double-precision floating point number that has greater mantissa and exponent accuracy than float
decimal	Decimal	$\approx \pm 1.0 \times 10^{-28}$ to $\pm 7.9 \times 10^{28}$	16	0	✓	A more precise decimal number that does not suffer from round off issues of `float` and `double`

C# Name	CTS Name	Range	Size	Default	CLS	Purpose
char	Char	Unicode values from 0x0000 to 0xFFFF (0 – 65,535)	2	0 or '\0'	✓	Represents a single UTF-16 character
string	String	Up to millions of characters	≈2n	null	✓	A contiguous sequence of characters (basic text)
DateTime	DateTime	1/1/0001 to 12/31/9999 CE	8	1/1/0001	N/A	Not really an intrinsic data type but it is extremely useful for storing dates and times
object	Object	Undefined	Varies	null	✓	Base class of all .NET types
var	N/A	Undefined	Varies	N/A		Implicit type defined by the value being assigned to it

As you can see, there are many useful intrinsic types, each suited for different usage scenarios. Knowing the types of data and the range of values each type can store will help you to determine which is best for your particular needs. We will examine many of these types in more detail later in the chapter.

4.4 Variables

Variables are the primary mechanism for storing state information, or data, in your programs. These variables can have values that remain unchanged for the life of a program, or they may change frequently, based on specific business rules. Variables may also remain active for the entire life of a program, or they may live only for the duration of one line of code. Variables are the cornerstone to the imperative programming paradigm which describes computation in terms of statements that change a program's state over time. However, it is not necessary to understand the theory of imperative programming to utilize variables in your own programs.

The types listed in Table 4-1 are not very useful until you create variables using those types. A variable in C# represents a location in memory that holds a value of a specific type. A variable is given a name to make accessing that memory location easy from code. When a variable is created, C# guarantees that the location in memory represented by that variable can only contain data of the specified type. The value of a variable can be assigned at the time it is created or at a later time in your code (delayed initialization). In summary, a variable is comprised of the following:

- Name
- Memory Location and Size
- Data Type
- Value

Since C# is a language managed by the .NET CLR, the details about the memory location of a variable is, for the most part, abstracted from the programmer. Basically, the .NET CLR is responsible for allocating memory and managing its usage. The amount of memory allocated is dictated by the data type and its initial contents. Therefore, the three items we generally need to concern ourselves with are: Name, Type and Value.

Variable Naming Rules

When choosing a name for a variable there are certain rules that must be followed and some guidelines that should be followed. First, the rules. Variables names…

- must start with a letter (upper or lower case) or an underscore "_"
- can contain any alpha-numeric or underscore after the first character
- cannot contain any spaces
- are case-sensitive (a ≠ A)
- cannot be the same name and case as a reserved keyword, such as "`for`", "`while`" or "`if`"
    - Technically you can "escape" any keyword with the "at" character "@" to use it as a variable identifier, such as "*@for*", but this practice is discouraged due to possible confusion.

There are also some well-defined guidelines that should be followed. Variable names…

- should be descriptive, avoiding abbreviations when possible
    - Try to avoid names like *temp*, *val*, *x*, etc…
    - However, sometimes variables like *x* make sense due to their usage, like as the horizontal component of a coordinate.
- should use a consistent case convention, such as "camel case" for local variables.
    - Camel case is the process of grouping multiple words together without any symbols where only the first letter of each word is capitalized, except the first word. These are example camel case variable names: *dateOfBirth*, *lastName*, *backgroundColor*, *milesPerGallon*
    - Variables declared outside of methods typically use Pascal case which is identical to camel case except the first letter is capitalized
- should only use acronyms when they are common knowledge in the given organization or industry
    - should capitalize both characters of two-character acronyms, except the first word of a camel-cased identifier
    - should capitalize only the first character of acronyms with three or more characters, except the first word of a camel-cased identifier
    - should not capitalize any of the characters of any acronyms, whatever their length, at the beginning of a camel-cased identifier

Single Variable Declaration

The syntax for declaring a variables adheres to one of the following patterns:

Syntax #1: `<data type> <name>;`

Syntax #2: `<data type> <name> = <initial value>;`

The first syntax demonstrates variable declaration only. In this instance, a variable is allocated in memory but no initial value is assigned. If the data type of the variable is a value type (all of the data types in Table 4-1 except `string` and `object` are value types) then they are given a default value automatically. For numeric variables this default value is typically 0. Reference types like `string` and `object`, on the other hand, are given a default value of `null`, which implies a lack of a value (we'll discuss value and reference types in detail later). Even though variables declared without explicit initial values are assigned default values automatically by the CLR, you cannot use these variables in any way until they have been assigned values. Failure to adhere to this rule will yield a compiler error with a description like: "Use of unassigned local variable 'x'".

The second syntax above demonstrates both variable declaration and initialization. This is the preferred method of variable declaration as it helps avoid the "unassigned local variable" compiler error. Typically, unless you have a specific value to assign to a variable due to algorithm requirements, you should assign to them what would normally be their default value. So, for an `int` variable you would typically assign it 0.

Variables must be declared within the body of a method (known as local variables) or within a `class` or `struct` but outside any method body (known as fields). Since we are not ready to discuss the `class` or `struct` user-defined types yet, we will focus on declaring variables within methods. Also, it is not possible to create global variables in C#. In Chapter 11, we will discuss `static` classes which demonstrate how to achieve similar results to global declarations. The following example demonstrates the creation and initialization of several local variables:

Listing 4-6. Variable Declaration

```
1 int x;
2 // Can't use x until it is initialized
3 x = 10;
4 int y = 5;
5 int z = y;
```

This code sample first creates an `int` variable called *x* but does not assign an initial value – by default it is assigned the value 0. However, the variable cannot be used yet. Next, in line 3, the *x* variable is overwritten with the value 10, after which *x* can be used for other purposes. In line 4, a new `int` variable *y* is created and initialized with the value 5. Finally, a new `int` variable *z* is created and assigned the value from the *y* variable, which is 5.

The following demonstrates, in simplistic detail, what is happening in memory as this code executes. The memory addresses are completely arbitrary and are just for illustration purposes. Visually, the values are added to memory from the bottom up, just like a stack of coins. In fact, the memory structure where these variables are stored is called a stack.

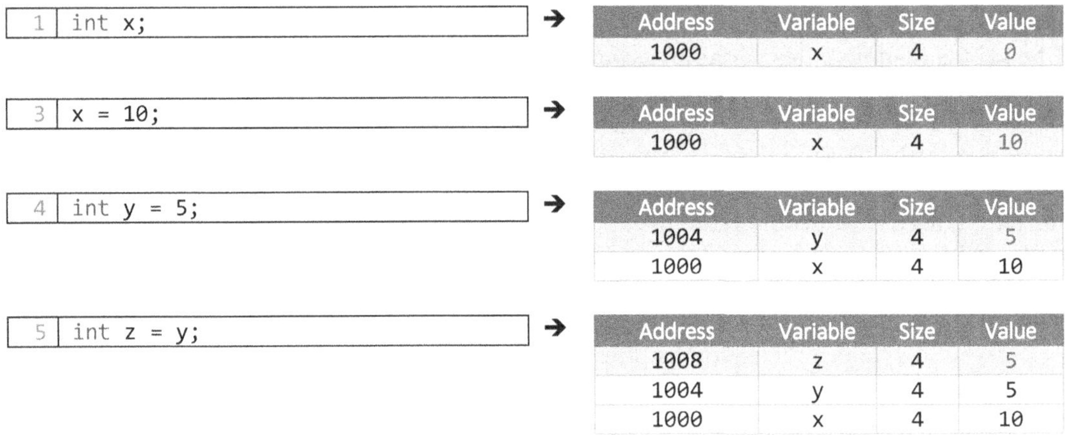

Address	Variable	Size	Value
1000	x	4	0

Address	Variable	Size	Value
1000	x	4	10

Address	Variable	Size	Value
1004	y	4	5
1000	x	4	10

Address	Variable	Size	Value
1008	z	4	5
1004	y	4	5
1000	x	4	10

Multiple Variable Declaration

It is possible to declare multiple variables of the same type in a single statement. The declaration begins with the data type, followed by comma separated variable names. Each variable may also be initialized with a value. The syntax for declaring multiple variables adheres to one of the following patterns:

Syntax #1:
```
<data type> <name1>, <name2>, …, <nameN>;
```

Syntax #2:
```
<data type> <name1>=<value1>, <name2>=<value2>, …, <nameN>=<valueN>;
```

The following example demonstrates the creation and initialization of multiple local variables per line:

Listing 4-7. Multiple Variable Declaration

```
int x, y, z;  // Can't use x, y or z until they are initialized
double d = 1.1, e = 2.2, f = 3.3; // d, e & f are declared & given initial values
// You can also mix and match initialized and uninitialized...
char ch1 = 'A', ch2, ch3 = 'C';  // Remember to assign a value to "ch2" before use!
```

The major benefit to declaring multiple variables in a single line of code is minimizing lines of code. However, the gain in vertical space reduction is frequently offset by cluttered, unreadable code. One approach to getting the biggest bang for your buck is to vertically align the variables as shown in Listing 4-8.

Listing 4-8. Lining Up Multiple Variable Declarations

```
int    x,          y,         z;
double d   = 1.1,  e = 2.2,   f   = 3.3;
char   ch1 = 'A',  ch2,       ch3 = 'C';
```

Whether or not you feel this is easier to read is really a matter of personal preference. In practice, declaring most variables on their own line of code is typically the easiest to read and debug.

I do have a preference for variable declaration. I find it very hard to read code when multiple variables are declared on the same line when they also define initial values. If I am declaring like variables with the express intent of assigning values at a later time I sometimes will choose to put them on a single line. However, since I am a big fan of assigning initial values, even when they correspond to the type's default, I tend not to use this technique much. By the way, the code samples in this book may violate some of my preferences based on space limitations.

Variable Scope

In C# global variables are not supported. In other words, you cannot declare a variable in a place where any other section of code in a program can access it directly. Instead, all variables must be declared within a `class`, `struct` or a method. Since we are not dealing with classes and structs yet, let's just consider method-level variable declaration. This type of declaration is also known as "local declaration". A variable declared within a method (local variable) is accessible only from within that method after its declaration. This accessibility is known as the variable's scope, which, in this case, is local to the method.

Actually, the scope of the variable is not defined by the method itself, but rather the set of curly braces "{ }" that comprises the method body. Since all methods are defined with a set of braces, which delimit a method's body, any variable declared within its braces is local to that scope.

It is also possible to have nested braces within another set of braces, also known as nested scopes. In this case, any variable declared within the inner set of braces would only be accessible in that scope, but a variable declared in the outer scope would be visible to the inner scope as long as it was declared *prior* to the inner scope.

Listing 4-9. Variable Scope

```
 1 static void Main(string[] args)
 2 {
 3   double outside = 0;
 4   if (true)
 5   {
 6     double inside = outside;
 7     Console.WriteLine(inside);
 8   }
 9   Console.WriteLine(outside);
10 }
```

In Listing 4-9 there are two variables declared within the Main() method. The first variable, *outside*, is available only to code contained within the Main() method after its declaration, or lines 3 – 9. It is also accessible from any nested scopes, such as the block of code following the "`if`" statement on line 4. This is demonstrated by the assignment of "outside" to "inside" on line 6. However, the *inside* variable is only available to the block of code it is defined in, so only lines 6 and 7. Once the closing brace on line 8 is executed, the *inside* variable ceases to exist.

It is very important to understand a variable's scope so as not to try to use a variable outside its legal area. If you do try to use a variable outside its scope the compiler will yield an error, such as: "The name 'XXX' does not exist in the current context".

Another issue you may run into is declaring two variables with the same name in the same or nested scope. A variable identifier must be unique to the scope in which it is defined. So, in the same example above, there can only be one variable called "outside" within the Main() method. Any attempt to declare a second variable with the same name will yield an error: "A local variable named 'outside' is already defined in this scope". Likewise, if you attempted to create a second "outside" variable within the "`if`" block on line 6, you would get a different error: "A local variable named 'outside' cannot be declared in this scope because it would give a different meaning to 'outside', which is already used in a 'parent or current' scope to denote something else".

4.5 Constants

Constants play much the same role in programming as variables. The most obvious difference, however, is that a constant's value cannot be changed after its declaration, hence the name "constant". The declaration of a constant looks very much like a variable declaration with the additional following requirements:

- The "`const`" keyword must precede the type name
- The constant must be assigned an initial value, either a literal value like 0 or another constant
- Simple arithmetic may be performed on the constant value, but not results of function calls or any other runtime created value

Constants generally share the same naming convention as variables. It is common to also find the old C standard of all upper case identifiers with underscores separating words. Examples: PI, TWO_PI, PI_OVER_4.

Listing 4-10. Example Constants

```
const double PI = 3.14159265359;
const double E = 2.71828182846;
const double TWO_PI = PI * 2;
const double piOver4 = PI / 4;
```

The most common reason to use constants is to avoid using literal values directly in code, especially with the potential to have those hard-coded value appear multiple times in code. Let's assume that we have code that requires the use of the 'pi' constant. We could use the literal value 3.14 wherever it is needed. However, if we decide later on that we need more precision from our calculation, we would need to find every occurrence of 3.14 and replace that value with a more precise one. Defining a constant would allow us to use that named value throughout our code providing a single point of contact to change its value. Then, any such changes would be instantly picked up by all code that references it.

Constants also help avoid the use of "magic numbers", or values that have context-specific meaning in a block of code. For instance, let's consider an application that requires us to track student records. We may need to categorize students by their grade level and store that value as a numeric entry in a database. We might implicitly know that the value '0' represents a preschooler, and that '4' is used for college students. However, anyone without that knowledge would not understand the significance of these numbers; so, using a named constant in their place would greatly assist their understanding.

Listing 4-11. Avoiding Magic Numbers with Constants

```
const int PreK = 0;
const int Elementary = 1;
const int MiddleSchool = 2;
const int HighSchool = 3;
const int College = 4;
```

4.6 Expressions, Statements and Blocks

Expressions

In natural language, expressions are similar to sentence fragments. Expressions are code instructions that yield a single result. Frequently, you will find expressions on the right-hand side of an assignment operator (=). Most of the time, expressions are part of larger statements and can also be joined together to make compound expressions.

Listing 4-12. Simple Expressions

```
1 double pi = 3.14159;
2 string name = "John Smith";
3 Console.WriteLine("Hello, " + name);
```

Literal expressions (aka literals) are numbers or strings typed "literally" into code and have no associated name. In the majority of cases, a literal expression is used as part of an assignment to a variable, used in conjunction with operators to create a new value, or as an argument to a method. In Listing 4-12, the number 3.14159 and the strings "John Smith" and "Hello, " are all literal expressions.

Name expressions (aka simple names) are variable or constant names, typically used as part of a compound expression or parameter to a method call. Both *pi* and *name* in Listing 4-12 are example names.

Compound expressions are expressions that are tied together using operators. Operators can include, but are not limited to: mathematical operators (+, -, *, /, %), comparison operators (<, >, <=, >=, ==, !=) and logical operators (&&, | |, ^). In line 3, the literal "Hello, " is concatenated with the *name* variable in a compound expression using the `string` "+" operator, the result of which is then passed as an argument to Console.WriteLine().

Invocation expressions are another type of expression which represent calls to methods. In the previous example, the call to Console.WriteLine() is an invocation – the method WriteLine() of the Console class is being called. An invocation expression always uses parentheses, between which any required arguments are passed. Looking closely at the single call to Console.WriteLine(), we can conclude that it actually comprises 4 different expressions:

1. Literal expression: "Hello, "
2. Name expression: *name*
3. Compound expression: "Hello, " + *name*
4. Invocation expression: Console.WriteLine()

Statements

Statements are similar to complete sentences in natural language. Most statements either end with a semicolon ";" or are separated by commas, where the last statement must end with a semicolon. Whitespace is typically not significant within statements, except within quotes; therefore, expressions can be separated by a single space, multiple spaces, tabs or even carriage returns.

Declaration statements are one of the most common forms of statement. A declaration statement consists of a data type and a name. Any time you create a variable you are using a declaration statement.

Assignment statements are also very common. Any time the state (value) of a variable changes, an assignment operator is typically used to do it. An assignment statement consists of three parts: an lvalue, assignment operator and an rvalue and follows the form:

```
<lvalue> = <rvalue>;
```

An **lvalue** is an expression that appears on the left-hand side of an assignment operator and typically refers to the memory location of a name expression. In effect, the name expression in lvalue returns a single value, the variable's address in memory. An **rvalue** is an expression that can be a single value or the result of a compound expression or invocation expression. That value is then stored in the memory location represented by lvalue. In simple terms, whatever value is on the right-hand side of the equal sign is stored in the variable on the left-hand side.

Blocks

A code block is a section of code delimited by curly braces. A block can contain 0 or many statements. Code blocks are typically associated with methods, `if` statements, `switch` statements and loops, all of which will be covered in greater detail later.
Blocks also represent scope boundaries. In other words, any variables or constants declared within those boundaries are, by default, accessible only within those boundaries. This definition will be extended later when we discuss object oriented programing, but for now this definition applies.

4.7 Operators

Mathematic Operators

When working with numeric values, such as `int`, `long`, `float`, `double` and `decimal`, it is frequently necessary to manipulate those values. Each of the numeric data types support the standard binary mathematical operations: addition, subtraction, multiplication and division. A binary operation simply means the operation requires two operands, or values, to calculate a result, one on either side of the operator. To make life simple, C# uses the standard "+" and "-" characters to represent addition and subtraction, respectively. Multiplication and division, on the other hand, use "*" and "/" since the "×" and "÷" symbols are not easily typed on a keyboard. Additional operators are also available to most numeric data types, as shown below.

Table 4-2. Binary Mathematic Operators

Binary Operator	Name	Purpose	Example (int/double)
+	Add	Adds two numbers together	5 + 7 ➔ 12 4.3 + 1.2 ➔ 5.5
-	Subtract	Subtracts one number from another	8 - 5 ➔ 3 8.7 - 1.4 ➔ 7.3
*	Multiply	Multiplies two numbers together	4 * 5 ➔ 20 3.2 * 1.4 ➔ 4.48
/	Divide	Divides one number by another	11 / 3 ➔ 3 12.25 / 6.25 ➔ 1.96
%	Modulus	Computes the remainder after a division	11 % 3 ➔ 2 12.25 / 6.25 ➔ 6.0
<<	Left shift	Shifts the first operand left by the number of bits specified by the second operand (integer-style numbers only). Effectively multiplies left operand by 2^n.	4 << 3 ➔ 32 ($4 \times 2^3 = 32$)
>>	Right shift	Shifts the first operand right by the number of bits specified by the second operand (integer-style numbers only). Effectively divides left operand by 2^n.	64 >> 4 ➔ 4 ($64 \div 2^4 = 4$)

Working with the mathematic binary operators is relatively straight-forward as long as you are using the same data type for both operands. However, things become a bit trickier when you start to mix and match data types using these operators. We'll look at this concept a bit later. For now, let's consider these operators using similar data types.

When performing addition, subtraction and multiplication, using either `int` or `double` for both operands, the result is what you would expect. However, division with `int` data types may not give you what you would normally expect if the divisor does not go evenly into the dividend. So, for the example "11 / 3", the answer is 3, or the whole number answer with no remainder. This sometimes causes consternation when doing an operation like "1 / 3" which yields 0. The same expression using `double` values will return a number to a precision of roughly 16 digits. So, "11.0 / 3.0" = 3.6666666666666667 and "1.0 / 3.0" = 0.3333333333333333.

Another warning about integer divide: if you attempt to divide by 0, an exception, or error, will be thrown. This will have the effect of crashing your application until such time as you learn about `try` blocks. Dividing by 0 with the `double` data type will not yield an error, however the result will be some variety of "infinity" based on the sign of the dividend.

The following demonstrates some expressions utilizing these operators:

Listing 4-13. Simple Mathematic Operators

```
static void Main(string[] args)
{
  int x = 10, y = 3;
  int z = x + y;
  Console.WriteLine("x + y = " + z);
  z = x - y;
  Console.WriteLine("x - y = " + z);
  z = x * y;
  Console.WriteLine("x * y = " + z);
  z = x / y;
  Console.WriteLine("x / y = " + z);
  z = x % y;
  Console.WriteLine("x % y = " + z);
  Console.ReadLine();
}
```

```
x + y = 13
x - y = 7
x * y = 30
x / y = 3
x % y = 1
```

Figure 4-6. Simple Mathematic Operators Output

Unary Operators

In addition to the binary operators listed above, there are two unary operators, unary+ and unary-. Unary operators are always found to the left of the target operand. Unary+ is actually only included to balance out the unary- operator, as it simply returns the value of the operand it is applied to. For instance, "+9" is simply "9". Unary-, on the other hand, is used to negate whatever operand it is applied to. "-9" is decidedly different than "9". But, unary- can also be used on compound expressions as well. Consider "-(6 + 3)" – the unary- operator is applied to the result of the contents of the parentheses, yielding a result of "-(9)" or simply "-9".

Increment and Decrement Operators

There are two specialized unary operators called the increment operator ++ and the decrement operator --. These operators are used to increment or decrement the operand they are applied to by 1. These operators can only be applied to variable operands, not to literals or constants. The basic syntax of these operators:

```
variable++     variable--
```

These operators can be used within expressions or can stand alone as complete statements. The increment and decrement operators can also appear prior to their operands as such:

```
++variable    --variable
```

When the operator appears to the right of the variable it is known as a postfix operation and when the operator appears to the left of the variable it is known as a prefix operation. When these operators are used as stand-alone statements there is not much difference in the outcome – either the variable is incremented or decremented by 1. However, if the operators are used within the context of a compound expression there is a distinct difference in how these operators are evaluated. When the prefix form of the operator is used the result of the operation is calculated prior to passing the result to other expressions in the compound expression. However, when the postfix form is used, the current value of the operand is passed to other expressions in the compound expression and then the operand is either incremented or decremented.

Listing 4-14. Increment and Decrement Operators

```
int x = 10;
int y = x++;  // x == 11, y == 10
int z = ++x;  // x == 12, z == 12

int v = z + x--;  // x == 11, v == 24
v = z + --x;      // x == 10, v == 22
x++;  // x == 11
```

As you can see, the more complex the expressions involving these operators, the harder it is to visually determine the resulting output. It is for this reason that you should use these operators in complex expressions sparingly. However, when used by themselves in stand-alone statements, they are very useful. We'll look at these operators in more detail when we discuss looping constructs in Chapter 7.

Many people claim that the prefix version of the operators are faster than their postfix counterparts. While this is technically correct, in practice you will probably never notice the difference unless you have need of extreme performance.

Compound Assignment Operators

The C-style languages have other specialty operators that allow for simultaneous mathematic operation and assignment. These operators replace statements, such as:

```
x = x + 2;
y = y - 10;
```

Notice that the rvalue expressions alter a single variable by some value then reassigns that result back into the variable. The above statements can be replaced with these compound assignment operators:

```
x += 2;
y -= 10;
```

The benefit of these operators, other than smaller code, is that the variables do not need to be evaluated twice, once in the rvalue expression and again in the lvalue expression. The result is improved execution efficiency. Additionally, these compound operators are very useful in `for` loops.

Table 4-3. Compound Assignment Operators

Operator	Purpose	Example
+=	Increments the target variable by a specified amount.	`x += 10;`
-=	Decrements the target variable by a specified amount.	`x -= 4;`
*=	Multiplies the target variable by a specified amount.	`x *= 8;`
/=	Divides the target variable by a specified amount.	`x /= 2;`
%=	Calculates the remainder of a division operation on a variable and assigns the result to that variable.	`x %= 3;`

Comparison Operators

One of the most crucial aspects of programming is being able to make decisions based on the comparison of two values. C# provides several operators to assist with this process. The result of each comparison operator is a `bool` value, or in other words: `true` or `false`.

Table 4-4. Comparison Operators

C# Operator	Algebraic Form	Common Name	Purpose
==	=	Equals	Compares two items for equality. For value types this operator typically compares the values of the operands. For reference types this operator typically compares the addresses of the operands to determine if they are actually the same object.
!=	≠	Not equals	Compares two items for inequality.
>	>	Greater than	Determines if the left operand is greater than the right operand.
<	<	Less than	Determines if the left operand is less than the right operand.
>=	≥	Greater than or equal to	Determines if the left operand is greater than or equal to the right operand.
<=	≤	Less than or equal to	Determines if the left operand is less than or equal to the right operand.

Comparison operators are most commonly used within loops and conditional statements, such as "`if`", so we'll hold off on the bulk of this discussion until those topics are introduced in Chapter 7.

Order of Operations

When using compound expressions to calculate a value it is important to know how and when the operators will be called. Let's say we have an expression: "5 + 3 + 2". Since addition is associative, the order that the operands are added together does not matter. The same would apply if we threw subtraction into the mix since addition and subtraction are also associative between each other.

Things start to get tricky when we also do either multiplication or division in conjunction with addition and subtraction. For instance, let's change our expression to: "5 + 3 * 2". Should the answer be 16 or 11? That depends on whether the add operation or multiply operation is done first. In C#, multiply has a higher priority than addition, so the answer would, in fact, be "5 + (3 * 2)" or 11. The following chart lists the order of operations for C# operators, from highest to lowest:

Table 4-5. Operator Precedence

Operator Precedence
( ) *parenthesis*
x++ x--
unary+ unary- ++x --x
* / %
+ -
<< >>
< > <= >=
== !=
= += -= *= /= %= <<= >>=

In the above chart, parenthesis take precedence over the unary operators, followed by *, /, %, then + and -, and finally the bit shift operators. Notice that some operators share the same precedence level. In that case, the operators are evaluated in the order they are encountered going left to right.

Some advice about operator precedence: if it is difficult to determine an expression's order of operations, it never hurts to add parenthesis around sub-expressions. It will generally increase readability and help with debugging.

4.8 Data Type Promotion

Occasionally, when mathematic expressions are executed, the two operands surrounding a binary operator may not be the same type. The way the operators are written in C#, both operands must be the same type. However, instead of causing the compiler to fail, one of the data types will be "promoted" to the other's type. Consider the following expression:

```
12 * 5.1 + 2
```

The compiler will see this as:

```
int * double + int
```

Since the first operation to execute is 12 * 5.1, based on operator precedence rules, the compiler has to decide if the 12 should become 12.0 or the 5.1 should become 5. Since the second choice would lead to data loss the compiler is designed to promote the `int` value to a `double`. Therefore, the expression becomes:

```
12.0 * 5.1 + 2
```

Then, the first operation is calculated, resulting in:

```
61.2 + 2
```

As you can see, the remaining operation is faced with the same problem again. And, once again, the `int` value is promoted to a `double`:

```
61.2 + 2.0
```

And the result is calculated as 63.2, which is a `double`.

The same type of promotion occurs with any other numeric data type mismatches, where the value with the least precision is substituted for an equivalent value using the higher precision type. Consider the following example:

Listing 4-15. Integer Promotion

```
short s = 12;
int i = 325;
long l = 1234567890123L;
var add = s + i + l;
```

Three different integer types (`short`, `int` and `long`) are being added together. Since the `long` value has the highest precision, the result will also be a `long`, which is implicitly typed within the `var` variable *add* (see section 4.9 for details about var).

Sometimes promotion is not an option and the mathematic operation cannot be calculated. This issue happens most frequently when you attempt to perform an operation on two operands that have the same precision, but one is signed while the other is not. A perfect example of this would be trying to add a `long` to a `ulong`. This is just not possible since there is no implicit conversion available between the two types. In those cases you will have to use explicit conversions to get a result which is covered in section 4.11.

4.9 Data Types Detailed

Now that we have looked at the basic usage of data types and variables it is time to dive a little deeper into specific types and their usage patterns. This section will not cover every data type listed in Table 4-1, but it will look at the most common and useful types of C#. The one very useful type that will not be covered here is the `string` data type as it is covered extensively in Chapter 6 due to the importance of text data handling.

System.Object – object

The `object` data type is the root data type from which all other types are defined. As a result, any variable type can be stored in an `object` variable. However, since the `object` type is a reference type, special handling of value types occurs to wrap those values in a reference type variable. This is called "boxing" and is discussed in section 4.10.

Since all data types are based either directly or indirectly from `object`, all data types automatically have members that are defined in `object`. These members are:

Table 4-6. Object Members

Name	Description
Equals()	Compares the variable to another for equality.
GetHashCode()	Gets the hash code for the `object`. A hash code is used to define the index of an item in a collection such as a Dictionary or HashTable.
GetType()	Gets the data type of the variable.
ToString()	Converts the variable to a `string`.

The most important method in the list, for our purposes, is the ToString() method. Since `object` contains this method, all other data types also contain this method. Therefore, if you have an `int` variable, called *x*, you can convert its value to a `string` by calling: x.ToString()

System.Int32 – int

The System.Int32 data type, `int` in C#, is the most commonly used integral style numeric data type in the .NET Framework. Unlike implementations of C and C++ where the exact size of the `int` data type is compiler dependent, an `int` in C# is always 32 bits. At the time .NET was being developed, 32-bit CPUs were prevalent throughout the computer industry, especially for machines running Windows. The `int` data type was defined to be exactly the size of a typical hardware register, thus providing an extremely efficient numeric type that could take advantage of CPU-native mathematic operations. It is possible, although unlikely, that the type could be redefined as a 64-bit entity in future releases of the .NET Framework since most machines are moving toward 64-bit operating systems, but the `long` data type fills that niche now.

The primary use for `int` is storing whole numbers that can be either negative or positive. The 32-bits consumed by the type allows for values between -2,147,483,648 and 2,147,483,647. Any attempt to store a value outside this range will result in an overflow causing the value to flip from negative to positive or vice versa. For instance, if you have a variable called *x* which has `int`.MaxValue assigned to it, or 2,147,483,647, and you execute *x*++, the result will be -2,147,483,648. This may not seem intuitive, but C# optimizes integer arithmetic to ignore overflows and allow this behavior. To alter this behavior so an OverflowException is thrown when an int "wraps over the edge" in this manner, you would have to surround the offending statement with a "checked" block as such:

Listing 4-16. Detecting Overflows

```
checked
{
  int x = int.MaxValue;
  x++;
}
```

Alternatively, you can also change your project's settings to automatically throw an OverflowException when overflows are detected on integer data types. In your project's properties window, select the "Build" tab, then select the "Advanced..." button. Inside the "Advanced Build Settings" dialog you will see the "Check for arithmetic overflow/underflow" checkbox.

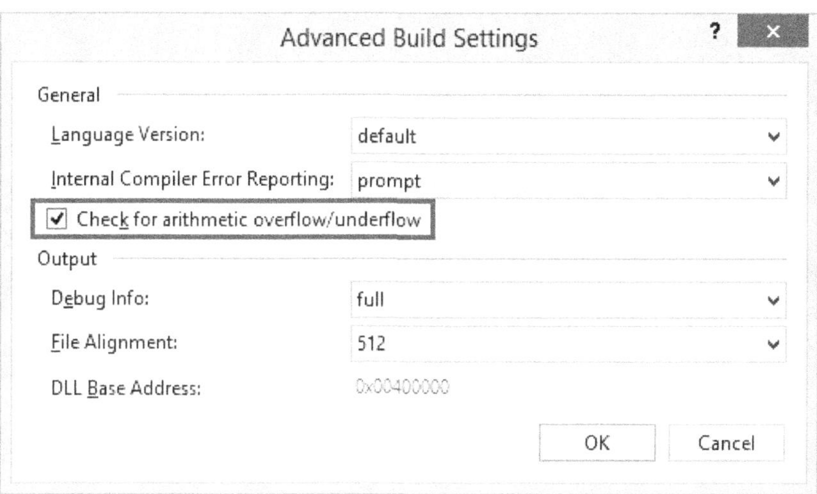

Figure 4-7. Overflow Check Build Setting

When selected, "checked" blocks are no longer required. However, when enabled and you wish to ignore overflows for a block of code you can use an "unchecked" block, which as you can probably guess, disables overflow checks within its curly braces.

One word of caution with overflows using literals and constants: if the compiler can determine you are going to cause an overflow based on math using literals and constants, the code will not compile.

I have a pet-peeve (actually, you'll learn I have many) about this concept of "silent" overflow and underflow. There may very well be some legitimate use of rollover, where adding 1 to int.*MaxValue yields* int.*MinValue without an error, however, most of the time this is a problem you want to detect.*

One mathematic operation which you cannot configure to be ignored is dividing by zero. By definition, dividing by zero results in infinity, which is not representable by an int value. As a result, if the operation is attempted, the runtime will throw a DivideByZeroException. At this point, since we have not discussed handling exceptions, it is best to avoid the situation entirely.

By default, all whole number literals in code are automatically assumed to be of type int, even if the value could fit in a type with a smaller memory footprint, such as short or byte. The default value for an int is 0; however, it is always good practice to supply your own initial value explicitly, even if it is 0. Doing this will prevent compiler exceptions where you may unintentionally attempt to use a variable prior to it being initialized.

Table 4-7. Common int Members

Static*	Name	Description
✓	MaxValue	Constant that represents the largest possible int value.
✓	MinValue	Constant that represents the smallest possible int value.
✓	Parse()	Attempts to parse a given string into an equivalent int value. Invalid input causes exceptions.
	ToString()	Converts the given int to a string.
✓	TryParse()	Attempts to parse a given text string into an equivalent int value.

**Note about static members: Static members are accessed directly from the data type they belong to. For instance, to call int's MinValue member, you would use "int.MinValue". Non-static members, also known as instance members, require an actual variable or constant of that data type to access them. So, if we had an int variable called "i" we would access the ToString() method as follows: "i.ToString()". Constants are also implicitly static which implies that they are accessed in much the same manner as static members. This will discussed in greater detail later in the book.*

Listing 4-17. int Usage

```
1  int id = 111223333;
2  Console.WriteLine("Your ID is: " + id.ToString());
3  
4  int minimum = int.MinValue;
5  Console.WriteLine("The smallest possible int is: " + minimum.ToString());
6  
7  int operand1 = 7;
8  int operand2 = 3;
9  int product = operand1 * operand2;
10 Console.WriteLine("The product of " + operand1 + " and " + operand2 + " is " +
     product);
11 Console.WriteLine("The quotient of " + operand1 + " and " + operand2 + " is " +
     operand1 / operand2);
```

In the above example, notice on line 2 that the *id* variable's ToString() method is being called then that result is appended to the string "Your ID is: ". The concatenated string is then output to the console using WriteLine(). In actuality, the call to ToString() prior to concatenation is not necessary as the "+" operator will automatically convert the integer into a string. That technique is demonstrated on lines 10 and 11. However, being explicit is sometimes preferred over brevity.

System.Int64 – long

If 32 bits of data are not sufficient for storing integer values in your application, the System.Int64, or long, data type doubles the number of bits. The interesting thing about binary math is that when the number of bits is doubled the resulting range of values is squared. A single additional bit would be sufficient to double the range of values. By adding another 32 bits it actually increases the upper bound of the legal values by a factor of 4 billion, or 2^{32}. This makes the upper bound of long 9,223,372,036,854,775,807. Correspondingly, the lower bound is also enlarged to -9,223,372,036,854,775,808.

You might think integer numbers with such a large range are only marginally useful, but there are many practical applications for data of this size. For instance, consider a social security number, which is comprised of 9 digits. An int is large enough to store a value of this size. However, what about a credit card number? That would require up to 16 digits, far larger than an int can store, but definitely within the capacity of a long which can hold 18 digits (almost 19 actually).

Just as with int, a long value cannot be divided by 0. Any attempt to do so would cause a DivideByZeroException to be thrown. Again, it is best to write code that avoids that eventuality.

When working with long literals, if the number you are working with is longer than 9 digits, then the suffix 'L' is required to instruct the compiler that the value is a long rather than an int. For example, a 13 digit number would need to be declared as such:

```
long longValue = 1234567890123L;
```

Failure to include the 'L' in this example would yield a compiler error.

Table 4-8. Common long Members

Static	Name	Description
✓	MaxValue	Constant that represents the largest possible long value.
✓	MinValue	Constant that represents the smallest possible long value.
✓	Parse()	Attempts to parse a given string into an equivalent long value. Invalid input causes exceptions.
	ToString()	Converts the given long to a string.
✓	TryParse()	Attempts to parse a given text string into an equivalent long value.

System.Double – double

When working with numbers that have decimal points, the double data type is the most versatile and optimized for typical computer hardware. The "double" name refers to its double-precision nature as compared to single-precision floating point numbers (float).

Unlike the integral number types (`int`, `long`, etc.) which are represented in computer memory without any loss of precision, `double` values are approximations. This has to do with the mechanism by which they are stored in memory, using IEEE standards (specifically, IEEE 754) for double-precision floating point values. As a result, a `double` is only precise to 15 or 16 digits. However, the ability to represent a given value may not extend to all 15 or 16 digits due to how base-10 floating point numbers are stored as binary. This can lead to a phenomenon known as "round-off errors" as extremely small pieces of imprecise data can lead to large discrepancies after repeated calculations. To avoid round-off, avoid using `double`s in repeated calculations where the least significant digits are important (i.e. the 15th or 16th digit). An example of this imprecision can be demonstrated with any irrational number, such as "pi", or rational numbers with infinite repeating decimal digits, such as 1/3. At some point these numbers with infinite fractional decimal values have to be approximated or rounded to fit within the given space for a `double`. We'll look at a specific problem related to round-off errors momentarily.

The default value for a `double` is 0. However, if you wish to use a literal 0 in code to represent a double it is preferred to use either 0.0 or 0D to avoid the implicit conversion from an `int` to `double` by the compiler (the "D" is the literal suffix for the `double` data type).

Unlike `int`, it is possible to divide a `double` by 0. Instead of an exception, the result will be either positive or negative infinity. These values are represented by the constants `double`.PositiveInfinity and `double`.NegativeInfinity.

Table 4-9. Common double Members

Static	Name	Description
✓	MaxValue	Constant that represents the largest possible `double` value.
✓	MinValue	Constant that represents the smallest possible `double` value.
✓	Epsilon	Constant that represents the smallest positive value greater than 0 that a `double` can represent. In practice, this value is seldom used.
✓	NaN	A constant value that represent a `double` that is not a valid number. The value equates to 0.0 / 0.0.
✓	NegativeInfinity	Constant that represents negative infinity. The value equates to -1.0 / 0.0.
✓	PositiveInfinity	Constant that represents positive infinity. The value equates to 1.0 / 0.0.
✓	IsNaN()	Determines if a given `double` is not a valid number.
✓	IsInfinity()	Determines if a given `double` is an infinite value, either positive or negative.
✓	IsPositiveInfinity()	Determines if a given `double` is a positive infinite value.
✓	IsNegativeInfinity()	Determines if a given `double` is a negative infinite value.
✓	Parse()	Attempts to parse a given `string` into an equivalent `double` value. Invalid input causes exceptions.
	ToString()	Converts the given `double` to a `string`.
✓	TryParse()	Attempts to parse a given text `string` into an equivalent `double` value.

An interesting problem arises due to the inexact nature of the `double` data type. Sometimes, due to rounding errors, two numbers that should be equal will not actually equate to `true` when using the "==" operator. Look at the following example:

Listing 4-18. Round-off Example

```
1  double high = 1.0;
2  double low = 0.0;
3  double diff = 0.0;
4
5  high -= 0.33D;
6  low += 0.67D;
7
8  bool equals = (high == low);
9  Console.WriteLine("high == low? " + equals);
10
11 diff = Math.Abs(high - low);
12 Console.WriteLine("Difference: " + diff);
```

In the example, both the *high* and *low* variables should equal 0.67 after line 6 executes. However, when compared with "==" on line 8, the result is `false`. The output on line 12 shows the difference between the two values which is extremely small, but significant enough to cause the two variables to be distinct.

```
high == low? False
Difference: 1.11022302462516E-16
```

Figure 4-8. Round-off Output

The difference between the two variables is approximately 0.000000000000000111 which prevents the two values from evaluating as equal. So, how can we get around this problem? One solution is to avoid using `double` and use `decimal` in its place. However, `decimal` is not optimized for mathematic operations since it is not a hardware type (a type that has specific instructions built directly into the CPU). Therefore, if we wish to continue using the faster `double` type we have to devise a solution that allows us to approximate equality.

Listing 4-19. Double Equality Approximation

```
const double marginOfError = 0.0000000001;
if (Math.Abs(high - low) < marginOfError)
{
  Console.WriteLine("high is approximately equal to low");
}
```

Subtracting low from high and obtaining the result's absolute value gives us the difference between the values as a positive number. If this value is less than a given margin of error, we can assume the values are approximately equal. The primary concern in the above example is determining an acceptable margin of error. If the margin is too small it might not detect relatively equal values. If the margin is too large it could result in false positives. In either case, it would be more beneficial to contain this logic within its own method making repeated tests more efficient. Methods will be discussed in more detail in Chapter 8. There are far more sophisticated methods for determining equality than the code in Listing 4-19 which are readily available online.

System.Decimal – decimal

The `decimal` data type is a specialized floating point numeric type that minimizes the effect of rounding errors exhibited by the `double` type. In fact, a `decimal` value is actually stored as a 96-bit integer with a scalar value indicating the position of its decimal point. The fact that the numbers are stored and manipulated internally using integer algorithms provides protection from round-off issues up to the least significant digit. Also, the type is capable of storing 28 digits which is almost twice the precision of `double` and more precise than what any typical application would require. The biggest drawback to the `decimal` type, besides its larger footprint in memory, is its lack of dedicated hardware support. Also, a `decimal` cannot represent values smaller than 10^{-28} or larger than 10^{28}. Due to its precision stability, especially when dealing with base-10 numbers, `decimal` is ideal for financial and monetary calculations.

Like all numeric values, the default value for `decimal` variables is 0. Since the `double` data type is implied whenever a literal value contains a decimal point, the suffix "M" must be used to explicitly treat a number as a `decimal` value. This distinction is especially important when assigning a literal value with more than 16 digits. For example, consider assigning the value pi to both a `double` and a `decimal` using 28 digits. The `decimal` assignment will retain all 28 digits in its value. The `double` will not be able to hold more than 15.

Listing 4-20. Decimal Literals

```
1 decimal piDecimal = 3.1415926535897932384626433832M;
2 double piDouble = 3.1415926535897932384626433832;
3
4 Console.WriteLine(piDecimal);
5 Console.WriteLine(piDouble);
```

```
3.1415926535897932384626433832
3.14159265358979
```

Figure 4-9. Decimal Literals Output

Notice in Figure 4-9 that the second line of output, for the `double` value, only shows 14 decimal places while the first output retains all 27. Also, the "M" suffix on line 1 of Listing 4-20 is required by the compiler since implicit conversions from `double` to `decimal` are prohibited.

Unlike other floating point types, dividing a `decimal` by 0 is not allowed and will result in a DivideByZeroException. Like integer types it is best to avoid that possibility by using defensive code rather than having to handle the exception.

Table 4-10. Common decimal Members

Static	Name	Description
✓	MaxValue	Constant that represents the largest possible decimal value.
✓	MinValue	Constant that represents the smallest possible decimal value.
✓	MinusOne	Represents the value -1 in decimal form.
✓	One	Represents the value 1 in decimal form.
✓	Zero	Represents the value 0 in decimal form.
✓	Ceiling()	Returns the smallest integral value that is greater than or equal to the specified decimal number.
✓	Floor()	Rounds a specified decimal number to the closest integer toward negative infinity.
✓	Round()	Rounds the specified decimal number to the given decimal place.
✓	Truncate()	Returns the whole number portion of the given decimal without rounding.
✓	Parse()	Attempts to parse a given string into an equivalent decimal value. Invalid input causes exceptions.
	ToString()	Converts the given decimal to a string.
✓	TryParse()	Attempts to parse a given text string into a decimal value.

There are actually many more members of decimal than are listed in Table 4-10 such as: Add, Subtract, Multiply and Divide. These methods exist to support languages that do not have an alias for the `decimal` type. Since C# does have a formal alias it is best to use the native operators: +, -, * and /.

System.Boolean – bool

The `bool` data type is used to store `true` or `false` values. This data type is the result of any Boolean logic comparison, commonly found in "`if`" statements. Due to their implicit use in logical comparisons, loops and branching statements, `bool` values are one of the most commonly used types within expressions without explicit declaration. Basically, you will be using `bool` all the time without necessarily creating variables of that type.

The only two values that a `bool` variable can accept are `true` and `false`, both of which are reserved words in C#. Some C-style programming languages will allow implicit conversion of numeric values into `bool` values, but C# is not one of them. Although a bit would be sufficient for storing the state of a `bool` variable, addressing limitations in .NET require that variables consume at least 1 byte.

We'll look at `bool` in far greater detail in when we discuss flow control and `if` statements in Chapter 7.

System.DateTime – DateTime

While DateTime is not an intrinsic data type it is still incredibly useful for storing dates and times. The range of legal values for this type is between January 1, 0001 12:00:00 AM and December 31, 9999 11:59:59 PM. The type can store times within that range to a precision of one ten-millionth of a second, also known as a "tick". Although the type is precise to 100 nanosecond increments, most operating systems will only yield times accurate to 15 milliseconds due to the use of the system clock. However, this limitation does not apply if the times are obtained from other sources, such as database fields, high-precision timers like the Stopwatch class, or manually entered values. DateTime is also aware of leap years and seconds and can store times based on time zone or UTC (Coordinated Universal Time). The default value for DateTime is equivalent to DateTime.MinValue, which is Januray 1, 0001 at 12:00 AM. There is no C# alias for this type.

To get the current date and time the DateTime type contains the Now and UtcNow properties, depending on whether you require the time formatted using the local time zone or universal time. If you are only interested in the date portion of a DateTime variable, the Date property returns the date with the time portion set to 12:00:00 AM as a new DateTime variable. Likewise, the TimeOfDay property returns only the time portion of the DateTime variable, but in another data type called TimeSpan.

Listing 4-21. DateTime Current Time Sample

```
DateTime now = DateTime.Now;
DateTime nowUtc = DateTime.UtcNow;
Console.WriteLine("Now: " + now);
Console.WriteLine("Now (UTC): " + nowUtc);

DateTime nowDateOnly = now.Date;
Console.WriteLine("Now (Date only): " + nowDateOnly);
TimeSpan nowTimeOnly = now.TimeOfDay;
Console.WriteLine("Now (Time only): " + nowTimeOnly);
```

```
Now: 4/10/2015 11:30:56 PM
Now (UTC): 4/11/2015 6:30:56 AM
Now (Date only): 4/10/2015 12:00:00 AM
Now (Time only): 23:30:56.5303532
```

Figure 4-10. DateTime Current Time Output

DateTime variables with specific values can be created using a special initialization method called a constructor. There are various forms of constructors for DateTime, but the most common are listed here:

Example #1: `DateTime date = new DateTime(2015, 1, 30);`

Example #2: `DateTime date = new DateTime(2015, 1, 30, 15, 14, 10);`

The first version accepts the year, month and day values, in that specific order, setting the time to 12:00 midnight. The second version accepts the same first 3 values as the first example, but it also assigns hours (in 24-hour format), minutes and seconds. It is also possible to convert a string value to a DateTime which will be discussed in section 4.12.

Dates can also be manipulated with a series of "Add" methods that correspond to the different date and time units, such as months, days, hours and minutes. Subtracting time span units requires the same methods, just with negative time span values. Multiple time units can be manipulated within a single statement by chaining the method calls together as shown in Listing 4-22 on line 7.

Listing 4-22. DateTime Manipulation

```
1 Console.WriteLine("Now (Date only): " + nowDateOnly);
2 DateTime lastYear = nowDateOnly.AddYears(-1);
3 Console.WriteLine("Last year: " + lastYear);
4 DateTime nextMonth = nowDateOnly.AddMonths(1);
5 Console.WriteLine("Next month: " + nextMonth);
6 // Add three months and five days
7 DateTime newDate = nowDateOnly.AddMonths(3).AddDays(5);
8 Console.WriteLine("New date: " + newDate);
```

```
Now (Date only): 4/10/2015 12:00:00 AM
Last year: 4/10/2014 12:00:00 AM
Next month: 5/10/2015 12:00:00 AM
New date: 7/15/2015 12:00:00 AM
```

Figure 4-11. DateTime Manipulation Output

The individual DateTime time units can also be retrieved from DateTime variables. The properties for the units are intuitively named and most are of type int. So, if you need the month, day and year units of a DateTime variable, access the Month, Day and Year properties, respectively. Additionally, there is a DayOfWeek property that returns an enum constant value that corresponds to the named day of the week and a DayOfYear year property that returns the sequential value of the day between 1 and 366.

Listing 4-23. DateTime Units

```
DateTime fireworks = new DateTime(2015, 7, 4, 20, 45, 0);
Console.WriteLine("Fireworks start on " + fireworks.DayOfWeek + " at " +
  fireworks.Hour + ":" + fireworks.Minute);
Console.WriteLine("It is on day " + fireworks.DayOfYear + " of the year " +
  fireworks.Year);
```

```
Fireworks start on Saturday at 20:45
It is on day 185 of the year 2015
```

Figure 4-12. DateTime Units Output

Table 4-11. Common DateTime Members

Static	Name	Description
✓	MaxValue	The largest possible DateTime value, 12/31/9999.
✓	MinValue	The smallest possible DateTime value, 1/1/0001.
✓	Now	The current date and time in the current time zone.
✓	UtcNow	The current date and time in universal time.
✓	Today	The current date with time set to 12:00 midnight.
	Date	The date portion of a DateTime variable.
	Day	The day of month portion of a DateTime variable (1 – 31).
	DayOfWeek	The day of week of a DateTime variable (Sunday – Saturday).
	DayOfYear	The day of year number of a DateTime variable (0 – 366).
	Hour	The hour or day portion of a DateTime variable (0 – 23).
	Millisecond	The millisecond portion of a DateTime variable (0 – 999).
	Minute	The minutes portion of a DateTime variable (0 – 59).
	Month	The month portion of a DateTime variable (1 – 12).
	Second	The seconds portion of a DateTime variable (0 – 59).
	TimeOfDay	The time portion of a DateTime variable (12:00:00 AM – 11:59:59 PM)
	Year	The year portion of a DateTime variable (1 – 9999).
	AddDays()	Adds the given number of days to the DateTime variable.
	AddHours()	Adds the given number of hours to the DateTime variable.
	AddMilliseconds()	Adds the given number of milliseconds to the DateTime variable.
	AddMinutes()	Adds the given number of minutes to the DateTime variable.
	AddMonths()	Adds the given number of months to the DateTime variable.
	AddSeconds()	Adds the given number of seconds to the DateTime variable.
	AddYears()	Adds the given number of years to the DateTime variable.
✓	Parse()	Attempts to parse a given string into an equivalent DateTime value. Invalid input causes exceptions.
	ToString()	Converts the given DateTime to a string.
✓	TryParse()	Attempts to parse a given text string into a DateTime value.

var

The var data type is not really a data type at all. Instead it is an implicit placeholder for another defined type. The var type is only legal for locally scoped variables (variables declared within a method), and the compiler determines their actual type based on what is stored in them. This means that anytime you create a local variable in a method, like Main(), you can use the var keyword in place of the variable's actual data type. If you store the value 10 in a var, the compiler will automatically make that variable an int. That variable is just as type-safe as any other explicitly declared int and can be passed to methods expecting an int argument as well. The compiler, IntelliSense and any other code will see the var variable for what it really is, so there is no performance penalty or chance of a type mismatch issue.

So, what is this var type/keyword good for? The var keyword was designed for use with anonymous types, which is far beyond the scope of this chapter, but can be quickly described as data types created "on-the-fly". Since any type created in that manner would not have a formal type name, var is used to implicitly define that type. Another use is to minimize typing where the data type can be easily discerned based on a constructor call. A good example of this would be when creating a Dictionary object as it requires a lengthy statement. For instance:

```
Dictionary<decimal, string> myDictionary = new Dictionary<decimal, string>();
```

Would become:

```
var myDictionary = new Dictionary<decimal, string>();
```

Both variable declarations are identical to the compiler, but the second example replaces the formal, explicit variable type with var. Clearly, it saves a lot of real estate in the code, and since the constructor (after the new keyword) defines what the type is there is no real confusion for anyone reading the code.

Even though the use of var saves a lot of typing, it is still highly recommended that any variable declaration that cannot be easily distinguished based on its assigned contents should still use an explicit type name. Keep the old adage in mind: just because you can do something doesn't mean you should. Overuse of the var keyword can make code extremely hard to read.

I try to use the var keyword sparingly as it can result in hard to read code. It does have its practical uses, such as with LINQ and streamlining overly verbose constructor calls, but beyond those I prefer explicit variable type declarations. I do, however, love to use it when creating a variable with a long constructor call as duplicating the name actually makes it harder to read (Dictionary example above).

4.10 Understanding Value & Reference Types

Data types in C# are divided into two categories: value types and reference types. Most of the built-in data types in Table 4-1 fall into the value type category, with the exception of string and object.

Stack and Heap

Programs in C# have two distinct regions of memory where variable data is stored. The ***stack*** is a small, efficient structure in memory (roughly 1MB in most implementations) that is ideal for small variable types that don't vary in size. The ***heap*** is a huge data structure that can store variable data that is larger than what can be stored in the stack, typically only by the maximum size of a process's memory. For 32-bit systems that value is 2GB and for 64-bit systems the size is much larger, on the order of 128GB. However, every individual object is still limited to 2GB on a 64-bit machine.

Value Types

Value type variables are stored in the stack. The term "value type" refers to how the memory location in the stack is actually the value of the variable. Therefore, when you create an `int` called *x* with the value 5 in a program, *x* is a 32-bit allocation (the size of an `int`) in the stack that stores the value 5. Whenever *x* is referred to in the program, the value 5 is actually used (because that is the value in the stack at the location of *x*). Value types must always contain a legal value, which is why all the basic numeric types have a default value.

All data stored in the stack has a finite lifetime. When a variable goes "out of scope" the memory that variable consumed is reclaimed by the stack and can be reused for other variables. Therefore, the lifetime of a value type variable is "deterministic", or the exact time of creation and destruction is known. Typically, the scope of a variable is determined by the set of curly braces it is defined in. The variable is created at the time it is declared and initialized and it is destroyed upon reaching the end curly brace in which it is defined.

Reference Types

Reference types, like value types, are also declared in the stack. However, the value stored in the stack is not the variable's data. Rather, it is an index into the heap where the actual variable data is stored. So, when you declare a variable of type `string` called *s* with the value "ABC", the variable *s* is created in the stack. This identifies that the variable *s* exists and is of type `string` so you can use it like any other variable in the program. However, the data "ABC" is allocated in the heap and the value of *s* in the stack is an index, or address, that refers to the location of "ABC" in the heap.

Since reference type variables point to locations in the heap for their data, not assigning an initial value to a variable leaves the stack value in an invalid state. This state is actually referred to by a special value called `null`. The variable still exists, essentially as a placeholder for future use. Any attempt to read a value out of that variable, except to compare it to `null`, will cause a NullReferenceException to be thrown. It is very common for programmers to use this `null` state to indicate that the variable is not initialized or has not yet been assigned a value. This is especially useful when reading records from databases where fields can be nullable to save space.

The lifetime of a reference type variable is not as clear-cut as its value type counterpart. Any data stored in the heap is managed by the .NET Garbage Collector. Periodically, the garbage collector is called by your program, typically out of your control. While it executes it looks for reference variables that are no longer in use. If it detects that a variable is no longer useful it will call that variable's finalizer and reclaim its memory for use by other variables. Since heap data tends to be quite large, this periodic cleansing method is typically more efficient than on-demand cleaning, as calling the garbage collector constantly would starve the rest of your program from getting CPU cycles. The downside to garbage collection is that you cannot be 100% certain when a variable is going to have its memory reclaimed. Even if a reference type variable falls out of scope, its memory payload may remain active for quite some time. This means the variable's cleanup is non-deterministic and you will have to use other techniques, such as the IDisposable pattern, to handle object teardown in a predictable manner.

Reference Types and the '=' Operator

When you have two value types, such as `int` variables, assigning one to the other has predictable results. Consider the following code sample:

Listing 4-24. Value Type Assignment

```
1 int x = 10;
2 int y = x;
3 x++;
```

Intuitively, you probably assume that the variable *y* will have the value 10 after the assignment. That assumption is correct. However, do you understand why? We've discussed that every variable has its own space in the stack, and for value types, the actual value of the variable is stored there. So, in the example above, there are two variables in the stack and therefore two distinct values. When the assignment operator is encountered in the assignment expression "*y* = *x*", the value from *x*'s location in the stack is copied to *y*'s location. So, in this case, the value 10 is copied into *y*'s stack location. Since these variables store their data in two distinct locations, any changes to either variable after the assignment is strictly contained to that specific variable. So, after line 3 executes, *x* becomes 11 but *y* remains 10. The chart below shows this in action. *Note: the addresses displayed are arbitrary values.*

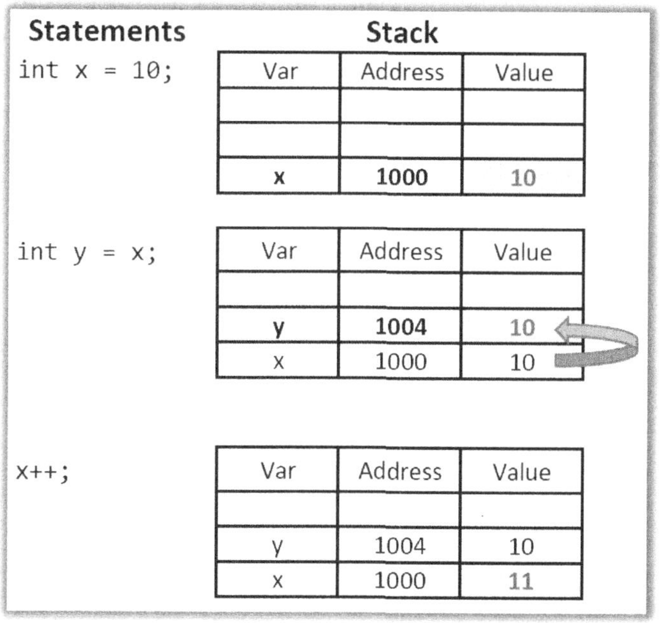

Statements / **Stack**

`int x = 10;`

Var	Address	Value
x	**1000**	10

`int y = x;`

Var	Address	Value
y	**1004**	10
x	1000	10

`x++;`

Var	Address	Value
y	1004	10
x	1000	11

Figure 4-13. Value Type Assignment Memory Graph

No real surprises… yet.

Now, let's take a look at a reference type's assignment operation. Since we have not really worked with any reference types as of yet (except `string` which is a special case for a later discussion) let's just use StringBuilder which is a commonly used utility class to construct `string` variables. Since it is a reference type we know three things:

- any variables of its type are created in the stack (like any data type variable)
- all of its data, or state, is stored in the heap
- the value stored in the stack is an address to the value in the heap

Examine the following sample:

Listing 4-25. Reference Type Assignment

```
1 StringBuilder s1 = new StringBuilder("ABC");
2 StringBuilder s2 = s1;
3 s1.Append("D");
```

The code in Listing 4-25 is analogous to the code in Listing 4-24. We create a variable of type StringBuilder, called *s1*, and assign to it a new instance with the value "ABC". We then instantiate a second StringBuilder called *s2* and assign to it the value of *s1*. Lastly, we make a change to *s1* by appending a 'D' character to the end of its data making the final value "ABCD". So, what's so special about this? Would it surprise you to know that after that last line of code that the value of *s2* is also "ABCD"? Wait, what? Remember, what is the default behavior of the '=' operator? It assigns a copy of the value in the stack of the right-hand variable into the value in the stack for the left-hand variable. What is in the stack for reference types? That's right, the address of that variable's contents in the heap. So, what actually happened in line 2 is that the address of *s1*'s heap location is copied into *s2*'s stack value. This implies that both *s1* and *s2* are pointing to the exact same data in the heap. You can see this in Figure 4-14:

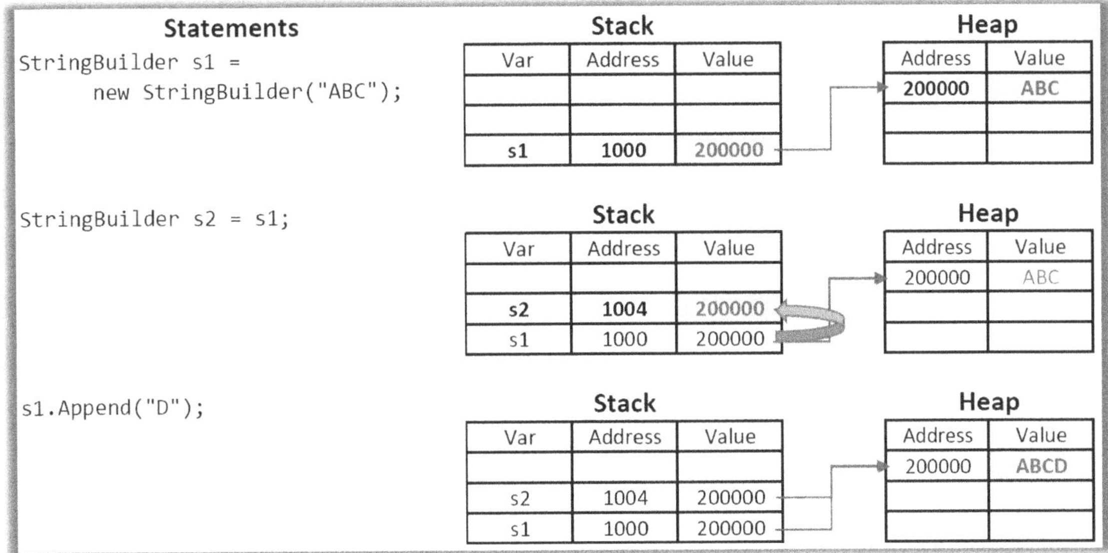

Figure 4-14. Reference Type Assignment Memory Graph

Don't forget that the default value for reference types is `null`. You can also explicitly assign `null` to a reference type variable using the "=" operator. When this happens, the value in the "Value" column of the stack will actually contain the value `null`, which implies it does not point to anything in the heap. That is why it is considered a "null reference" and will throw exceptions if you try to read the variable's contents.

As you can see, working with reference types has some gotchas, but as long as you remember that "=" produces different results with reference types than with value types you should be ok. We will look at this situation again when we discuss passing parameters by-value and by-reference.

Nullable Value Types

As mentioned above, it can be very useful to store the value `null` in reference types to indicate the variable is uninitialized or that the value represents an empty field in a database. Unfortunately, value types cannot be assigned `null` values because value type variables must always be assigned a legitimate value. That would seem to be a limitation, especially since numeric types in a database can definitely be nullable. Fortunately, in C# 2.0, a new data structure called Nullable<T> was added to address this very issue. Essentially, Nullable<T> is a wrapper around whatever value data type you wish to be nullable. The formal syntax for creating a Nullable variable is:

```
Nullable<T> nullVar = new Nullbale<T>(initialValue);
```

Where *T* is the value type, like `int`, that you wish to make into a nullable variable and ***initialValue*** is the initial value to assign to the variable. Once initialized it is possible to assign any legitimate value of type *T* into the variable as well as `null`.

The downside to the formal Nullable syntax is that it is very cumbersome to implement. To work around this issue, C# has a bit of "syntactic sugar" sprinkled onto it to make Nullable types much friendlier. Instead of using Nullable<*T*> to define the type a programmer can use *T*?, where, again, *T* can be any value data type:

```
T? nullVar = initialValue;
```

Regardless of which syntax is used to create the variable, once it has been initialized it can be used almost the exact same way a variable of type *T* is used, except now it can be assigned or compared to `null`.

Listing 4-26. Nullable Values

```
// Assign 10 to nullable int n1 and null to n2
Nullable<int> n1 = new Nullable<int>(10);
Nullable<int> n2 = new Nullable<int>();
Console.WriteLine(n1);
Console.WriteLine(n2);

// Do the same but with simplified C# syntax for n3 & n4
int? n3 = 10;
int? n4 = null;
Console.WriteLine(n3);
Console.WriteLine(n4);

// Re-assign value to n3
n3 = 20;
// Check n4 for null
if (n4 == null)
{
  Console.WriteLine("n4 is null");
}
```

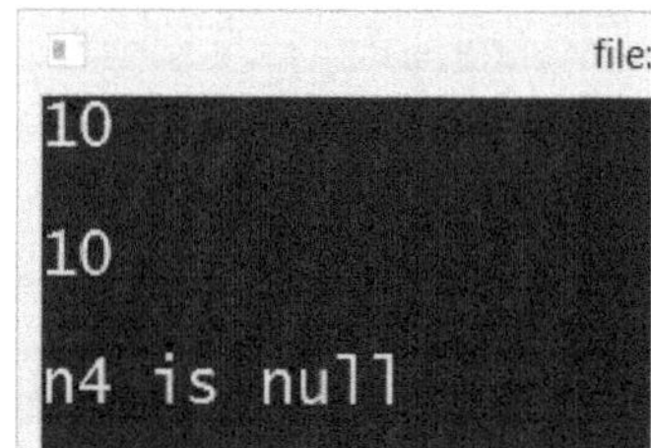

Figure 4-15. Nullable Output

Notice the blank spaces in the output of Figure 4-15. This is the result of attempting to print a `null` value.

One issue you will encounter with Nullable types is when you attempt to copy their value into a non-Nullable variable. The problem is that the compiler cannot know whether or not the Nullable variable contains a legitimate value or `null` – that can only be determined at runtime. Since a non-Nullable variable cannot contain `null`, the compiler prevents any direct assignment from a Nullable to non-Nullable variable using the "=" operator. You could use an `if` statement to check for `null` first and then use the "Value" property of the Nullable variable to do the assignment. However, there is a special operator, called the null-coalescing operator "??", which simplifies this process. The "??" operator is a binary operator where the left operand is the Nullable variable and the right operand is the value to use if the left operand is null. Therefore, if the Nullable variable contains a legal value that is the value used as the result of the expression. Otherwise, the right operand is used.

Listing 4-27. Use of null-Coalescing Operator

```
int? n = null;
// Cannot assign n directly to x, so use ?? operator
int x = n ?? 0;   // x will be assigned the value 0 since n is null

n = 10;
x = n ?? 0;       // Now x will be assigned the value 10 since n is a legal value
```

Boxing

Boxing is a fairly complicated technique that many programmers run into without even realizing it. As we've discussed, value types tend to store their data directly in the stack where the variable is defined. Reference types declare a variable in the stack, but the value in the stack is a reference, or pointer, to a location in the heap where the variable's data is actually stored. These lines can be blurred when a value type, such as an `int` variable, is stored in an `object`, which is a reference type. Essentially, the `object` variable becomes a wrapper (or a box) and the `int` value is moved to the heap. When the value is read from the boxed object, the value is said to be "unboxed". Unboxing requires the runtime to validate that the data in the heap matches the expected data type and then create a new value type variable on the stack to copy the boxed contents to.

There is a fairly large downside, performance-wise, to boxing and unboxing. To access a value type variable's data is single instruction, which is why stack-based variables are considerably faster than heap-based variables that require a second look-up into the heap to find the data. Boxing causes any value type variables to be treated like reference type variables, including the extra look-up and periodic processing by the garbage collector rather than the fall-out-of-scope cleanup employed by the stack.

Listing 4-28. Boxing and Unboxing

```
1 int x = 10;
2 // Box the data into an object:
3 object o = x;  // The value of o (10) is now stored in the heap
4 
5 // Now, unbox the variable back into an int.
6 // Notice that it requires an explicit cast to int:
7 int y = (int)o;// Now x will be assigned the value 10
```

The process of boxing and unboxing is simple in code, but can definitely impact performance. Note that in line 7, when *o* is unboxed into variable *y* that we have to do a special cast to `int`. That is because an `object` can contain anything and the compiler would otherwise have no way of knowing what is coming out of *o*. The concept of type casting is discussed in section 4.11.

Boxing is something I pay close attention to as it can severely degrade performance. In older versions of .NET a very useful type called ArrayList made extensive use of boxing. The ArrayList type is a dynamically expandable list of `objects`. Since every element in the list is an `object`, you could use this structure to store a list of anything. The downside is that an ArrayList of `int` values would require every value to be boxed/unboxed when added/accessed. The List<T> class was introduced to alleviate this problem.

4.11 Data Conversions

In programming it is frequently necessary to convert a variable of one data type into another. One of the most common conversions employed is transforming a value of almost any type into a `string`. Since all data types derive from the type called `object`, all data types naturally possess a ToString() method which converts a value to a `string`. However, converting to and from any other types requires other techniques.

Implicit & Explicit Conversions

Some data types can be converted to another type directly with an assignment statement. This type of translation is known as implicit conversion. For instance, it is possible to take a value of type `int` and assign it directly to a `long` variable without any additional code. This type of conversion is not common as it is only allowed when there can be no loss of data. Consider going the other direction, converting a `long` into an `int`. Since a `long` can hold values both smaller and larger than an `int`, the C# compiler prevents any attempt to implicitly convert values in that direction. Therefore, to convert between data types where implicit conversions are not available the programmer must use an explicit technique. We will look at those techniques after we discuss widening and narrowing conversions.

Widening Conversions

Widening conversions are when a smaller data type is converted into a larger data type. It is only possible if the larger data type can represent every possible value from the smaller type. In the example above, when converting from an `int` to a `long`, every possible value of the `int` can be represented by a `long` so this qualifies as a widening conversion. Widening conversions, such as this, are typically permitted to be done implicitly.

Narrowing Conversions

Narrowing conversions are the opposite of widening conversions, where the programmer wishes to convert from a larger format data type to a smaller one. One important feature of C# is that it tries to keep you from losing data. You must use explicit conversion techniques to inform C# that you are doing the conversion intentionally, not accidentally.

System.Convert

The System.Convert class contains many methods to convert from one built-in data type to another built-in type. The methods are named using the CTS naming conventions for the intrinsic types; therefore, there is no method named "ToInt()", but there is a "ToInt32()" method. Since all C# program files, by default, have a `using` directive to include the System namespace, it is not typically necessary to type "`System.Convert.`" prior to each command. Instead, just use "`Convert.`" as a prefix to the method names. The following is a list of the common conversion methods available in the System.Convert class:

Table 4-12. Common System.Convert Methods

Static	Name	Description
✓	ToBoolean()	Converts the given input to a bool.
✓	ToByte()	Converts the given input to a byte.
✓	ToChar()	Converts the given input to a char.
✓	ToDateTime()	Converts the given input to a DateTime.
✓	ToDecimal()	Converts the given input to a decimal.
✓	ToDouble()	Converts the given input to a double.
✓	ToInt16()	Converts the given input to a short.
✓	ToInt32()	Converts the given input to an int.
✓	ToInt64()	Converts the given input to a long.
✓	ToSByte()	Converts the given input to an sbyte.
✓	ToSingle()	Converts the given input to a float.
✓	ToString()	Converts the given input to a string. Not commonly used since all variables already have a ToString() method.
✓	ToUInt16()	Converts the given input to a ushort.
✓	ToUInt32()	Converts the given input to a uint.
✓	ToUInt64()	Converts the given input to a ulong.

The available conversion methods, shown in Table 4-12, allow the programmer to convert between virtually all of the built-in data types to another. However, not all data type conversions can be applied universally to all other data types, even if the method is provided. For instance, converting from a DateTime to an sbyte using Convert.ToSByte() will cause an InvalidCastException to be thrown, which makes sense since there is no logical relationship between those two types. Also, providing a value that is not legal for the output type can also cause an exception, even if providing similar input, but in another form, succeeds. Consider the example below:

Listing 4-29. Simple Conversion

```
1 double d1 = 5.5;
2 // This conversion will succeed:
3 int i1 = Convert.ToInt32(d1);
4 string s1 = "5.5";
5 // This conversion will fail:
6 i1 = Convert.ToInt32(s1);
```

The first conversion on line 3, going from a double to int, succeeds. However, the second conversion, on line 6, fails when converting from a string, even though the underlying value is the same. In the first case, the value is rounded up from 5.5 to 6 when converting to an int. The conversion from string is much stricter regarding the format of the input, so it fails when it encounters the decimal point. Basically, the string version must have the input in a legitimate integer format prior to the conversion call. There is a second version of the ToInt32() method that also accepts an IFormatProvider which alleviates this problem, but that is beyond the scope of this chapter. Just be aware, some of the conversion functions may fail if the given input does not meet the criteria of the specific method.

Using these conversion methods we can explicitly execute narrowing conversions. Be cautious! Some conversions just are not possible no matter how hard you try. Later, when you learn about "`if`" statements, you can use conditional tests to make sure the conversion you are about to perform is legal. For now, we'll just ensure we only use legal values.

Listing 4-30. Narrowing Conversion Using Convert.ToInt32

```
long l = 12345L;
// Can't do this:
//    int i = l;
// So, instead do this:
int i = Convert.ToInt32(l);
```

A word of caution about converting from `string` to another data type… Since it is common to have a user type data into a console app or enter values into a UI text box, it is frequently necessary to convert these `string` values into other types, like `int` and `float`. The Convert methods can definitely do this work. Just be aware that any malformed input will typically yield a FormatException. Instead, I propose that you work with the target data type's Parse() and TryParse() methods discussed in section 4.12.

Casting

Another form of explicit conversion is called casting. Instead of calling a method to convert a value to a different data type, the explicit cast operator is used. This operator is unary and always precedes the value being converted. The operator is comprised of a set of parentheses containing the desired destination type within those parentheses. Due to the relatively simple syntax this methodology is sometimes considered easier than using the Convert class methods. In addition, the casting operators tend to be more forgiving than the Convert class methods.

One of the most common use of casting is to temporarily convert an `int` to a `float` to carry out a division operation. Consider a problem where an instructor needs to determine the percentage of problems a student answered correctly on a test. Assume the student answered 93 problems out of 100 correctly. You intuitively know that the student answered 93%, or 0.93, correctly. However, if both the *numberCorrect* and *totalPoints* variables are of type `int`, dividing *numberCorrect* by *totalPoints* would yield a value of 0. This is the case even if the value you are attempting to assign the result to is a `float`. Remember, `int` does not retain decimal places, so the result is truncated to the next lowest whole number, which is 0 since it is the next lowest number from 0.93. To resolve this issue, cast the first value to `float`. The second value will implicitly be promoted to a `float` during the division operation, although it is also perfectly acceptable to cast both values.

Listing 4-31. Explicit Cast Operator

```
long l = 12345L;
int i = (int)l;  // Casts from long to int

float f = 1.5F;
i = (int)f;      // Casts from float to int, truncating 1.5 to 1

// Using casts to calculate percentage using ints and floats
int score = 93;
int totalPoints = 100;

// The following result of pct is 0, not 0.93 due to int math.
float pct = score / totalPoints;

// To get the expected result cast score to a float
//   Note: totalPoints is implicitly promoted to float.
pct = (float)score / totalPoints;

// Or explictly cast both operands to float
pct = (float)score / (float)totalPoints;
```

Converting from string to another data type, like int or float, can also be very useful, especially if you are reading in values from the Console.ReadLine() method which only returns string. However, the explicit casts from string to the other built-in data types are, for the most part, not provided. This is because it would be common for the input data to be in an incorrect format. Instead, if you wish to convert from a string to another built-in data type, use that data type's Parse() or TryParse() method.

4.12 Parsing

Parsing is the process of converting a text value into another form. Most built-in data types support this type of conversion via their Parse() and TryParse() methods. The end goal of either method is to convert a string to the required data type. However, Parse() will throw an exception upon failure while TryParse() will simply return false.

Parse()

The following data types support the Parse() method:

bool	byte	sbyte	char
decimal	double	float	int
uint	long	ulong	short
ushort	DateTime		

Since the Parse() method is static, the mechanism for accessing the method is <type>.Parse(). All of the various Parse() methods accept a single string as input and returns a value of the type that the method is called upon. Some of the types have optional ways of calling Parse() with additional parameters that customize how to parse the input value. Let's take a look at the single `string` input cases first, then we'll look at the other calls.

Listing 4-32. Parsing

```
1  string input = "123";
2  int i = int.Parse(input);
3  Console.WriteLine("The int is: " + i);
4
5  input = "123.45";
6  double d = double.Parse(input);
7  Console.WriteLine("The double is: " + d);
8
9  input = "true";
10 bool b = bool.Parse(input);
11 Console.WriteLine("The bool is: " + b);
12
13 input = "January 12, 2015 2:00 PM";
14 DateTime dt = DateTime.Parse(input);
15 Console.WriteLine("The DateTime is: " + dt);
```

```
The int is: 123
The double is: 123.45
The bool is: True
The DateTime is: 1/12/2015 2:00:00 PM
```

Figure 4-16. Parsing Output

As you can see, calling Parse() for any data type follows the same pattern and is relatively straight-forward. Rather than demonstrating every single data type's Parse() method, the above sample shows the basic pattern for each class of type (integral, decimal, Boolean and dates). The problem you will encounter with this technique of parsing is when the input value is not in a valid format for the type you are attempting to parse into. Let's assume, for instance, that *input* is initialized with "ABC" instead of "123" on line 1. When line 2 attempts to execute, you will see the following in Visual Studio:

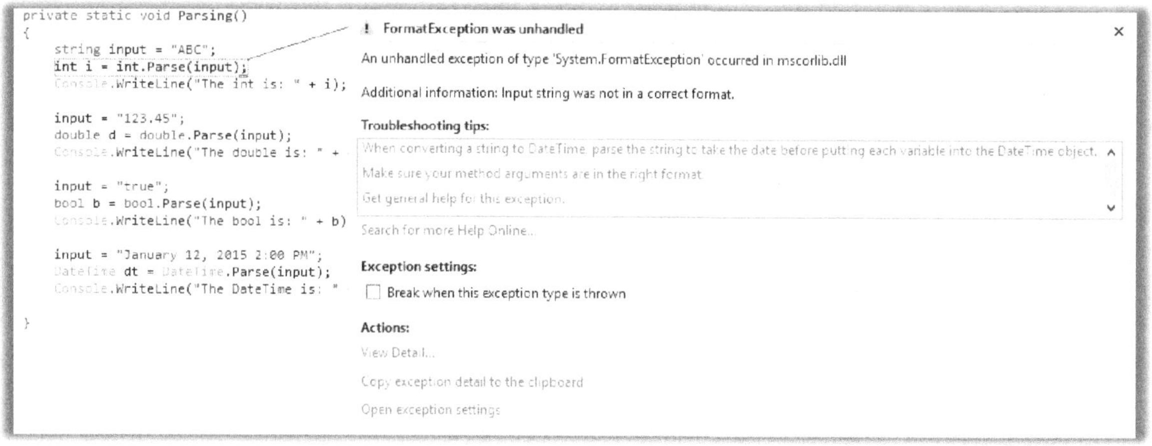

```
private static void Parsing()
{
    string input = "ABC";
    int i = int.Parse(input);
    Console.WriteLine("The int is: " + i);

    input = "123.45";
    double d = double.Parse(input);
    Console.WriteLine("The double is: " +

    input = "true";
    bool b = bool.Parse(input);
    Console.WriteLine("The bool is: " + b)

    input = "January 12, 2015 2:00 PM";
    DateTime dt = DateTime.Parse(input);
    Console.WriteLine("The DateTime is: "

}
```

FormatException was unhandled

An unhandled exception of type 'System.FormatException' occurred in mscorlib.dll

Additional information: Input string was not in a correct format.

Troubleshooting tips:

When converting a string to DateTime, parse the string to take the date before putting each variable into the DateTime object.

Make sure your method arguments are in the right format.

Get general help for this exception.

Search for more Help Online...

Exception settings:

Break when this exception type is thrown

Actions:

View Detail...

Copy exception detail to the clipboard

Open exception settings

Figure 4-17. Parse() Exception

Clearly, if we are attempting to author robust code, this is not the correct way. If this application is running outside of the context of Visual Studio, the result is a crash. To prevent that from occurring in a production environment you would need to wrap that code within a `try` block. We'll talk in great detail about exception handling in Chapter 9, but for right now, here's a preview what the code looks like to protect against crashes:

Listing 4-33. Parse() Within a try Block

```
string input = "ABC";
try
{
  int i = int.Parse(input);
  Console.WriteLine("The int is: " + i);
}
catch (Exception ex)
{
  Console.WriteLine("Could not parse to int: " + ex.Message);
}
```

Essentially, the code that can potentially cause problems is nestled within the `try` block. If a problem occurs the code is redirected to the `catch` block below it. If the code succeeds then the `catch` block is bypassed and code continues to execute after the `catch` block close brace. Again, it is not expected that you fully understand what is happening here since it is a topic we'll investigate in great detail later.

As mentioned earlier, several data types support additional arguments being sent to Parse(). This is to support the various formats that data types may appear as when saved in a `string`. Consider the following two numeric values:

- 12345678.90
- $12,345,678.90

These are technically the same values although the first value lacks any special formatting while the second is in the default currency format for the culture "English (United States)". So what happens when we try to parse these values into a `decimal`?

Listing 4-34. Parsing Currency

```
1 string input = "12345678.90";
2 decimal dec = decimal.Parse(input);
3 input = "$12,345,678.90";
4 dec = decimal.Parse(input);
```

Everything works great for the first call to `decimal`.Parse(). However, when line 4 executes we get that nasty FormatException again. The problem is, by default, the various Parse() methods will only accept input when the `string` is in its simplest form for that data type without any extraneous characters. Clearly, that is not the case in the second example. So, how can we fix this? Another version of the `decimal`.Parse() method accepts three arguments:

```
public static decimal Parse(string s, NumberStyles style, IFormatProvider provider);
```

The first argument, *s*, is the same as with the other Parse() calls, it is the input string. The second argument, *style*, represents the different formats and characters that may appear in the input string. Some of the valid styles are: AllowLeadingSign, AllowThousands, AllowCurrencySymbol and AllowDecimalPoint. There is also an additional style, called Currency, which is a combination of those formats. Finally, the *provider* argument allows the programmer to specify the culture to use when handling special characters and formatting. For instance, not all countries use "$" as their currency symbol, nor do they all use "," as their thousands separator. By specifying a culture, those specific details can be compensated for. So, to correct our program to handle the currency input, the code would look like:

Listing 4-35. Parsing Currency with Extended Formatting

```
dec = decimal.Parse(input, NumberStyles.Currency, CultureInfo.CurrentCulture);
```

Note: for the above code to work, a using directive must be added to the top of the code file:

```
using System.Globalization;
```

Notice for the second argument, the value "`NumberStyles.Currency`" was chosen to indicate we are accepting values formatted with currency characteristics. The last argument indicates that we are looking for formats that correspond to the local culture, wherever the program happens to be running. If the program runs on a computer in France then it would automatically look for Euros instead of dollars. You could also identify a specific culture by using the following for argument 3:

Listing 4-36. Specifying a Culture

```
CultureInfo en_us = CultureInfo.GetCultureInfo("en-US");
dec = decimal.Parse(input, NumberStyles.Currency, en_us);
```

The code "en-US" specifies the language English for the United States. To get the culture for Mexican Spanish the code would be "es-MX". A quick search for "C# Language Culture Codes" on the Internet will give you a complete list for your programming needs. Alternatively, you could call "`CultureInfo.GetCultures(CultureTypes.AllCultures)`", but you would have to know in advance specifically what you are looking for.

Other data types will have a similar argument list if you are looking to accept enhanced formats for that specific type.

TryParse()

Besides Parse(), all of the data types listed in the previous section also support the TryParse() method. Unlike Parse(), this method will not cause exceptions to be throw if the input data is not in the correct format. Instead, the return value from the method is a `bool` that indicates if the parsing succeeded. That is fantastic, because then all we need is an "`if`" statement (which we'll cover in detail later) to deal with bad input. Hold on a second... If the return value from the method is always `true` or `false` then how do we get the parsed result? It turns out that C# has a special type of input argument that can also be used to return a value. This special type of argument is called an "`out`" parameter. This actually deals specifically with passing variables by-reference which is a topic that we'll look at closely in Chapter 8. However, since the syntax is relatively simple there is no reason not to use it right now.

Listing 4-37. TryParse()

```
string input = "123";
int i;

if (int.TryParse(input, out i) == true)
{
  Console.WriteLine("The input value is " + i);
}
else
{
  Console.WriteLine("Bad input value!");
}

input = "ABC";
if (int.TryParse(input, out i) == true)
{
  Console.WriteLine("The input value is " + i);
}
else
{
  Console.WriteLine("Bad input value!");
}
```

```
The input value is 123
Bad input value!
```

Figure 4-18. TryParse() Output

As you can see, the statement on line 4 is a bit more complex than a call to `int`.Parse(), but if we break it down into smaller chunks it is manageable. First, notice that we are using an "`if`" statement to test the result of the expression. Since we know the TryParse() method will return a `bool` we can test the result for `true` or `false`. Typically, programmers try to code with the positive result as the primary code path so we will look for `true` in our code. So, for the result of TryParse() to be `true`, the value of *input* must be safely converted into an `int`. That's where the second argument to TryParse() comes in. Notice that we are passing *i* to the method, but we are also adding a special operator, `out`, in front of the variable name to indicate that the argument will act as another return value. In essence, if the value of *input* can be converted to a `int`, then *i* will contain that parsed value upon completion of the call to TryParse().

In Listing 4-37 *the result of the TryParse() method is compared to* `true` *using the "==" operator. This is actually superfluous since the result of the call will already be either* `true` *or* `false` *which can be directly tested by the* `if` *statement. I decided that since we have not looked at* `if` *statements yet that the more verbose syntax would be appropriate.*

TryParse() also contains other versions of the call that accept additional parameters, much like Parse(). So, to format extended values, the call will look very similar to Listing 4-35:

Listing 4-38. TryParse() with Extended Formatting

```
string input = "$12,345,678.90";
decimal dec;
if (decimal.TryParse(input, NumberStyles.Currency, CultureInfo.CurrentCulture,
    out dec) == true)
{
  Console.WriteLine("The decimal is: " + dec);
}
```

4.13 Summary

C# contains a variety of data types right out of the box to support numbers, text and dates. The data types are used to create variables, or named locations in memory, which can be used in expressions to calculate values based on formulas.

Constants are like variables except their values cannot change after they've be assigned. These are used to avoid "magic numbers" or numeric literals that have special meaning but only within the context of the program.

Comments can be used to annotate your code without actually affecting the compiled result. Special comments, called XML Comments, can be used to add IntelliSense to your programs and can be exported for use by other tools, like document creation utilities.

Operators are used to manipulate single variables or two variables. Special operators, compound assignment operators, can calculate expressions and assign the results to a variable.

Variables come in two flavors, value type and reference types, which is determined by their data types. Value types store their data in the stack while reference types store their data in the heap. Special care must be taken when creating and assigning values to reference type variables.

Converting data from one type to another can be done using System.Convert, casting and parsing. Each technique has its advantages and drawbacks and some thought should be used when determining the correct technique for a given situation.

Later, we'll look at the `string` data type in more details as well as using arrays and lists to store series of values in one variable.

5

5. Arrays and Lists

One of the features of programming that is practically required for any robust solution is the creation of variables. As you have seen, variables can be created based on a wide variety of data types, including numerical, textual and temporal values. What happens when you need to store multiple items of the same type? Does that mean for every unique value you are required to create a new variable, such as: name1, name2, name3, etc…? Fortunately, the answer to that question is "no" - C# has specialized structures to handle groups of related data, called arrays. Later, we'll also expand our knowledge by using dynamic lists, another mechanism for storing like data.

5.1 One-Dimensional (1D) Arrays

Arrays are groups of like data that are organized into single variables. In the case of one-dimensional arrays, the group is linear, or it has only a single dimension. We'll look at higher dimensional arrays later, but for now let's focus on the simple case. Assume you are asked to write a program that will hold five names. The code might end up looking something like this:

Listing 5-1. Multiple Like Variables

```
string name1 = "Bill";
string name2 = "Joan";
string name3 = "Steven";
string name4 = "Angella";
string name5 = "John";
```

Although the code is functional, you can see how this can get to be unwieldy, especially as the number of names increases. So, if we need to store 100 names does that mean we require 100 unique variables? Unfortunately, if you follow the above pattern, the answer would be "yes". While this approach may work for simple examples and small sets of data it quickly becomes apparent there must be a better way. Enter the array…

Arrays are defined as contiguous sets of like data. In C#, arrays are linear in that they consume a single, contiguous block of memory. Each entry, or element, of the array is essentially a unique variable all to itself and does not have any particular ties to previous or later values in the same array. The position, or index, of each element in the array is determined by the programmer and may or may not have contextual meaning. In other words, in your application it may not matter that the elements in the arrays are presented in a given order. However, it is just as likely that the element positions are significant based on the business logic of the program. Consider a pill box you can purchase at a pharmacy. The pill box is divided into 7 cells for you to put pills into. This pill box is essentially a seven element array, where each element of the array is a pill that must be taken on the given day. In this example, the index of each element has importance as it relates to a given day of the week.

C# Array Rules

Before we look at a practical example of an array, let's look at some of the rules regarding arrays in C#. Some of these rules are similar to other languages; however, do not make any assumptions that a feature of arrays in another language directly applies to C# arrays.

- Array indices are 0-based
- All elements of an array must be of the same data type
- Arrays are immutable
- Arrays are reference types
- All elements are given default values
- Arrays are stored in a contiguous block of memory

These rules can be a little tough to understand for those that have not worked with programming before, so let's look at each one in detail.

Array Indices Are 0-based

Every element in an array is addressable (accessed) by index. So, if you are looking for the 3rd element in an array that position must be translated into a valid index. In C#, array indices are 0-based, which means the counting of index positions starts at 0, not 1. So, the first element in an array is at index 0, while the 2nd is at index 1 and the 3rd element is at index 2. A simple formula is pretty easy to derive from this pattern: index = position - 1. It is critical that when you access an array that you never request an element with an index of less than 0. Likewise, it is also necessary to never attempt to access an element after the last valid position. So, if you create an array using the "pill box" example discussed above, it would have 7 elements, but the valid indices would be 0 through 6. It is a very common mistake for beginners to attempt accessing the last element as index 7, but this is guaranteed to cause an IndexOutOfRangeException.

It is only appropriate to mention that it is technically possible to create an array with an arbitrary first index value, other than 0. This technique requires the use of Array.CreateInstance() and will not be discussed in this book due to its very infrequent usage.

All Elements of an Array Must Be of the Same Data Type

When you create an array, like any other variable, you must specify its data type. If you create an array of `int` values, every element in the array must be an `int`. It is possible to create an array of `object` values, which would allow any element to be any type, but this practice is strongly discouraged as it can lead to unmaintainable, or just plain old sloppy, code.

Arrays Are Immutable

This particular rule is one you are likely to run into and curse the developers of C# for implementing it. The word immutable simply means "unable to be changed". In this context it means an array created with 5 items will forever have 5 items. There is no built-in mechanism for growing or shrinking an array in C#. Therefore, when creating an array it is essential to create it with a sufficient capacity for your needs. There are techniques for manually changing the size of an array using memory copying techniques which will be discussed later on in the chapter.

Arrays Are Reference Types

There is a formal `class` called System.Array which all user-defined arrays are based from. As such all arrays are declared in the stack, like any variable type, but their data is stored in the heap. This allows arrays to have large sets of elements without concern for exhausting the stack.

All Elements Are Given Default Values

When an array is created without initial values for its elements, C# will automatically provide default values based on the data type that comprises the array. All numeric types are given the value 0. All reference types are set to `null`.

Arrays Are Stored in a Contiguous Block of Memory

When an array is created, a single, contiguous block of memory in the heap is allocated to store all of the elements. This has several advantages, most of which are abstracted from the programmer's view. Specifically, when accessing elements in an array by index, the position of a specific element can be quickly calculated knowing the starting address of the array, the size of each element and the index of the item. The formula looks something like:

```
ElementAddress = ArrayStartAddress + (ElementSize × Index)
```

Fortunately, this is all done behind the scenes, so when you wish to get a given element you only need its index and the address is calculated for you.

Creating a One-Dimensional Array

Creating an array requires one of the following different syntaxes. Common to all of the syntaxes is the array variable declaration:

```
<data type>[] <array name>;
```

Where <data type> is the type of data stored in each element of the array and <array name> is the name of the array variable. Notice that the data type is followed immediately by a set of square brackets, which identifies the variable as an array of that data type. In other C-style languages, these brackets follow the variable name instead of the type. However, C# makes the distinction that the array is more closely associated to the type rather than the variable. Also, in other C-style languages, the size of the array would be identified within these brackets, but that syntax is not permitted in C#. By leaving the array's size undefined in the variable declaration any size array of the correct data type can be stored in the variable. Just like other reference types, the default value for an uninitialized array is null, therefore if you want to do anything useful with the array it must be initialized using one these syntaxes:

Syntax #1:
```
<data type>[] <array name> = new <data type>[size];
```

Syntax #2:
```
<data type>[] <array name> = new <data type>[size] { <value list> };
```

Syntax #3:
```
<data type>[] <array name> = new <data type>[] { <value list> };
```

Syntax #4:
```
<data type>[] <array name> = { <value list> };
```

The first syntax is used when you need to create an array with a specific size but do not have a default set of values to supply for the elements in the array. The other three are variations of the same theme. Each creates an array with a specific size and default set of values to pre-populate the array's elements. Since these three variations accomplish the same goal, the last syntax is usually preferred as it is more concise. The following is an example of the different syntaxes creating arrays of string values, simplifying the code in Listing 5-1:

Listing 5-2. Simple string Arrays

```
1 string[] names1 = new string[5];
2 string[] names2 = new string[5] { "Bill", "Joan", "Steven", "Angela", "John" };
3 string[] names3 = new string[] { "Bill", "Joan", "Steven", "Angela", "John" };
4 string[] names4 = { "Bill", "Joan", "Steven", "Angela", "John" };
```

Besides line 1, each of the statements in Listing 5-2 creates identical arrays containing the same five names. If we need to populate *names1* with values we would need to use indexer syntax which we will look at in the next section.

Array Indexer Syntax

Once an array has been initialized it is possible to access the elements within by utilizing the array's indexer. An array's indexer is a special operator that accepts a parameter of type int that corresponds to an element's position in the array. As mentioned previously, the index value must be between 0 and the length of the array minus one. The syntax of the indexer is the same whether it appears in an expression as an lvalue or rvalue.

Listing 5-3. Array Indexer Example

```
string[] names1 = new string[5];
// Populate the elements of the array, indexer as lvalue
names1[0] = "Bill";
names1[1] = "Joan";
names1[2] = "Steven";
names1[3] = "Angela";
names1[4] = "John";
// Retrieve elements of the array, indexer as rvalue
string name = names1[3];  // Angela
Console.WriteLine("1st name: " + names1[0]);
```

The above example demonstrates how to populate the array *names1* created in Listing 5-2 after initialization. There is no limit to how many times you can write to or read from an element of an array. Each element, in a way, acts like an independent variable, so you can think of the above array as a group of 5 `string` variables.

There is no restriction to the type of data that can be made into an array. The next example shows how to create an array of integers and manipulate the values by using the array's indexer.

Listing 5-4. Integer Array

```
// Assume we want an array of the first 10 prime numbers, but only the first 8
// are known at array creation time.
// Use '0' placeholders for the unknown values since we need 10 elements.
int[] primes = { 2, 3, 5, 7, 11, 13, 17, 19, 0, 0 };

// Now, assign the missing values (9th and 10th elements).
// Remember, index is 0-based, so we access indices 8 & 9!
primes[8] = 23;
primes[9] = 29;

// Print the 5th prime number - element index 4.
Console.WriteLine("The 5th prime number is " + primes[4]);
```

Here's what the above code looks like in memory (remember, the addresses are arbitrary for illustration purposes only):

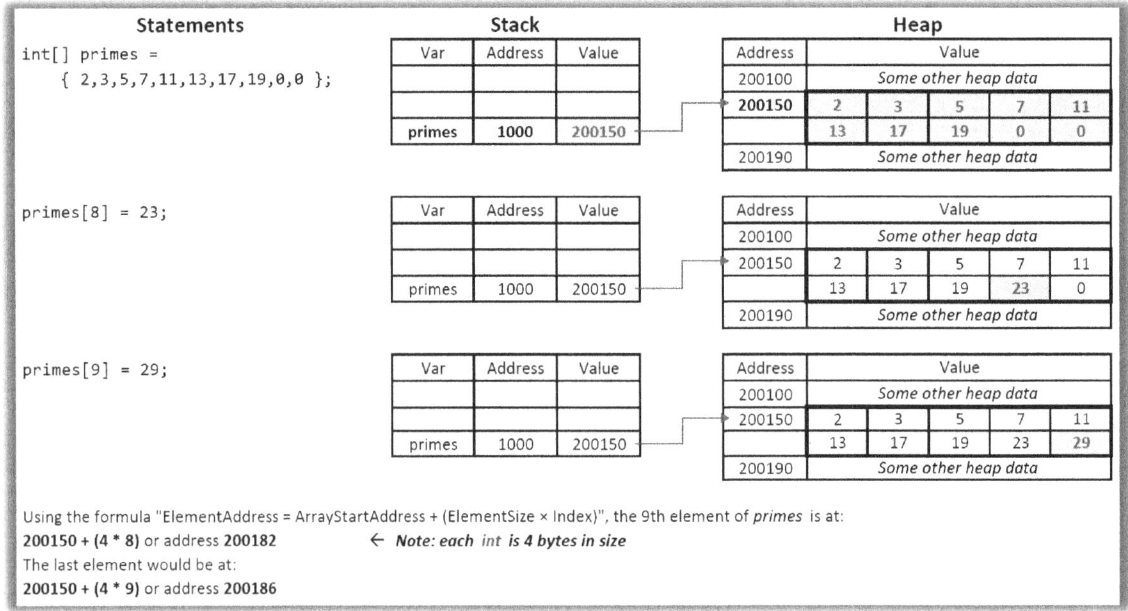

Figure 5-1. Example Array Memory Usage

5.2 Array Members

Arrays in C# have many members to assist with writing code using them. Some of the most important members involve obtaining the size of the array, the first valid index and the last valid index. Some members require using the Array class handle to access the members, just like Console. Other members are accessed from the array variable itself, known as an *instance* of an array. Either way, the dot operator is used to access the members.

Table 5-1. Important Array Class Members

Static	Name	Description
✓	BinarySearch()	Attempts to find an item in the array using a binary search algorithm. This method requires the array be in sorted order.
✓	Clear()	Resets a range of elements in the array to their default value.
✓	ConstrainedCopy()	Copies the contents of one array to another, rolling back changes upon failure.
✓	Copy()	Copies the contents of one array to another, supporting both 32-bit and 64-bit array lengths.
✓	IndexOf()	Attempts to find a specific element in the array. Returns the found index or -1.
✓	LastIndexOf()	Similar to IndexOf() but searches in reverse order.
✓	Resize()	Resizes a one-dimensional array.
✓	Reverse()	Reverses the order of the elements in the array.
✓	Sort()	Sorts the array. This method requires that the type be *comparable* (contains methods to determine equality of objects of the array element type). Otherwise a separate comparer object can be used to determine relational equality of elements.

Listing 5-5. Array Class Members

```
// Create array of primes out of order
int[] primes = { 29, 17, 7, 5, 23, 13, 3, 19, 11, 2 };

// Find the value '5' - will return -1 since array is unsorted
int index = Array.BinarySearch(primes, 5);
Console.WriteLine("The value '5' is currenlty at index " + index);
// Sort the array and find the value '3' again.
// This version of BinarySearch avoids boxing the input.
Array.Sort(primes);
index = Array.BinarySearch<int>(primes, 5);
Console.WriteLine("Now, the value '5' is at index " + index);

// Clear the last two elements of the array
Array.Clear(primes, 8, 2);

// Get the index of the value '29' when missing
index = Array.IndexOf<int>(primes, 29);
Console.WriteLine("The value '29' is at index " + index);
// Re-add missing numbers and search again
primes[8] = 23;
primes[9] = 29;
index = Array.IndexOf<int>(primes, 29);
Console.WriteLine("Now, the value '29' is at index " + index);
```

```
file:///C:/Users/Bruce/SkyDrive/Learning C Sharp/Samples/Chapte
The value '5' is currenlty at index -1
Now, the value '5' is at index 2
The value '29' is at index -1
Now, the value '29' is at index 9
```

Figure 5-2. Array Class Member Output

A common feature of the array commands issued in Listing 5-5 is that they all start with "Array." and the first parameter is *primes*, or the array being manipulated. The first call, on line 5, executes a binary search for the item "5". For a binary search to work the list of items must already be in a sorted order. A binary search simply takes the list of values and checks if the middle value equals the search target. If not, the half of the values that must contain the target, based on whether the target is greater or less than the middle value, is tested using the same logic. The binary search fails since *primes* is not sorted and the result of the call is -1. Since *primes* is an array of `int` values it already has the logic necessary for sorting which is done on line 9 (for custom types special methods must be added to allow sorting). The next call to Array.BinarySearch() is a little different. Notice "<int>" just prior to the parameter list – it signifies the use of a generic method. How this works is not important at this time. What does matter is that it forces the call to only accept a value of type `int` and it avoids boxing the value since the other BinarySearch() call accepts an `object`.

The call to Array.Clear() on line 14 resets the last to values in the array to 0. This call can also reset the entire list, not just two elements by adjusting the last two parameters to 0 and *primes*.Length.

The Array.IndexOf() calls that follows also use the generic syntax with "<int>" (there is a non-generic version as well). IndexOf() returns the 0-based index where the item is found. If not found, the return value is -1.

Table 5-2. Important Array Instance Members

Name	Description
Clone()	Performs a shallow clone on the array. If the array element type is a reference type the same references will be in the source and destination array.
CopyTo()	Copies the array to another.
GetLength()	Gets the length of the array's specified dimension. If the array is one-dimensional the required parameter is 0. For multi-dimensional arrays the parameter corresponds to the 0-based dimension that the length is being determined for.
GetLowerBound()	Gets the smallest valid index for the given dimension of the array. See GetLength() for a description of the parameter.
GetUpperBound()	Gets the largest valid index for the given dimension of the array. See GetLength() for a description of the parameter.
Length	Returns the total number of elements, in all dimensions, of the array.
Rank	Gets the total number of dimensions in the array. A one-dimensional array would return 1.

Listing 5-6. Array Instance Members

```
1 string[] names = { "Bill", "Joan", "Steven", "Angela", "John" };
2 // Clone the names array into the clone variable
3 string[] clone = (string[])names.Clone();
4 
5 // Verify that the 3rd elements are equal
6 Console.WriteLine(names[2]);
7 Console.WriteLine(clone[2]);
8 
9 // Use the CopyTo method copy the array
10 string[] copy = new string[5];
11 names.CopyTo(copy, 0);
12 Console.WriteLine(copy[2]);
13 
14 // Print the properties of the names array
15 Console.WriteLine("Length: " + names.GetLength(0) + "  LB: " +
     names.GetLowerBound(0) + "  UB: " + names.GetUpperBound(0));
```

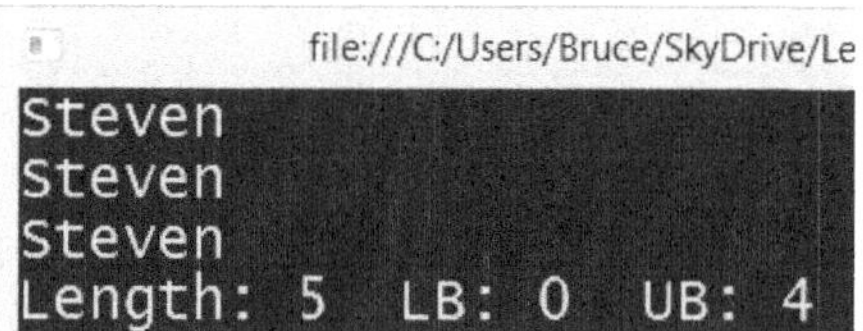

Figure 5-3. Array Instance Members Output

The code in Listing 5-6 demonstrates the use of instance members of an array. Notice that the biggest difference is that instead of "Array." preceding each call, a specific array name is used. The first line create a string array called *names* and prepopulates it with five names. Line 3 creates a copy of this *names* array by using the Clone() method. Since the output of this method is an object, it is necessary to use some conversion technique to store that result in the appropriate type. In this case, a cast is used to convert the result to string[]. A similar method is executed on line 11 called CopyTo() which, like Clone(), makes a copy of the source array *names*. However, instead of an array being returned from this method, the destination array is passed as the first argument to CopyTo(). Finally, the last line outputs the length, lower bound and upper bound of *names*. Note that the upper bound is one less than the length. This is a critical distinction about array indexing which will also come into play when looping through arrays, discussed in chapter 7.

5.3 Dynamic Arrays

One major limitation of C# arrays is that their size cannot be changed once initialized. It is possible to change the individual elements of an array using the indexer operator demonstrated earlier in the chapter, but the number of elements remains fixed. In other words, the array size is immutable. Wouldn't it be nice if, once an array is filled up, it could be expanded to fit more elements? How about shrinking an array if some elements are no longer required? Both options are technically possible, however, at a cost of memory and performance.

Resizing an Array

Consider an array of 10 elements of type int, called "int[] *values*". If we required the array to expand to 20 elements there is nothing that can be done directly to that array. Instead, it is necessary to create a new array with 20 elements, copy the contents of *values* into the first 10 elements of the new array, then reassign the new array into the *values* variable. Fortunately, there is also the Array.Resize() method which performs the very same operations, just with fewer steps.

Listing 5-7. Resize Array

```
// Resize array to add next value
int[] primes1 = { 2, 3, 5, 7, 11, 13, 17, 19, 23, 29 };

// Make a new array one element larger than primes1
int[] newArray = new int[primes1.Length + 1];

// Copy the values in primes1 to newArray, starting at newArray's 1st index (0)
primes1.CopyTo(newArray, 0);

// Reassign newArray back into the primes1 variable
primes1 = newArray;

// Assign the next prime number into the new last index of primes1
primes1[10] = 31;

// Another approach, using Array.Resize (fewer commands)
int[] primes2 = { 2, 3, 5, 7, 11, 13, 17, 19, 23, 29 };
Array.Resize<int>(ref primes2, primes2.Length + 1);
primes2[10] = 31;
```

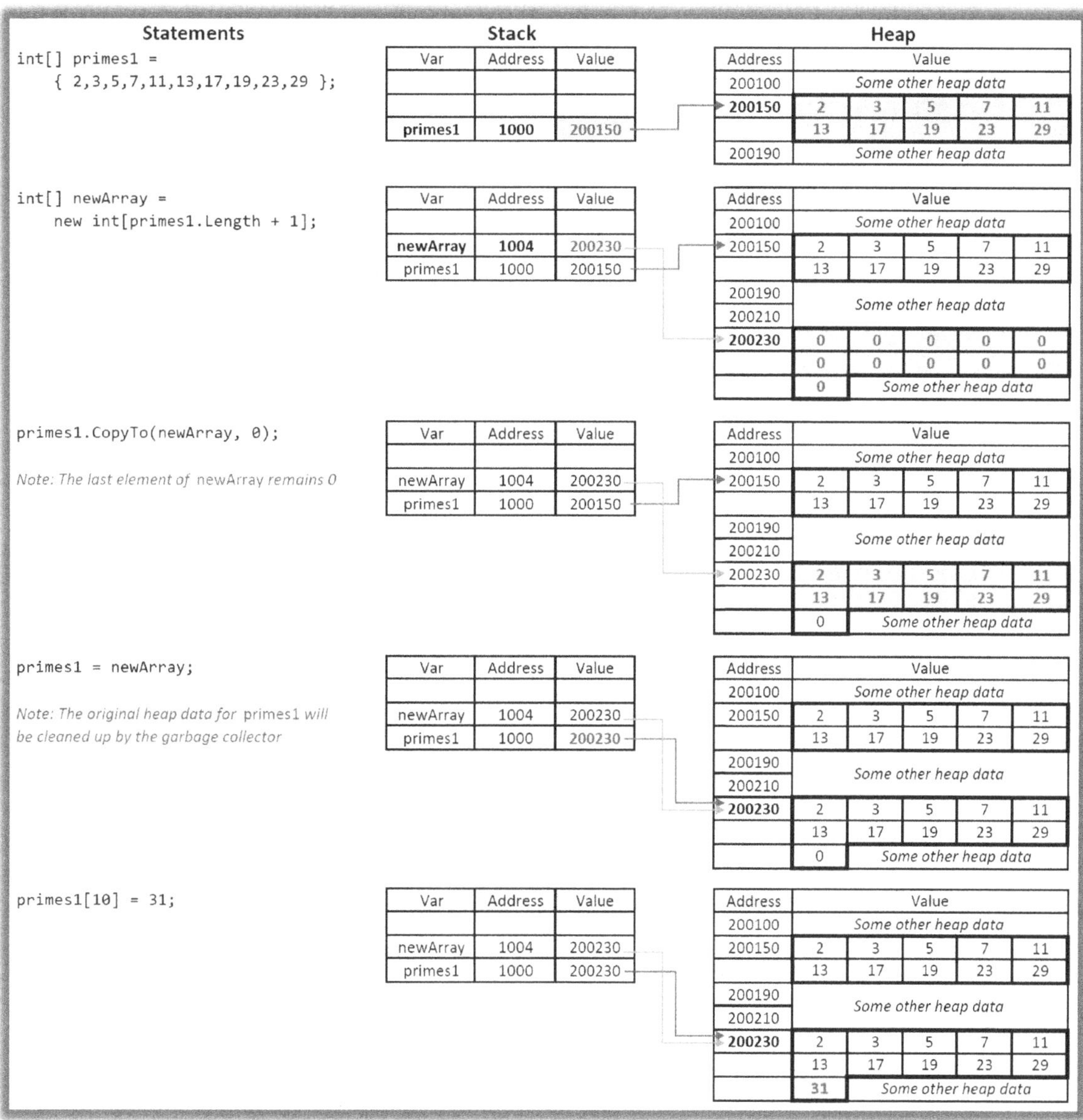

Figure 5-4. Array Resize Details

Inserting Elements into an Array

Insertion of an element within an array requires a similar, albeit complicated, technique. First, a new array is created that is one larger than the original. Second, the values to the left of the index where the new data is to be inserted are copied to the new array in the exact same position as the original. Next, the new item is inserted into the desired position. Finally, the values to the right of the new value's index are copied from the original array to the new one, with the destination index one greater than the source. The new array variable value can then be assigned to the original variable to make it look like the original array was modified rather than creating a new one.

Listing 5-8. Array Element Insertion

```
char[] letters = { 'A', 'B', 'D', 'E' };

// Create a new array with one extra element
char[] newLetters = new char[letters.Length + 1];

// Copy the first 2 elements from letters into newLetters
Array.Copy(letters, 0, newLetters, 0, 2);

// Place 'C' into 3rd element of newLetters
newLetters[2] = 'C';

// Copy last
Array.Copy(letters, 2, newLetters, 3, 2);

// Reassign newLetters back into the letters array
letters = newLetters;

// Set newLetters to null since we no longer need it
newLetters = null;
```

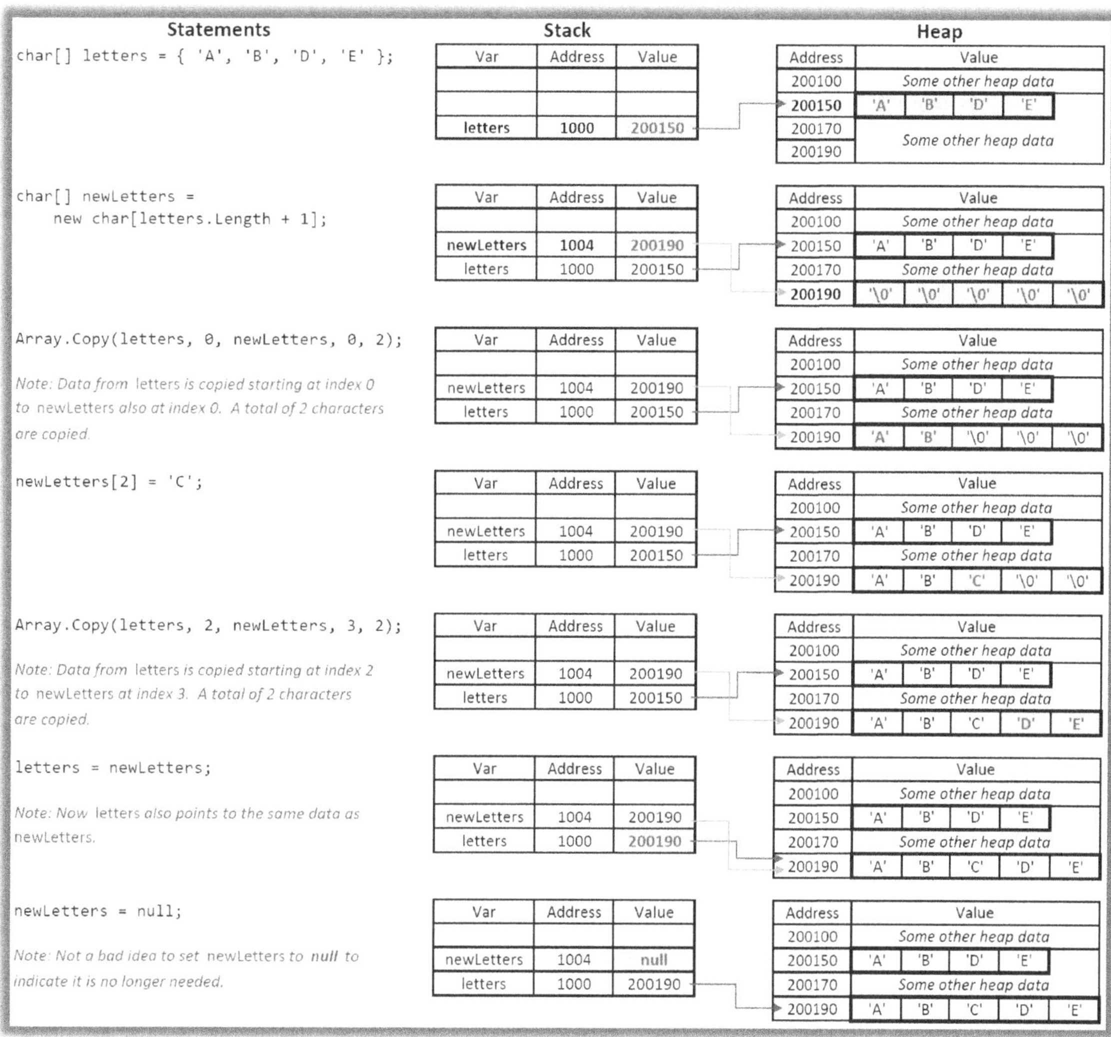

Figure 5-5. Array Element Insertion Details

After seeing how to manipulate arrays, making them appear to be dynamic, you may be wondering if it is worth the effort. For most programmers, the answer would be "no", which is why arrays are considered to be immutable and best left at their original sizes. The good news is that there are other data structures, like generic lists, which provide many of the same features of an array but are designed to be fully dynamic. This does not mean arrays are not useful. For most applications, arrays will perform faster and consume less memory than other structures of similar functionality.

5.4 Two-Dimensional (2D) Arrays

All examples up to this point have dealt with linear data. It is possible, however, to create arrays in multiple dimensions. For instance, a multiplication table could be considered a two-dimensional array, where the indices of the first dimension represent the rows and the indices of the second dimension represent the columns.

Dimension 0 ↓

Dimension 1 →

	0	1	2	3	4	5	6	7	8	9
0	0	0	0	0	0	0	0	0	0	0
1	0	1	2	3	4	5	6	7	8	9
2	0	2	4	6	8	10	12	14	16	18
3	0	3	6	9	12	15	18	21	24	27
4	0	4	8	12	16	20	24	28	32	36
5	0	5	10	15	20	25	30	35	40	45
6	0	6	12	18	24	30	36	42	48	54
7	0	7	14	21	28	35	42	49	56	63
8	0	8	16	24	32	40	48	56	64	72
9	0	9	18	27	36	45	54	63	72	81

Figure 5-6. Multiplication Table as a Two-Dimensional Array

The above multiplication table would be declared as an array as follows:

```
int[,] mult = new int[10, 10];
```

As you can see, the declaration for a two-dimensional array is very similar to a one-dimensional array with the major difference being the use of a comma between the square brackets. The initialization of the array is also very similar with the size of the individual dimensions also separated by a comma. In this case both dimensions are the same size, 10 elements each for a total of 100 elements. Initializing the above array would be best handled by a nested for loop. However, we can also hard-code the entries using a similar initializer syntax to what is used by one-dimensional arrays:

Listing 5-9. Two-dimensional Array Initialization

```
1  int[,] mult = new int[10, 10]
2    {
3      {0, 0, 0, 0, 0, 0, 0, 0, 0, 0},
4      {0, 1, 2, 3, 4, 5, 6, 7, 8, 9},
5      {0, 2, 4, 6, 8,10,12,14,16,18},
6      {0, 3, 6, 9,12,15,18,21,24,27},
7      {0, 4, 8,12,16,20,24,28,32,36},
8      {0, 5,10,15,20,25,30,35,40,45},
9      {0, 6,12,18,24,30,36,42,48,54},
10     {0, 7,14,21,28,35,42,49,56,63},
11     {0, 8,16,24,32,40,48,56,64,72},
12     {0, 9,18,27,36,45,54,63,72,81}
13   };
```

In a way, the initialization of a two-dimensional array mimics set of sets. The outer set of braces corresponds to the array data as a whole. Inside that set of braces are comma separated sets of other braces. Each of these inner brace sets represents a row of values. So, line 3 of the example is assigning the first row of data for the array, where each value separated by a comma represents the column value for that row.

Row-Major Order

Two-dimensional (2D) arrays are stored and accessed using a scheme known as "row-major order". In the case of C# arrays, this implies that the first index of the array represents the row and the second represents the column, such as:

```
array[row, column]
```

This also has implications in the way 2D arrays are stored in memory. Just like 1D arrays, 2D arrays consume a contiguous chunk of memory in the heap. In row major order, all of the row values are contiguous in memory and the first column value of the next row immediately follows the last column value of the previous row. Consider and array with the following declaration:

Listing 5-10. Simple 2D Array

```
int[,] demo = new int[2, 3]
{
  { 1, 2, 3 },
  { 4, 5, 6 }
};
```

This array *demo* has 2 rows and 3 columns and is stored in memory as a list of 6 elements: 1, 2, 3, 4, 5 and 6. A relatively simple formula is used to identify the address of any element in a two-dimensional array. First, we need to know a few things about the array that we are accessing, namely the type of array, the dimensions, and which element (row & column) being accessed:

Array: `type`[R, C] ← R = rows, C = columns
Base address (BA): 20000 (purely arbitrary value)
Element size (ES): Number of bytes in each element
Row size (RS): ES * C
row & *col*: The row and column of the item we are trying to get address for
Element address (A): BA + (RS * *row*) + (ES * *col*)

So, if you are interested in getting the element at index [3, 2] of the array with the definition `int`[5, 4], the formula would read:

RS = 4 * 4 = 16 (`int` *consumes 4 bytes and there are 4 columns in the array)*
A = 20000 + (16 * 3) + (4 * 2) = 20056

Let's see if this makes sense by looking at the sample array in memory. Create an array with the following specification:

Listing 5-11. Two-Dimension Array Memory Example

```
int[,] A = {
  { 23, 54, 61, 12 },
  { 51, 16, 32, 47 },
  { 48, 31,  9, 71 },
  { 88, 11, 91,  5 },
  { 19, 27, 44, 39 }
};
```

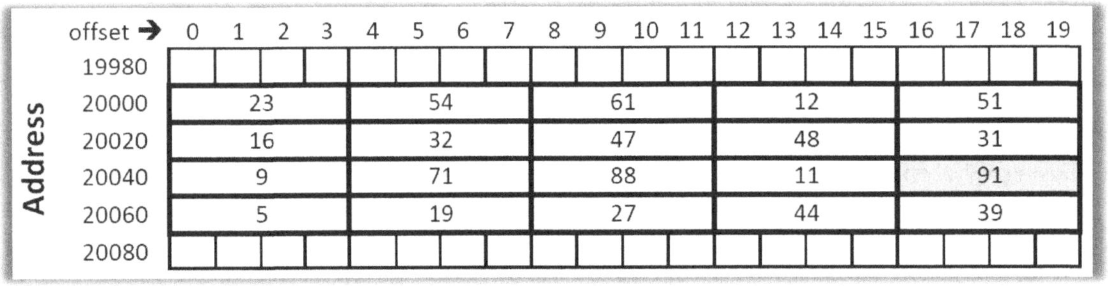

Address / offset →	0	1	2	3	4	5	6	7	8	9	10	11	12	13	14	15	16	17	18	19
19980																				
20000	23				54				61				12				51			
20020	16				32				47				48				31			
20040	9				71				88				11				91			
20060	5				19				27				44				39			
20080																				

Figure 5-7. 2D Array Memory Map

As you can see in the memory map, the address of the item is at 20040 + offset 16, which is 20056. Fortunately, unless you like to do custom memory access for 2D arrays, there is a pre-built syntax which allows you to get the item by index. So, to retrieve the value at row 3, column 2 (0-based, of course), you could use the following statement:

```
int value = A[3, 2];
```

In the background C# will calculate the address of that particular element and retrieve the value at that address, storing it in the *value* variable. Likewise, if you wish to change the value at a specific location, let's say row 0, column 3, you could use the exact same array indexer syntax but as an lvalue instead of an rvalue:

```
A[0, 3] = 99;
```

In this example, the value 12 would be replaced with 99.

So, if the indexer syntax is so simple, why did we bother with the exercise of using the address formula? This was done to demonstrate how 2D arrays are stored and accessed in memory. The memory map should also show how difficult it would be to change the number of columns in an array in a dynamic fashion. Since the rows are stored consecutively, inserting a new column would require adding a new value at the end of each row. Adding extra rows is far easier since the new data would only appear at the end of the existing memory graph. However, just like 1D arrays, this technique would still require a "create and copy" operation, costly in both memory and CPU time.

2D Array Methods

The methods that apply to 1D arrays also apply to 2D arrays. However, unlike the calls against 1D arrays, where 0 was always passed as a parameter to the methods, the calls against 2D arrays can accept a 0 or 1. The following methods can accept 0 or 1 depending on which dimension the method should operate on:

Table 5-3. Important 2D Array Methods

Name	Description
GetLength()	Passing 0 returns the length of the array's 1st dimension. Passing 1 returns the length of the 2nd dimension.
GetLowerBound()	Passing 0 returns the smallest legal index of the array's 1st dimension. Passing 1 returns the smallest legal index of the 2nd dimension.
GetUpperBound()	Passing 0 returns the largest legal index of the array's 1st dimension. Passing 1 returns the largest legal index of the 2nd dimension.
Length	Accepts no arguments and returns the total number of elements in the array.

Listing 5-12. Using 2D Array Methods

```
int rows = A.GetLength(0);
int cols = A.GetLength(1);

Console.WriteLine("Array size: " + rows + " x " + cols + " = " + A.Length);

int rowLowIndex = A.GetLowerBound(0);
int rowHighIndex = A.GetUpperBound(0);
int colLowIndex = A.GetLowerBound(1);
int colHighIndex = A.GetUpperBound(1);

Console.WriteLine("Valid row indices: " + rowLowIndex + " - " + rowHighIndex);
Console.WriteLine("Valid column indices: " + colLowIndex + " - " + colHighIndex);
```

file:///C:/Users/Bruce/SkyDrive/Learning C

```
Array size: 5 x 4 = 20
Valid row indices: 0 - 4
Valid column indices: 0 - 3
```

Figure 5-8. 2D Array Methods Output

5.5 Jagged Arrays

Consider a problem where you are required to store the high temperature for each day of the year. You contemplate using a 1D array, where each day of the year is stored consecutively in an array with 365 or 366 elements as such:

```
double[] temps = new double[365];
```

However, you decide that looking up a specific date would be too complicated since the linear date would need to be calculated (i.e. February 1 would be at index 31). Next, you consider a 2D array where months are mapped to the array's rows and the days of the month are mapped to the array's columns. The array would be defined as:

```
double[,] temps2 = new double[12,31];
```

This approach would provide much easier access to specific elements. However, as you may have guessed, there is some storage inefficiency in that each month does not actually have 31 days. This inefficiency may be acceptable, but there is another approach that works very much like a 2D array, but provides for different 2nd dimension lengths.

Jagged arrays are a special construct that essentially allows the programmer to create a one-dimension array where each element is also one-dimensional array. Each of these "nested arrays" is completely independent from one another and their varying lengths are what gives the jagged array its name and appearance.

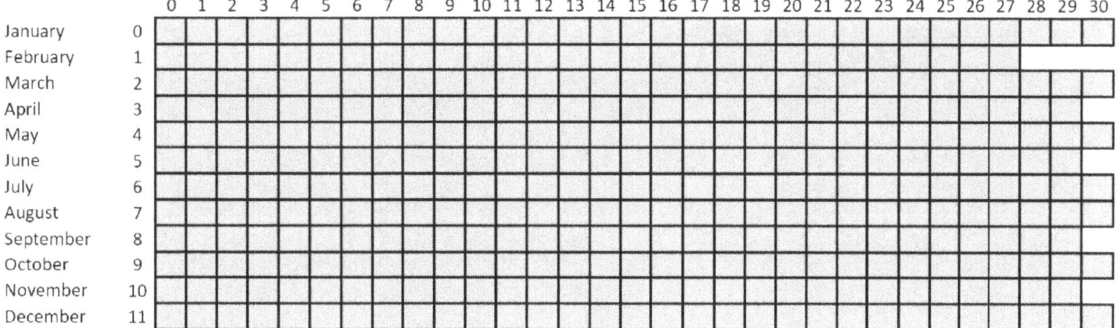

Figure 5-9. Jagged Array Example

The following creates a jagged array that defines the above example:

Listing 5-13. Jagged Array Creation

```
1  double[][] jagged = new double[12][];
2  jagged[0] = new double[31];
3  jagged[1] = new double[28];
4  jagged[2] = new double[31];
5  jagged[3] = new double[30];
6  jagged[4] = new double[31];
7  jagged[5] = new double[30];
8  jagged[6] = new double[31];
9  jagged[7] = new double[31];
10 jagged[8] = new double[30];
11 jagged[9] = new double[31];
12 jagged[10] = new double[30];
13 jagged[11] = new double[31];
```

Notice the syntax of the jagged array variable does not use a comma like a standard 2D array uses. Instead, this syntax indicates the variable is an array of arrays, hence the double brackets "[][]". Also, notice that when the array is initialized only the first array size is supplied. This essentially means we are creating a 1D array of 12 elements where each element, instead of being a simple type, is actually an array of `double` values of undefined length. Each of these nested arrays is initialized independently as seen in lines 2 through 13.

Jagged Array Indexing

Indexing a jagged array is very similar to indexing a 2D array, except, once again, you must use the double bracket syntax instead of the comma syntax to access both dimensions. Also, since each array is independent from the others, the upper bound of one nested array will not necessarily match another. Therefore, more care must be taken to ensure only legal indices are used.

Continuing with the example in Listing 5-13, populate the high temperatures with the values provided for the following dates:

Date	Temperature
January 4	57.4°
March 17	75.2°
May 30	80.1°
July 4	92.1°
September 12	90.7°
October 31	69.1°
December 11	67.8°

Listing 5-14. Assigning Values to a Jagged Array

```
jagged[0][3] = 57.4;
jagged[2][16] = 75.2;
jagged[4][29] = 80.1;
jagged[6][3] = 92.1;
jagged[8][11] = 90.7;
jagged[9][30] = 69.1;
jagged[11][10] = 67.8;
```

Probably the most complicated part of this example is remembering that arrays are 0-based, so the index for "January" is 0, not 1. The same goes for the day of the month. Retrieving a value from the jagged array once again uses the same indexer syntax as assignment, just on the opposite side of the assignment operator. Therefore, reading the value for June 17th and November 16th would look like:

Listing 5-15. Reading Values from a Jagged Array

```
double june17 = jagged[5][16];
double november16 = jagged[10][15];
```

Perhaps, one of the more challenging aspects of working with jagged arrays is getting the lengths and bounds of the various elements. We will once again be using the jagged array defined in Listing 5-13 to demonstrates these methods. We'll start by retrieving the length and bounds of the outer array, the one that is defined by the first set of brackets and represents months in our example.

Listing 5-16. Getting Outer Array Properties of a Jagged Array

```
int months = jagged.Length;
Console.WriteLine("The outer array contains " + months + " nested arrays");

int monthLowIndex = jagged.GetLowerBound(0);
int monthHighIndex = jagged.GetUpperBound(0);
Console.WriteLine("Valid row indices: " + monthLowIndex + " - " + monthHighIndex);
```

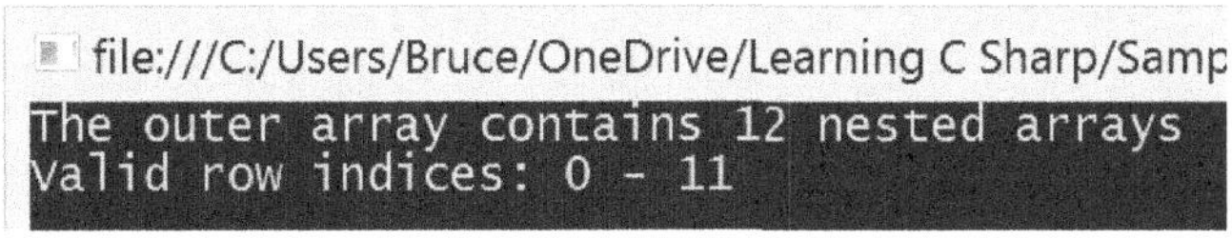

```
file:///C:/Users/Bruce/OneDrive/Learning C Sharp/Samp
The outer array contains 12 nested arrays
Valid row indices: 0 - 11
```

Figure 5-10. Jagged Array Outer Array Output

If this looks familiar it should. It is identical to how you would access these members for any one-dimensional array. Remember, a jagged array really is a 1D array, where each element is another array.

Here comes the tricky part - how to access the nested array properties. In our example, since each element of the outer array is essentially a `double[]`, you can retrieve an element of the outer array into a variable of that type as such:

```
double[] january = jagged[0];
```

Then you can once again apply any of the 1D methods to this variable called *january*. Alternatively, you can bypass the temporary variable altogether and access the methods of a nested array all in one statement:

```
int janLength = jagged[0].Length;
```

In terms of performance it makes little difference which technique is used to access the nested arrays' members. It really comes down to a meter of personal preference. Both are demonstrated in the following example.

Listing 5-17. Accessing Nested Arrays in a Jagged Array

```
// Two temp variable technique
double[] january = jagged[0];
int janLength = january.Length;
Console.WriteLine("January has " + janLength + " values.");

// One temp variable technique
int febLength = jagged[1].Length;
Console.WriteLine("February has " + febLength + " values.");

// Inline technique
Console.WriteLine("March has " + jagged[2].Length + " values.");
```

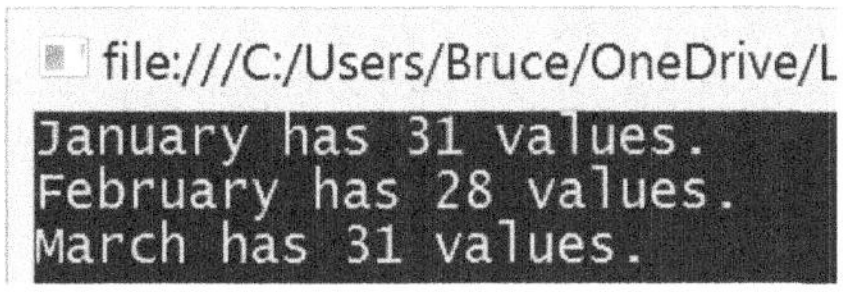

```
file:///C:/Users/Bruce/OneDrive/L
January has 31 values.
February has 28 values.
March has 31 values.
```

Figure 5-11. Nested Array Output

5.6 Generic Lists

Without a doubt, arrays are very powerful and useful data structures. However, one recurring issue with arrays is that once they are defined it is very tricky to modify their size. To be fair, arrays do exactly what they are intended to do. In fact, most languages define arrays to be static in size, so this is not just a short-coming of C#. It really comes down to memory management. There is no way to define a contiguous block of memory for an array and guarantee there will be enough additional memory immediately succeeding it for it to grow into indefinitely. We have seen memory allocation and copying techniques which facilitates an imitation dynamic array, but the code is fairly involved and not at all efficient. In reality, it is best to leave arrays alone once they are defined except in performance-demanding applications.

However, don't fret - C# provides another data structure that gives us the performance of a 1D array with a truly dynamic memory management framework. This data structure is called a generic list, sometimes shown as List<T>. The beauty of the generic list is that it actually uses a 1D array internally and does all of the memory shifting for us by providing methods to add, insert and remove elements. In addition, generic lists use a buffered memory approach to avoid costly re-allocations every time a single element is added or inserted. Generic list elements can be accessed using the same indexer syntax employed by 1D arrays.

You may be wondering about the "generic" name and what implications it has on this data structure. Generics are a style of programming where a type or a method is defined in code to work with other data types that are not defined at design time. The "unknown type" is referred to within the angle braces "<" and ">". In the case of a generic list, that type is referred to as "T" and simply means you can create a list of a specific type, like `int` or `string`. Then, when you create a generic list variable in your code, the compiler actually creates a new type in the final code that ensures your list variable can only work with the specified type. Therefore, a `List<int>` can only add items of type `int`. It is not necessary at this time to fully understand how generics are implemented in C#, just how to utilize them in your code.

To incorporate generic lists into your programs you should ensure the following `using` directive is at the top of your C# code files (Note: this directive is added to every new code file by default):

```
using System.Collections.Generic;
```

Next, declaring and initializing a generic list requires the following syntax:

```
List<type> listName = new List<type>();
```

After the generic list is initialized there are several useful methods that can be invoked to manipulate the list. The following list is not the complete set of methods that can be used on a generic list but the other methods are a bit too complicated to investigate at this time due to their use of predicates and other functional programming techniques.

Table 5-4. Important List<T> Methods

Name	Description
Capacity	Gets or sets the total size of the current array buffer containing the list data.
Count	Gets the number of items currently in the list.
Add()	Adds a new item to the end of the list.
AddRange()	Adds a group of items to the end of the list.
BinarySearch()	Uses a binary search algorithm to find an item in the list.
Clear()	Clears all items from the list.
Contains()	Determines if an item is currently contained in the list.
CopyTo()	Copies the contents of the list into an array of the same data type. The destination array must be pre-initialized to an adequate size.
IndexOf()	Gets the first index of the given item in the list (-1 if not found).
Insert()	Inserts an item into the list at a specific index.
InsertRange()	Inserts a group of items into the list at a specific index.
LastIndexOf()	Gets the last index of the given item in the list (-1 if not found)
Remove()	Removes the first occurrence of the given item from the list.
RemoveAll()	Removes all occurrences of the given item from the list.
RemoveAt()	Removes an item at a specific index.
RemoveRange()	Removes a range of items from the list.
Reverse()	Reverses the items in the list.
Sort()	Sorts the list. Requires the type of items in the list must be comparable to each other.
ToArray()	Copies the contents of the list to a new array.
TrimExcess()	If the difference between Capacity and Count is greater than 10% of the list size the excess space is reclaimed by the CLR.

Listing 5-18. Generic List Usage

```
List<char> chars = new List<char>();
// Add several characters to the end of the list, resulting in { 'B', 'C', 'E' }
chars.Add('B');
chars.Add('C');
chars.Add('E');
// Insert 'A' at the front of the list to get { 'A', 'B', 'C', 'E' }
chars.Insert(0, 'A');
// Insert 'D' in between 'C' and 'E', at index 3
chars.Insert(3, 'D');

// Display Count and Capacity of list
Console.WriteLine("List Count: " + chars.Count + "   Capacity: " + chars.Capacity);

// Copy contents of list to an array using CopyTo()
char[] charArray = new char[5];
chars.CopyTo(charArray);

// Copy contents of list to an array using ToArray()
char[] charArray2 = chars.ToArray();

// Use indexer to access an item in the list
char ch = chars[2];
Console.WriteLine("Character at index 2: " + ch);
// Use indexer to change an item in the list
chars[0] = 'a';
Console.WriteLine("Character at index 0 is now: " + chars[0]);
```

file:///C:/Users/Bruce/SkyDrive/Le

```
List Count: 5   Capacity: 8
Character at index 2: C
Character at index 0 is now: a
```

Figure 5-12. Generic List Output

Generic List Capacity

As mentioned earlier, generic lists store data in an internal buffered array. This simply means that an array is used to store the individual items, but the array is initialized to contain more elements than required. As you are aware, resizing arrays is an expensive proposition. Therefore, when an item is being added to the list and the capacity of the array is not sufficient to store the new item, a new array is allocated that has a buffer twice the size of the previous. The old contents are copied to the new buffer and the new item is added. Unlike using 1D arrays, this entire process is hidden from the programmer with generic lists.

Listing 5-19. Generic List Capacity

```
// Create a list with first 8 numbers of the Fibonacci sequence which
// will fill the initial list buffer to capacity
List<int> fib = new List<int>();
fib.Add(1);
fib.Add(1);
fib.Add(2);
fib.Add(3);
fib.Add(5);
fib.Add(8);
fib.Add(13);
fib.Add(21);
Console.WriteLine("Initial fib Count: " + fib.Count + "   Capacity: " +
    fib.Capacity);

// Add one more item and report the new capacity
fib.Add(34);
Console.WriteLine("Add item fib Count: " + fib.Count + "   Capacity: " +
    fib.Capacity);

// Remove excess capacity
fib.TrimExcess();
Console.WriteLine("TrimExcess fib Count: " + fib.Count + "   Capacity: " +
    fib.Capacity);
```

```
file:///C:/Users/Bruce/SkyDrive/Learning C Sharp/
Initial fib Count: 8   Capacity: 8
Add item fib Count: 9   Capacity: 16
TrimExcess fib Count: 9   Capacity: 9
```

Figure 5-13. Generic List Capacity Output

Generic List Constructors and Bulk Insertion

As shown in Listing 5-19, adding individual items to a generic list can be rather verbose. To alleviate this problem it is possible to pass an array of items of the same type as the list to the method that creates the list. Recall that the command to create a generic list has the syntax:

```
List<type> ListName = new List<type>();
```

This syntax is known as a constructor call. A constructor is a specialized method used for creating a variable of a non-built-in type. The give-away that indicates a constructor method is being called is the "`new`" keyword. The example above and all generic lists created in this section use the default constructor syntax, which accepts no argument. This is only one possible way to call the constructor for a generic list. Two other constructors are available, one that accepts a value indicating the initial capacity of the list, the other accepts another data structure, like an array, to pre-populate the list with values. We will look much more closely at constructor semantics later in the book when we discuss object-oriented programming. For now, just be aware that there can be multiple ways of creating variables of complex types, like generic lists.

Similarly, there are methods like AddRange() and InsertRange() that allow for bulk insertion of items into a list after initialization. Both techniques are demonstrated in the following example:

Listing 5-20. Generic List Creation and Bulk Insertion

```
// Create an array with the first 8 Fibonacci numbers and pass that to list
// constructor
int[] fibArray = { 1, 1, 2, 3, 5, 8, 13, 21 };
List<int> fibList = new List<int>(fibArray);

// Create another array with the next 4 numbers and add it to the list
int[] fibNext = { 34, 55, 89, 144 };
fibList.AddRange(fibNext);
```

5.7 Summary

In programming it is frequently necessary to store data in contiguous blocks that are addressable as a single variable. Arrays are very capable data structures for storing like data in a single dimension, two dimensions, or even three or more dimensions. While these arrays are efficient data structures, their inability to add, insert or remove items without complex memory management limits their usefulness regarding dynamic data. Generic lists close that hole by providing 1D array functionality with the complex memory management of dynamic array built-in. These data structures will become even more useful when we look at loops in later chapters.

There are many other extremely useful collection-style data structures in C#, like dictionaries, linked lists, stacks and queues which may be of interest to you.

6

6. Character Data

Computers have many ways of displaying data to a user. Most operating systems offer a graphical user interface that can display pictures, graphs, videos and 3D simulations. For some types of information graphics are well suited for the task. However, at some point, the written word typically comes into play and, in many environments, dominates the user interface. As a result, the ability to read, manipulate, format and display text is a critical skill. In fact, since most of the demos in this book utilize a Console Application for their user interface, you will become quite familiar with many techniques for working with textual data.

In this chapter we will start by reviewing the `char` data type as it is the fundamental unit of text in C#. Then we will look at the `string` data type in detail, learning how to create, manipulate and format text. We will also look at a helper class called StringBuilder which optimizes the process of manipulating text data.

6.1 System.Char – char

The character, or `char`, data type is the fundamental unit of text in C#. As the name implies, the type's entire purpose is to store a single character of text. Each `char` variable stores 2 bytes worth of data, which corresponds to a numeric value between 0 and 65,535. Each one of these numeric values maps to a character in various languages such as English, Hebrew, Arabic, Greek and virtually every other language on the planet. These characters conform to a formatting standard known as Unicode (UTF-16 to be precise) which ensures text will be rendered identically on all machines that support the standard. In actuality some languages are so complex, due to the use of diacritics (accent marks, modifiers, etc.) and compound sounds, that a single `char` may not be sufficient to store a single glyph, or symbol. In those cases multiple char variables are blended together to make a single glyph. This topic is beyond the scope of this course as we will be focusing on English for our text.

The `char` data type supports ASCII which for many decades was the only set of characters representable on computers. ASCII stands for American Standard Code for Informational Interchange and is a set of 128 characters that contains all of the printable characters of the English language, plus several dozen reserved characters for special computer operations. When Unicode was defined all of the printable characters of ASCII were migrated to the new format with the same value mappings to maintain backwards compatibility.

Table 6-1. 7-bit ASCII Table

Dec	Hex	Char	Esc	Dec	Hex	Char	Dec	Hex	Char	Dec	Hex	Char
0	00	*null*	\0	32	20	*space*	64	40	@	96	60	`
1	01	SOH		33	21	!	65	41	A	97	61	a
2	02	STX		34	22	"	66	42	B	98	62	b
3	03	ETX		35	23	#	67	43	C	99	63	c
4	04	EOT		36	24	$	68	44	D	100	64	d
5	05	ENQ		37	25	%	69	45	E	101	65	e
6	06	ACK		38	26	&	70	46	F	102	66	f
7	07	BEL		39	27	'	71	47	G	103	67	g
8	08	*backspace*	\b	40	28	(	72	48	H	104	68	h
9	09	*tab*	\t	41	29	)	73	49	I	105	69	i
10	0A	*linefeed*	\n	42	2A	*	74	4A	J	106	6A	j
11	0B	VT		43	2B	+	75	4B	K	107	6B	k
12	0C	FF		44	2C	,	76	4C	L	108	6C	l
13	0D	*carriage return*	\r	45	2D	-	77	4D	M	109	6D	m
14	0E	SO		46	2E	.	78	4E	N	110	6E	n
15	0F	SI		47	2F	/	79	4F	O	111	6F	o
16	10	DLE		48	30	0	80	50	P	112	70	p
17	11	DC1		49	31	1	81	51	Q	113	71	q
18	12	DC2		50	32	2	82	52	R	114	72	r
19	13	DC3		51	33	3	83	53	S	115	73	s
20	14	DC4		52	34	4	84	54	T	116	74	t
21	15	NAK		53	35	5	85	55	U	117	75	u
22	16	SYN		54	36	6	86	56	V	118	76	v
23	17	ETB		55	37	7	87	57	W	119	77	w
24	18	CAN		56	38	8	88	58	X	120	78	x
25	19	EM		57	39	9	89	59	Y	121	79	y
26	1A	SUB		58	3A	:	90	5A	Z	122	7A	z
27	1B	*escape*	\e	59	3B	;	91	5B	[	123	7B	{
28	1C	FS		60	3C	<	92	5C	\	124	7C		
29	1D	GS		61	3D	=	93	5D	]	125	7D	}
30	1E	RS		62	3E	>	94	5E	^	126	7E	~
31	1F	US		63	3F	?	95	5F	_	127	7F	*delete*

In Table 6-1 each character of the ASCII scheme is shown. Unprintable characters, or those without keyboard equivalents, are shaded. Notice that each character has a decimal and hexadecimal equivalent. When working with characters it is common to reference either the glyph directly or its hexadecimal equivalent when a keyboard key is not available. Also, in C#, some special characters, such as *tab* and *linefeed*, can be represented by an escape sequence (we'll look at hexadecimal encoding and escape sequences momentarily). From this chart it is obvious that English was the only concern of this encoding scheme. Even other Latin alphabets, such as Spanish, cannot be fully represented by characters in this list. The globalization of computers and the use of the Internet forced most operating systems to support Unicode by the late 1990's. As mentioned previously, to maintain backwards compatibility with ASCII, the first 128 values of Unicode are identical. Since .NET was built around Unicode from the beginning, there should be very few migration concerns regarding any software you write.

Representing char Values

The char data type is a value type therefore any value stored in a char variable is stored exclusively in the stack. Like other value types the variable is cleaned out of the stack when it falls out of scope. The delimiter for a char literal value is the apostrophe. The most direct way to create a char variable is to use the following syntax:

```
char <variable> = '<glyph>';
```

Here's an example that creates a char called *ch* and stores within it a lowercase *x*.

```
char ch = 'x';
```

It is also possible to initialize a char using either the decimal or hexadecimal equivalents. However, the (char) cast must be used as there are no implicit conversions from numeric data types to char.

Listing 6-1. Initializing char Values

```
// Creating a char from the literal character 'a'
char a = 'a';
// Creating a char from the decimal value of 'b'
char b = (char)98;
// Creating a char from the hexadecimal value of 'c'
char c = (char)0x63;
```

The first assignment in the above example is straight-forward – the literal character "a" is being assigned to the char variable *a*. The second assignment is casting the decimal value 98 into a char type then assigning that result to the variable *b*. The third example does basically the same thing as the second, however the numeric value is in hexadecimal notation, using a prefix of "0x". The digits that follow the "0x" prefix must be either 0 – 9 or A – F since those are the legal digits for hexadecimal (base-16) numbers.

Hexadecimal values may not be as intuitive as decimal values, however, base-16 is much more closely related to base-2 (binary) than base-10 (decimal) which explains its prevalence in computer science. Essentially, a base-10 number requires 10 unique symbols to represent the "units" values, or single-digit numbers, which are 0–9. Base-16 requires 16 such symbols, and since we only have 10 numeric symbols in our base-10 society, 6 had to be created. Instead of designing brand new symbols (which many have proposed) the first 6 alphabet letters are used immediately following 9. Therefore, counting in hexadecimal would look like: 0, 1, 2, 3, 4, 5, 6, 7, 8, 9, A, B, C, D, E, F, 10, 11, 12, … , 19, 1A, 1B, 1C, 1D, 1E, 1F, 20, … In most usage scenarios the alphabet letters are case insensitive.

Whenever a literal character cannot be represented by a keyboard key I prefer hexadecimal notation. In fact, Unicode values are specified as base-16 values in virtually all documentation.

So, what happens when we wish to use a character outside of ASCII's range? In this case you have basically three choices:

- Use the `(char)` casting technique discussed in Listing 6-1.
- Find the glyph you wish to use in "charmap.exe" or other tool and copy and paste it to your code.
- Find the Unicode value for the glyph and use the "\u" escape sequence in the char's literal definition.

We've already covered the first option, so let's look at option 2. Run the Character Map tool in Windows by executing the following keyboard commands: ⊞+R, then type "charmap" (or you can use your operating system's search function and look for "Character Map").

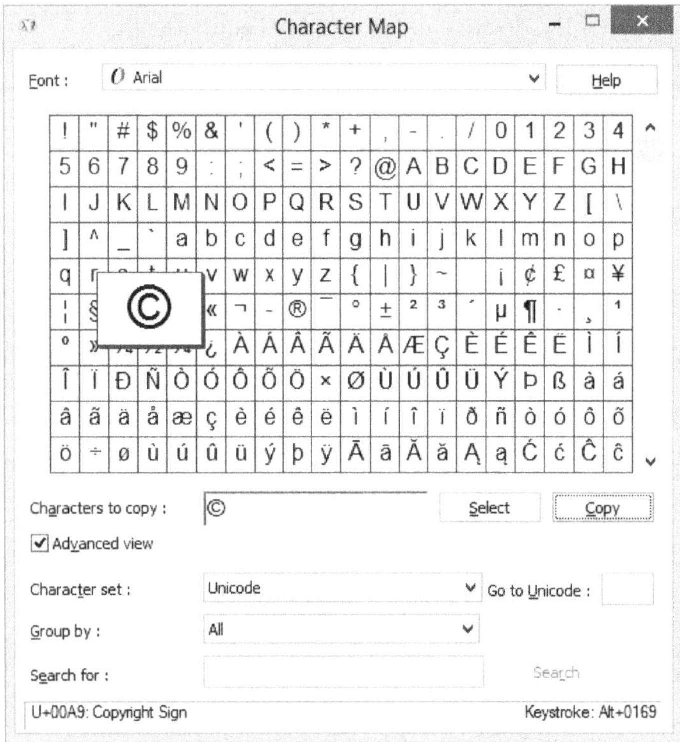

Figure 6-1. Character Map Application

In this tool you can search for specific characters by name, or browse through the list until you find what you are looking for. If you select a glyph it is enlarged and information about that character is displayed at the bottom. If you double-click on a glyph, or click the "Select" button, in it will appear in the "Characters to copy" text box. Clicking the "Copy" button will move that character to the clipboard. You can then paste that glyph directly into your code as such:

```
char ch = '©';
```

If you prefer, you can use the third technique, using the "\u" escape sequence in the char literal. The hexadecimal number you will require is shown in the bottom-left hand of the status bar of the Character Map tool when a glyph is selected. In the case of the copyright sign, the code is "U+00A9". We are only interested in the "00A9" part, and it is embedded in the character literal as such:

```
char copyright = '\u00A9';
```

When output to the screen or a file the *copyright* variable will show '©'.

Notice in the last example that the single glyph is represented by 6 letters "\u00A9". Normally, putting this many letters between apostrophes would cause a compiler error since a char can only store a single letter. This demonstrates one of many escape sequences that are legal within a char literal value. Whenever the backslash "\" character is encountered in a char literal the compiler understands that the next letter, or several letters, will covey a special meaning. In this case the letter immediately following the backslash is "u" which requires the next 4 letters to be a hexadecimal value corresponding to a Unicode character.

There are many other useful escape sequences valid for a character, most of which are shown here (escape sequences that are not typically used are excluded from this list):

Table 6-2. C# char Escape Sequences

Escape Sequence	Meaning	Example	Output
\u*XXXX*	Unicode character, must contain 4 hexadecimal digits	'\u00A9'	©
\x*XXXX*	Unicode character, can contain 1 to 4 hexadecimal digits (missing leading digits assumed to be 0)	'\xA9'	©
\'	The apostrophe character	'\''	'
\"	The quote character	'\"'	"
\0	A null, or undefined character	'\0'	*N/A*
\n	Newline character. Advances to the next line.	'\n'	*N/A*
\r	Carriage return. Moves the cursor back to the start of the line. '\r' and '\n' are typically paired together.	'\r'	*N/A*
\t	Tab character. Advances the cursor to the next tab stop, typically every 8 characters.	'\t'	*N/A*
\\	Backslash character.	'\\'	\

Useful char Members

Like other data types, char contains many methods to simply certain tasks. The following list contains some of the more useful methods of char:

Table 6-3. Useful char Members

Static	Name	Description
✓	GetNumericValue ()	Gets the numeric value of a char value, or -1 if not a number.
✓	GetUnicodeCategory ()	Gets the Unicode category that the given character belongs to.
✓	IsControl()	Determines if the given character is a control character (special ASCII unprintable character).
✓	IsDigit()	Determines if the given character is a numeric digit, ie. 0-9.
✓	IsLetter()	Determines if the given character is a letter.
✓	IsLetterOrDigit()	Determines if the given character is a letter or a digit.
✓	IsLower()	Determines if the given character is a lowercase letter.
✓	IsNumber()	Determines if the given character is a numeric value. In addition to 0-9 this will also detect values such as ½, ¼ and ^{2}.
✓	IsPunctuation()	Determines if the given character is a punctuation mark.
✓	IsSeparator()	Determines if the specified character is a separator character like space or line feed.
✓	IsSymbol()	Determines if the given character is a symbol like $ and #.
✓	IsUpper()	Determines if the given character is a uppercase letter.
✓	IsWhiteSpace()	Determines if the specified character is a white space character like space.
✓	ToLower()	Converts the given character to lowercase. If not applicable the original character is returned.
✓	ToUpper()	Converts the given character to uppercase. If not applicable the original character is returned.

Listing 6-2. Sample char Member Calls

```
UnicodeCategory cat = char.GetUnicodeCategory('©');
Console.WriteLine("Category of '@': " + cat);

double value = char.GetNumericValue('9');
Console.WriteLine("Numeric value of '9': " + value);

Console.WriteLine("'9' is a symbol? " + char.IsSymbol('9'));
Console.WriteLine("'$' is a symbol? " + char.IsSymbol('$'));
Console.WriteLine("'a' is lowercase? " + char.IsLower('a'));
Console.WriteLine("'a' is uppercase? " + char.IsUpper('a'));
```

```
Category of '@': OtherSymbol
Numeric value of '9': 9
Numeric value of 'a': -1
'9' is a symbol? False
'$' is a symbol? True
'a' is lowercase? True
'a' is uppercase? False
```

Figure 6-2. Sample char Member Output

While characters are very useful on their own, the majority of your programming will use characters within the context of strings, which is a sequence of characters.

6.2 System.String – string

The `char` type is useful for storing a single character of Unicode text. A `string` is used to store a consecutive set of characters as a single entity. In math, and other disciplines, a string is a sequence of symbols. In C#, it is not unreasonable to think of a `string` as an array of characters, although that is not entirely accurate. We'll get to that in a bit. Let's start by looking at some of the important facts about the `string` class.

- Strings are composed of a consecutive group of char values.
- Strings can theoretically contain up to roughly 2GB of data, or one billion characters.
- Strings are reference types, therefore the character data is stored in the heap.
- Being a reference type implies the default value for a `string` variable is `null`.
    - Don't try to access `string` contents or members without first initializing it.
- Strings are immutable, meaning the contents cannot be changed once created.
- Strings are delimited by quote characters unlike characters which use apostrophes.
- Strings use the same escape sequences as characters.

Creating String Variables

There are several different techniques for creating a `string` variable. The first is a process we have already used - assigning a `string` literal to a variable:

```
string name = "Some String";
```

The next technique is to use the `string`'s constructor syntax. There are actually 8 different ways to create a `string` using a constructor call, but most are infrequently used. In fact the following three are the only ones you will likely ever use.

Constructor #1: `string s1 = new string(char[]);`
Constructor #2: `string s2 = new string(char[], int, int);`

Constructor #3: `string s3 = new string(char, int);`

The first constructor creates a string from a char array. So, if the array contains 10 characters the new string will also contain those same 10 characters, in the same order. The second constructor is a slightly different version of the first. A char array is also used as the basis for the string's data; however, you can specify a subset of the array, passing in the starting index and number of chars to use in the string. The last constructor allows you to create a string of repeating characters. The character to repeat is the first argument and the number of repetitions is the second.

Another way strings can be created is the result of a method call. For instance, when you call Console.ReadLine(), the result of that method is a new string object. You can then store the result of that call in a new string variable as such:

```
string input = Console.ReadLine();
```

Finally, strings can also be created as the result of operators in expressions. Consider the following statement:

```
string concat = "ABC" + "DEF" + "GHI";
```

In this statement the compound expression "ABC" + "DEF" + "GHI" is evaluated and the result "ABCDEFGHI" is placed in a new string called *concat*. By the way, combining strings in this manner is called concatenation, hence the name of the variable, *concat*.

In the event you wish to create a new string variable but you do not wish to assign any data to it you can assume the default value null or assign it the value string.Empty. The value string.Empty is the same value as "", two consecutive quotes, which is a legal string value with no characters and a length of 0.

My preference is to use string.Empty instead of "". The primary reason is to avoid confusing the two quote symbols with four apostrophes '''' or a quote character inside two apostrophes '"'. As you can see, they look almost identical. Additionally, I prefer to initialize all strings to string.Empty to avoid the dreaded NullReferenceException.

Listing 6-3. String Creation Example

```
char[] chars = { 'A', 'B', 'C', 'D', 'E' };

// Create a string from a literal
string name = "John Smith";

// Create a string based on the chars array
string s1 = new string( chars );
// Create a string of 10 '=' symbols
string s2 = new string('=', 10);
// Create a 3 char string based on the chars array starting at index 2, or "CDE"
string s3 = new string(chars, 2, 3);

// Create a string from a method
string input = Console.ReadLine();

// Create a string by concatenating 3 literals
string concat = "ABC" + "DEF" + "GHI";
```

String-Specific Escape Sequences

Strings utilize the same "\" escape sequences as char. However, one critical difference about strings is that they support surrogate pairs and characters that require 4 bytes instead of the customary 2. Essentially, some special character modifiers can be applied to a Unicode character, such as accent marks, which require more space than 2 bytes. Strings will string treat these special characters as a single glyph when displayed. The escape sequence for these 4 bytes characters is "\UXXXXXXXX", where the block of 8 'X' symbols represents exactly 8 hexadecimal digits. We will not be using this particular feature of C# in this book, but it is still good to store this information in the back of your mind in the event you require enhanced globalized strings in your code.

One other special feature of strings, regarding escape sequences, is the ability to disable special characters. Consider the following file path as stored in a string variable:

```
string path1 = "C:\\users\\john\\documents\\test.txt";
```

As you can see, it is very important to escape each backslash with another backslash, otherwise some of the text would be interpreted as special characters, such as the '\' paired with the 't' character. If you prefer, you can also turn off escape sequences in the entire string by adding a "@" prefix before the first quote of the string literal as such:

```
string path2 = @"C:\users\john\documents\test.txt";
```

Each backslash in this second example literally means backslash. As you can see, this technique is especially useful when working with Windows file system paths.

6.3 String Members

The `string` class contains many members useful for the detection of `string` fragments contained within a string, manipulating the contents of a `string` or formatting other data types into a string. One detail which will be expanded upon shortly is that none of these methods actually change the size or contents of an existing `string` as they are immutable. Instead, the result of the operation typically is a new `string` containing the modified data. However, in practice, this limitation is not much of a burden since the C# language is designed to treat `string` objects like value types even though they are actually reference types. Before we get into all of that, however, let's take a quick look at the members of the `string` class. We'll actually delve a little deeper into some of these methods than we have for previous topic, mostly because of the importance of text handling in programming.

Table 6-4. Key string Members

Static	Name	Description
	CompareTo()	Compares the `string` that this method is called on with another.
	Contains()	Determines if a `string` contains another `string` fragment.
	EndsWith()	Determines if a `string` ends with the given `string` fragment.
	IndexOf()	Gets the index where one `string` is located within another. If not found the result is -1.
	Insert()	Inserts a `string` fragment into another `string`.
	LastIndexOf()	Gets the last index where one `string` is located within another. If not found the result is -1.
	Length	Returns the number of characters in the `string`.
	PadLeft()	Adds spaces or other character to the start of the `string` to make the total length a specified value.
	PadRight()	Adds spaces or other character to the end of the `string` to make the total length a specified value.
	Remove()	Removes a specified range of characters from the `string`.
	Replace()	Replaces a pattern of characters with another `string` fragment.
	Split()	Splits a `string` into a `string` array based on a delimiter character.
	StartsWith()	Determines if a `string` starts with the given `string` fragment.
	Substring()	Extracts a string fragment from a `string`.
	ToLower()	Converts the entire `string` to lowercase characters.
	ToUpper()	Converts the entire `string` to uppercase characters.
	Trim()	Trims all whitespace from the beginning and end of a `string`.
	TrimEnd()	Trims all whitespace from the end of a `string`.
	TrimStart()	Trims all whitespace from the beginning of a `string`.
✓	Compare()	Compares two `string` objects for <, == or >.
✓	Concat()	Concatenates, or combines, a series of `string` objects into a single `string`.
✓	Copy()	Creates a copy of a `string`.
✓	Empty	Returns a `string` object with no character data.

Static	Name	Description
✓	Equals()	Tests two `string` objects for equality.
✓	Format()	Formats a string using parameter substitution and data type formatting rules.
✓	Intern()	Stores a `string` in a special memory location so that other `string` variables with the same text can share the same memory.
✓	IsInterned()	Determines if a given `string` is interned.
✓	IsNullOrEmpty()	Determines if a `string` object is set to `null` or contains no character data.
✓	Join()	Combines an array of `string` values into a single `string`.

Basic String Manipulation

When working with text data you may be in a situation where you are required to modify the contents of a `string`. First, let's consider a simple example: you have a `string` with the contents "ABC" and you wish to add the letter "D" to the end of it. The `string` type can utilize the "+" and "+=" operators to concatenate text, or you can use the named methods `string`.Concat() and `string`.Join(). Following is an example demonstrating this scenario:

Listing 6-4. String Concatenation

```
1 string abc = "ABC";
2 // Add 'D' to the end of abc:
3 abc = abc + "D";
4 // Now add an 'E':
5 abc += "E";
```

The variable *abc* is initialized to "ABC". After line 3 the contents of *abc* are "ABCD". Finally, after line 5 the value is "ABCDE". However, there is one crucial piece of information that was overlooked in this process: strings are supposed to be immutable, or, in other words, not modifiable. The results, however, indicate a different outcome. In reality, strings are very much like arrays in that they cannot grow or shrink without extensive memory manipulation. In fact, this is the process that is occurring on line 3:

- A new `string` is created in the process of concatenating the contents of *abc* and "D".
- The result of the concatenation is stored in heap memory.
- The variable *abc* is pointed to the new heap location.
- The original heap data that contained "ABC" is reclaimed by the garbage collector.

So, what looks like an innocuous concatenation is actually a fairly complex procedure. The operation on line 5 goes through the exact same process, meaning these two concatenation operations both involve costly memory manipulation. It is for this reason that repeated concatenations on `string` data is strongly discouraged. However, as long as performance and memory are not primary concerns for your application, several concatenations are not overly costly. For repeated concatenations consider the buffered string class called StringBuilder which will be discussed a bit later in the chapter.

PadLeft() and PadRight()

These two methods add spaces (or other specified character) to the start or end of the string that they are called upon. This technique is especially useful if you need to display text in a tabular format where the contents in rows of data must line up. For PadLeft(), the spaces are added to the start of the string to make the entire length of the string match the requested number of characters. As you probably guessed, PadRight() adds the spaces to the end of the string. If the requested total length is less than the pre-existing text length these method will do nothing except return the original string.

Listing 6-5. String Padding

```
string test = "ABCDE";
// Add 5 spaces to the front of test
string left = test.PadLeft(10);
// Add 5 '+' to the end of test
string right = test.PadRight(10, '+');

Console.WriteLine(left);
Console.WriteLine(right);
```

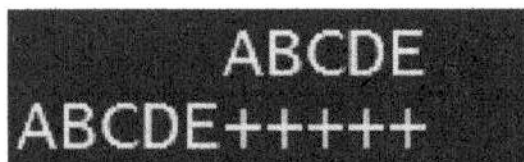

Table 6-5. Padding Output

Trim(), TrimStart() and TrimEnd()

The Trim methods remove whitespace, such as the space character and carriage returns, from a string. The Trim() method removes whitespace from both ends of a string, preserving non-whitespace characters. TrimStart() and TrimEnd() remove whitespace from the beginning or end of a string, respectively. Again, the original contents of the string being trimmed remain unchanged and the result of the method calls contain the changed values. These methods can result in an empty string, but not a null string.

Listing 6-6. String Trimming

```
string text = "    A string with whitespace.      ";
Console.WriteLine("Original Len:   " + text.Length + " '" + text + "'");

string ts = text.TrimStart();
Console.WriteLine("TrimStart Len: " + ts.Length + " '" + ts + "'");

string te = text.TrimEnd();
Console.WriteLine("TrimEnd Len:   " + te.Length + " '" + te + "'");

string trim = text.Trim();
Console.WriteLine("Trim Len:      " + trim.Length + " '" + trim + "'");
```

```
Original Len:  35 '    A string with whitespace.      '
TrimStart Len: 31 'A string with whitespace.      '
TrimEnd Len:   29 '    A string with whitespace.'
Trim Len:      25 'A string with whitespace.'
```

Figure 6-3. String Trimming Results

Insert(), Remove() and Replace()

These three methods provide functionality for modifying the contents of a string. The Insert() method inserts a given text fragment into another string at the provided index. Remove() deletes text from the string given an index and number of characters to remove. Replace() searches for all occurrences of a given text fragment and replaces it with another. If you wish to remove text from a string use Replace() supplying string.Empty as the replacement text. Remember, these methods do not actually modify the original string, they create a new one.

Listing 6-7. Insert, Remove and Replace

```
string text = "Now the time for   all good men...";
Console.WriteLine(text);

// Add the word "is " in the correct position, at index 4
text = text.Insert(4, "is ");
Console.WriteLine(text);

// There are too many spaces between "for" and "all".  Remove 2 at index 19.
text = text.Remove(19, 2);
Console.WriteLine(text);

// The text is not very modern.  Change "men" to "people"
text = text.Replace("men", "people");
Console.WriteLine(text);
```

```
Now the time for   all good men...
Now is the time for   all good men...
Now is the time for all good men...
Now is the time for all good people...
```

Figure 6-4. Insert, Remove and Replace Output

Substring()

The Substring() method provides a mechanism for extracting a fragment of text from a `string`. There are two ways to call this method. The first requires the index of the character to start extracting text from in addition to the number of characters to extract. The second version only accepts the starting index and retrieves all characters from that point up to the end of the `string`.

There are two ways calling Substring() can go sideways (semi-technical term for code that fails)... The first is if you provide a starting index that is outside the bounds of the `string` for either version of the method. The second way is if you ask for more characters than are available in the `string` when calling the first version of the method. Either scenario results in an exception.

Listing 6-8. Substring

```
string text = "The Eagle has landed.";

// Extract the word Eagle:
string eagle = text.Substring(4, 5);
Console.WriteLine(eagle);

// Extract everything after 'has ':
string theRest = text.Substring(14);
Console.WriteLine(theRest);
```

```
Eagle
landed.
```

Figure 6-5. Substring Output

ToLower() and ToUpper()

The methods ToLower() and ToUpper() return a completely lowercase or uppercase version of a `string`. These methods determine which letters require modification based on the computer's locale. Characters that do not support casing, like numerals and punctuation, remain unchanged.

Listing 6-9. String Casing

```
string text = "THis IS a SAmpLe StRINg.";

string lower = text.ToLower();
Console.WriteLine("Lower: " + lower);
string upper = text.ToUpper();
Console.WriteLine("Upper: " + upper);

// Use a combination of Substring, ToUpper and ToLower
string correct = text.Substring(0, 1).ToUpper() + text.Substring(1).ToLower();
Console.WriteLine("Correct: " + correct);
```

```
Lower: this is a sample string.
Upper: THIS IS A SAMPLE STRING.
Correct: This is a sample string.
```

Figure 6-6. String Casing Output

Comparing Strings

Unlike most other reference types, string variables can be compared to each other using the standard comparison operators (==, !=, >, >=, <, <=). In addition, several members of the string class are geared specifically to compare string contents to other string objects. Some methods are static and others are instance members which implies some are accessed via "string." and the others require a variable. Unless otherwise specified, all of these comparison techniques are case sensitive, so A ≠ a.

CompareTo()

The CompareTo() method compares a string to another to determine if they are equal or if one is less than or greater than the other based on region-specific alphabetic rules. The method is called using one string as a handle while the other is passed in as an argument. The result is an int with the value 0 if both strings are equal, -1 if the handle string is less than the argument string or 1 if the handle string is greater than the argument string.

Listing 6-10. string.CompareTo()

```
string test1 = "This is a test.";
string test2 = "This is another test.";

int comp = test1.CompareTo(test2);
// If result is 0, strings are equal, -1 if test1 < test2, 1 if test1 > test2
Console.WriteLine("Result of string compare is: " + comp);
```

```
Result of string compare is: -1
```

Figure 6-7. string.CompareTo() Results

Equals()

The Equals() method tests two `string` values for equality. Unlike CompareTo(), Equals() is called using the "`string.`" handle and two `string` values are passed to the method. The `bool` result is `true` if the values are equal, `false` otherwise.

Listing 6-11. string.Equals()

```
string test1 = "This is a test.";
string test2 = "This is another test.";

bool result = false;
result = string.Equals(test1, test2);
Console.WriteLine("test1 equals test2: " + result);
```

```
test1 equals test2: False
```

Figure 6-8. string.Equals() Output

IsNullOrEmpty()

This method is exceptionally useful for testing if a `string` has been properly initialized and if it has any character data. Use this method to avoid accessing the contents of a `null string` which causes NullReferenceExceptions. Because the result of this method is a `bool` value, it is especially useful within an `if` statement. Like the CompareTo() method, this is called using the "`string.`" handle.

Listing 6-12. string.IsNullOrEmpty()

```
string nullString = null;
if (string.IsNullOrEmpty(nullString))
{
  Console.WriteLine("The given string is null or empty.");
}
```

```
test1 is null or empty: False
```

Figure 6-9. string.IsNullOrEmpty() Output

Contains(), StartsWith() and EndsWith()

The methods Contains(), StartsWith() and EndsWith() check if the given `string` contains the requested value. The difference between the methods is that the first method, Contains(), checks for existence of a string fragment within any part of the given string. The other two, StartsWith() and EndsWith(), check for the fragment's existence at the beginning or end of the given string, respectively. StartsWith() and EndsWith() can also be called in a case-insensitive manner by providing a StringComparison parameter. As these are instance methods, they require the handle of a string object.

Listing 6-13. string Containment Checks

```
string text = "Out with the old, in with the new.";
bool result = text.Contains("old");
Console.WriteLine("text contains 'old': " + result);

result = text.StartsWith("out");
Console.WriteLine("text starts with 'out': " + result);

result = text.StartsWith("out", StringComparison.CurrentCultureIgnoreCase);
Console.WriteLine("text starts with 'out' case insensitive: " + result);

result = text.EndsWith("dog");
Console.WriteLine("text ends with 'dog': " + result);
```

```
text contains 'old': True
text starts with 'out': False
text starts with 'out' case insensitive: True
text ends with 'dog': False
```

Figure 6-10. string Containment Results

IndexOf, LastIndexOf()

The IndexOf() and LastIndexOf() methods help you to locate a text fragment within a string. If found, the index of the first character is returned. If the fragment is not found then the methods return -1. Since a fragment may be present multiple times within a string, both methods can also accept a starting index to skip over either the beginning or ending of the string, depending on which method is being called. By default, the searches are case sensitive, but it is also possible to perform a case insensitive search.

Listing 6-14. IndexOf() and LastIndexOf()

```
string text = "A penny saved is a penny earned.";
int index = -1;

// Find the first occurrence of "penny" in text
index = text.IndexOf("penny");
Console.WriteLine("The first occurrence of 'penny' is at: " + index);
// Look for the next occurrence of "penny" after the first found one
index = text.IndexOf("penny", index + 5);
Console.WriteLine("The second occurrence of 'penny' is at: " + index);
// Look for the next occurrence of "penny" after the second found one
// Will return -1 which means "not found"
index = text.IndexOf("penny", index + 5);
Console.WriteLine("The third occurrence of 'penny' is at: " + index);

// Now look for "penny" starting from the end of the string...
index = text.LastIndexOf("penny");
Console.WriteLine("The last occurrence of 'penny' is at: " + index);

text = "The early bird catches the worm";
string search = "the";
// Look for the text contained in 'search' variable in a case-insensitive manner
index = text.IndexOf(search, StringComparison.CurrentCultureIgnoreCase);
Console.WriteLine("The first occurrence of 'the' is at: " + index);
// Look for the next occurrence of "the" after the first found one
index = text.IndexOf(search, index + 3, StringComparison.CurrentCultureIgnoreCase);
Console.WriteLine("The second occurrence of 'the' is at: " + index);
```

```
The first occurrence of 'penny' is at: 2
The second occurrence of 'penny' is at: 19
The third occurrence of 'penny' is at: -1
The last occurrence of 'penny' is at: 19
The first occurrence of 'the' is at: 0
The second occurrence of 'the' is at: 23
```

Figure 6-11. IndexOf() and LastIndexOf() Output

Advanced String Manipulation

Split()

The `string`.Split() method provides a mechanism for breaking a larger `string` into several smaller ones. By default, whitespace characters are used as delimiters to create the individual substrings, but custom delimiters can be supplied. The result of the Split() call is a `string[]` where each element in the array is one of the substrings. The delimiters are not included in any of the elements.

Listing 6-15. Split() Example

```
string socrates = "The only true wisdom is in knowing you know nothing";
// Split the quote into words using the default whitespace chars for delimiters
string[] words = socrates.Split();

Console.WriteLine("Quote: \"" + socrates + "\"");
Console.WriteLine("String split into " + words.Length + " words");
Console.WriteLine("First word: " + words[0]);
Console.WriteLine("Last word: " + words[words.GetUpperBound(0)]);

string picasso = "Computers are useless.  They can only give you answers.";
Console.WriteLine("\nQuote: \"" + picasso + "\"");
char[] delimiters = {' ', '.'};
// Split using space and . as delimiters, ignoring blank results
words = picasso.Split(delimiters, StringSplitOptions.RemoveEmptyEntries);
// Use a foreach loop to show all split words
foreach (string word in words)
{
  Console.WriteLine(word);
}
```

```
Quote: "The only true wisdom is in knowing you know nothing"
String split into 10 words
First word: The
Last word: nothing

Quote: "Computers are useless.  They can only give you answers."
Computers
are
useless
They
can
only
give
you
answers
```

Figure 6-12. Split() Output

Join()

Opposite of Split() is the Join() method. Given a `string[]` you can recombine the individual elements into a single `string`. The required arguments to this method are the `string` used to combine the individual items together (such as a space) and the `string[]` containing the items to join.

Listing 6-16. Join() Example

```
string[] items = { "This", "is", "a", "sample", "string" };
string joined = string.Join(" ", items);
Console.WriteLine("The joined string is: " + joined);
```

```
The joined string is: This is a sample string
```

Figure 6-13. Join() Output

6.4 String Formatting

So far you've seen techniques for creating, concatenating, searching, comparing, splitting and joining `string` values. There is another vital technique for working with text data – formatting. Consider a `decimal` with the value 123456.78. If you are required to format this value using the local currency rules, and to use extra space characters to right justify the result to fit in a table column that is 15 characters wide, the output of the formatting would look like this (dots used to emphasize space characters):

```
····$123,456.78
```

The `string`.Format() method provides the power to achieve these results. Before we look at the most complex scenarios, however, we'll take a look at value substitution.

Value Substitution

Assume that a user is instructed to input their name and that value is stored in a `string` variable called *name*. The program is then required to output to the console window a salutation followed by the name and some other greeting text. Based on current knowledge, the desired output may be achieved using the following code:

Listing 6-17. Traditional String Concatenation

```
Console.Write("Please enter your name: ");
string name = Console.ReadLine();

string output = "Hello, " + name + ", how are you doing today?";
Console.WriteLine(output);
```

For simple text, like the above example, standard `string` concatenation is sufficient to carry out the desired task. However, once you must concatenate many items together, this technique can result in hard to read code and is error prone. Instead, you can use `string`.Format() with value substitutions to achieve the same results.

The `string`.Format() method accepts a single format `string` followed by an arbitrary number of arguments. Then, anywhere in the format `string` that a special escape sequence is encountered, that escape sequence is substituted by one of the following arguments. The method has the following syntax:

```
string.Format("<format>", arg0, arg1, arg2, …, argn-1);
```

Where <format> is a format string that contains literal text to pass directly to the output of the method as well as special escape sequences to substitute with one of the arguments (arg_0 through arg_{n-1}). The argument list is 0-based, therefore the last argument has an index of "n-1" when there exists a total of "n" elements. A value substitution escape sequence in the format string has the following syntax:

```
{<arg#>}
```

Where <arg#> is the 0-based argument number to substitute at that specific location in the format string. So, to substitute an argument into the format string, use a curly brace delimiter around the argument number you wish to substitute, such as "{0}". The same substitution can be used an unlimited number of times, just ensure that all indices refer to legitimate values. Keep in mind that since the "{" and "}" characters have special meaning in the format string if you need to output one of those characters you need to double it up: "{{" and "}}". The code in Listing 6-17 can be replaced with this example using string.Format():

Listing 6-18. Value Substitution

```
Console.Write("Please enter your name: ");
string name = Console.ReadLine();

string output = string.Format("Hello, {0}, how are you doing today?", name);
Console.WriteLine(output);
```

```
Please enter your name: William
Hello, William, how are you doing today?
```

Figure 6-14. Value Substitution Output

In the above example, the Format() method detects the "{0}" escape sequence in the format string (which was highlighted for your benefit) and substitutes that with the value of the argument at index 0 which is the *name* variable. As mentioned, the same argument can be referenced many times in a format command, so if the *name* variable is required to be substituted twice, the following example is possible:

```
string output = string.Format("Hello, {0}.  I always liked the name {0}.", name);
```

Now the output would look like:

```
Hello, William.  I always liked the name William.
```

Figure 6-15. Argument Reuse Output

It does not matter what type of variables are used for arguments as the Format() command will call their "ToString()" methods to convert them to a string when substituting. Remember, in C# every object has a ToString() method, but some types may not be equipped to provide useful string representations. All of the built-in types, however, do have well-defined ToString() methods so this is only an issue when dealing with custom types. Also, the arguments do not have to be variables, they can be literal values or expressions as well. The following example demonstrates multiple arguments of different types.

Listing 6-19. Multiple Value Substitution

```
int x = 6;
double y = 0.5;
string output = string.Format("The square of {0} is {1}, and {0} * {2} = {3}",
  x, x * x, y, x * y);
Console.WriteLine(output);
```

```
The square of 6 is 36, and 6 * 0.5 = 3
```

Figure 6-16. Multiple Value Substitution Output

Not only are there more arguments in this example, they are of different types. Plus, two of the arguments are actually expressions. Also, notice that the order that the arguments are used is not entirely sequential: {0}, {1}, {0}, {2}, {3}. The following mapping is used when the argument substitutions are evaluated by Format():

{0} ➔ x
{1} ➔ $x * x$
{2} ➔ y
{3} ➔ $x * y$

As a reminder, it is not legal to use an argument index when no argument exists at that position. If, in the above example, the Format() method encountered the escape sequence "{4}", then a FormatException would be thrown causing the program to terminate. Needless to say, it is important that formatting code only references arguments that exist in the argument list. However, it is perfectly acceptable, if a bit sloppy, to have arguments in the list that are never used by the Format() command.

Value Alignment and Spacing

Not only can values be inserted into strings using value substitution, they can also be formatted to a specific size and alignment. The functionality is similar to the PadLeft() and PadRight() methods of string in that the total number of characters used in the substitution can be defined as well as whether the padding occurs prior to or following the value. To control the spacing of a substitute value, a comma followed by a numeric value indicating the total spacing is added after the argument number in the escape sequence:

```
{<arg#>,<spacing>}
```

The <spacing> value can be positive or negative. Positive values indicate right-justification, or equivalent to the output of the PadLeft() method, where extra spaces are added prior to the value. Negative values are equivalent to the PadRight() method where extra spaces are added following the value. In either case, spaces are added to the output string only if the substituted value is smaller than the defined spacing number. So, if the provided spacing value is 10 or -10 and the substitute value is already 12 characters wide, no spaces are added and no truncation will occur.

Listing 6-20. Alignment and Spacing

```
// Create some variables representing people
int id1 = 12345;
int id2 = 555;
string name1 = "John Smith";
string name2 = "Jane Doe";
int age1 = 7;
int age2 = 25;

// Output a header
Console.WriteLine("ID     NAME           AGE");
Console.WriteLine(new string('-', 25));  // Print string of 25 '-' characters

// Format the people variables so they line up in a table
string fmt = string.Format("{0,6} {1,-15} {2,2}", id1, name1, age1);
Console.WriteLine(fmt);
fmt = string.Format("{0,6} {1,-15} {2,2}", id2, name2, age2);
Console.WriteLine(fmt);
```

```
ID     NAME           AGE
-------------------------
 12345 John Smith       7
   555 Jane Doe        25
```

Figure 6-17. Alignment and Spacing Output

As you can see from the example, formatting with alignment and spacing enables simple tabular output. Typically, text substitutions will utilize left justification (negative spacing values) and numeric substitutions will utilize right justification (positive spacing values).

Type Formatting

In addition to alignment and spacing, individual value substitutions may also specify how to format the value being substituted. All the previous examples rely on the default ToString() output for each argument being substituted. However, many data types can utilize pre-defined or custom format codes to alter their text format. Like the spacing parameter, the format code specifier appears after the argument index in the escape sequence, but this one appears after a colon, not a comma:

```
{<arg#>:<format code>}
```

If both spacing and type formatting are to be done with the same value they must appear in the following order:

```
{<arg#>,<spacing>:<format code>}
```

So, what can the `<format code>` specifier be? In fact, it can be almost any `string` value, but it typically is a single character or a character followed by a number known as the *precision specifier*. Making matters more interesting is that each data type defines its own list of legal format codes, some of which are designed to work with regions and cultures and others which are custom-defined by the programmer. All built-in data types support the format code "G" which represents the standard, most compact output for that type.

Rather than attempt to define an exhaustive list here, which would be impractical, we'll examine some of the most commonly used format codes for common data types. All of the example output assumes American English for the culture and language.

Integer Format Codes

Table 6-6. Integer Format Codes

Code	Description	Ex.	Value	Output
C or c	Uses culture-specific currency format.	C	12345 -12345	$12,345.00 ($12,345.00)
C# or c#	Same as "C" but includes the number of decimal places to display.	C0 C3	12345 12345	$12,345 $12,345.000
D# or d#	Decimal format outputs the value using the specified number of digits, padding with leading 0's as necessary.	D8	12345 -12345	00012345 -00012345
E#	Outputs the number in exponential format where the precision specifier indicates the number of decimals to display.	E3	12345	1.235E+004
e#	Same as "E#" but the output includes a lowercase "e".	e3	12345	1.235e+004
G or g	General output for the type.	G	12345	12345
G# or g#	If the precision specifier is smaller than the number of digits being formatted, then the output will be in exponential format ('E' case dependent on 'G' or 'g'), otherwise it simply displays all digits.	G2 G8	12345 12345	1.2E+04 12345

Code	Description	Ex.	Value	Output
N or n	Uses the formal number format for the region. In the case of US English, this includes thousands separators and 2 decimal places.	N	12345 -12345	12,345.00 -12,345.00
N# or n#	Same as "N" but includes the number of decimal places to output.	N0	12345	12,345
X or x	Formats the number into hexadecimal (base-16) format where the letters A – F are upper or lowercase based on the case of X.	X x	6173 6173	181D 181d
X# or x#	Same as X, but specifies the total size of the output, left-padding 0's as necessary.	X8	6173	0000181D

The format codes listed in Table 6-6. Integer Format CodesTable 6-6 work for most integral style number types, such as `int`, `uint`, `long`, `ulong`, `short`, `ushort` and `byte`. Just be aware, the unsigned types will never output negative values.

Decimal Format Codes

Table 6-7. Decimal Format Codes

Code	Description	Ex.	Value	Output
C or c	Uses culture-specific currency format.	C	12345.67 -12345.67	$12,345.68 ($12,345.68)
C# or c#	Same as "C" but includes the number of decimal places to display.	C0 C3	12345.678 12345.678	$12,346 $12,345.678
E#	Outputs the number in exponential format where the precision specifier indicates the number of decimals to display.	E3	12345.678	1.235E+004
e#	Same as "E#" but the output includes a lowercase "e".	e3	12345.678	1.235e+004
F# or f#	Uses fixed point notation where the precision specifier indicates the number of decimal places.	F0 F4	12345.678 12345.678	12346 12345.6780
G or g	General output for the type.	G	12345.678	12345.678
G# or g#	Formats using fixed point notation if the precision specifier is sufficiently large to display all significant digits, exponential notation otherwise.	G2 G8	12345.678 12345.678	1.2E+04 12345.678
N or n	Uses the formal number format for the region. In the case of US English, this includes thousands separators and 2 decimal places.	N	12345.678 -12345.678	12,345.68 -12,345.68
N# or n#	Same as "N" but includes the number of decimal places to output.	N0 N4	12345.678 12345.678	12,346 12,345.6780
P# or p#	Outputs the value using the culture-specific percentage format. The precision specifier indicates the number of decimal digits to output.	P0 P2	0.318512 0.318512	32 % 31.85 %
R or r	The round-trip format displays all of the necessary numeric data to be able to parse the value back to its original data type.	R	1.0 / 3.0	0.33333333333333331

The format codes listed in Table 6-7 apply to `double`, `float` and `decimal` (except for "R" which `decimal` does not support).

In the following example, you will notice that the string.Format() method is never called. Instead, the Console.WriteLine() method is used with the exact same syntax. The only difference between the calls is that while string.Format() returns a string with the formatted data, Console.WriteLine() outputs the formatted string directy to the console window.

Listing 6-21. Pre-defined Numeric Format Codes

```
int x = 12345;
Console.WriteLine("int");
Console.WriteLine("0. {0}", x.ToString());
Console.WriteLine("1. {0,13:C} {1,13:C} {0,13:C3}", x, -x);
Console.WriteLine("2. {0,13:D8}", x);
Console.WriteLine("3. {0,13:E3} {0,13:e3}", x);
Console.WriteLine("4. {0,13:G} {0,13:G2} {0,13:G8}", x);
Console.WriteLine("5. {0,13:N} {1,13:N} {0,13:N3} {0,13:N0}", x, -x);
Console.WriteLine("6. {0,13:X} {0,13:x}", x / 2 + 1);  // x / 2 + 1 = 6173

double d = 12345.678;
Console.WriteLine("double");
Console.WriteLine("0. {0}", d.ToString());
Console.WriteLine("1. {0,13:C} {1,13:C} {0,13:C3}", d, -d);
Console.WriteLine("2. {0,13:E3} {0,13:e3}", d);
Console.WriteLine("3. {0,13:F0} {0,13:F2} {0,13:F4}", d);
Console.WriteLine("4. {0,13:G} {0,13:G2} {0,13:G8}", d);
Console.WriteLine("5. {0,13:N} {1,13:N} {0,13:N4} {0,13:N0}", d, -d);
double pct = 0.318512;
Console.WriteLine("6. {0,13:P0} {0,13:P2}", pct);
d = 1.0 / 3.0;
Console.WriteLine("7. {0:R}", d);
```

```
int
0. 12345
1.    $12,345.00  ($12,345.00)   $12,345.000
2.      00012345
3.    1.235E+004    1.235e+004
4.         12345       1.2E+04         12345
5.     12,345.00    -12,345.00    12,345.000         12,345
6.          181D          181d
double
0. 12345.678
1.    $12,345.68  ($12,345.68)   $12,345.678
2.    1.235E+004    1.235e+004
3.         12346      12345.68    12345.6780
4.     12345.678       1.2E+04     12345.678
5.     12,345.68    -12,345.68   12,345.6780         12,346
6.          32 %       31.85 %
7. 0.33333333333333331
```

Figure 6-18. Pre-defined Numeric Format Codes Output

Notice on lines 4, 8, 14 and 18 that there are two arguments passed to the Format() method, one is the variable being formatted and the other is the negative value of that variable. So, within the format strings on these lines, the second escape sequence points to the negative values by referencing the argument `{1}`. The numbers at the beginning of each output line are there to associate the source code to the output.

Custom Numeric Format Codes

The previous tables itemize some of the pre-defined format codes for numeric values, most of which utilize region-aware formatting. Sometimes, however, it is useful to be able to define custom formatting when the pre-defined formats are insufficient for your needs.

A major difference between pre-defined and custom format codes is that only one pre-defined format code may be applied to an argument at a time but many custom format codes can be applied simultaneously. Combining multiple custom format codes together forms something known as a mask.

The following codes can be used with all numeric data types, although some of the codes do not apply to all types (such as fractional format codes with integral numeric types).

Table 6-8. Custom Numeric Format Codes

Code	Description
`0`	The "0" represents a placeholder in the output. If a corresponding digit exists in the input argument then that digit is output, otherwise a 0 is put in its place.
#	The "#" represents a placeholder in the output. If a corresponding digit exists in the input argument then that digit is output, otherwise nothing is put in its place.
.	Determines the location of the decimal point in the output.
,	The "," code has two different meanings. It can be used as a group separator in conjunction with the "0" and "#" placeholders. It can also be used as a number scaling specifier where each comma divides the input by 1000.
%	This format code multiplies the input argument by 100 and inserts the localized percentage symbol in its place.
‰	This format code multiplies the input argument by 1000 and inserts the localized per mille symbol in its place.
`E0` or `e0`	Formats the number using exponential notation where the number of "0" characters indicates the 0-padding to use in the exponent portion of the output. The case of the "e" in the format code indicates what the output case of the "e" will be.
`E+0` or `e+0`	Formats the number using exponential notation where the number of "0" characters indicates the 0-padding to use in the exponent portion of the output. The "+" character indicates that a sign operator always appears prior to the exponent value.
`E-0` or `e-0`	Same as "E+0" but the "-" character indicates that the exponent's sign should only be shown if negative.
'*text*'	Any text contained within the apostrophes is copied directly to the output.
;	The semicolon acts as a section separator that allows the definition of three independent format groups, one for positive inputs, one for negative inputs and the other for inputs with the value 0.

Listing 6-22. Custom Numeric Format Codes

```
double d = 12345678.9012;
Console.WriteLine("A1. {0:0.000}", d);
Console.WriteLine("A2. {0:#,##0.000}", d);
Console.WriteLine("A3. {0:0.000E+000}", d);
Console.WriteLine("A4. {0:0.0e0}", d);

double pct = 0.318512;
Console.WriteLine("B1. {0:0.00 %}", pct);
Console.WriteLine("B2. {0:0.00 ‰}", pct);
Console.WriteLine("B3. {0:0.000E+000}", pct);
Console.WriteLine("B4. {0:0.0e0}", pct);

// Phone number stored as long
long phone = 8885551212;
Console.WriteLine("C1. {0:(000) 000-0000}", phone);
// Social Security Number as int
int ssn = 123456789;
Console.WriteLine("C2. {0:000-00-0000}", ssn);

// Tri-section
Console.WriteLine("D1. {0:0.000;(0.0);-0-}", 123.45678);
Console.WriteLine("D2. {0:0.000;(0.0);-0-}", -123.45678);
Console.WriteLine("D3. {0:0.000;(0.0);-0-}", 0);
```

```
A1. 12345678.901
A2. 12,345,678.901
A3. 1.235E+007
A4. 1.2e7
B1. 31.85 %
B2. 318.51 %
B3. 3.185E-001
B4. 3.2e-1
C1. (888) 555-1212
C2. 123-45-6789
D1. 123.457
D2. (123.5)
D3. -0-
```

Figure 6-19. Custom Numeric Format Codes Output

Note: Due to a limitation of the Consolas font in the console window, ‰ is rendered as % on line B2.

DateTime Format Codes

DateTime values have a unique set of format codes specifically tailored for formatting date and time values. In addition to the standard, region-aware codes, there are a slew of specifiers for formatting individual time span components like years, hours and minutes. First, let's look at the built-in, region-aware codes. The date formats for a given machine's culture is defined in the Control Panel's "Region" dialog:

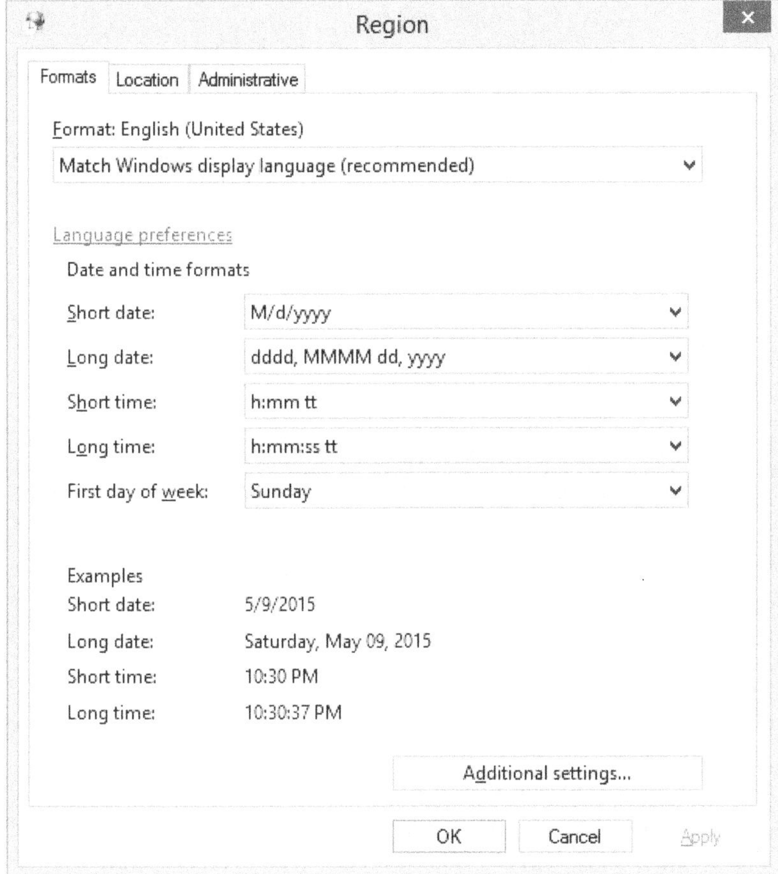

Figure 6-20. Region Date and Time Formats

The test value used for all of the DateTime format codes below is:

```
October 9, 2014 1:05:23 PM
```

In addition, all of the output corresponds to the default settings for a Windows 8.1 machine using the default U. S. English culture settings.

Table 6-9. DateTime Format Codes

Code	Description	Output
d	Short date format.	`10/9/2014`
D	Long date format.	`Thursday, October 09, 2014`
f	Full date & time format with short time.	`Thursday, October 09, 2014 1:05 PM`

Code	Description	Output
F	Full date & time format with long time.	Thursday, October 09, 2014 1:05:23 PM
g	General date & time format with short time.	10/9/2014 1:05 PM
G	General date & time format with long time.	10/9/2014 1:05:23 PM
M or m	Month & day format.	October 09
O or o	Round-trip date & time format.	2014-10-09T13:05:23.0000000
R or r	RFC 1123 format.	Thu, 09 Oct 2014 13:05:23 GMT
s	Sortable date & time format.	2014-10-09T13:05:23
t	Short time format.	1:05 PM
T	Long time format.	1:05:23 PM
u	Universal sortable date & time format.	2014-10-09 13:05:23Z
U	Universal full date & time format.	Thursday, October 09, 2014 8:05:23 PM
Y or y	Year & month format.	October, 2014

The following code demonstrates these date & time format codes in action:

Listing 6-23. DateTime Format Codes Example

```
DateTime dt = DateTime.Parse("March 22, 2015 11:55:05 AM");
Console.WriteLine("d. {0:d}", dt);
Console.WriteLine("D. {0:D}", dt);
Console.WriteLine("f. {0:f}", dt);
Console.WriteLine("F. {0:F}", dt);
Console.WriteLine("g. {0:g}", dt);
Console.WriteLine("G. {0:G}", dt);
Console.WriteLine("m. {0:m}", dt);
Console.WriteLine("o. {0:o}", dt);
Console.WriteLine("r. {0:r}", dt);
Console.WriteLine("s. {0:s}", dt);
Console.WriteLine("t. {0:t}", dt);
Console.WriteLine("T. {0:T}", dt);
Console.WriteLine("u. {0:u}", dt);
Console.WriteLine("U. {0:U}", dt);
Console.WriteLine("y. {0:y}", dt);
```

```
d. 3/22/2015
D. Sunday, March 22, 2015
f. Sunday, March 22, 2015 11:55 AM
F. Sunday, March 22, 2015 11:55:05 AM
g. 3/22/2015 11:55 AM
G. 3/22/2015 11:55:05 AM
m. March 22
o. 2015-03-22T11:55:05.0000000
r. Sun, 22 Mar 2015 11:55:05 GMT
s. 2015-03-22T11:55:05
t. 11:55 AM
T. 11:55:05 AM
u. 2015-03-22 11:55:05Z
U. Sunday, March 22, 2015 6:55:05 PM
y. March, 2015
```

Figure 6-21. DateTime Format Codes Output

Custom DateTime Format Codes

Although there are many built-in DateTime format codes, there may still be a need to create custom date or time formats. Just like custom numeric format codes, these custom DateTime codes may be combined. If you wish to use a single character custom format code by itself, like "d", you must prepend a "%" in front of the code to distinguish it from the built-in codes, such as:

```
{0:%d} {1:%H}
```

The test value used for all of the custom DateTime format codes below is:

```
July 4, 2002 6:25:09.475 PM
```

Listing 6-24. Custom DateTime Format Codes

Code	Description	Output
d dd ddd dddd	Corresponds to the day portion of the value. d = day of the month with no 0 padding dd = day of the month with leading 0 padding ddd = abbreviation of the day of the week dddd = full name of the day of the week	d: 4 dd: 04 ddd: Thu dddd: Thursday
f ... fffffff	Fractions of a second. The number of "f" characters corresponds to the decimal places displayed. Milliseconds would be "fff".	f: 4 ff: 47 fffffff: 4750000

Code	Description	Output
F … FFFFFFF	Same as lowercase "f" except trailing 0's are ignored.	F: 4 FF: 47 FFFFFFF: 475
g	Era, such as A.D.	A.D.
h hh	Corresponds to the hours portion of the DateTime value in 12-hour format. The single "h" has no leading 0 padding but the double "hh" prepends a 0 for hours less than 10.	h: 6 hh: 06
H HH	Corresponds to the hours portion of the DateTime value in 24-hour format. The single "H" has no leading 0 padding but the double "HH" prepends a 0 for hours less than 10.	H: 18 HH: 18
K	Time zone information, if available.	-07:00
m mm	Corresponds to the minutes portion of the DateTime value. The single "m" has no leading 0 padding but the double "mm" prepends a 0 for minutes less than 10.	m: 25 mm: 25
M MM MMM MMMM	Corresponds to the month portion of the value. M = month with no 0 padding MM = month with leading 0 padding MMM = abbreviation of the month MMMM = full name of the month	M: 7 MM: 07 MMM: Jul MMMM: July
s ss	Corresponds to the seconds portion of the DateTime value. The single "s" has no leading 0 padding but the double "ss" prepends a 0 for seconds less than 10.	s: 9 ss: 09
t tt	Corresponds to the "meridiem" portion of the DateTime value (AM/PM). The single "t" yields the first letter only while the double "tt" yields both.	t: P tt: PM
y yy yyy yyyy	Corresponds to the year portion of the value. y = 2-digit year from 0 to 99 (no padding) yy = 2-digit year from 0 to 99 (0 padding) yyy = minimum 3-digit year (0 padding) yyyy = 4-digit year (0 padding)	y: 2 yy: 02 yyy: 2002 yyyy: 2002
z zz zzz	Represents the hours offset from UTC z = hours offset from UTC, (no padding) zz = hours offset from UTC, (0 padding) zzz = hours and minutes offset from UTC	z: -7 zz: -07 zzz: -07:00
:	Default time separator (culture specific)	:

Listing 6-25. Custom DateTime Format Codes Example

```
// Create a date time object from a string
DateTime dt = DateTime.Parse("July 4, 2002 6:25:09.475 PM");
// Make the date time use the local time zone
dt = DateTime.SpecifyKind(dt, DateTimeKind.Local);
// Print the "round-trip" format for the DateTime:
Console.WriteLine("Custom Formats for {0:O}", dt);

Console.WriteLine("d-dddd.      {0,-8:%d} {0,-8:dd} {0,-8:ddd} {0,-8:dddd}", dt);
Console.WriteLine("f-fffffff.   {0,-8:%f} {0,-8:ff} {0,-8:fff} {0,-8:fffffff}", dt);
Console.WriteLine("F-FFFFFFF.   {0,-8:%F} {0,-8:FF} {0,-8:FFF} {0,-8:FFFFFFF}", dt);
Console.WriteLine("g.           {0,-8:%g}", dt);
Console.WriteLine("h,hh,H,HH.   {0,-8:%h} {0,-8:hh} {0,-8:%H} {0,-8:HH}", dt);
Console.WriteLine("K.           {0,-8:%K}", dt);
Console.WriteLine("m.           {0,-8:%m} {0,-8:mm}", dt);
Console.WriteLine("M.           {0,-8:%M} {0,-8:MM} {0,-8:MMM} {0,-8:MMMM}", dt);
Console.WriteLine("s.           {0,-8:%s} {0,-8:ss}", dt);
Console.WriteLine("t.           {0,-8:%t} {0,-8:tt}", dt);
Console.WriteLine("y.           {0,-8:%y} {0,-8:yy} {0,-8:yyy} {0,-8:yyyy}", dt);
Console.WriteLine("z.           {0,-8:%z} {0,-8:zz} {0,-8:zzz}", dt);
```

```
Custom Formats for 2002-07-04T18:25:09.4750000-07:00
d-dddd.      4        04       Thu      Thursday
f-fffffff.   4        47       475      4750000
F-FFFFFFF.   4        47       475      475
g.           A.D.
h,hh,H,HH.   6        06       18       18
K.           -07:00
m.           25       25
M.           7        07       Jul      July
s.           9        09
t.           P        PM
y.           2        02       2002     2002
z.           -7       -07      -07:00
```

Figure 6-22. Custom DateTime Format Codes Output

The above example demonstrates the custom DateTime format codes in action, one-at-a-time. However, the real power of the custom formats is revealed when multiple codes are used in conjunction with one another.

Listing 6-26. Combined Custom DateTime Format Codes

```
// Create a date time object from a string
DateTime dt = DateTime.Parse("July 4, 2002 6:25:09.475 PM");
// Simulate pre-built region formats
Console.WriteLine("Short date: {0:M/d/yyyy}", dt);
Console.WriteLine("Long date:  {0:dddd , MMMM dd, yyyy}", dt);
// Custom US formats
Console.WriteLine("MM/dd/yyyy: {0:MM/dd/yyyy}", dt);
Console.WriteLine("Custom:     {0:dddd, MMMM dd @ h:mm tt}", dt);
// Format that can be used for a filename
Console.WriteLine("Filename:   {0:yyyy_MM_dd_HH_mm_ss}", dt);
```

```
Short date: 7/4/2002
Long date:  Thursday , July 04, 2002
MM/dd/yyyy: 07/04/2002
Custom:     Thursday, July 04 @ 6:25 PM
Filename:   2002_07_04_18_25_09
```

Figure 6-23. Combined Custom DateTime Format Codes Output

ToString() Variations

If you only need to format a single value, many of the built-in types support a version of the ToString() method that accepts an argument that represents a format string. The format string for these calls does not accept the curly brace delimiters or the argument number like the string.Format() command. Instead, just provide the format codes you wish to format the data with. This technique only allows formatting of the data, not spacing. So if, in addition to the formatting, spacing is required, use the PadLeft() or PadRight() methods directly on the output of ToString().

DateTime values also support this custom version of ToString(). Additionally, there are other ToXXXXString() methods that can be called using a DateTime value, such as ToLongDateString(). The following code demonstrates these calls.

Listing 6-27. ToString() Variations

```
int i = 12345;
string output = i.ToString("X8");
Console.WriteLine(output);

decimal money = 12345.67M;
output = money.ToString("C");
Console.WriteLine(output);

// Add padding to the output prior to printing
output = money.ToString("C").PadLeft(12);
Console.WriteLine(output);

// You can also call ToString() directly on a literal
output = 123456789.ToString("000-00-0000");
Console.WriteLine(output);

// DateTimes have some special ToString variations
DateTime date = DateTime.Parse("2001-10-12 17:35:44");
output = date.ToString("D");
Console.WriteLine(output);
output = date.ToLongDateString();
Console.WriteLine(output);
output = date.ToShortDateString();
Console.WriteLine(output);
output = date.ToLongTimeString();
Console.WriteLine(output);
output = date.ToShortTimeString();
Console.WriteLine(output);
```

```
00003039
$12,345.67
  $12,345.67
123-45-6789
Friday, October 12, 2001
Friday, October 12, 2001
10/12/2001
5:35:44 PM
5:35 PM
```

Figure 6-24. ToString() Variations Output

String Formatting Using Interpolation

In C# 6.0, a new type of `string` formatting was introduced, known as `string` interpolation. Instead of using index numbers that map to the list of arguments passed to the `string`.Format() method, the values you wish to insert are written directly inline in the format `string` itself. This simplifies the task of mapping argument numbers to the actual arguments and eliminates the possibility of accessing elements beyond the legal list of arguments.

Interpolation does not actually utilize an explicit method call. Instead, the formatting is done implicitly when a string literal is preceded by a "$" character. Inside the interpolation string, the "{ }" delimiters will directly reference the literals, constants or variables that you wish to format, including optional spacing and format codes, using the same syntax as traditional formatting.

Listing 6-28. String Interpolation Example

```
decimal money = 12345.67M;
string name = "John Doe";
int hours = 80;
DateTime payday = DateTime.Parse("May 1, 2015");

string s = $"{name} earned {money:C} on {payday:d} for {hours} hours of work.";
Console.WriteLine(s);
```

```
John Doe earned $12,345.67 on 5/1/2015 for 80 hours of work.
```

Figure 6-25. String Interpolation Output

As you can see in the example, no call to string.Format is executed, and there are no arguments being passed. Instead, each of the local variables are inserted directly into the string in their respective locations. Also, the values being interpolated do not have to be local variables. Any value that is visible in scope where this process is being implemented can be used. Visual Studio 2015 (and newer) even provides IntelliSense popups when the [{] key is pressed. Like regular string formatting, if you need to put a literal "{" or "}" in the output you need to use two of those characters in the interpolation string: "{{" and "}}".

I have been a huge proponent of the string.Format() command since inception – so much so that I developed a version that was compatible with Visual Basic 6 which I worked with frequently way back then. With interpolation I feel that text formatting has reached a new level of sophistication which even new programmers can appreciate. Let's face it, the argument substitution of string.Format() can be a bit daunting. Interpolation brings the power without as much pain.

6.5 StringBuilder

One of the biggest drawbacks to the string data type is its immutability. Once created, a string variable's contents cannot be changed. As you have seen, you can assign a new string to an existing string variable, but every time this is done a memory and CPU penalty is incurred. In other languages, such as C and C++, the character data of a string can be manipulated by changing the value at a given character's index. However, even then you are not allowed to modify the length of the `string`, just the individual characters. So, what is a programmer to do? Just accept the performance hit associated with continually allocating new strings? Absolutely not! What we need is a buffered `string` which the .NET Framework provides with the StringBuilder class.

The StringBuilder type, defined in the System.Text namespace, uses an internal character buffer to contain its text data. The buffer is at least as large as the data it contains and can grow as demands are made upon it. By default, a StringBuilder object will allocate 16 characters for its buffer and will double in size anytime a change will result in a buffer overrun. The largest possible `string` that a StringBuilder can contain is roughly 2 billion characters, although allocating such a large chunk of memory can lead to a host of problems such as OutOfMemoryExceptions. For practical purposes the size of the object's buffer should be limited to far smaller chunks of memory, thousands or millions of characters. This is more of a limitation to how the CLR allocates memory and deals with fragmentation than a problem with the StringBuilder type itself. Once manipulation of the StringBuilder is complete, calling ToString() on the object will retrieve the text contents to be used elsewhere in your program.

StringBuilder Creation

Creation of a StringBuilder object requires the use of one of its constructors, complete with the `new` operator. As of C# 6.0 there are six different ways to create a StringBuilder, but the following three are the most commonly used.

Syntax #1: `StringBuilder <name> = new StringBuilder();`

Syntax #2: `StringBuilder <name> = new StringBuilder(<capacity>);`

Syntax #3: `StringBuilder <name> = new StringBuilder(<initial string>);`

The first syntax creates a StringBuilder with a blank buffer of 16 characters. This is the appropriate constructor to use if you are unable to predetermine the final size of the `string` data and have no initial character data to initialize the buffer with.

The second example creates a StringBuilder object with a buffer set to the size provided as the constructor's argument. This versions is especially useful if you have an idea ahead of time what the final `string` size will be.

The final constructor is used when you have an initial `string` with which to prepopulate the StringBuilder. When a `string` is passed to this version of the constructor, the buffer is sized to the input text length, so the object's Capacity and Length properties will be equal. If a `null` `string` is passed to the constructor then the buffer text is initialized with `string`.Empty and a default size of 16.

StringBuilder Members

Unlike the string data type, all of the members of StringBuilder are instance members, which means you must use a variable of type StringBuilder to access them.

Table 6-10. Key Members of StringBuilder

Name	Description
Append()	Appends the given value to the end of the StringBuilder. If the value is not a string or char the ToString() member is automatically called on that value prior to its appending. This method may trigger an automatic re-allocation of memory for the buffer.
AppendFormat()	Uses the string.Format() syntax to add a new string to the end of the StringBuilder.
AppendLine()	Appends a new line to the end of the string.
Capacity	Gets or sets the number of characters in the StringBuilder's buffer. This cannot shrink the buffer size, only increase its capacity.
Clear()	Clears the contents of the StringBuilder's buffer and sets the Length property to 0, but does not shrink the buffer capacity.
EnsureCapacity()	Ensures that the buffer contains at least as many characters as the value provided. If the capacity is already larger than the given value, no action occurs.
Insert()	Inserts a value at the specified location in the StringBuilder's buffer. If the value is not a string or char the ToString() member is automatically called on that value prior to its insertion. This method may trigger an automatic re-allocation of memory for the buffer.
Length	Gets the number of "used" characters in the StringBuilder.
Remove()	Removes a range of characters from the StringBuilder's buffer. Any characters remaining in the buffer to the "right" of the removed data is moved to the start of the removal range.
Replace()	Replaces all occurrences of a given string fragment with another. If the size of the search fragment is different than the replacement fragment then the buffer contents are adjusted accordingly.
ToString()	Extracts the string data from this StringBuilder.

Listing 6-29. StringBuilder Example

```
StringBuilder sb1 = new StringBuilder();
StringBuilder sb2 = new StringBuilder(100);
StringBuilder sb3 = new StringBuilder(null);
Console.WriteLine($"sb3 Length: {sb3.Length}   Capacity: {sb3.Capacity}");

StringBuilder sb4 = new StringBuilder("This is a good place for a string");
Console.WriteLine($"sb4: {sb4}");
Console.WriteLine($"sb4 Length: {sb4.Length}   Capacity: {sb4.Capacity}");

// Insert the word 'really' after  'is':
sb4.Insert(8, "really ");
Console.WriteLine($"sb4: {sb4}");
Console.WriteLine($"sb4 Length: {sb4.Length}   Capacity: {sb4.Capacity}");

// Add several characters to the end
sb4.Append("...");
Console.WriteLine($"sb4: {sb4}");
Console.WriteLine($"sb4 Length: {sb4.Length}   Capacity: {sb4.Capacity}");

// To extract the string from the StringBuilder:
string output = sb4.ToString();
```

```
sb3 Length: 0   Capacity: 16
sb4: This is a good place for a string
sb4 Length: 33   Capacity: 33
sb4: This is really a good place for a string
sb4 Length: 40   Capacity: 40
sb4: This is really a good place for a string...
sb4 Length: 43   Capacity: 80
```

Figure 6-26. StringBuilder Output

StringBuilder Performance

Many times I have stated that StringBuilder is superior in performance to the `string` data type if many manipulations occur. That last statement is critical. For text that does not change StringBuilder objects are far more inefficient, since they will underutilize their allocated memory and have a larger code execution footprint. However, as soon as repeated concatenation occurs, the `string` type is left in the dust. In the next example, a single character is appended to a `string` a number of times and the same is done with a StringBuilder. This code was executed on a fairly beefy i7 processor with 16GB of RAM, and even then the `string` type shows its weakness with mutable data.

Listing 6-30. StringBuilder vs. string Performance

```
int[] iterations = { 1000, 10000, 100000, 1000000 };
DateTime start, end;
foreach (int count in iterations) {
  Console.WriteLine($"{count:N0} Iterations");
  // string concatenation
  string s = string.Empty;
  start = DateTime.Now;
  for (int i = 0; i < count; i++) {
    s += 'A';
  }
  end = DateTime.Now;
  Console.WriteLine($"string: {(end-start).TotalMilliseconds:N0} ms");
  GC.Collect();
  // StringBuilder appends
  StringBuilder sb = new StringBuilder();
  start = DateTime.Now;
  for (int i = 0; i < count; i++) {
    sb.Append('A');
  }
  end = DateTime.Now;
  Console.WriteLine($"StringBuilder: {(end-start).TotalMilliseconds:N0} ms");
  Console.WriteLine(new string('=', 30));
  GC.Collect();
}
```

```
1,000 Iterations
string: 2 ms
StringBuilder: 0 ms
==============================
10,000 Iterations
string: 20 ms
StringBuilder: 0 ms
==============================
100,000 Iterations
string: 1,801 ms
StringBuilder: 1 ms
==============================
1,000,000 Iterations
string: 455,585 ms
StringBuilder: 5 ms
==============================
```

Figure 6-27. StringBuilder vs. string Performance Output

First, let's be clear that the StringBuilder does not operate instantaneously, even if the output claims 0ms elapsed. This is due to the system clock not having a high-enough resolution to detect the actual time elapsed. It is clear that for a small number of iterations, `string` can hold its own against a StringBuilder. However, as soon as the iteration count jumps above 1,000, there is no contest. In fact, at 1,000,000 iterations, the `string` code takes a whopping 7½ minutes compared to StringBuilder's 5ms (or 91,117 times as long). Again, this code will execute at different speeds on different hardware, but the proportions between the two techniques will remain relatively similar. What's the moral of the story? Don't use `string` variables to perform repeated concatenations!

6.6 String Internment

This last topic is a fairly advanced one, and will not likely affect your day-to-day programming tasks. However, it is sometimes important to recognize what the CLR is doing to your string data under the covers. Text data tends to be one of the largest consumers of memory in programs. This is especially true when the same text is used repeatedly throughout an application.

In addition to stack and heap storage which we've touched on previously, the CLR maintains a data structure in memory called the "intern pool", which is a table of unique strings. By default, any `string` literal encountered by the compiler will automatically be placed in this pool. Therefore, any `string` variable that is assigned this value will also share that interned memory. Remember, any change to the data of a `string` actually creates another `string` in memory which that variable then points to, resulting in a non-interned `string`. By this description, any strings created at runtime will generally be non-interned and consume its own memory in the heap.

There is a `static` method of the `string` datatype that provides a mechanism for interning text data, called `string`.Intern(). This will intern the `string` provided as an argument and returns the reference to the interned `string` data, or a reference to an existing interned `string` that contains the exact same text. Be careful, however, as any interned `string` may live in memory for the life of your application (or even beyond as the CLR may remain in memory after a program terminates).

To determine if a string is already interned, call `string`.IsInterned(). If the `string` argument is found in the intern pool a reference to that `string` is returned, otherwise `null`. This is contrary to most examples in the .NET Framework where an "Is…()" method returns a `bool`.

Again, this topic is not critical to your programming success. However, in a managed environment like .NET, it is always a good idea to understand what "magic" is being performed behind the scenes to make your applications work smoothly and efficiently.

6.7 Summary

Considering that a complete chapter was devoted fully to the handling of text data it should be obvious that it is a very important concept to not only understand but to master.
Even Microsoft, one of the pioneers of graphical user interfaces (GUI), adopted a very textual environment in its modern UIs, like Windows 8 and 10, especially in their mobile offerings.

Characters (char) are the basis for text in C# and they represent a single glyph or symbol of text. The string datatype embodies the concept of stringing together many characters as a whole unit. Text can be searched, indexed, compared trimmed, case changed, split into multiple strings or joined back together. Modifying string variables is not efficient due to their immutable nature so care must be taken when repeatedly changing text. Text can be formatted with the string.Format() command, variables' ToString() methods or using string interpolation with "$". Finally, for text data that will frequently change, the StringBuilder class provides a buffered string, replete with methods for appending, inserting and deleting text.

7

7. Flow Control

Most of the programs we have experimented with up to this point have been fairly simplistic and linear. In other words, the program begins at the first line of the Main() method, followed by some number of statements, then it terminates when the Main() method exits. Very little has been done with regards to making decisions about how the program should proceed based on user input or repeating a group of statements a number of times to accomplish a given task. These concepts are critical for making your software useful, and with a little practice you will be utilizing them in your own code, making simplistic programs into full-fledged applications. In fact, it is nearly impossible to write robust applications without the topics that will be discussed in this chapter.

7.1 Boolean Logic

The ability to make decisions in your programs is a crucial process that delivers a much more robust and sophisticated application, both in terms of usability and functionality. For instance, consider a program that asks the user to enter their name, regardless of whether it is done in a console window or Windows application. After the user commits their input you may have several things to consider:

- Is the text entered an empty `string`?
- Does the text conform to expected input patterns?
- Does the input text match a record in your database?

Notice that each of these items is essentially a question you are asking about the user's input. At each step, a "yes" or "no" response to each question may require different responses and actions taken by the program. However, before we can jump into the syntax for asking questions in our C# code, we need to fully understand the possible answers: `true` and `false`.

Boolean (Logical) Expressions

When you ask a person a question that should result in a yes/no response, that is known as a "closed question". Computers are very good at representing closed questions as their entire makeup is essentially a series of 0's and 1's, where 0 represents "no" and 1 represents "yes". Computers, at least of the digital variety, are not so good dealing with questions that result in "maybe" answers without a great deal of added logic. Fortunately, most of the time a simple yes or no will be sufficient for determining what action to take based on the question. However, before we continue, let's start using the values "`true`" and "`false`" to represent "yes" and "no", respectively. As you may recall from section 4.9, these values are what comprise the data type `bool`. The `bool` type name is shorthand for Boolean, and is named after a prominent 19th century mathematician and logician George Boole. Clearly, Mr. Boole did not have a direct role in the development of computers and programming languages; however, his contributions to the world of algebraic logic was so influential that it earned him immortality in modern computer science. In fact, many computer languages support a Boolean type, even if it is not explicitly named thusly.

A Boolean expression, or logical expression, is any expression that results in a `true` or `false` answer. In fact, the simplest logical expressions are the values `true` and `false`. The next simplest Boolean expressions are those that utilize the equality and comparison operators (==, !=, <, >, <=, >=), such as:

```
x == 5          y > 10        str.Length <= 20
```

Finally, any method that returns a `bool` value is also a logical expression.

Compound Logical Expressions and Logical Operators

In Boolean logic, the answer to any question is either `true` or `false`. That part is fairly straight-forward. However, sometimes the question being proposed is a complex question, comprised of several parts. Consider the following question:

Do you have experience repairing cars and can you start on Monday?

This inquiry is clearly asking two individual questions:

- *Do you have experience repairing cars?*
- *Can you start on Monday?*

Notice that the two questions are joined by the conjunction "and", implying that for you to be hirable you must satisfy both questions in a positive manner. In fact, if you cannot repair cars there's really no reason to ask you the second question. This represents a concept known as short-circuiting, which is an optimization technique used by C# to eliminate unnecessary work.

Now consider the following question:

Can you write programs using C++ or C#?

Again, this inquiry is actually two separate questions:

- *Can you write programs using C++?*

- *Can you write programs using C#?*

The difference here is that the conjunction joining the questions is "or", which implies that answering either question in the affirmative will yield a positive result. You may be able to answer both questions positively, but that is not a requirement. If either question yields a `true` response then the other answer is insignificant (at least in terms of C# logic).

Let's formalize these concepts as they relate to C# as well as introduce a few other Boolean logical operators.

And – &&

The "and" operator, represented by two ampersands "&&", is a binary operator used to compare the results of two independent questions, otherwise known as Boolean expressions. For the result of the operation to be `true`, ***both*** subordinate expressions must also be `true`. If either Boolean expression is `false` then the result is also `false`. Assume two logical expressions with the values `A` and `B`. They can be evaluated together with the "&&" operator as follows, with the result being placed in `R`:

```
R = A && B
```

The only possible way for `R` to be set to `true` is if both `A` and `B` are `true`. The following is the truth table for "&&" that demonstrates this result:

Table 7-1. Truth Table for &&

A	B	A && B
false	false	false
false	true	false
true	false	false
true	true	true

The "&&" operator is known as a short-circuiting operator. In other words, if the left-hand Boolean expression `A` is `false`, there is no reason to evaluate the right-hand expression `B` as there is no value of `B` that can result in an overall `true` value. There is also a non-short-circuiting version of the "and" operator, known as "bitwise and", represented by a single ampersand "&", but since it typically results in slower code it is infrequently used except for bitwise operations.

Or – ||

The "or" operator, represented by two pipes "||", is a binary operator used to compare two Boolean expressions. This operator is also formally known as the "inclusive or" operator, but it is hardly ever referred to in that manner. For the result of the operation to be `true`, ***either*** subordinate expression must be `true`. If both logical expressions are `false` then the result is also `false`. Using the same expression names as before, this is how the "or" operator is implemented:

```
R = A || B
```

The only possible way for R to be set to false is if both A and B are false. The following is the truth table for "||" that demonstrates this result:

Table 7-2. Truth Table for ||

A	B	A||B
false	false	false
false	true	true
true	false	true
true	true	true

The "||" operator is also a short-circuiting operator. In other words, if the left-hand Boolean expression A is true, there is no reason to evaluate the right-hand expression B as there is no value of B that can result in an overall false value. There is also a non-short-circuiting version of the "or" operator, known as "bitwise or", represented by a single pipe "|", but just like the "&" operator, it is hardly ever used.

Exclusive Or – ^

The "exclusive or" or "xor" operator, represented by a single caret "^", is a binary operator used to compare two Boolean expressions. In plain English, this operator means "one or the other, but not both". For the result of the operation to be true, ***either*** subordinate expression must be true, but ***not both of them***. It is for this reason it is given the "exclusive" moniker, since the truth value of one value must be exclusive of the other. Here is what the operation looks like:

```
R = A ^ B
```

The following is the truth table for "^":

Table 7-3. Truth Table for ^

A	B	A ^ B
false	false	false
false	true	true
true	false	true
true	true	false

The "^" operator is not a short-circuiting operator since both expressions must be evaluated to ensure they have opposite values. In day-to-day use, the standard "inclusive or" operator is used with much higher frequency since programmers typically are looking for either value to be true without necessarily caring if both are true. However, in disciplines relating to graphics and encryption "xor" is used much more frequently.

Not – !

The final operator we'll look at is the "logical negation" operator or "not" operator, represented by a single exclamation point "!". Unlike the other logical operators, this is a unary operator used to negate or reverse the value of a single logical expression. So, any logical expression immediately following the "!" operator will have its value negated. Here is what the operation looks like:

```
R = !A
```

The following is the truth table for "!":

Table 7-4. Truth Table for !

A	!A
false	true
true	false

This operator is heavily used in programming as it can be helpful to know what the opposite value of a Boolean expressions is. Consider a program that loops while a given `bool` variable *quit* is `false`. Since most loops only continue executing while their test condition evaluates to `true`, it would be necessary to negate *quit* to continue iterating, like this:

```
while (!quit) { /* loop body */ }
```

For your reference, the following table encompasses all four of the logical operators. Note that the unary "not" operator only references the expression `A`.

Table 7-5. Complete Truth Table

A	B	A && B	A || B	A ^ B	!A
false	false	false	false	false	true
false	true	false	true	true	true
true	false	false	true	true	false
true	true	true	true	false	false

Order of Operations

When tying multiple logical expressions together using the operators illustrated above it is important to understand their order of precedence, just as you would with standard arithmetic operators. The following table lists these operators in order from highest precedence to lowest.

Table 7-6. Logical Operator Precedence

Operator Precedence
!
&
^
|
&&
||

So, in an expression such as:

```
A || B && C ^ D
```

The operations will be executed as if the following parentheses were added:

```
A || ( B && ( C ^ D ) )
```

This example demonstrates a key point – if the logical expression is overly complex it may be best to manually introduce some parenthetical grouping, making the compound expression both easier to read and debug.

I almost always use parentheses in compound logical expressions. It removes ambiguity from the expression and, quite frankly, just looks better. Consider these two expressions:

1. `x > 0 || y > 0 && y < 10`
2. `(x > 0) || (y > 0 && y < 10)`

Both expressions will evaluate to the same result, but I believe #2 is both easier to read and clearer in its intentions. It should be apparent that the y conditions are to be evaluated as a whole, reducing the expression to a more manageable "`A||B`" pattern.

7.2 Decision Making

Now that we know how to create expressions using Boolean logic, it is time to start using them to make decisions in our code. There are several techniques for making decisions based on the outcome of a logical expression, such as the "`if`" statement, the "`if / else`" construct, the ternary conditional operator "`?:`" and the "`switch`" statement. Each of these techniques has its pros and cons and one may be better suited for a given situation than another. Regardless of which technique is used, the outcome is the same – a decision is made and your code can respond to it accordingly.

if

As mentioned earlier, there are several techniques for making decisions based on the outcome of a Boolean expression, but the "`if`" statement is the most versatile, by far. This statement is used to evaluate the result of a simple or compound logical expression and execute one or more statements only if the result of the logical expression is `true`. The logical expression being tested ***must*** be contained within a set of parenthesis. The statement(s) to execute when `true` is known as the "then" statement(s). If the expression evaluates to `false`, then the statements following the "then" statement(s) are executed next, bypassing the "then" code entirely.

```
if (<Logical Expression>) < then statement >;
```

OR

```
if (<Logical Expression>)
    < then statement >;
```

If the "then" portion of code contains more than one statement, wrap that code in a code block (curly braces):

```
if (<Logical Expression>)
{
    < then statements >;
}
```

I almost always use code blocks (last example) regardless of the number of lines within the then *block. This is an example of using structured programming techniques to make code more readable. I also prefer to place the open brace "{" on the following line even with the "i" in "if". This is a common standard but it is also common to see the open "{" immediately following the closing ")" of the "if" statement.*

The following example shows how to use an `if` statement to evaluate both simple and compound logical expressions, using all of the various syntaxes and formatting shown above.

Listing 7-1. if Statement Examples

```
int x = 5, y = 10;

// Simple logical expressions
if (x == 5)  Console.WriteLine("x equals 5");

if (x > 0) {
  Console.WriteLine("x is greater than 0");
}

if (x != 10)
{
  Console.WriteLine("x is not equal to 10");
}

// Compound expressions
if (x >= 0 && y >= 0)
{
  Console.WriteLine("x & y are positive");
}

if (x < 0 && y < 0)
{
  Console.WriteLine("x & y are negative");
}

if ((x > 0 && x <= 10) && (y > 0 && y <= 10))
{
  Console.WriteLine("x & y are between 1 and 10");
}
```

```
x equals 5
x is greater than 0
x is not equal to 10
x & y are positive
x & y are between 1 and 10
```

Figure 7-1. if Statement Output

if – else

So, with the `if` statement we are able to test a particular condition and execute code based on when that condition evaluates to `true`. What happens if we also want to take a particular action when the expression evaluates to `false`? We could have a second `if` statement immediately following the first `if` statement which tests for the exact opposite condition of the first `if`'s logical expression like this:

Listing 7-2. Handling the False Condition

```
if (x > 0)
{
  // Do something
}
if (x <= 0)
{
  // Do something else
}
```

The good news is there is a special statement called "`else`" which allows us to do the same thing without the extra `if` statement and its logical expressions.

```
if (<Logical Expression>)
{
    < then statements >;
}
else
{
    < else statements >;
}
```

The "else" block can also consist of a single statement without the use of curly braces, but only the structured example is demonstrated above. This code not only looks cleaner, but it eliminates the possibility of the second `if` condition from accidentally overlapping the first's condition or missing a range of values altogether. With the `if` - `else` construct *only one* of the statement blocks will execute, either the "then" or the "else" block.

Listing 7-3. if – else Example

```
string name = "John";
DateTime bday = DateTime.Parse("5/9/1990");

if (name == "John")
{
  Console.WriteLine("A special welcome for John!");
}
else
{
  Console.WriteLine("Who are you?");
}

if (bday.Month >= 1 && bday.Month <= 3)
{
  Console.WriteLine("You were born in the first quarter.");
}
else
{
  Console.WriteLine("You were not born in the first quarter.");
}
```

```
A special welcome for John!
You were not born in the first quarter.
```

Figure 7-2. if – else Output

if – else if – else

The first two if constructs, `if` and `if - else`, are great for testing one of two conditions, respectively. However, as a programmer you will frequently find yourself needing to test multiple conditions. Enter the `if - else if - else` pattern:

```
if (<Logical Expression>)
{
     < then statements >;
}
else if (<Logical Expression>)
{
     < then statements >;
}
else
{
     < else statements >;
}
```

As you can see in the example syntax, the initial `if` statement block is followed by an "`else if`" statement block which contains its very own logic expression. In fact, if you ignored the `else` keyword it would look like a regular `if` statement. Finally, the `else` block is always at the end of the construct. Actually, `else` is not a requirement of this construct so that block can be omitted if it is not required. Essentially, the `else` statement acts as a "catch-all" which is executed when all other conditional expressions evaluate to `false`.

Since C# ties all of the blocks of the `if` - `else if` - `else` pattern together into a single construct, only one of the logical expressions will evaluate to `true`; therefore, only that block's code will execute. It is entirely possible to write the `else if`'s logical expression in such a way that it overlaps the condition of the `if`'s logical expression. In this case the first logical expression encountered that evaluates to `true` will be the code block that executes and the rest are ignored. It is also possible to have an unlimited number of `else if` blocks if the logic of your code requires more than three conditions. Just remember, the `if` statement is always first and the `else` statement is always last with any number of `else if` statements in between.

The following example determines the Cartesian quadrant of a sample point, a common problem given to students in Algebra classes.

Listing 7-4. if - else if - else Example

```
int x = 2, y = -4;

// Determine the quadrant of the (x, y) coordinate
if (x > 0 && y > 0)
{
  Console.WriteLine($"({x}, {y}) is in quadrant I");
}
else if (x < 0 && y > 0)
{
  Console.WriteLine($"({x}, {y}) is in quadrant II");
}
else if (x < 0 && y < 0)
{
  Console.WriteLine($"({x}, {y}) is in quadrant III");
}
else if (x > 0 && y < 0)
{
  Console.WriteLine($"({x}, {y}) is in quadrant IV");
}
else
{
  Console.WriteLine($"({x}, {y}) is on one of the axes");
}
```

```
(2, -4) is in quadrant IV
```

Figure 7-3. if -else if - else Output

Nested if Statements

Sometimes, none of the aforementioned "`if`" constructs are sufficient for solving a particular problem. Instead, the required logic may lend itself to another technique called nested `if` statements. Essentially, a standard `if` statement or one of the other `if` constructs is used to narrow down the problem scope. Inside the "then" block another `if` statement is used to further narrow down the possible states until you obtain a desired match. This is especially useful for more complex tests where you need to narrow down the possibilities for the state of one variable before tackling the state of another. In the example in Listing 7-4, the `if` statements test the states of both the *x* and *y* variables in the same complex expression. Using nested `if` statements, the code could be re-written as such:

Listing 7-5. Nested if Statement

```
int x = -6, y = 10;

// Determine the quadrant of the (x, y) coordinate
if (x == 0 || y == 0)
{
  Console.WriteLine($"({x}, {y}) is on one of the axes");
}
else if (x > 0)
{
  if (y > 0)
  {
    Console.WriteLine($"({x}, {y}) is in quadrant I");
  }
  else  // y < 0
  {
    Console.WriteLine($"({x}, {y}) is in quadrant IV");
  }
}
else  // x < 0
{
  if (y > 0)
  {
    Console.WriteLine($"({x}, {y}) is in quadrant II");
  }
  else  // y < 0
  {
    Console.WriteLine($"({x}, {y}) is in quadrant III");
  }
}
```

```
(-6, 10) is in quadrant II
```

Figure 7-4. Nested if Statement Output

Although this code accomplishes the same goal as the previous sample, it does require several more lines of code. However, it is often acceptable to sacrifice brevity if maintainability or simplicity can be achieved. It is always important just to ensure that the construct you choose does not adversely affect performance. Typically, if statements are relatively lightweight and the difference in execution time between the constructs is negligible, especially in the context of business applications.

In reality, there is nothing special about nested if statements as the "then" blocks can contain any C# statements including if.

Testing for Null Values

One of the most important uses of if statements is to test reference type variables for null. If you try to access the members of a null variable the result will be a thrown NullReferenceException. This is typically an undesirable result. Even if you handle the exception with a try block, the application will take a performance hit. Rather than allow the exception it is better to test the object you are referencing prior to accessing its members. The test itself is very simple:

```
if (<variable> == null)
```

Another possibility:

```
if (<variable> != null)
```

Note that <variable> must be a reference type or a nullable value type (see section 4.10) for this statement to compile.

What happens if you are really interested in using one of the members of the variable you must test for null in a logical expression? In this case you can do the test for null first followed by the logical expression involving the variable's member. A good example of this occurs when testing the length of a string variable for a specific value. Since a string can be null, accessing its Length property prior to validating that the string is valid and initialized will cause the dreaded NullReferenceException. Assuming we have a string variable called *str*, the following if statement will test it for null followed by a check of its length:

```
if (str != null && str.Length > 0)
```

The order of the logical expressions is critical. Remember, the && operator is a short-circuiting operator, meaning that if the left-hand expression is false the right-hand expression will not be evaluated. Therefore, the expression "str.Length > 0" is completely ignored if *str* is equal to null. With the string datatype there is a static method called string.IsNullOrEmpty() which does something similar to our test - please review Character 6 for more information.

Strings are not the only data type that benefits from this test - any reference type object that you wish to interrogate should also be tested in a similar manner. If many members of the target variable must be accessed, a single if statement testing for null with all of the member access inside the "then" block will also suffice:

```
if (<variable> != null)
{
    // In this block you can access <variable>'s members with impunity
}
```

The ?? and ?. Operators

We've already looked at a special operator "??" called the null-coalescing operator. Recall that this operator is used to test a variable for null prior to assigning the value to another variable or pass it to a method. In a way, it can be used as a replacement for an if statement.

Consider you have a string variable called *str* and that you are uncertain of its contents. You want to assign its contents to another variable, *output*, but only if it is not null. If it is null, then you wish to assign a default string instead. From what you have learned, an if statement can easily be employed to do just this. However, the "??" operator can do the same thing in a much simpler statement.

Listing 7-6. if vs. ??

```
string str = null;
string output = null;

// Using if
if (str != null)
{
  output = str;
}
else
{
  output = "default";
}

// Using ??
output = str ?? "default";
```

In this example, since *str* is initialized to null, *output* is assigned the value "default" regardless of which comparison technique is used.

Another operator, "?.", introduced in C# 6.0 (also called the null-conditional operator), is used in a very similar manner. However, instead of just testing a variable for null it can also be used to access members of the object in a safe manner. If either the variable or its member is null then the operator will return null. Otherwise the requested member is accessed normally. This is exceptionally useful if you are trying to access the member of a member of the variable, or even further nested members.

The "?." operator actually has several usage patterns. The first is to read properties or fields of a variable. For instance, a string variable contains a Length property. If the string variable, called *str* in this case, is null, reading the Length value as follows will cause a NullReferenceException:

```
int length = str.Length;
```

Instead, we can read the value using the "?." operator into a nullable `int`. If *str* is `null`, then so will be *length*:

```
int? length = str?.Length;
```

You still need to test *length* for `null` before using it, so we have not really avoided any significant work in this case. You will find this operator usage most beneficial when accessing multiple nested members of a variable. Just be aware that this usage scenario only allows read access to variable members. Trying to assign a value to a member using "?." will yield a compiler error.

The next usage pattern of the "?." operator is to access methods of an object. If the object is `null` the method call is simply ignored and any expected result will be `null` as well. If you were to use the same *str* variable and call the StartsWith() method using the standard "." operator, and *str* is `null`, then a NullReferenceException is thrown. Using "?." avoids this issue as the method would not be called. Again, the result will be `null` in this case.

```
bool? startsWith = str?.StartsWith("A");
```

Overall, these operators are used to streamline your C# code, but the underlying compiled code will still use the more verbose `if` logic. Syntactic sugar, such as this, simply makes your logic easy to express and read.

The ?: Operator

One final specialized operator that takes the place of an `if` statement is the "?:" operator. Also known as the conditional operator or the ternary operator, this operator contains a logical expression to evaluate and returns one of two other expressions based on the result of the logical expression. The syntax of this operator is:

```
<result> = <logical expression> ? <true result> : <false result>;
```

Unlike the "??" and "?." operators, the "?:" is not exclusively for use with `null` values. Instead, the logical expression can test any condition, so long as the result of that expression is a `bool`. If the result of the logical expression is `true` then the value of <true result> is returned from the conditional operator. Likewise, if the result of the logical expression is `false`, the value of <false result> is returned from the conditional operator.

Listing 7-7. Conditional Operator

```
string str = null;
int length = 0;

// Using if
if (str == null)
{
  length = 0;
}
else
{
  length = str.Length;
}

// using ?:
length = str == null ? 0 : str.Length;

// Possibly easier to read with parens:
length = (str == null) ? 0 : str.Length;
```

Safe Array Indexer Syntax

One item that was glossed over when arrays were introduced is accessing elements of an array where the array itself, or any of its elements, may be null. When creating an array without a list of values to initialize that array it becomes hazardous to assume any element in the array is properly initialized. In fact, each element will be set to whatever the default value is for the type of array being created. For numeric types, the elements will all be set to 0. However, for reference types, each element will be set to null. If the array is subsequently sparsely populated, there will be many remaining elements with the value null.

So, let's assume we have an array with the following declaration:

```
string[] array = new string[10];
```

This array will initially contain 10 string objects, all set to null. If we were to try to access the Length property of any one of these string elements without first checking for null we would trigger a NullReferenceException.

```
int length = array[0].Length;  // This triggers a NullReferenceExcpetion
```

Let's analyze the problem we would encounter doing this. First, the element at "array[0]" is evaluated. Since we did not pre-initialize the array with legitimate string values that expression will return null. Next, the Length property is accessed on that string returned from the previous expression. The problem is that expression returned null. Since a null object does not actually point to a real object the runtime has no choice but to throw the exception.

Now, let's look at the problem we might encounter when the array itself is null. In that case we can't even get to a particular element in the array because it simply doesn't exist.

Because of this eventuality, a special operator "?[ ]" was created (as of C# 6.0). This one behaves just like the "?." except instead of accessing a member of the of the array we are trying to access an element in the array. If the array is null the operator will short-circuit and return null.

```
int? length = array?[0].Length;
```

So, assuming *array* in this statement is null, the variable *length* will also be set to null. So far, so good. But what happens if the element at index 0 is null? Then, the previous statement would fail with an exception. But, with our handy "?." operator we can ensure that the Length property is never called if the element is null:

```
int? length = array?[0]?.Length;
```

Finally, what if we want the result of the operation to never return null? Instead, maybe we want the expression to return 0 if either the array is uninitialized or the element we are accessing is null. In that case we can exchange the nullable int for a standard int and use the null-coalescing operator to default the result to 0 in the event of null.

```
int length = array?[0]?.Length ?? 0;
```

Wow, that's a lot of question marks in one statement! However, the number of if statements we avoided may make this syntax a bit more appealing. It really depends on what you are trying to accomplish and what level of terseness in your code you are willing to accept.

The specialized operators "??", "?.", "?[]" and "?:" are all extremely useful. However, overuse of these operators can easily lead to unreadable code. Consider this code to constrain an int *between two values* min *and* max*:*

```
int min = 0, max = 10, value = 15;
value = value < min ? min : value > max ? max : value;
```

Although this produces the desired result (value *is set to 10) the code is incredibly hard to follow. Even with strategically placed parenthesis it is tough to read. Sometimes a few* if *statements are preferred just for the readability factor.*

7.3 The switch Statement

One of the more powerful decision-making statements is the switch control statement. This statement is used to execute a specific block of code based on the value of a variable. In a way switch works like a series of if - else if statements testing the same variable for different values. One primary difference is that the variable being evaluated must be a discrete type, such as int, long, char and string. The switch statement is also ideal for enum types which will be discussed at a later time (see Listing 10-6). The values being compared against the variable must be known at compile-time, therefore they are either constants or literals.

Let's start with the basics. The switch statement is declared using the following syntax:

```
switch (<variable>)
{
     // Case labels
}
```

Again, <variable> must be a type that can contain a discrete list of values and must be compatible with const. This means types like int, long, char and string will work, but not DateTime, float or double. Inside the switch code is a list of case labels (the values being compared to the switch variable) and execution is transferred to the first matching label upon reaching of the switch statement. There can also be a default label that acts like the else block for if statements. Each case label block must issue a jump command like break or return prior to the next group of case labels. Failure to do so will yield a compiler error. Just be aware that the break statement will continue executing code immediately after the switch's terminating brace whereas return will exit whatever method the code is executing within. The syntax of a case label block is:

```
case <const value>:
     // Some statements to execute;
     break;  // or return;
```

Notice that the case block does not require delimiting curly braces like most C# blocks. They can be used, but since each case block must end with a jump statement the compiler is able to determine the limits of the blocks without them.

The following is a simple example using an int variable as the target of the switch statement.

Listing 7-8. Simple switch Statement

```
int value = 3;
switch (value)
{
  case 1:
    Console.WriteLine("The value is 1");
    break;
  case 2:
    Console.WriteLine("The value is 2");
    break;
  case 3:
    Console.WriteLine("The value is 3");
    break;
  default:
    Console.WriteLine($"Unexpected value of {value}");
    break;
}
```

```
The value is 3
```

Figure 7-5. Simple switch Output

In the code sample above, the variable *value* is the target of the `switch` statement. Since the value of *value* is 3, execution is transferred to the "`case 3:`" label upon entering the `switch` block. Text is output to the console window and then the `break` command is executed causing the program to continue after the close brace of the `switch` statement block on line 16.

The order of the `case` labels in a `switch` is not significant as there can only be one possible match among the list of cases. If no match is made but there is a `default` label then execution is transferred to that label block. Otherwise all of the `case` labels will be bypassed and code will continue executing after the `switch`'s closing brace. Multiple case labels can be grouped together if they are to execute the same code block upon a match. The following sample illustrates how this is achieved:

Listing 7-9. Grouped case Labels

```
char ch = 'A';
switch (ch)
{
  case 'A': case 'E': case 'I': case 'O': case 'U':
    Console.WriteLine("ch is an uppercase vowel");
    break;
  case 'a':
  case 'e':
  case 'i':
  case 'o':
  case 'u':
    Console.WriteLine("ch is a lowercase vowel");
    break;
  default:
    Console.WriteLine("ch is not a vowel");
    break;
}
```

```
ch is an uppercase vowel
```

Figure 7-6. Grouped case Labels Output

As you can see, the grouped `case` labels can be on the same line or on separate lines. The general consensus is to use whichever is more readable for the given example.

Even though the switch statement is very powerful there are some serious limitations in its implementation in C#. First, no `case` fall-through is permitted. In other words there must be a `break` or similar statement after each `case` block. Therefore, you cannot have a `case` label with some specific statements to execute for that condition and then have execution jump into the next `case` block and execute the statements contained within that block. Second, all `case` labels must use either constants or literals. This implies that the conditions you are testing cannot be evaluated at runtime. Third, there is no way to test for a range of values without explicitly identifying each possible value in that range. So, if you want to test for values 1 – 10, you must have ten discrete case labels.

switch Jump Commands

break

So far in all of the examples each case block has terminated with a break statement. As mentioned, when break is encountered within a case block execution is redirected immediately to the end of the entire switch block, bypassing any remaining case labels.

return

The other jump command discussed is the return statement. This statement causes program execution to jump to the very end of the method that the switch statement is contained in. This can be useful if you are in a method where the switch statement is being used to calculate and return a value based on the value of the switch variable.

goto case

Another less frequently used jump command is "goto case <x>", where <x> represents one of the defined case label constants within the switch statement. This is useful if you want to execute the logic of a given case label block and then execute the statements within another case label afterwards.

Listing 7-10. goto case Example

```
string packageType = "priority";
decimal fee = 0M;

switch (packageType)
{
  case "firstclass":
    fee += 0.59M;
    break;
  case "priority":
    fee += 5.99M;
    goto case "firstclass";
  case "freight":
    fee += 19.99M;
    break;
}
Console.WriteLine($"The fee is {fee:C}");
```

```
The fee is $6.58
```

Figure 7-7. goto case Example Output

Notice when *packageType* is set to "priority" that execution is first passed to the "priority" label and 5.99 is added to *fee*. Then code execution is redirected to the "firstclass" label causing another 0.59 to be added to *fee* before finally exiting the `switch` statement. Using this technique any number of `case` labels can be chained together. Just be very careful to avoid endless loops which can happen if label *A* jumps to label *B* which jumps back to label *A*!

continue

The `continue` jump command is only useful if the switch statement is contained within a loop construct like `while` or `for`. It causes program execution to immediately jump to the next iteration of the loop that the `switch` block resides in. Later in the chapter we'll look at loop constructs and discuss `continue` in more detail.

throw

The `throw` command is used to throw an exception from the current location. Since we have not discussed structured exception handling yet we'll save this command for that section.

7.4 Iteration Statements

An "iteration statement" is a fancy term for a "loop". Within your code it is frequently desirable to execute a given block of code a number of times to achieve desired results. Consider reading a file from the hard drive one byte at a time. It would be incredibly impractical to write a sequential set of C# statements to read a file that may be arbitrary in length byte-by-byte. So if you need to read 1000 bytes that would equate to 1000 read statements. With a loop, however, you can surround a single read command with a special loop construct and achieve the same results with far less code. This is only one small example of how loops can improve the robustness of your code.

The for Loop

The `for` loop is one of the most recognizable C-style statements. It is so popular that it is also available in C++, Java and, of course, C#. The `for` loop is used to execute a block of code a specific number of times based on the value of a logical condition which is evaluated immediately prior to each iteration of the loop. The syntax of the `for` loop takes time to get used to, so don't feel you have to understand it fully right off the bat. Here's the formal syntax of the `for` loop:

```
for (<initialization>; <logical condition>; <iterators>)
{
    // for loop body contains statement(s) to execute;
}
```

As you can see, the for statement is composed of 4 sections, 3 sections that control the loop and the loop body. The for loop body does not actually require braces if only one statement is contained within, but including them can make the code easier to read.

<initialization>: This section is where the variable(s) being used to control the loop is initialized and is only executed once before any other part of the loop construct. Typically, the loop control variable is an integral value, like int or long, and would be initialized to a value that makes sense for the loop. If you are using the loop to iterate through the indices of an array, this variable would typically be initialized to 0. The variable(s) used within this section can be declared outside and above the loop or they can be fully declared and initialized within this section. Just be aware that any variable declared in this section can only be used within the for loop.

<logical condition>: This section contains a logical expression that evaluates to a bool and it is executed at the start of every iteration of the loop. The logical expression typically utilizes the variables initialized in the initialization section. If the expression returns true the loop body will execute. If it evaluates to false the loop terminates and control is returned immediately after the close brace of the for block. It is entirely possible that the loop body will never execute if this expression initially evaluates to false.

<iterators>: This section contains statements that are executed at the end of each iteration of the loop. Typically, it will contain increment or decrement statements (i++, ++i, i--, --i) or arithmetic assignment statements (i+=2, i-=10) involving the variables initialized in the initialization section.

Loop body: This section contains the statement or statements that are executed for every iteration of the loop. Since the variables declared in the initialization section are available for use within the loop body you can use them for specific purposes like indices of an array or a general purpose counter. It is considered bad practice to modify the loop control variables from within the body.

The following are samples of for loops solving fairly typical problems requiring iteration.

One-Dimensional Arrays and for Loops

Listing 7-11. Looping Through One-Dimensional Array

```
int[] primes = { 1, 2, 3, 5, 7, 11, 13, 17, 19, 23 };

// Loop through each index of primes:
for (int i = 0; i < primes.Length; ++i)
{
  Console.WriteLine($"Prime #{i+1} = {primes[i]}");
}
```

```
Prime #1 = 1
Prime #2 = 2
Prime #3 = 3
Prime #4 = 5
Prime #5 = 7
Prime #6 = 11
Prime #7 = 13
Prime #8 = 17
Prime #9 = 19
Prime #10 = 23
```

Figure 7-8. Looping Through One-Dimensional Array Output

Let's break down this `for` loop in detail. We are creating a loop to iterate through each element of the array *primes*. The initialization section contains the statement "`int i = 0`". We will be using this variable *i* as the index value to access the array elements, and we are assuming that the array will start at index 0 (safe assumption for all standard arrays).

The logical condition that keeps the loop running is: "`i < primes.Length`". Essentially, what this is saying is "while the value of *i* is less than the length of *primes* continue executing the loop". Note that the comparison operator employed is "<" and not "<=". This is an important distinction. Since we intend to access the elements of *primes* through its indexer operator "[ ]" we need to ensure that only legal indices are requested. Since this array contains 10 elements we only want to access indices 0 – 9. Since the Length property returns the number of elements in the array (10) we need to make sure we only use values up to one less than that. That is why we continue executing the loop only while *i* is **less than** the array's length. If we used "<=" then we'd eventually access index 10 which would cause an IndexOutOfRangeException to be thrown.

The next section is the iterator section where we are augmenting the value of *i* by one after each iteration of the loop. In practical terms it doesn't matter if you use *i*++ or ++*i* as the statement will be executed by itself after each iteration and before the next check of the logical condition. Technically ++*i* is faster but we're talking microseconds (if even that). Without this section *i* would never be incremented and the loop would execute forever.

Finally, we get to the body of the loop. It is only one statement so the braces could be omitted, but for consistency they are included. Using interpolation, the value of *i* + 1 is printed (because *i* is 0-based) followed by the value at *primes*[*i*]. If "+ 1" is not present, then the output would start with "`Prime #0 = 1`".

Using for Loops for Calculations

The next example will print a list of Fibonacci numbers using a `for` loop. The Fibonacci sequence of numbers starts with { 1, 1 } and then each successive number is equal to the sum of the previous two. This will be different from the previous loop as the loop control variable is only used as a counter to limit the number of times the loop will execute.

Listing 7-12. Using for to Calculate the Fibonacci Sequence

```
// Fibonacci sequence
int fib0 = 1;
int fib1 = 1;
// Print first two "seed" numbers
Console.Write($"{fib0} {fib1} ");
for (int i = 0; i < 10; ++i)
{
  // Next number in sequence is the sum of the previous 2
  int sum = fib0 + fib1;
  fib0 = fib1;
  fib1 = sum;
  Console.Write($"{sum} ");
}
Console.WriteLine();
```

```
1 1 2 3 5 8 13 21 34 55 89 144
```

Figure 7-9. Fibonacci Sequence Output

So far, each loop's iterator section has used simple increment statements. What if we need to skip values? This next example calculates the squares of the first 10 even numbers.

Listing 7-13. Calculating Even Squares

```
for (int i = 2; i <= 20; i+=2)
{
  Console.WriteLine($"The square of {i} is {i * i}");
}
```

```
The square of 2 is 4
The square of 4 is 16
The square of 6 is 36
The square of 8 is 64
The square of 10 is 100
The square of 12 is 144
The square of 14 is 196
The square of 16 is 256
The square of 18 is 324
The square of 20 is 400
```

Figure 7-10. Calculating Even Squares Output

Once again this loop uses the loop control variable as a counter *and* as part of the calculation taking place within the loop body. Also, notice that the iterator section augments *i* by 2 after each iteration.

Two-Dimensional Arrays and for Loops

Now, let's move into trickier territory. Suppose we have a two-dimensional array and we want to first populate the array using `for` loops and then output the array using more `for` loops. The good news is that this technique is actually relatively straight-forward using nested `for` loops. When you have a 2D array each element is accessed via row and a column index values where the row represents the first dimension and the column represents the second. We need to create two `for` loops: one whose loop control variable represents the row index and another nested loop whose loop control variable represents the column index.

Listing 7-14. Two-Dimensional Arrays and for Loops

```
int[,] mult = new int[12, 12];
// Create a multiplication table
for (int row = 0; row <= mult.GetUpperBound(0); ++row)
{
  for (int col = 0; col <= mult.GetUpperBound(1); ++col)
  {
    mult[row, col] = (row + 1) * (col + 1);  // + 1 because we don't want 0's
  }
}

// Print the multiplication table
for (int row = 0; row <= mult.GetUpperBound(0); ++row)
{
  for (int col = 0; col <= mult.GetUpperBound(1); ++col)
  {
    Console.Write($"{mult[row, col],3} ");
  }
  Console.WriteLine();
}
```

```
 1   2   3   4   5   6   7   8   9  10  11  12
 2   4   6   8  10  12  14  16  18  20  22  24
 3   6   9  12  15  18  21  24  27  30  33  36
 4   8  12  16  20  24  28  32  36  40  44  48
 5  10  15  20  25  30  35  40  45  50  55  60
 6  12  18  24  30  36  42  48  54  60  66  72
 7  14  21  28  35  42  49  56  63  70  77  84
 8  16  24  32  40  48  56  64  72  80  88  96
 9  18  27  36  45  54  63  72  81  90  99 108
10  20  30  40  50  60  70  80  90 100 110 120
11  22  33  44  55  66  77  88  99 110 121 132
12  24  36  48  60  72  84  96 108 120 132 144
```

Figure 7-11. Two-Dimensional Arrays and for Loops Output

Let's look at some of the key differences between these loops and the ones we examined previously. First, notice that we are using "<=" in the logical condition. The reason for the change is because we are using the GetUpperBound() method of the array. Unlike Length which returns the total number of elements in the array, this method returns the largest valid index for the requested dimension, which is 0 or 1 in this case. Since the value returned is legal for us to access as an index value we must include it in the test calculation, hence the "<=" operator instead of "<". Next, notice that we nested the loop for *col* within the loop for *row*. What this does is loop from 0 to 11 for *row*, and for each of these values of *row*, loops 0 to 11 for *col*. This guarantees that every possible combination of *row* and *col* are calculated (144 possibilities in all).

One of the biggest stumbling blocks when using `for` loops to iterate through array indices is deciding when to use "<" or "<=". This depends on what you are using as your "end condition" value. If you are using Length or GetLength() you will almost always use "<" since those values are always one greater than the last legal index. However, if you use GetUpperBound(), then that value is a legal index in the given dimension and you can safely use "<=". If you get an IndexOutOfBoundsException thrown in your code, chances are high that you used the wrong comparison operator, "<=" instead of "<". Likewise, if the value stored in the last index of the array is incorrect or not output you probably used "<" instead of "<=".

The foreach Loop

The `for` loop is a very versatile iteration statement that can be used for many different purposes. The `foreach` loop, however, is tailored to perform a very specific task – iterate linearly through a one-dimensional array or collection, like List<T>. Additionally, the `foreach` construct utilizes a single variable that is the same type as the collection being stepped through. At each iteration of the loop the variable will contain the next item in the collection. The loop will automatically terminate once all items have been iterated through so there is no chance of incorrectly accessing items out-of-bounds. In most instances the foreach loop has similar execution speed as a for loop, but it can be marginally slower under certain circumstances. For business applications this difference is typically negligible and outweighed by the benefits of implementing an arguably cleaner construct.

The foreach loop syntax requires two variables, the collection being stepped through and a variable that will contain each collection value as it iterates.

```
foreach (<type> <item> in <collection>)
{
    // foreach loop body contains statement(s) to execute;
}
```

Where:

<type>: This represents the data type for the items contained within the collection. It is common to see the keyword "var" here since the type can typically be implicitly determined.

<item>: This represents the temporary variable to store each item in the collection at every iteration of the loop.

<collection>: The collection can be one of many types as long as it contains something called an enumerator. An enumerator is a special code construct that keeps track of the current item and next item in a collection and notifies the loop when there are no more items to process. One-dimensional arrays and virtually all collection types within the System.Collections namespace all support enumeration. If the collection being iterated through does not contain any items the loop body will never execute.

Here are some examples of the foreach loop in action.

Listing 7-15. Simple foreach Loop

```
int[] primes = { 1, 2, 3, 5, 7, 11, 13, 17, 19, 23 };
// Loop through each element of primes:
int i = 0;
foreach (int prime in primes)
{
  Console.WriteLine($"Prime #{++i} = {prime}");
}
```

```
Prime #1 = 1
Prime #2 = 2
Prime #3 = 3
Prime #4 = 5
Prime #5 = 7
Prime #6 = 11
Prime #7 = 13
Prime #8 = 17
Prime #9 = 19
Prime #10 = 23
```

Figure 7-12. foreach Loop Output

Notice that to duplicate the output from the code in Listing 7-11 an extra `int` variable *i* had to be added outside the loop. If we didn't care about the sequence number in the output that variable could have been omitted making the loop code even simpler. The next example makes use of a `string[]` and does not keep track of the sequence number.

Listing 7-16. Another Sample foreach Loop

```
string[] names = { "Bill", "Cathy", "David", "Emily", "Gerard" };
foreach (var name in names)
{
  Console.WriteLine(name);
}
```

```
Bill
Cathy
David
Emily
Gerard
```

Figure 7-13. string[] foreach Loop Output

There are some very important rules to follow when using `foreach`. First, it is important that you do not modify the collection being iterated through while the `foreach` loop is executing. At best you will receive strange results. At worst the program will throw an exception. Next, ensure that the collection is a valid object prior to using in a `foreach` loop. If the object is `null` the CLR will throw an exception. Finally, try not to use "`object`" as the loop variable's data type as it will box elements of collections containing value types. Instead, either use the exact type that the collection contains or use `var` to have the compiler determine the type implicitly at compile-time.

The while Loop

If your loop does not require a counter or index (`for`) and you are not looping through a collection (`foreach`) then the `while` loop is probably the best choice. The `while` loop is actually similar to a `for` loop that only has a logical condition section defined in its construct. Essentially, a `while` loop continues executing while a given logical expression evaluates to `true`. The logical expression is evaluated before each iteration of the loop so it is entirely possible that the loop body will never execute if the expression initially evaluates to `false`. The `while` loop has the following syntax:

```
while (<logical expression>)
{
    // loop body contains statement(s) to execute;
}
```

Like the other loops it is important that the logical expression eventually evaluates to `false` so the loop can terminate normally. If you use a counter variable as part of the logical expression don't forget to increment or decrement it within the loop body as seen in this example:

Listing 7-17. Sample while Loop

```
// Output the squares of the first 10 numbers
int i = 1;
while (i <= 10)
{
  Console.WriteLine($"{i}² = {i*i}");
  ++i;
}
```

```
1² = 1
2² = 4
3² = 9
4² = 16
5² = 25
6² = 36
7² = 49
8² = 64
9² = 81
10² = 100
```

Figure 7-14. Sample while Loop Output

The following is a slightly more complex example where the user is prompted for input until they enter the word "quit".

Listing 7-18. Processing User Input Using while

```
string input = string.Empty;
while (input != "quit")
{
  Console.ForegroundColor = ConsoleColor.White;
  Console.Write("Enter a name: ");
  Console.ForegroundColor = ConsoleColor.Yellow;
  input = Console.ReadLine();
  Console.ForegroundColor = ConsoleColor.Cyan;
  Console.WriteLine($"You entered '{input}'.");
}
Console.ResetColor();
Console.WriteLine("Done");
```

```
Enter a name: Bill
You entered 'Bill'.
Enter a name: Jill
You entered 'Jill'.
Enter a name: Joe
You entered 'Joe'.
Enter a name: quit
You entered 'quit'.
Done
```

Figure 7-15. Processing User Input Output

The do Loop

Also known as the do...while loop, the do loop is virtually identical to the while loop in functionality except the logical expression that determines if the loop should continue is performed ***after*** each iteration of the loop. This implies that the loop body will always execute at least once. The do loop has the following syntax:

```
do
{
    // loop body contains statement(s) to execute;
} while (<logical expression>);
```

The next example utilizes a do loop and if statements to play a simple number guessing game.

Listing 7-19. Number Guessing Game Using do Loops

```
Random rnd = new Random();
int target = rnd.Next(100) + 1;
int guess = 0;
int count = 0;
do
{
  Console.Write("Enter a number between 1 and 100: ");
  string input = Console.ReadLine();
  if (int.TryParse(input, out guess))
  {
    if (guess < target)
    {
      Console.WriteLine("Too low.");
    }
    else if (guess > target)
    {
      Console.WriteLine("Too high.");
    }
    ++count;
  }
} while (guess != target);
Console.WriteLine($"You got it in {count} guesses!");
```

```
Enter a number between 1 and 100: 50
Too high.
Enter a number between 1 and 100: 25
Too high.
Enter a number between 1 and 100: 12
Too low.
Enter a number between 1 and 100: 18
Too high.
Enter a number between 1 and 100: 15
You got it in 5 guesses!
```

Figure 7-16. Number Guessing Game Output

The first two lines create a random number generator then gets a random number between 1 and 100 and places the value into *target*. The do loop then continues to execute while *guess* is not equal to *target*. Within the loop the user is prompted to enter a number which is parsed into *guess* and then compared to *target*. If the numbers do not match then the user is notified. Once the loop terminates the user is notified how many guesses it took to reach the correct answer.

As you can see, with loops and Boolean logic, the programs you can write become more sophisticated and useful.

Controlling Loops

Just like the `switch` statement, loops can utilize special jump commands to exit a loop prior to normal completion or skip to the next iteration of the loop. This is the preferred technique rather than changing the loop control variable manually. We'll revisit these commands here as they have slightly different effects inside loops than when used within `switch` statements.

break

The `break` command exits the loop immediately and resumes program execution on the line following the closing brace of the loop body (or the line after the loop body if no braces are present). If the loop that is "broken" out of is part of another loop body, only the inner-most loop will terminate execution.

The following example uses a `do` loop set to execute while the variable *i* is less than 10. However, we arbitrarily set a condition within the loop body that will break out of the loop once *i* equals 4.

Listing 7-20. Using break to Terminate a Loop

```
int i = 0;
do
{
  Console.WriteLine($"i = {i}");
  if (i == 4)
  {
    break;
  }
  ++i;
} while (i < 10);
```

return

The `return` command immediately exits the method (and the loop) it is contained within. This call bypasses any conditional logic established by the loop and will also exit nested loops regardless of the degree of nesting. Since we have not investigated methods yet we'll save the example until then.

continue

The `continue` command does not actually exit the loop it is called within. Rather, it will jump to the next iteration of the loop. In the case of `for`, the next code executed will be the iterator section followed by the logical condition section. In a `foreach` loop, the execution will continue with the next item in the collection being placed in the loop variable. With `while` and `do`, the program immediately jumps to the logical condition test either at the top of the loop body or the bottom for the two loop types, respectively. From here if the logical condition fails (`for`, `while`, `do`) then the loop terminates, otherwise the next iteration is executed.

Listing 7-21. Using continue to Skip to Next Iteration of a Loop

```
// Calculate the sum of the even numbers from 1 to 20
int total = 0;
for (int i = 1; i <= 20; ++i)
{
  if (i % 2 == 1)  // An odd number modulus 2 == 1
  {
    continue;      // Skip to the next loop iteration
  }
  total += i;
}
Console.WriteLine($"Total: {total}");  // Output:   Total: 110
```

It is true that we could have written the previous example with an iterator that skip counts by 2 eliminating the need for the modulus test as well as the `continue` command.

throw

This command throws an exception from the line it is called on. Where the program next executes is entirely dependent upon how exception handling is implemented in the code. We'll look at this in Chapter 9.

goto

The `goto` command allows you to define labels within the code that you can do a "hard jump" to. There are limits to how far you can jump, namely within the same method. Overusing `goto` can have a negative impact on the readability and maintainability of your code so use it sparingly.

Listing 7-22. Using goto to Exit a Nested Loop

```
for (int x = 0; x < 10; ++x)
{
  for (int y = 0; y < 10; ++y)
  {
    for (int z = 0; z < 10; ++z)
    {
      if (x * y * z == 27)
      {
        goto EndOfLoop;  // Jump to the EndOfLoop label
      }
    }
  }
}
EndOfLoop:
Console.WriteLine("At end of loop");
```

The inner-most loop contains an arbitrary test that will cause a jump to the *EndOfLoop* label once $x = 1$, $y = 3$ and $z = 9$. We could not effectively use `break` or `continue` to do the job since they would only affect the "z" loop.

The use of the `goto` command is one of the most hotly contested topics among programmers. One camp is adamant about avoiding its use at all costs, and in practical terms almost all scenarios using the command can be rewritten to avoid it. However, the other camp insists that it can be the right tool for the right job. I personally fall mostly into the first camp as I feel hard jumps are tough to debug and maintain. That being said, the `goto` command is very useful for breaking out of nested loops, without using `return` or adding special flags that need to be monitored at each nested level. My suggestion – just don't overuse it.

The Infinite Loop

One thing programmers typically try to avoid is the infinite loop. An infinite loop will either run forever until the program is forcefully terminated or until memory is exhausted. While infinite loops may seem like a bad idea, and generally they are, if you have no clear terminal condition to use in a loop construct's logical expression, or the terminal condition is a moving target, then an infinite loop may be desirable. Each loop construct (except `foreach`) has a syntax for creating infinite loops. The following examples are the simplest form for each one:

```
for ( ; ; )
```

```
while (true)
```

```
do
{
    ...
} while (true);
```

```
StartOfLoop:
    ...
    goto StartOfLoop;
```

Then, within the loop, use a `break`, `return` or `goto` statement to exit the loop once a specified event occurs. Since a loop of this type is intended to run forever until you manually cause it to terminate, great care must be taken to avoid programs that do not terminate when expected.

7.5 Summary

As you have learned in this chapter robust programs almost always require decision-making structures and iteration statements. Without those constructs programs are monolithic lists of sequential statements that cannot easily handle changing conditions based on user input or mutable data.

The `if`, `if-else` and `if-else if-else` statements give you the ability to test variables for specific values and execute code specific for those conditions. The `switch` statement is a structured programming construct that provides an easily readable list of candidate cases to test a variable for. We also looked at advanced `null` condition operators: "`??`", "`?.`" and "`?[]`" and the ternary operator "`?:`".

Then we started looking at repetition or iteration statements which allow us to write code that is repeated based on a specified condition. The `for` loop is good for looping through multi-dimensional arrays or collections where the index of values is important within the loop body. The `foreach` loop is ideal for looping through one-dimensional arrays and collections when all we care about are the elements within those collections. Both `while` and `do` loops provide a simple logical condition-based iteration structure that is more customizable than the `for` loop.

With these tools in your toolbox you can now start to write much more sophisticated programs, especially once you've mastered custom methods, the next topic in this book.

8

8. Methods

In the days of BASIC (Beginners All-purpose Symbolic Instruction Code) source code was organized by line numbers. Code would start executing from the lowest line number and continue executing the next lowest line number until reaching the end of the program. It was possible to branch to other portions of code by using the `GOTO` command which allowed for more sophisticated programs. Later a `GOSUB` command (short for **GO**to **SUB**routine or **SUB**procedure) was added that would allow the program to jump to a specific line number then return back to the line where the `GOSUB` command was issued. This was very useful as it allowed programmers to encapsulate functionality within a unit of code that could be called from various locations when that functionality was required. This concept is available in most modern languages as well; however, since line numbers are not frequently used anymore, a named approach is employed.

8.1 Method Basics

Modularization is the process of grouping blocks of code into self-contained, reusable units. These units can be repeatedly called when that code is required by your program. In most procedural languages, like C and Pascal, these units are called functions. In object-oriented languages these units are called methods, but the only real difference is the name. Since C# is an object-oriented language we will refer to these units as methods.

Why do we need methods? Let's consider an application used by a bank that manages mortgages and other loans. The formula for calculating the monthly payment of an interest installment loan is as follows:

$$P_m = \frac{Pr(1+r)^N}{(1+r)^N - 1}$$

We'll translate this formula into C# code later, but let's just say it is a fairly complex calculation requiring several variables and multiple calculations. Now, if we want to use this formula in our program we have two choices. The first choice is to include the translated code inline wherever we need to use it. The second choice is to create a method that performs the calculation and then call the method as needed. The problem with the first choice is, besides repeating code throughout your program, if the formula needs to be modified then it must be changed in multiple places. This could become a serious problem if the code is not modified exactly the same in all locations. By encapsulating the formula into a single function we avoid this problem completely. Refactoring into a method also promotes code reuse, speeding up development and testing.

A method in C# must belong to a `class` or `struct` (also known as user-defined types) just as Main() is a member of the Program class. We'll look at the effects of creating classes in addition to Program later on, but for right now we'll only consider adding methods to Program. The following are the rules governing method creation, many of which are very similar to the rules governing variables:

- A method must be defined within a `class` or `struct`
- A method must have a name that follows the same requirements as a variable, summarized below:
  - must start with a letter (upper or lower case) or an underscore "_"
  - can contain any alpha-numeric or underscore after the first character
  - cannot contain any spaces
  - are case-sensitive (a ≠ A)
  - cannot be the same name and case as a reserved keyword, such as "`for`", "`while`" and "`if`"
- Methods can accept any number of parameters (including zero)
- Methods can return one value of any type or no value (`void`)
  - All code paths in non-`void` methods must return a value of the defined type using the "`return`" keyword
- Methods can be overloaded (share the same name) as long as the input parameter type lists are different for each same-named method
- There is no limit to the number of statements allowed in a method

There are also some well-defined guidelines that should be followed. Method names…

- should be descriptive, avoiding abbreviations when possible. Plus, since methods indicate an action, a verb tends to be part of the name. Examples:
  - *Load(), Save(), Delete(), Print(), DownloadFile()*
- should use a consistent case convention, such as Pascal case, which is the Microsoft standard for C# methods.
  - Pascal case is the process of grouping multiple words together without any symbols where the first letter of each word is capitalized. These are example Pascal case method names: *CalculateArea(), SaveToFile(), Export(), TryParse()*
- should only use acronyms when they are common knowledge in the given organization or industry
  - should capitalize both characters of two-character acronyms
  - should capitalize only the first character of acronyms with three or more characters

Methods should be limited in scope. In other words, each method should be defined to perform a single, well-defined task. If your business logic requires multiple actions to be performed in succession it might be best to create several methods and chain them together by calling them in sequence. This way, if you ever need to execute only one of the tasks by itself, or run the tasks in a different sequence, the methods themselves would not need to be changed, only the order in which they are called. This promotes code reuse instead of rewriting the exact same logic in multiple places.

8.2 Method Syntax

Because you have worked with Program.Main() since the first program you wrote, method syntax should already be somewhat familiar. However, that one example is insufficient for describing all of the possible ways to write a method. Just be aware that all of the features of the syntax will not make sense immediately as they pertain to more advanced topics. Like all things we've studied so far we'll take it slow. Here's the formal syntax of a method:

```
[<access>] [static] [async] [<poly>] <type> <name>([<parameter list>])
{
        // Method body
}
```

As you can see there are many parts to this construct, and many of them are optional as indicated by the square brackets. Technically, only the `<type>` and `<name>` parts are required. For your information, the computer science name for a method definition is "signature". Here are detailed descriptions and use cases for each portion of the signature:

`<access>`: The access modifier is an optional keyword that identifies what can access this method. The `private` keyword (which is the default if omitted) indicates that the method can only be called from other methods of the same `class` or `struct`. The `public` keyword, on the other hand, indicates that the method can be accessed from other user-defined types. There are three other access modifiers (`internal`, `protected` and `protected internal`) which can also be applied but they will not make any sense until we discuss libraries and inheritance. For now, we can either leave this section blank or explicitly mark the method `private`.

`[static]`: There are two types of methods - instance and static methods. Instance methods require an instance (variable) of the user-defined type that the method is defined in, whereas `static` members do not. What this means is that to access an instance method you need to call it using a variable of its type. Consider a `string` variable called *s*. To access the StartsWith() method you would use "*s*" as the handle prior to the dot operator as such: *s*.StartsWith(). This implies that the StartsWith() method directly applies only the variable you are calling it on. Alternatively, methods marked with the `static` keyword belong to the user-defined type not to a particular instance so when you access it you would use the `class` or `struct` name as the handle. This is how to call the WriteLine() method of Console - you do not need to create a variable of type Console before executing that method, you simply call: Console.WriteLine(). Another rule about `static` methods is that `static` methods can only directly call other static methods of a user-defined type. Instance members are not restricted in this manner. Notice that Main() is marked with the static keyword which requires any methods we add to the Program class that will be called from Main() to also be marked static. We're not done with this concept and it will be revisited when we discuss creating class and struct types.

[async]: The async keyword is used with multi-threaded code and is one of the most advanced features of C#. As such, it will not discussed at this level.

[<poly>]: This optional section relates to how derivatives of the user-defined type will relate to the method. Some of the keywords that can be used here are virtual, abstract, override and sealed. As this topic relates to polymorphism it will not be discussed at this time.

<type>: This corresponds to the required return type of the method. One of the requirements of a method is that it either returns a value of a specified type or is marked with void. Consider a method that will calculate the area of a circle. Since the formula for this calculation utilizes the value "pi" (~3.14159) which is a double, the return value will also be a double. Likewise, a method that determines the number of times a specific character appears in a string would return a whole number, so its return type would likely be an int. However, not all methods require a return value. A method that prints a value to the console window would not necessarily need to return any value to the caller. In this case the return value would be void.

<name>: The name of the method is how callers will access it. As such, it is very important that the name be descriptive and directly related to the method's functionality. As discussed in the aforementioned "rules" section, method names must adhere to specific rules. Typically, the name of the method will consist of at least one word that corresponds to an action (verb), such as "Save()". However, a single word is not always sufficient for describing the action that the method performs. In those cases, additional descriptive words are appended after the verb, such as "SaveToFile()" or "DrawToWindow()". Since methods are the primary interface to user-defined types, descriptive names are critical in designing a clear API (application programming interface).

[<parameter list>]: For many methods additional information must be provided by the caller to carry out the specified task. This additional information is defined as parameters in the method signature. Each parameter in the list looks very much like a variable definition defined in a method and they are separated by commas. The syntax for each parameter also has additional modifiers in the following format:

```
[ref|out] [params] <type> <name> [= <default>]
```

For right now we are only interested in the <type> and <name> portions and we'll discuss the others a bit later in the chapter. The <type> of the parameter indicates what type of value must be passed in for this parameter. The <name> indicates how this parameter will be referenced within the method. Essentially, each parameter acts like a local variable in the method.

In case you were wondering what the differences are between a parameter and an argument, here you go: A parameter is part of the code definition (signature) of a method. It is one of the defined values accepted by the method. An argument, on the other hand, is the value passed to a method when called. In C#, the default mapping of arguments to parameters is done by position. Therefore, the first argument maps to the first parameter, and so on. In the real world, programmers interchange the two terms quite frequently, but the formal definitions are adhered to within this book to minimize confusion.

Enough background information. Let's look at some sample problems and methods that solve those problems.

Problem 1. Output text to the console

This is a fairly straight-forward problem. You need to create a method that accepts a string and outputs that string to the console window. We'll create a void method called PrintString() that accepts an argument of type string. Then, we'll call this method from Main() to demonstrate its functionality.

Listing 8-1. Simple void Method

```
using System;

namespace Methods
{
  class Program
  {
    static void Main(string[] args)
    {
      PrintString("This is a string");

      Console.WriteLine("Press <ENTER> to quit.");
      Console.ReadLine();
    }

    static void PrintString(string output)
    {
      Console.WriteLine(output);
    }
  }
}
```

```
This is a string
Press <ENTER> to quit.
```

Figure 8-1. Sample void Method Output

Because this is our first example of custom methods the entire code listing is shown. This is so you can see where everything is supposed to go. Future examples will focus exclusively on the methods. In C# it does not matter if Main() comes before or after the custom methods as long as they are both defined at the same level within their parent `class`, which is called Program by default for console applications.

Program execution starts on line 7, the entry point of Main(). Next, line 8 is executed, but since it is just an open brace nothing actually occurs. Line 9 is the next line to execute. Here is the call to PrintString() which causes a jump to line 15. Before the jump, the literal `string` argument "This is a string" is mapped to the `string` parameter *output* of PrintString(). This *output* parameter is actually a new variable scoped to the PrintString() method and contains a copy of the value passed to it. Therefore, inside the method, *output* can be used just like any variable declared within the method. In this case, all that is occurring is sending that variable as an argument to Console.WriteLine(). After the call to WriteLine() completes, execution of PrintString() terminates and control is returned to Main() after line 9. Note: if PrintString() was required to return a value (not `void`) then the method would have ended with a `return` statement. The rest of Main() prompts the user to press the Enter key and waits for that key press to terminate the program.

Problem 2. Output text to the console using supplied color

In this problem we are asked to do almost the same thing as problem 1. The major difference is that this method will require a second argument to be passed in that specifies the color to print the text with. If you recall from Chapter 3, the ConsoleColor `enum` provides a list of available colors that can be used as the foreground color of the output text. So, the second parameter of the method is of that ConsoleColor data type.

Listing 8-2. Enhanced Print Method

```
static void PrintStringUsingColor(string output, ConsoleColor color)
{
  // Remember the current ForegroundColor so we can set it back
  ConsoleColor originalColor = Console.ForegroundColor;

  // Change the color of the Console's foreground and output the text
  Console.ForegroundColor = color;
  Console.WriteLine(output);

  // Now reset the color back to the original before exiting
  Console.ForegroundColor = originalColor;
}

static void Main(string[] args)
{
  string text = "Another test string";
  PrintStringUsingColor(text, ConsoleColor.Cyan);

  Console.WriteLine("Press <ENTER> to quit.");
  Console.ReadLine();
}
```

```
Another test string
Press <ENTER> to quit.
```

Figure 8-2. Enhanced Print Method Output

Instead of looking at this example line-by-line let's take a look at the major changes. First, the `namespace` and `class` definitions were omitted to save space – you most definitely need them to compile the code. Next, the position of Main() is after our custom method, just to prove that the order is not important to the compiler. You may decide that it looks best to have Main() as the first method of Program, but it is not required. Notice that the new method, PrintStringsUsingColor(), has an additional parameter called *color*. This will be used to assign a color to the console for the text being printed. We also use a temporary, local variable, *originalColor*, inside the method to retain what the console's foreground color was at the time the method started executing. This way we are able to reset the foreground color to the value of *originalColor* prior to exiting the method.

In Main(), where PrintStringsUsingColor() is called, a `string` variable called *text* is created which will act as the first argument to the method. Don't worry that the parameter name is *output* and the argument name is *text*, the compiler uses type and position, not name, to map arguments to parameters. Also, this demonstrates that variables as well as literals can be used as arguments to methods. For the second argument, ConsoleColor.Cyan is used as the color for printing the text.

Problem 3. Calculate the area of a rectangle

The first two examples were `void` methods, or methods that don't return a value. One of the key features of methods is the ability to return a value. Using this technique we are able to translate mathematical formulas into C# where the parameters of the method are the formula inputs and the method return value is the formula output. We'll start with a very simple formula, calculating the area of a rectangle. Recall from basic geometry that the formula to calculate rectangle area is:

$$Area = width \times height$$

Using this formula we can construct the prototype of the method. A prototype is simply another name for the method's signature. Assuming the inputs and outputs are values that contain decimals, the prototype could be:

```
static double GetRectangleArea(double width, double height)
```

Then, the actual method could be written as:

Listing 8-3. Calculate Rectangle Area

```
static double GetRectangleArea(double width, double height)
{
  double area = width * height;
  return area;
}
```

Notice that the last line of the method is a `return` command that passes the value of *area* back to the caller. The use of the *area* variable is strictly for readability. For a simple method, such as this, you may omit that variable and directly use the result of the calculation as the return value:

Listing 8-4. Calculate Rectangle Area Without Temp Variable

```
static double GetRectangleArea(double width, double height)
{
  return width * height;
}
```

Calling either version of the above method is almost the same as calling the methods in the previous examples except with these you can accept a return value.

Listing 8-5. Calling GetRectangleArea()

```
double area = GetRectangleArea(12.5, 7);
Console.WriteLine($"The area is {area}");
```

```
The area is 87.5
```

Figure 8-3. RectangleArea() Output

If you only need the result of the method call for output purposes, you can also omit the *area* variable and call the method inline as follows:

Listing 8-6. Calling GetRectangleArea() Without Temp Variable

```
Console.WriteLine($"The area is {GetRectangleArea(12.5, 7)}");
```

Problem 4. Calculate Mortgage Payment

Let's look at a more difficult problem, calculating the monthly payment for a mortgage. Recall the formula is:

$$P_m = \frac{Pr(1+r)^N}{(1+r)^N - 1}$$

Clearly, this formula requires more inputs than out previous examples, so let's identify what they are and give them better names than *P*, *r* and *N*.

> *P* = Loan principal, or amount borrowed. We'll rename this to *principal*.
> *r* = Monthly interest rate as a decimal (annual rate divided by 12). We'll call this *rate*.
> *N* = Number of monthly payments, also called the term. We will call this *term*.

Because we are dealing with money, we would normally use `decimal` instead of `double` for the currency variables. However, the problem with round-off typically only occurs with repeated calculations so we'll just use `double` for this example. In addition, the order of the parameters is relatively arbitrary but we'll choose an order that makes sense for this particular problem, as shown in the following prototype:

```
static double GetMonthlyPayment(double principal, double rate, int term)
```

Now, all that's left is to translate the formula into C# code to calculate the result and return the value from the method. Many mathematical problems require operations more advanced than adding and multiplying. In this example we are going to need to raise a value to a specified power. To do this we will utilize the Math class which contains many helper methods, one of which is called Pow().

Listing 8-7. Mortgage Calculator Method

```
static double GetMonthlyPayment(double principal, double rate, int term)
{
  // Get rate in terms of monthly amount in decimal form
  rate = rate / 12.0 / 100.0;    // Or: rate /= 1200;
  // Since Math.Pow is expensive, calculate (1 + r)^N  only once
  double rateN = Math.Pow(1.0 + rate, term);
  double numerator = principal * rate * rateN;
  double denominator = rateN - 1;
  double result = numerator / denominator;
  return result;
}
```

Once again temporary variables are used to make the code easier to read. First, *rate* must be recalculated to be in terms of monthly interest rate and in decimal form. So, if the input is 4.0, representing 4%, we need to divide by 12 and then 100. You may be wondering if it is wise to change *rate* inside the method. Since *rate* is a value type this is a brand new variable in the stack exclusive to this method, meaning any change to it will not affect any data outside the method. We'll peek at passing by reference in a little while, but for right now know it is safe. Next, the $(1 + r)^N$ portion is calculated and saved in a temporary variable, *rateN*, so the Math.Pow() method is invoked only once. This type of optimization is common where the cost of calculating a value is greater than the cost of using another variable. Once we have *rateN* the *numerator* and *denominator* of the formula are calculated which allows us to arrive at the result.

Calling GetMonthlyPayment() is relatively straight-forward as shown in the following excerpt from Main():

Listing 8-8. Calling GetMonthlyPayment()

```
double principal = 540000;
double rate = 3.75;
int term = 360;

double monthly = GetMonthlyPayment(principal, rate, term);
Console.WriteLine($"The monthly payment is {monthly:C}");
```

Problem 5. Mortgage chart

So far we've only called each custom method once from our programs. The real power of methods is exhibited when we call them multiple times with different inputs. We'll continue using the GetMonthlyPayment() to demonstrate multiple calls to the same method. A useful tool for real estate agents is a chart listing potential monthly payments for various housing prices and prevailing interest rates. A client would, at a glance, know what they can afford. Using nested `for` loops we can build such a chart. We will also use another method called PrintMortgageChart() to do this rather than add all of the code directly to Main().

Listing 8-9. PrintMortgageChart()

```
 1 static void PrintMortgageChart(double startAmount, double startRate)
 2 {
 3   const double rows = 20;
 4   const double cols = 8;
 5   const double rateIncr = 0.25;
 6   const double amtIncr = 20000;
 7   double amount = startAmount;
 8   double rate = startRate;
 9
10   // Print header
11   Console.Write(" MORTGAGE");
12   for (int col = 0; col < cols; ++col)
13   {
14     Console.Write($"{rate,7:0.00}%");
15     rate += rateIncr;
16   }
17   Console.WriteLine();
18   Console.WriteLine(new string('-', 73));
19
20   for (int row=0; row<rows; ++row)
21   {
22     rate = startRate;  // for each row, reset the rate back to startRate
23     Console.Write($"{amount,9:C0}");  // print mortgage amt for each row
24     for (int col=0; col<cols; ++col)
25     {
26       double monthly = GetMonthlyPayment(amount, rate, 360);
27       Console.Write($"{monthly,8:N0}");
28       rate += rateIncr;  // increment rate
29     }
30     Console.WriteLine();
31     amount += amtIncr;   // increment principal amount
32   }
33 }
```

Lines 3 through 8 declare constants and variables that will be used in the method, including the number of rows and columns in the chart and how much to increment the rate and mortgage amount for each cell advancement in the chart. Lines 10 through 18 print the chart header which includes the various interest rates the mortgage amounts are calculated with. The remainder of the method contains the nested loops to print the individual cells of the chart. Notice the strategic use of spacing in the format strings as well as Console.Write() and Console.WriteLine() depending on if a carriage return is warranted at specified locations. Calling this method with the following arguments:

```
PrintMortgageChart(300000.0, 3.0);
```

produces this output:

```
MORTGAGE   3.00%   3.25%   3.50%   3.75%   4.00%   4.25%   4.50%   4.75%
--------------------------------------------------------------------------
$300,000   1,265   1,306   1,347   1,389   1,432   1,476   1,520   1,565
$320,000   1,349   1,393   1,437   1,482   1,528   1,574   1,621   1,669
$340,000   1,433   1,480   1,527   1,575   1,623   1,673   1,723   1,774
$360,000   1,518   1,567   1,617   1,667   1,719   1,771   1,824   1,878
$380,000   1,602   1,654   1,706   1,760   1,814   1,869   1,925   1,982
$400,000   1,686   1,741   1,796   1,852   1,910   1,968   2,027   2,087
$420,000   1,771   1,828   1,886   1,945   2,005   2,066   2,128   2,191
$440,000   1,855   1,915   1,976   2,038   2,101   2,165   2,229   2,295
$460,000   1,939   2,002   2,066   2,130   2,196   2,263   2,331   2,400
$480,000   2,024   2,089   2,155   2,223   2,292   2,361   2,432   2,504
$500,000   2,108   2,176   2,245   2,316   2,387   2,460   2,533   2,608
$520,000   2,192   2,263   2,335   2,408   2,483   2,558   2,635   2,713
$540,000   2,277   2,350   2,425   2,501   2,578   2,656   2,736   2,817
$560,000   2,361   2,437   2,515   2,593   2,674   2,755   2,837   2,921
$580,000   2,445   2,524   2,604   2,686   2,769   2,853   2,939   3,026
$600,000   2,530   2,611   2,694   2,779   2,864   2,952   3,040   3,130
$620,000   2,614   2,698   2,784   2,871   2,960   3,050   3,141   3,234
$640,000   2,698   2,785   2,874   2,964   3,055   3,148   3,243   3,339
$660,000   2,783   2,872   2,964   3,057   3,151   3,247   3,344   3,443
$680,000   2,867   2,959   3,054   3,149   3,246   3,345   3,445   3,547
```

Figure 8-4. PrintMortgageChart() Output

Incrementally, we are getting more sophisticated code by implementing methods and some of the other techniques we have learned. However, there are more things we need to learn about methods before moving on to other topics.

8.3 Passing Arguments By Value and By Reference

It may not come as a surprise that there are different ways arguments can be passed to methods. Specifically, arguments can be passed "by value" or "by reference". By default, all arguments are passed by value. This is especially true regarding constants and literals which can only be passed by value. Variables, on the other hand, have no such constraint and methods can define their parameters to accept variable arguments using either technique. To understand the difference we first need to see what actually happens inside a method with respect to the parameter list and the stack.

Passing Arguments By Value

When arguments are passed to a method by value, a copy of that argument's value is what is actually sent. That means if an `int` variable called *x* with the value of 5 is passed to a method by value, the 5 is what is sent, not *x* itself. Inside the method a new variable is created in the stack, using the name and type assigned to the parameter, with the value 5. Therefore, the parameter and the argument are physically distinct variables and changing the value of one does not affect the other. These types of parameters are known internally by the compiler and CLR as "in parameters".

Listing 8-10. Passing By Value Example

```
static void MethodByValue(int value)
{
  value *= 2;
  Console.WriteLine($"MethodByValue(): value = {value}");
}

static void Main(string[] args)
{
  int x = 5;
  Console.WriteLine($"Main(): x = {x}");
  MethodByValue(x);
  Console.WriteLine($"Main(): x = {x}");
}
```

```
Main(): x = 5
MethodByValue(): value = 10
Main(): x = 5
```

Figure 8-5. Passing By Value Output

Passing Arguments By Reference

Passing variables to a method by reference is very different internally than passing variables by value. When a method's parameter is marked with the "`ref`" keyword, instead of a new variable being created in the stack that is local to that method, the very same variable is used. Even if the method's parameter has a different name than the argument being passed in, the compiler knows to treat them as the same item in memory. This, of course, has the effect of linking any changes to that variable in the method to the external variable. This is also why constants and literals cannot be passed by reference – they are not variables contained in the stack so they cannot be manipulated in this manner. These types of parameters are known internally by the compiler and CLR as "in/out parameters"

Listing 8-11. Passing By Reference Example

```
1 static void MethodByReference(ref int value)
2 {
3   value *= 2;
4   Console.WriteLine($"MethodByReference(): value = {value}");
5 }
6
7 static void Main(string[] args)
8 {
9   int y = 10;
10   Console.WriteLine($"Main(): y = {y}");
11   MethodByReference(ref y);
12   Console.WriteLine($"Main(): y = {y}");
13 }
```

```
Main(): y = 10
MethodByReference(): value = 20
Main(): y = 20
```

Figure 8-6. Passing By Reference Output

First, notice that in the code, on line 1, the *value* parameter is marked with the `ref` keyword. This tells the compiler to treat this parameter differently than a parameter passed by value. The *value* variable points to the exact same memory location as the *y* variable inside Main() whch is being passed to the method. Therefore, any changes to *value* inside MethodByReference() is immediately reflected in the *y* variable of Main(). Next, notice that in the call to MethodByReference(), *y* is also marked with `ref`. This is a requirement, kind of like the reference and dereference operators (& and *) of C and C++. Don't worry if you forget it, though – the compiler will complain until you add the keyword. Now, when the code is executed you can see that the value of *y* has changed after the call to MethodByReference().

So, why would we do this? Remember, methods are limited to a single output value. If we require multiple return values there are only a few things we can do to support that. You can encapsulate multiple values in an array and use the array as a return type. This is problematic if the values you need to return are different data types. We could use an `object[]` as the return type, but that may lead to boxing and the caller would also have to have explicit knowledge as to the exact contents of each index to use the array properly. Another alternative would be to use a `struct` or `class` to encapsulate the data. In many cases this would be an appropriate solution, but it could be overkill for simple problems. We'll definitely look at this approach in future chapters, but we'll table that idea for right now. So, let's look at a realistic example that makes use of passing arguments by reference – converting a decimal number into feet and inches.

Listing 8-12. Convert Double to Feet & Inches

```
static void ConvertToFeetInches(double value, ref int feet, ref int inches)
{
  // Determine the number of feet by removing fractional part
  feet = (int)value;
  // Get the fractional part by subtracting feet from value
  value -= feet;
  // Get inches by multiplying remainder of value by 12
  inches = (int)(value * 12);
}

static void Main(string[] args)
{
  int feet = 0;
  int inches = 0;
  double length = 7.25;
  ConvertToFeetInches(length, ref feet, ref inches);
  Console.WriteLine($"{length} feet = {feet}' {inches}\"");
}
```

```
7.25 feet = 7' 3"
```

Figure 8-7. Convert Double to Feet & Inches Output

In the code, both the *feet* and *inches* parameters of ConvertToFeetInches() are marked with the `ref` keyword but *value* is not since that is being used exclusively as input to the method. The calculation above is well commented so we won't focus on that here. Let's look at Main() instead. There are three variables created in Main() to pass to the method: *feet, inches* and *length*. When the call to ConvertToFeetInches is made, both the *feet* and *inches* argument are marked with `ref` just as they are in the method signature. After the call, both of those variables will retain any changes made in the method, which, in this case, are the results of the calculation.

Passing Arguments By Reference - out

Another style of argument, also passed by reference, is called an `out` parameter. The `out` parameter style functions almost identically to the `ref` parameter style of passing by reference; however, `ref` parameters *may* be changed by the called method but `out` parameters *must* be changed by the called method. These types of parameters are known internally by the compiler and CLR as "out parameters"

Recall the TryParse() methods of the built-in data types, which were discussed in section 4.12, require an `out` parameter to store the result of the parsing operation if successful and return `true` or `false` based on their success. We could follow that same pattern and rewrite the ConvertToFeetInches() method into TryConvertToFeetInches():

Listing 8-13. Using out Parameters

```
static bool TryConvertToFeetInches(string input, out int feet, out int inches)
{
  double value = 0;
  if (double.TryParse(input, out value))
  {
    feet = (int)value;
    value -= feet;
    inches = (int)(value * 12);
    return true;
  }
  else
  {
    feet = 0;
    inches = 0;
    return false;
  }
}

static void Main(string[] args)
{
  int feet = 0;
  int inches = 0;
  string value = "8.83333";
  if (TryConvertToFeetInches(value, out feet, out inches))
  {
    Console.WriteLine($"{value} feet = {feet}' {inches}\"");
  }
}
```

```
8.83333 feet = 8' 9"
```

Figure 8-8. Using out Parameters Output

Unless you have a reasonable need to pass parameters by reference use the default mechanism – passing by value. There is a good reason that passing by value is default, because most of the time the caller does not expect their variables to change. When a parameter is marked with `ref` or `out` the expectation is that the values **will** *change so there are no surprises. This issue gets a little muddy when reference type variables are passed by value since their contents can be altered. Wait, what?!? Keep reading…*

8.4 Passing Reference Types to Methods

Now that you have a good understanding of passing variables by value and by reference let's turn the world a bit upside-down. What we discussed so far is passing *value types* to methods, but passing reference types to methods works a bit differently. We've only worked with a few reference types up until now, namely arrays and StringBuilder objects (`string` does not count here because they behave more like value types), so we'll only use those types in our discussion.

Recall what happens when you pass a variable by value to a method. A new variable is created in the method which implies a new value is added to the stack. What is actually passed to the method is a copy of the argument's value. In the case of a reference type variable, recall what is stored in the stack for that variable – the address to its data in the heap. So, in effect the argument and parameter will each have a separate slot in the stack but both of their values will point to the same location in the heap for the data! That means if you change the contents of either variable both will show the same change. In other languages like C++ you could mark a parameter with the keyword `const` to ensure the method actually gets a copy of the variable contents and leaves the original variable contents untouched. Unfortunately, C# has no such ability so any time you pass a reference type variable to a method there is a chance that it can be modified whether you like it or not.

To understand how this process works, let's look at some simple examples passing both value type and reference type variables by value and by reference.

Example 1. Passing Value Type By Value

Here is a value type being passed to a method by value and its corresponding call from Main():

Listing 8-14. Value Type Passed By Value

```
static void ValueTypeByValue(int value)
{
  value *= 2;
}

static void Main(string[] args)
{
  int a = 10;
  ValueTypeByValue(a);
}
```

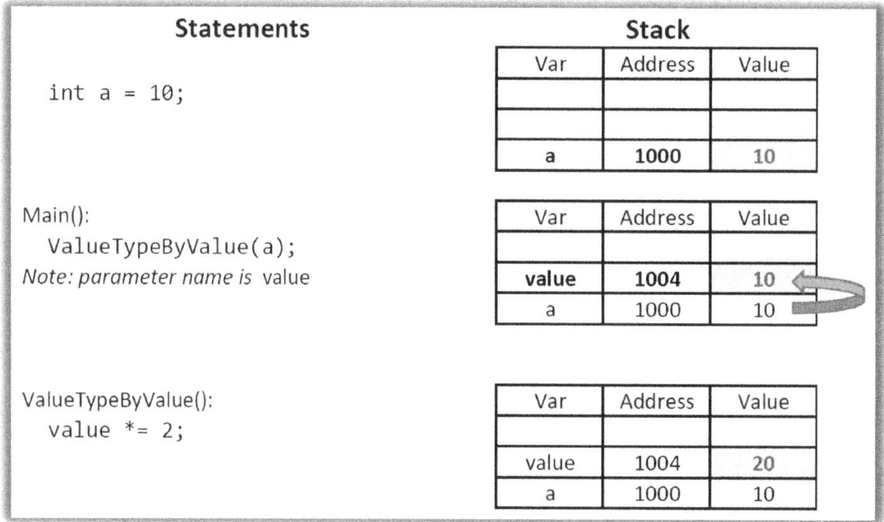

Figure 8-9. Value Type Passed By Value Memory Map

This example is very straight-forward. Because the *value* parameter is passed by value the argument *a* is not modified as a result of the method call.

Example 2. Passing Value Type By Reference

Here is the same basic code except this time the value type variable is passed to the method by reference:

Listing 8-15. Value Type Passed By Reference

```
static void ValueTypeByRef(ref int value)
{
  value *= 2;
}

static void Main(string[] args)
{
  int b = 10;
  ValueTypeByRef(ref b);
}
```

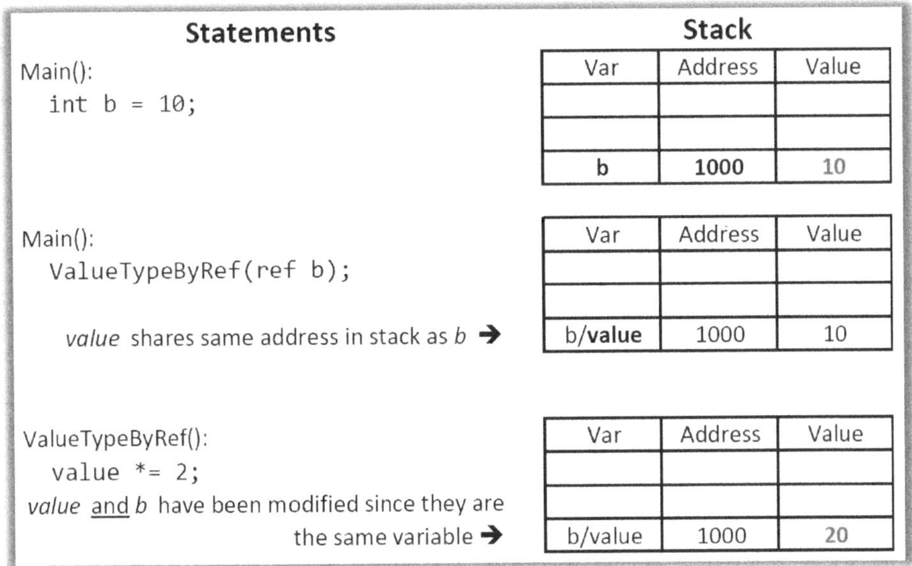

Figure 8-10. Value Type Passed By Reference Memory Map

Since the variable *value* shares the same exact location in memory as *b*, it should come as no surprise that modifying one will impact the other.

Example 3. Passing Reference Type By Value

Here things start to get more interesting. Remember, when you pass a reference type variable to a method by value, the contents of that variable can change. This is counter-intuitive based on what you learned in Example 1. However, look at the code, then the memory map, to see what is actually going on behind the scenes and it might start making sense…

Listing 8-16. Reference Type Passed By Value

```
static void RefTypeByValue(StringBuilder value)
{
  value.Append("D");
}

static void Main(string[] args)
{
  var c = new StringBuilder("ABC");
  RefTypeByValue(c);
}
```

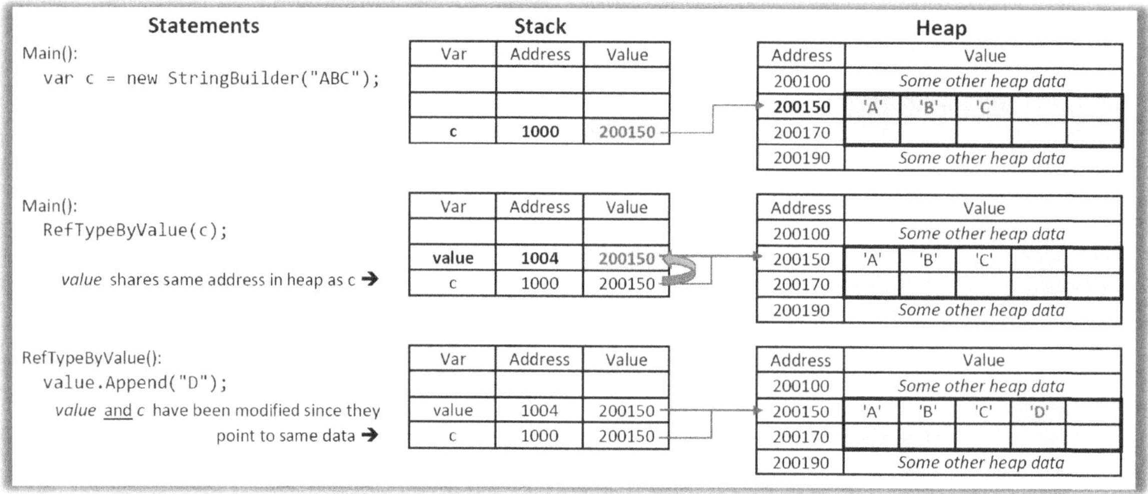

When you pass a variable by value to a method, a copy of the variable's value is passed to the method to use as the value of the parameter variable. In the case of a reference type, the value of the variable is the address to its data in the heap. So, making changes to one of the variable's data effectively changes them both. This really isn't any different than when you create a reference type variable and then assign it to another using the equals operator "=". Yes, you have two distinct variables in the stack, but they both point to the same heap data.

Example 4. Passing Reference Type By Reference

OK, so if you can change a reference type variable's contents when you pass it by value to a method, what possible purpose could there be to pass a reference type variable by reference? There actually is a legitimate reason to do this. By passing the variable by value the method has access to the variable's contents in the heap. However, when you pass a variable by reference you are passing the actual variable to the method. This allows you to change the stack value of the variable which means you not only can change the contents of the reference type variable, you can actually change where the variable points in the heap. This implies you can have the variable point to another location in the heap or even set the reference to `null`.

Repeating Example 3 only with `ref` parameters would server no actual purpose as the results would be identical as passing by value. Instead, let's use a practical example where this technique is absolutely required - swapping variables. If you have two variables that need to be swapped, like in a sorting algorithm that must reorder a list, using a method to do the swapping requires direct access to the variables themselves, not just their values. Hence the need to pass the variables to the method by reference. This requirement applies to value type and reference type variables alike.

The swap method is actually simple. Assume two values of the same type are parameters, called *a* and *b*, and they are both marked `ref`. First, a temporary variable of the same type as *a* and *b* is created, called *temp*. Next, *a* is assigned to *temp*. Then, *b* is assigned to *a*, followed by *temp* being assigned to *b*. Without the input parameters being passed by reference, all of the assignments would be local in scope and once the method terminates there would be no apparent change. Here is an example using StringBuilder objects as the variables to swap.

Listing 8-17. Swap()

```
static void Swap(ref StringBuilder a, ref StringBuilder b)
{
  var temp = a;
  a = b;
  b = temp;
}

static void Main(string[] args)
{
  var s1 = new StringBuilder("DEF");
  var s2 = new StringBuilder("ABC");
  Console.WriteLine($"Before swap: {s1}{s2}");
  Swap(ref s1, ref s2);
  Console.WriteLine($"After swap: {s1}{s2}");
}
```

```
Before swap: DEFABC
After swap: ABCDEF
```

Figure 8-11. Swap() Output

Let's take a look at what's going on in memory when this code is executed – pay attention, this one gets a bit involved:

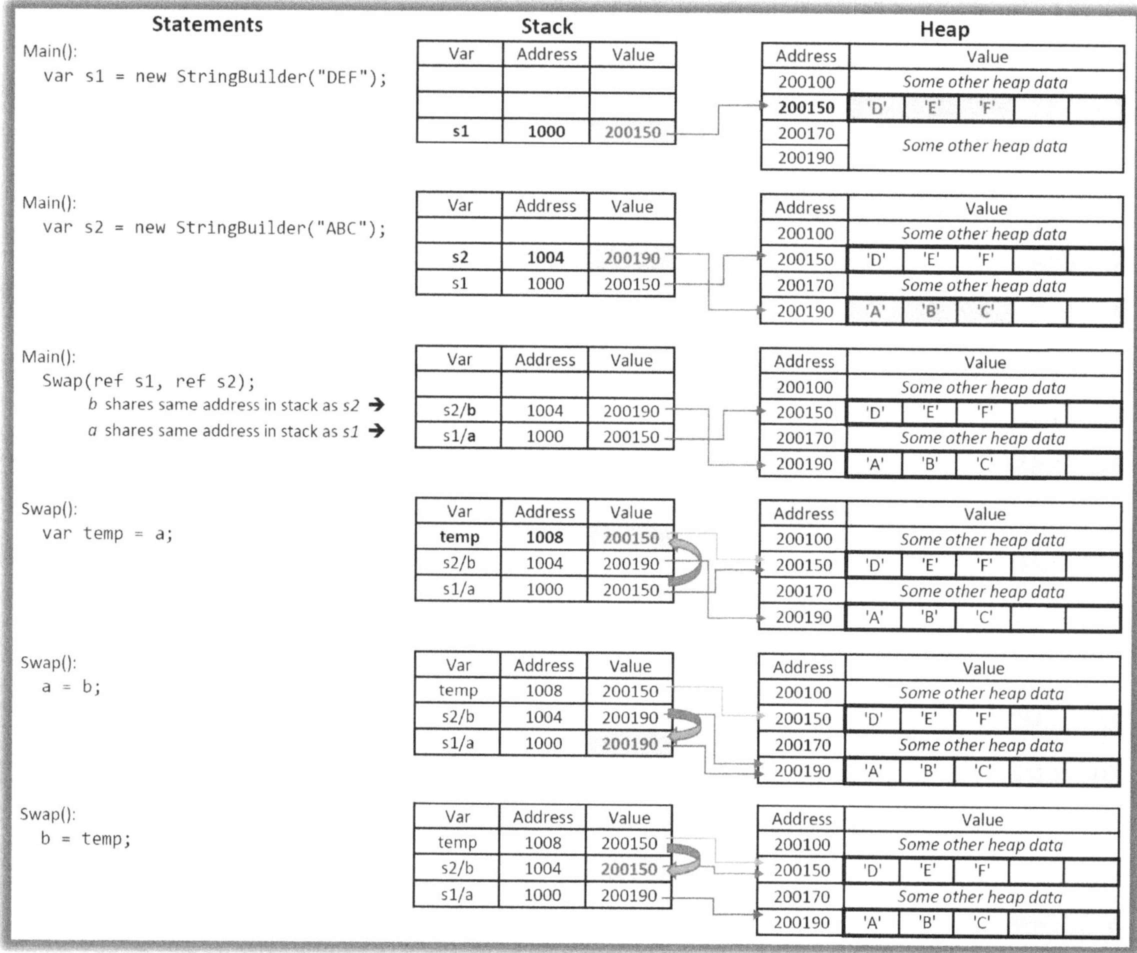

Figure 8-12. Swap() Memory Map

Even though StringBuilder objects are used in this example, the same basic operations would occur if Swap() accepted `int` variables instead, just without the heap's involvement.

Now, before you throw this book into your fireplace, just be aware you only really need to know the net effects of passing variables by value and by reference, not the grizzly details of what is happening deep inside the CLR's memory manager. However, it is always good to understand the details to help explain unexpected results.

8.5 Overloads

An interesting feature of many programming languages, including C#, is the ability to define multiple methods in a `class` or `struct` with the same name, called overloading. Initially, it may appear that the caller would have no way of knowing which method is being invoked – after all they have the same name. Don't worry, there are specific rules that prevent this type of ambiguity from occurring in your code:

- Overloaded methods share the exact same name, including spelling and case.
- Each overloaded method must have a unique input signature. In other words, the list of parameters defined for each method must be unique based on their types and order.
  - The return value is not considered when determining uniqueness.
- Overloaded methods should typically perform the same functionality just from a different set of inputs.
- Overloaded methods may call a common method to constrain core functionality to one location. Otherwise, the business logic may be spread among many different methods making maintenance complicated.

So, why is this technique important? Consider a program that can perform a specific set of tasks but the input required by those tasks is different based on circumstances. For instance, you may have a program that provides code to apply processing to an image and the method is called SmoothImage(). However, there are three different ways to provide an image to the method:

- As a local file
- As a byte array
- As a web URI

Here's what the signatures of these method may look like:

```
static void SmoothImage (string imageFilename)

static void SmoothImage (byte[] imageData)

static void SmoothImage (Uri imageAddress)
```

In turn, each of these methods would resolve the image data based on the given source. Once the image data is retrieved by the method the same processing is applied no matter the source, possibly by calling a `private` method called SmoothInternal() that accepts a common data type.

Alternatively, each method could be uniquely named, such as SmoothImageByFilename(), SmoothImageByByteArray() and SmoothImageByUri(). There is no one "correct" approach. In this example since there are only three overloads it may make more sense to have three unique method names. However, for a method like Console.WriteLine(), which has 19 unique ways of calling it, overloading makes more sense than creating 19 unique method names.

Listing 8-18. Overloads Example

```
static long Power(int num, uint power)
{
  long total = num;
  for (uint i = 0; i < power - 1; ++i)
  {
    total *= num;
  }
  return total;
}

static decimal Power(decimal num, uint power)
{
  decimal total = num;
  for (uint i = 0; i < power - 1; ++i)
  {
    total *= num;
  }
  return total;
}

static double Power(double num, uint power)
{
  double total = num;
  for (uint i = 0; i < power - 1; ++i)
  {
    total *= num;
  }
  return total;
}

static void Main(string[] args)
{
  int intBase = 5;
  uint power = 3;
  long power1 = Power(intBase, power);
  Console.WriteLine($"{intBase} ^ {power} = {power1}");

  decimal decBase = 4.2M;
  power = 4;
  var power2 = Power(decBase, power);
  Console.WriteLine($"{decBase} ^ {power} = {power2}");

  double dblBase = 6.3;
  power = 2;
  var power3 = Power(dblBase, power);
  Console.WriteLine($"{dblBase} ^ {power} = {power3}");
}
```

```
5 ^ 3 = 125
4.2 ^ 4 = 311.1696
6.3 ^ 2 = 39.69
```

Figure 8-13.Overloads Output

In this example there are 3 Power() methods, one that accepts an int and uint, one that accepts a decimal and uint, and one that accepts a double and uint. Notice in Main() that when each of these methods are called, the compiler must determine which is the best match based on the input parameters. The calls on lines 40 and 45 also emphasize how the return value plays no part in determining which overload to call as the compiler must implicitly decide the type due to the use of var.

Overloading can get a bit fuzzier when implicit type conversion is relied upon. Let's assume that the first overload, Power(int, uint), was omitted. Now, the compiler will have issues trying to determine which remaining overload is appropriate to call since an int can be implicitly converter to both a decimal and a double:

```
int intBase = 5;
uint power = 3;
long power1 = Power(intBase, power);
Console.WriteLi    decimal Program.Power(decimal num, uint power) (+ 1 overload)

decimal decBase    The call is ambiguous between the following methods or properties: 'Program.Power(decimal, uint)' and 'Program.Power(double, uint)'
power = 4;
```

Figure 8-14. Ambiguous Call

In this instance you could either convert *intBase* to one of the valid types, decimal or double, or you would have to re-add the first overload to directly support int parameters. Just be aware if you use the first technique, converting the input parameter, the output type will no longer be a long; therefore, *power1*'s type would also require changing.

So, which technique should you use, overloads or unique method names? I actually get asked this question quite often. The short answer is whichever suits your purposes. If your application is completely C# then either technique is fine. However, once you get into more sophisticated environments like creating WCF or Web API services, you'll find that overloads are either frowned upon or completely disallowed. One thing that is nice about unique method names is you avoid the call ambiguity issue shown in the last example. There is one place that overloads are absolutely required – creating constructors for classes and structs which are topics coming in later chapters.

8.6 Parameter Arrays

Parameter arrays are a very useful mechanism for specifying a parameter in a method that can accept a varying number of elements. Consider the `string`.Format() method which can accept an arbitrary number of arguments to insert into a formatted `string`. Unlike using a standard array as a parameter which would require the caller to formally create an array prior to passing the values, a parameter array is created "on-the-fly". In effect, the caller passes multiple arguments that are compressed into a single array parameter in the method. There are several requirements that must be adhered to when using parameter arrays:

- Only one parameter array is permitted per method.
- The parameter array is marked with the `params` keyword and must be an array type, such as: `params int[]`.
- The parameter array must be the last parameter in the method signature.
- Parameter arrays must be passed by value.
- All of the elements in the parameter array must be of the same data type (polymorphic derivatives are permitted).
- If no arguments are passed to the parameter array the parameter array will be empty (0 length, not `null`).

The following example uses a parameter array to calculate the average of an arbitrary number of `double` arguments:

Listing 8-19. Parameter Array Example

```
static double Average(params double[] values)
{
  double sum = 0;
  if (values.Length > 0)
  {
    foreach (double value in values)
    {
      sum += value;
    }
    return sum / values.Length;
  }
  // If you get here there were no values - return 0
  return 0;
}

static void Main(string[] args)
{
  double average = Average(12.1, 13.5, 7.5, 9.2, 7.0, 15.3);
  Console.WriteLine($"The average is: {average:0.00}");
}
```

```
The average is: 10.77
```

Figure 8-15. Parameter Array Output

The method Average() accepts a parameter array, called *values*, which contains a list of `double` values. Notice that in the method itself, *values* is treated like a standard `double[]`. The only indication that it is different is the keyword `params` in the method signature. In Main(), where Average() is called, there are 6 `double` literals being used as arguments to the method. So, at the time the call is executed, these 6 values are packed together into an array and passed to Average().

Truthfully, the need for `params` is limited, but when you have a method that must accept an arbitrary number of like elements this may be the best way to implement that functionality. This is especially true when you compare it to the alternative - creating an overload for every possible number of input parameters!

8.7 Optional Parameters and Named Arguments

Consider a method that accepts 30+ arguments. I know this is a ridiculous amount of items, but it has been done before - look at Microsoft's Office interop libraries for .NET. Here is one method prototype from Microsoft.Office.Interop.Word.DocumentClass:

Listing 8-20. Very Long Method Signature

```
public virtual LetterContent CreateLetterContent(string DateFormat,
  bool IncludeHeaderFooter, string PageDesign, WdLetterStyle LetterStyle,
  bool Letterhead, WdLetterheadLocation LetterheadLocation, float LetterheadSize,
  string RecipientName, string RecipientAddress, string Salutation,
  WdSalutationType SalutationType, string RecipientReference,
  string MailingInstructions, string AttentionLine, string Subject, string CCList,
  string ReturnAddress, string SenderName, string Closing, string SenderCompany,
  string SenderJobTitle, string SenderInitials, int EnclosureNumber,
  ref object InfoBlock, ref object RecipientCode, ref object RecipientGender,
  ref object ReturnAddressShortForm, ref object SenderCity, ref object SenderCode,
  ref object SenderGender, ref object SenderReference);
```

The hard part about calling this method is that you may not have every single piece of information necessary to fill in all of the arguments. In that case, you have to decide what should be used for arguments you don't have a value for. Should the `object` values be `null`? Should the `string` arguments be `string`.Empty? What about the `bool` and `float` values? Hopefully, documentation that accompanies the libraries you are using identifies the defaults. However, there is a much simpler technique that the developer of these libraries can use - optional parameters and named arguments.

An optional parameter is exactly what it sounds like, a parameter whose use is optional. If an argument is provided for a parameter then the argument's value is used by the method. However, if the argument is missing a default value, provided in the method signature, is used in its place. Let's use the Power() method as an example:

Listing 8-21. Optional Parameter Example

```
1  static long Power(int num, uint power = 2)
2  {
3    long total = num;
4    for (uint i = 0; i < power - 1; ++i)
5    {
6      total *= num;
7    }
8    return total;
9  }
10
11 static void Main(string[] args)
12 {
13   long power = Power(3, 3); // Result is 27
14   power = Power(4);         // Result is 16
15 }
```

The Power() method written above is almost identical to the one found in Listing 8-18. The only difference is the inclusion of a default value after the *power* parameter is defined. In this case, the default value is 2. In Main(), on line 13 when Power() is called, the set of arguments includes all required and optional parameters so no defaults are used. However, the second call, on the next line, only provides the argument that maps to the *num* parameter. Because of this omission, the value 2 is automatically used in the body of the Power() method. Some rules to consider when using optional parameters:

- Optional parameters must appear after all required parameters in the parameter list of a method signature.
- The default value must be a constant, literal or constructor call for a value type or `struct`.
- If an optional parameter is a reference type, the only default that can be supplied is `null` or the result of the `default` operator passed that type. Example: `default`(StringBuilder)

Named arguments work hand-in-hand with optional parameters. Consider the extreme example again, with 30+ parameters. Assuming most of these parameters are optional and you only have a value for the last one you would have a lot of empty values to provide defaults for. However, you can specifically identify the mapping of arguments to parameters by using the names of the parameters as part of the argument when calling the method. The following method accepts 4 arguments, only one of which is required, and calculates a number based on the place values provided.

Listing 8-22. Simple Optional Parameter Method

```
static int PlaceValues(int ones, int tens = 0, int hundreds = 0, int thousands = 0)
{
  return ones + (tens * 10) + (hundreds * 100) + (thousands * 1000);
}
```

If, when called, only the *ones* argument is passed, then that will be the return value as the defaults for each optional parameter is 0. However, what if we wanted to call this method providing different combinations of the optional parameters? The following demonstrates this option:

Listing 8-23. Names Arguments

```
int num = PlaceValues(5);    // Result: 5
num = PlaceValues(5, thousands: 4);  // Result: 4005
num = PlaceValues(5, hundreds: 3, thousands: 4);  // Result: 4305
num = PlaceValues(thousands: 5, hundreds: 2, tens: 8, ones: 0);  // Result: 5280
```

There is nothing special about the first call to PlaceValues() as the required parameter, *ones*, is supplied and the remaining 3 arguments are omitted leaving them to their default values. The second call shows how to identify a parameter by name. Since the *ones* argument is supplied without a name it relies on its position in the parameter list. The second argument is identified as mapping to the *thousands* parameter by explicitly identifying the parameter name followed by a colon ":" then the value. The third version is almost the same as the second with an added named argument, *hundreds*. The last one supplies all 4 arguments using name mapping, including the required parameter. Also notice the argument order is completely reversed from the parameter list. Here are some rules that describe this previous example:

- Non-named arguments automatically map to their corresponding parameters in positional order.
- Once a named argument is supplied all remaining arguments in the method call must also be named.
- Required parameters may be mapped to using named arguments but all required parameters must be accounted for otherwise the compiler will flag the call as an error.

By the way, IntelliSense uses square brackets to identify optional parameters:

```
// Named arguments
int num = PlaceValues(5);
            int Program.PlaceValues(int ones, [int tens = 0], [int hundreds = 0], [int thousands = 0])
```

Figure 8-16. Optional Parameters in IntelliSense

8.8 Method Parameter Conditions

Every method has its own specific logic regarding what is acceptable for the values passed to its parameters. Sometimes the only condition is that the value be of the correct data type which will be dealt with by the compiler. However, it is often the case that a parameter may only be a subset of the total possible values representable by a given data type. It is fairly common then to have conditional tests at the start of each method body, validating the parameters prior to execution of the method body's logic.

Consider a method that has a single string parameter called *input*. Your business logic specifies that *input* must be non-null and contain at least one character. The simplest way to deal with this situation is to use an if statement to test the condition on the first line of code in the method:

Listing 8-24. Testing Parameters

```
static void TestMethod1(string input)
{
  if (string.IsNullOrEmpty(input)) throw new ArgumentNullException("input");
  // Rest of method body...
}
```

In this code, the *input* parameter is tested for validity. If the test for validity fails, an exception is thrown, in this case an ArgumentNullException. Although we have not looked at exceptions in detail yet it is fairly simple to explain what happens here. In the event *input* is null or empty the code instructs the CLR to throw an ArgumentNullException. Immediately, the CLR tries to identify whether or not this code has an appropriate try/catch handler to redirect to, starting with this method and propagating out to its caller, then that method's caller, etc. Since our code has no such handler the result is an unhandled exception with a debug popup notifying us in Visual Studio where the problem occurred. Clearly, that is not an ideal and robust solution for production, but it does quickly let you know, as a programmer, that there was a failure in the business logic constraints. Since this could easily have been a result of user error, such as if they typed in a blank name, we'll need a better way of dealing with unhandled exceptions, and that will occur in a future chapter. For now, just be aware that when these occur due to coding errors you should immediately fix the offending code.

Every parameter in your methods should be tested in some manner prior to method body execution to avoid unwanted program states. In the event that a parameter can legitimately be any legal value for that data type then no testing is required. However, you'll find more often than not, that this is not the case. An advanced concept called "Code Contracts" can also be used to validate incoming parameter values.

I cannot emphasize enough how important this technique is for production-grade code. Code contracts are truly the way to go, but simple if tests are adequate. This is also one of the few places I eschew the use of braces with if statements as there is typically only one line of code in the "then" statement. Either way, try to embrace this technique as it will greatly enhance your code and should impress any potential employers in an interview.

8.9 Recursion

Recursion is an advanced technique used to solve problems that require repeated calculation of the same function or formula. Instead of using a loop to carry out the required task, a method will call itself either directly or indirectly until completion of its work. Clearly, not all problems are suited for this technique and it requires a bit of thought. Typically, recursive algorithms are designed to obtain an answer by breaking a problem down into smaller sub-problems which are, in turn, again broken into yet smaller sub-problems. Recursion is heavily used in functional programming languages, like F# and Lisp. C# supports functional constructs as well, but is an imperative language at its heart.

Many mathematical problems are well-suited for recursive implementation. A great example of a mathematical problem that can be solved with iteration or recursion is the factorial function. A factorial is the product of all numbers between 1 and a given non-negative number. So, the factorial of 5, written `5!`, would be 5 × 4 × 3 × 2 × 1 = 120. The last operation (× 1) is typically omitted because it doesn't change the value of the answer. First, here is what the problem would look like solved using a loop:

Listing 8-25. Factorial Using Iteration

```
static long FactorialLoop(uint number)
{
  long result = 1;
  for (uint i = number; i > 1; --i)
  {
    result *= i;
  }
  return result;
}
```

This code is very concise, although if we eschewed the use of curly braces in the loop body it would be even shorter. The code loops from the given number down to 1 (not inclusive) multiplying *result* buy the loop counter at each step. The result is then returned to the caller. Notice that *result* is initialized to 1. This is due to the rule that `0!` is equal to 1.

Believe it or not, the recursive solution is even shorter as we can take advantage of the "`?:`" operator to do the conditional testing for completion:

Listing 8-26. Factorial Using Recursion

```
static long FactorialRecursive(uint number)
{
  return (number > 1) ? FactorialRecursive(number - 1) * number : 1;
}
```

Seriously, that is the entire code listing. Let's break down what is going on in this code. Assume someone called this method using 4 as the input argument. That implies *number* is 4 the first time FactorialRecursive() is entered. The "`?:`" operator tests if *number* is greater than 1. Since it is this method then returns the result of calling this method recursively with *number* – 1, or 3, times *number* which is 4. So, before this method exits it must evaluate FactorialRecursive(3) and multiply that answer by 4. Now, we are in FactorialRecursive() a second time, but this time *number* is 3. The same test occurs implying the result of this particular call will be FactorialRecursive(2) * 3. One more time we are in FactorialRecursive() with *number* equaling 2. The result of this call will be FactorialRecursive(1) * 2. Finally, we get into FactorialRecursive()

one last time. Since *number* is 1, the result of the "? :" operation is the literal value 1, since the conditional test (*number* > 1) is `false`. This stops the recursion and the stack unwinds resulting in the final answer of 24. What this looks like in linear terms is:

FactorialRecursvie(FactorialRecursvie(FactorialRecursvie(1) * 2) * 3) * 4

Two things are certain about recursive methods: they are very powerful and they can be incredibly hard to read and write. One thing that is interesting about this set of examples is that the longer iterative code will typically execute faster than the shorter recursive code. If that seems strange, keep in mind that whenever a method is called the input parameters require stack entries, resulting in extra memory usage and computation cycles. In our example, calling FactorialRecursive(4) requires the *number* parameter to be added to the stack 4 times before each one is popped off the stack as their particular instance of the method exits and returns a value. There are other minor performance penalties incurred when calling methods which also tend to be greater than the cost of executing a loop. Like loops, one must be careful to provide an exit from recursive calls. Otherwise, the stack will eventually run out of space causing your program to crash.

It seems that the gain from using recursive methods is marginal at best. In fact almost all recursive algorithms can be implemented using standard iteration techniques. However, the elegance of recursion sometimes outweighs the simplicity of standard looping techniques. Compilers utilize recursion when analyzing code grammar and converting source code into machine code. Games and simulations also use recursion for determining shortest paths between two points in a maze.

Earlier it was mentioned that functional programming languages also make heavy use of recursion. That is because functional techniques don't rely on state change like imperative programming languages. What does this mean? Notice in the iterative method FactorialLoop(), the code requires 2 variables, *result* and *i*, that must change values to calculate the answer. FactorialRecursive() has no such variables as it relies on the result of function calls to calculate the results.

Recursion is a very powerful tool that can yield elegant code or a debugging nightmare. Due to the ease of using breakpoints and watches in the Visual Studio debugger, I tend to use the iterative approach for most business applications. I save recursion for those times when it clearly makes the most sense to use that approach. How much you use recursion will depend entirely on the type of problems you are attempting to solve. We'll look at additional functional programming techniques much later in the book.

8.10 Summary

Methods are a fundamental part of programming and we'll rely on them heavily throughout the remainder of this text. Methods enhance code reuse and maintainability and reduces the size of your main routines. A method may have a single return value of any type, or return nothing (`void`). Methods may also accept 0 or many arguments from the caller.

Parameters to methods can be of any type and are treated like local variables within the methods. Arguments may be passed to the method parameters either by value (default) or by reference. By reference parameters may modify the incoming argument whereas `out` parameters must modify the argument. Essentially, when an argument is passed by value, a copy of the value is sent, and when an argument is passed by reference, the actual variable is sent. Reference type variables can be modified by a called method regardless of how it is sent. Plus, when a reference type variable is passed by reference the entire variable can be swapped with another or even set to `null`.

Methods may share the same name as long as their parameter lists are different using a process called overloading. The return value is not considered part of a method signature and therefore doesn't contribute to a method signature's uniqueness.

Arguments can automatically be assembled into an array of items in a single parameter when using parameter arrays. Parameter arrays allow for an arbitrary number of arguments to be passed to a method.

Parameters can be required, by default, or made optional by providing default values in the method signature. If an argument is omitted where an optional parameter is positioned in the signature, the default value is used for that parameter. Arguments can also be identified by name instead of position. This allows you to skip over many parameters that can be left at their default value.

All methods should test the validity of incoming parameters prior to use within a method body. If an invalid value is detected then an exception should be thrown indicating a problem to the caller.

Finally, recursion provides a new technique for solving iterative problems. Although it is powerful, it is a skill that takes a lot of practice to hone.

9

9. Structured Exception Handling

Let's face it, nobody writes perfect programs. For that matter, there are no perfect programmers, either. That being said there are techniques you can use to mitigate problems that may pop up from time to time in your applications. To support robust and fault tolerant programs, most languages feature error checking of some form. Almost all modern languages use a technique called Structured Exception Handling which encompasses programming structures specific to listening for and trapping errors when they occur and dealing with the repercussions appropriately.

When I teach classes in person I tend to get a laugh when I state that "users are evil". Clearly, that is an extreme statement, but it does highlight a point. Whatever your program allows a user to do they will eventually do it, and sometimes it will not be in the order or manner you expect. Therefore, it is incumbent on you to anticipate all the possible ways your users will attempt to break your application intentionally or accidentally. Structured exception handling is a key weapon in your arsenal to defend against the evil that users do.

9.1 Exceptions

First let's look at the term "exception". Merriam-Webster defines the word as "someone or something that is different from others". That is essentially what an exception means in C# as well. However, let's alter the definition to say "code that runs differently than expected". But, what does this actually mean in terms of writing programs that do not crash? By the end of this chapter you will have a full understanding of this concept, but we need to bite off little chunks one piece at a time.

In C# there is a `class` called Exception that represents something bad that happened in code (basically, an error). Therefore, an exception is both a concept and a real entity. Instead of being just an error code, an `object` of this type contains many other key pieces of information. The following is a list of the key properties of Exception that you can use to help determine what kind of problem occurred and how best to resume execution of your code. All of the members in this list are instance members, meaning a variable of type Exception is needed to access these values.

Table 9-1. Exception Members

Name	Description
Data	A dictionary that contains key/value pairs of data pertaining to the exception.
HelpLink	A `string` that represents a URL containing information about the exception details.
InnerException	This property contains an optional Exception object, useful for embedding original exception details within a new Exception to be thrown.
Message	A text description of the problem that occurred.
Source	The name of the application or object that the exception originated from.
StackTrace	The list of methods executed to arrive at the method where the exception occurred.
TargetSite	The method that threw the exception.
GetBaseException()	This method determines the inner-most InnerException which identifies the root cause of the exception being thrown.

Most of the time in code you will not actually get plain Exception objects when an error occurs. Instead, you will likely receive one of Exception's derivatives, which are more specific versions of the Exception type. Derivatives are a fairly advanced topic that we don't need to address here, as long as we understand their usage. An example of an Exception derivative is DivideByZeroException which occurs when you attempt to divide an integer by zero. DivideByZeroException has all the same properties as Exception but the Message value will be tailored to that specific exception type.

9.2 The try-catch Construct

At the heart of C# structured exception handling is the `try-catch` structure, or `try` structure for short. Any code that has the potential for causing an exception should be contained within a `try` structure's `try` block. Interestingly enough, there are very few statements that are guaranteed not to throw an exception. One such statement is declaration of a value type variable initialized with a literal or constant value. Reference type declarations with no initialization (or initialized to `null`) also will not cause exceptions. Beyond that, almost everything else is capable of throwing exceptions. Therefore, almost all of the code you write is a candidate for inclusion into a `try` block.

When code placed in a `try` block causes an exception to be thrown, execution is immediately redirected to an appropriate `catch` clause, if one can be identified. Assuming a `catch` clause is found, code in its block is executed and then execution jumps to the end of the `try/catch` blocks. There is no way to jump back into the `try` code block once code has been redirected to a `catch` block, even with the use of a `goto` command. For this reason, code inside a `try` block is frequently concise, containing only several statements that perform a very specific task. Multiple `try` blocks can be written sequentially within a method; however, it is usually best to create multiple methods and chain them together with sequential calls.

The `try` block syntax varies depending on what you are trying to accomplish. This type of code block is one of the few that requires curly braces to delimit its contents. The first syntax we'll look at will protect your application from crashes but ignores the specifics about the exception that was thrown. Use this one only if you don't care what type of error occurred and will perform the same routine regardless of exception type.

Syntax #1:

```
try
{
     // "protected" code to wrap within the try block
}
catch
{
     // code to execute when an error occurs
}
```

Here is a code example demonstrating this syntax:

Listing 9-1. Basic Exception Handling

```
1 try
2 {
3   int x = 1;
4   int y = 0;
5   int z = x / y;  // Force a DivideByZeroException
6 }
7 catch
8 {
9   Console.WriteLine("Not sure what happened, but there was an error!");
10 }
```

This syntax is good to get you started with basic exception handling but it lacks the ability to provide detailed information about what exception occurred, where it occurred and why it occurred. Sometimes this technique leads to "silent failures", or errors in your code that are never observed or properly handled. Also be aware that code executed inside a `catch` block is no longer protected by the `try` block. Any exceptions thrown here could potentially be unhandled.

The division operation on line 5 is explicitly written to force an exception of type `DivideByZeroException` to be thrown (remember, you cannot divide `int` values by 0). Since the `catch` clause does not specify an exception type, any exception thrown within the `try` code block will be directed there. All we know at this point is that an error occurred. We know by looking at the code exactly what happened but the program cannot divine that information. So, a generic error message is written to the console and code continues to execute after line 10.

Instead of the previous syntax, consider using one of the next examples which, at the least, provide the exception type so you can deal with specific execution errors.

Syntax #2:

```
try
{
    // "protected" code to wrap within the try block
}
catch (<Exception Type>)
{
    // code to execute when an error occurs
}
```

Here is a modified form of the previous code sample that includes the exception type in the `catch` clause:

Listing 9-2. Typed catch Clause

```
try
{
  int x = 1;
  int y = 0;
  int z = x / y;  // Force a DivideByZeroException
}
catch (DivideByZeroException)
{
  Console.WriteLine("You divided by zero!");
}
```

This example provides a bit more detail when an exception occurs because it provides the specific type of exception that is thrown. Furthermore, this allows the error message printed to the console to be a bit more specific about the nature of the problem.

Do you notice a potential issue with this example? What happens if the exception thrown is not of type DivideByZeroException? In this case there is no appropriate `catch` clause to deal with the exception and the exception will propagate to the caller of this method and eventually go unhandled - exactly what we are trying to avoid. The way this particular code is written there is no way another exception type could be thrown; however, let's assume there is. How do we deal with that? By adding more `catch` clauses. This next example adds an additional `catch` clause to handle any other exception type:

Listing 9-3. Multiple Typed catch Clauses

```
try
{
  int x = 1;
  int y = 0;
  int z = x / y;  // Force a DivideByZeroException
}
catch (DivideByZeroException)
{
  Console.WriteLine("You divided by zero!");
}
catch (Exception)
{
  Console.WriteLine("Not sure what happened, but there was an error!");
}
```

Notice the second `catch` clause? It is listening for exceptions of type Exception. Due to polymorphism, which have yet to learn, this clause acts as the "catch-all" for any type of exception, similar to `else` in an `if` statement or `default` in a `switch` statement. It is important, if you use this technique, that the Exception `catch` clause always be the last one. The reason is because it can handle any type of exception. If it was first in the list then any specific `catch` clauses written afterwards would be unreachable. Sometimes the Exception `catch` clause is referred to as the "default catch clause" as it is capable of handling any exception type and should usually be part of any `try/catch` block.

Unfortunately, even this previous example has limitations. Remember the list of Exception class members itemized in Table 9-1? None of the previous examples allow us to access these members since we have no valid reference to an Exception object. This can be remedied quite simply by adding a variable name after each `catch` clause exception type.

Syntax #3:

```
try
{
      // "protected" code to wrap within the try block
}
catch (<Exception Type> <name>)
{
      // code to execute when an error occurs
}
```

Due to the way code block scope works, each `catch` clause can use the same name for the exception variable. The next example is a bit more involved than the previous to demonstrate more of the capabilities of exception handling.

Listing 9-4. Typed catch Clauses with Variable Names

```
int x = 0, y = 0, z = 0;
string input = string.Empty;
try
{
  // Ask user for two numbers and convert to ints
  Console.Write("Please enter a number: ");
  input = Console.ReadLine();
  x = Convert.ToInt32(input);
  Console.Write("Please enter another number: ");
  input = Console.ReadLine();
  y = Convert.ToInt32(input);

  // Divide x by y
  z = x / y;
  Console.WriteLine($"{x} / {y} = {z}");
}
catch (DivideByZeroException ex)
{
  Console.WriteLine($"Error: {ex.Message}");
}
catch (FormatException ex)
{
  Console.WriteLine($"Error: {ex.Message}; input: {input}");
}
catch (Exception ex)
{
  Console.WriteLine($"Unknown error: {ex.Message}");
}
```

```
Run # 1
Please enter a number: 15
Please enter another number: 0
Error: Attempted to divide by zero.
Run #2
Please enter a number: 7
Please enter another number: 2.1
Error: Input string was not in a correct format.; input: 2.1
Run #3
Please enter a number: 8
Please enter another number: 2
8 / 2 = 4
```

Figure 9-1. Exception Output from Various Inputs

In this example we are prompting the user for two numbers, which are read from the console as `string` values, attempting to convert the inputs into `int` variables and then performing a division operation. Along the way, many possible errors can occur. The two most likely ones are converting a `string` that is not a number into an `int` and possibly dividing by zero. We've already looked at DivideByZeroException so its inclusion in the `catch` clause list should be obvious. The next `catch` clause looks for exceptions of type FormatException. These will occur for many different reasons, but the Convert methods are notorious throwers of that exception type.

The first run of the code is instigating a DivideByZeroException by providing 0 as the second input value. At first glance, the second run seems like it will work just fine, but it also has an issue - trying to convert a `double` into an `int` using Convert.ToInt32() which doesn't allow truncation by default. The third, and final, run completes without error and is able to display the results.

Here are some of the highlights about the code that are bit different from the previous examples:

- All of the variables used in the `try` block are declared outside of the `try` block. This is done for good reason. Notice how *input* is referenced within the second `catch` clause? We could not do this if it was declared inside the `try` block since they belong to different sibling scopes. Just be aware that the value types are assigned literal values and the reference type, *input*, is assigned the innocuous value `string`.Empty, so no exception should occur due to the declarations.
- The default `catch` clause is last among the three `catch` clauses.
- Each `catch` clause utilizes the same variable name, *ex*, to hold the exception details. Because they are defined in different sibling scopes it is acceptable to use the same variable name.
- Because the exception details are held in the variable *ex*, we are able to obtain the exception's Message value and display it to the console.

This example can be used as a "boilerplate" for typical exception handling code. Clearly, the exception types will be different based on what you are calling within the `try` block, but the layout will be virtually identical.

If you were curious about what exceptions may be thrown by the calls you make on Base/Foundation Class Library methods, metadata provides that information. If you select a method of interest in code, right-click it and select "Go To Definition" (or hit F12), the comment above the method metadata will display the known exceptions thrown by that method.

I almost exclusively use the name ex *for my exception variables. In many examples, even on MSDN Online, the name* e *is frequently used. I am not a fan of that name since it is commonly used as the event argument name for event handler methods. Since most event handlers are added automatically it is a pain to always have to change their names. Instead, I adopted* ex *long ago and have not looked back since.*

9.3 The finally Block

In addition to the single `try` and multiple `catch` blocks that a `try` structure contains, there is also an optional `finally` block. The `finally` block must be the last portion of the `try` structure and the code within the `finally` block's body will always execute regardless of whether an exception was thrown or not. This block is very useful for tidying up after yourself by disposing of variable instances and ensuring the state of your program is the same no matter what path was taken in the `try` structure.

The syntax of the finally block is extremely simple. The `finally` keyword is used followed by a block of code containing statements that must be executed prior to leaving the `try` structure:

```
try
{
    // "protected" code to wrap within the try block
}
catch (<Exception Type> <name>)
{
    // code to execute when an error occurs
}
finally
{
    // this code always executes prior to leaving the try structure
}
```

The `finally` block is also another good reason to declare variables, used inside of the `try` structure, prior to the `try` keyword. The variables are then initialized inside the `try` block. This way, the `finally` block has access to those variables, just like the individual `catch` blocks discussed earlier. One word of caution - code inside the `finally` block is unprotected, just like `catch` blocks, so an exception thrown here could potentially be unhandled.

The following example demonstrates the patter of declaring a variable outside the `try` block, initializing and using the variable within the `try` block and disposing of the variable in the `finally` block:

Listing 9-5. try Block with finally

```
1 StringBuilder sb = null;
2 try
3 {
4   sb = new StringBuilder();
5   sb.Append("This is a string!");
6   Console.WriteLine(sb);
7 }
8 catch (Exception ex)
9 {
10   Console.WriteLine($"Error: {ex.Message}");
11 }
12 finally
13 {
14   sb?.Clear();
15 }
```

As you can see, the variable *sb* is declared prior to the `try` statement but left uninitialized. It is initialized to a valid StringBuilder within the `try` block. Then, in the `finally` block, *sb* is cleared, allowing it to be used later in the code by another algorithm. Take note at the use of the "`?.`" null-condition operator on line 14. This ensures that *sb* is not `null` prior to calling Clear(). Using an `if` statement instead, the `finally` block would look like:

Listing 9-6. Alternate finally Block

```
finally
{
  if (sb != null)
  {
    sb.Clear();
  }
}
```

It does not matter which technique you use, just ensure you write safe code within the `finally` block. The last thing you want is to start tracking down exceptions thrown from your `finally` blocks.

A less common pattern is the `try-finally` construct which excludes `catch` clauses entirely. Unlike `try-catch-finally`, this construct will not handle any exceptions thrown within the `try` block. Instead, it is up to the caller to ensure the exception is handled. However, the `finally` block is still executed either after the `try` block is complete or if execution is redirected to a higher `catch` block in the call stack. If there is no higher `catch` block in the call stack then the program will end with an unhandled exception. There is no guarantee that the `finally` block will execute under those circumstances.

9.4 Exception Propagation

We've already discussed how exceptions thrown from within a `try` block need an appropriate `catch` clause to keep the program from terminating due to an unhandled exception. This is only part of the story. Sometimes, you may not want to handle an exception at a given location, instead handing off that responsibility to the caller.

Most programs do not consist of just a Main() method. Instead, Main() will call other methods, which, in turn, will call yet other methods. If, in one of the methods called, an exception is thrown but not handled then it is up to the caller of that method to handle the exception. If the exception is not handled there then that method's caller is responsible for handling the exception. This process continues until either the exception is handled or there are no callers left, as in Main(). This process is called traversing the call stack. The following code demonstrates this process:

Listing 9-7. Exception Propagation

```
static void Main(string[] args)
{
  try
  {
    A();
  }
  catch (Exception ex)
  {
    Console.WriteLine($"Error: {ex.Message}");
  }
}

static void A()
{
  B();
}

static void B()
{
  C();
}

static void C()
{
  int x = 1, y = 0, z = 0;
  z = x / y;
}
```

Main starts with a `try` construct and a call within its block to A(). A() proceeds to call B() which then calls C(). Inside C() we purposely force a DivideByZeroException to be thrown. Since there is no appropriate `try-catch` construct at this level, the runtime starts crawling up the call stack to find an appropriate `catch` handler. First, it checks B() for a `catch` clause. Since C() was not called within the context of a `try` block the runtime will keep traversing the call stack to A(). A()

also did not have a try block so the final step up the call stack brings us to the original caller, Main(). Since A() was called within a try block, and there is a catch clause that can handle this exception, the exception is finally handled at that point. If Main() did not call A() within a try block, or there was no appropriate catch clause, then the program would have terminated with an unhandled exception.

9.5 Throwing Exceptions

Throwing exceptions is not solely at the discretion of the CLR. In your own code you may decide that some invalid state warrants an exception to be raised. An example of this would be at the beginning of a method, when a parameter is determined to be invalid for the call. Instead of silently failing by returning a default value from the method or just ignoring the parameter altogether, it may be most appropriate to throw an exception such as ArgumentException. Throwing an exception involves the use of the throw keyword and an appropriate exception object. The typical syntax for throwing an exception takes this form:

```
throw new <Exception type>(<arguments>);
```

The place where this code is executed is known as the throw point and the exception object's TargetSite property will contain the method that the throw statement is located in. In this example we are creating a Divide() method that takes two double parameters and attempts to divide them. Since double allows division by zero, code is added to throw an exception if a 0 is passed in for the *divisor* parameter.

Listing 9-8. Throwing an Exception

```
1 static double Divide(double dividend, double divisor)
2 {
3   if (divisor == 0)
4   {
5     throw new ArgumentException("Parameter divisor cannot be 0");
6   }
7   return dividend / divisor;
8 }
```

Notice that an ArgumentException object is created and used as the argument of the throw command. Also note that the ArgumentException object is initialized with a string representing the Message property of the exception. Different exception types have different parameters for their constructor calls, but most contain at least a parameter for the Message property. Use IntelliSense or Visual Studio's help feature to determine which constructor is best for your needs. Another key feature of throwing an exception is that any remaining code in the current method is skipped, so if divisor is 0 then the code on line 7 will never execute.

If a throw statement occurs within a try block it is possible that the exception will be handled by one of its catch handlers. If that is the desired behavior then there's nothing left to do. However, if you intended for that exception to be thrown to the caller then you will have to re-throw the exception from inside the catch block. This is done with a simple throw command by itself with no arguments.

Listing 9-9. Re-throwing an Exception

```
static double Divide(double dividend, double divisor)
{
  try
  {
    if (divisor == 0)
    {
      throw new ArgumentException("Parameter divisor cannot be 0");
    }
    return dividend / divisor;
  }
  catch (Exception)
  {
    throw;  // re-throw the exception to the caller
  }
}
```

Because we have no need for an exception variable, *ex* is omitted from the catch clause. The variable could be included but will yield a warning from the compiler due to an unused local variable.

Although it is legal to re-throw an exception variable with a command like "throw ex;" it is not recommended as it will change the throw point from its original location to where the re-throw is done, destroying the original exception's call stack. This is why "throw;" is recommended for re-throwing purposes.

When re-throwing exceptions, instead of simply passing the same exception object up to the caller, you may wish to throw a new exception. What if it is also important not to lose the original exception in the process? This is the purpose of the InnerException property of exceptions: to embed an exception object within another. Then, the handler of the exception can get information from the new exception that was thrown or the embedded InnerException which contains the original exception information. This technique is particularly useful if the user interface of the application displays exception information to the user but the original exception is too technical for the typical user to understand.

Listing 9-10. Re-throwing Embedded Exceptions

```
static void Main(string[] args)
{
  try
  {
    MethodA();
  }
  catch (Exception ex)
  {
    string padding = "";
    do
    {
      Console.WriteLine($"{padding}{ex.Message}");
      ex = ex.InnerException;
      padding += " ";
    } while (ex != null);
  }
}

static void MethodA()
{
  try
  {
    MethodB();
  }
  catch (Exception ex)
  {
    throw new Exception("Exception from A()", ex);
  }
}

static void MethodB()
{
  try
  {
    MethodC();
  }
  catch (Exception ex)
  {
    throw new Exception("Exception from B()", ex);
  }
}

static void MethodC()
{
  throw new Exception("Exception from C()");
}
```

```
Exception from A()
 Exception from B()
  Exception from C()
```

Figure 9-2. Re-throwing Embedded Exceptions Output

In MethodA() and MethodB(), when the exception from the called method is handled, a new exception is thrown (lines 27 and 39). However, instead of losing the information contained in *ex*, it is embedded in the new exception by passing it as an argument to the *innerException* parameter of its constructor. In Main(), the `catch` block utilizes a `do` loop to iterate through each of the InnerException property values of the handled exception. At each step of the loop, *ex* is set to *ex*'s InnerException value until it returns `null`. The *padding* `string` is used for formatting the output with indents showing the hierarchical relationship of the exceptions. This could have also been done with recursion, but this code is easier to follow.

9.6 Exception Filters

Exception filters are add-ons to `catch` clauses to provide additional conditional filtering to determine the appropriate `catch` block to handle an exception. The `catch` clause is immediately followed by the "`when`" keyword and a logical expression surrounded by parenthesis.

```
catch (<exception type> ex) when (<logical expression>)
```

There is no limit to what the logical expression actually does, as long as it returns `true` or `false`. It can be a simple test condition, a method call or a compound expression. A common use of this technique is to combine multiple exception types in one `catch` block.

Listing 9-11. Exception Filter Example

```
1  try
2  {
3    throw new ArgumentException();
4  }
5  catch (Exception ex) when (ex is ArgumentException || ex is ArgumentNullException)
6  {
7    Console.WriteLine($"Bad argument error: {ex.Message}");
8  }
9  catch (Exception ex)
10 {
11   Console.WriteLine($"Generic error: {ex.Message}");
12 }
```

The `when` expression on line 5 checks if the *ex* variable is of type ArgumentException or ArgumentNullException using the "`is`" operator. By the way, that is the purpose of the "`is`" operator - to determine if a reference type variable is a particular type and returns `true` for a match, `false` otherwise. If *ex* is one of those types then this is the appropriate `catch` block to execute. Otherwise it will move to the next `catch` clause. Since the second `catch` clause is also trapping on the `Exception` type, it will only be reached if *ex* is not one of the types filtered on in the previous `catch` clause. This technique can greatly simplify `try` structures with many distinct exception types to handle.

9.7 Custom Exception Types

C# does not limit programmers to using only those exceptions defined in the Base and Framework Class Libraries. Custom exception types can be defined using `class` inheritance which can then be utilized just like any other exception type. Since inheritance has not yet been discussed this topic will not be covered at this time.

9.8 Summary

Structured exception handling is fundamental to the creation of robust production-grade code. Using `try-catch` structures a programmer can detect specific errors and deal with the results of those errors accordingly. The `finally` block always executes giving the programmer a convenient place to clean up variables that are no longer required. Exceptions propagate from the point which they are triggered to that method's caller, and that method's caller, etc., until an appropriate `catch` handler is found or the top of the call stack is reached. The programmer can `throw` exceptions as well, indicating to callers that a problem has occurred. The `catch` clauses can also be filtered to make error handling more efficient and concise.

10

10. Introduction to Object-Oriented Programming

C# is a multi-paradigm programming language which provides incredible flexibility to programmers as they are not forced to use one particular technique. For the record, C# supports the following paradigms:

- Procedural – Code is executed as a series of method calls to achieve a desired result.
- Functional – Computation is the evaluation of functions without the need for state-full changes to data.
- Event-driven – The flow of program execution is governed by events or triggers typically instigated by a user, threads, timers or hardware interrupts.
- Object-oriented – Programming is centered on objects that contain data and methods to manipulate that data.

Up to now, most of the examples in this book focused on the procedural aspects of C#, where you create methods that call one another to achieve a desired goal. Object-oriented programming (OOP) shifts the focus away from the methods and onto the objects (`struct` and `class` constructs) that contain those methods. In reality, the style of object-oriented programming employed by C# is a mix of both traditional procedural programming and OOP.

Object-oriented programming is centered on the concept of objects. Objects are simply instances, or variables, of a given type. A type can be one of the following data structures:

- `enum`
- `struct`
- `class`
- `interface`

Custom entities of these types are known as user-defined types. These next chapters will focus on creating these types.

There will be a learning curve adapting to the techniques used by OOP. Learning to transition from maintaining your state variables in Main() to utilizing self-contained objects takes a bit to get used to. However, like all hard topics thus far we'll take it slow so you have time to absorb the nuances of shifting to this paradigm.

10.1 Enumerations (enums)

An `enum` is the simplest form of user-defined type and consists of a set of named, integral constants. Unlike typical integral constants, an `enum` provides a mechanism of limiting a variable of that type to the values in the named set. This is especially useful when using `enum` types as parameters to methods since IntelliSense will display the list of possible values when typing a call to them in code. By default, `enum`s contain `int` constants but they can be defined to contain any of the integral types except `char`. Here are some rules that must be followed when defining enumerations:

- An `enum` is usually defined directly within a `namespace`, but it can also be defined within a `class` or `struct`.
- An `enum` type name must follow the same rules as variable names.
    - Name must start with a letter or underscore.
    - Successive characters can be any alphanumeric character or underscore.
    - No whitespace allowed.
- The constants within an `enum` must also follow the same naming rules.
- By default, the first constant in an `enum` has the value 0, with each successive, comma separated constant being one greater than the previous.
- Individual constant values can be assigned specific values. Any constants that are not assigned explicit values will use sequential numbering starting from the last defined value.
- By default, `enum` types contain `int` values but can be defined to contain one of the following types:
    - `byte`, `sbyte`, `short`, `ushort`, `int`, `uint`, `long` or `ulong`

Creating enums

For `enum`s that utilize the default type and numbering, the syntax appears as follows:

```
enum <name> { <comma-separated constant names> };
```

If the `enum` is to contain values other than `int`, the syntax becomes:

```
enum <name> : <type> { <comma-separated constant names> };
```

To define an `enum` that contains the days of the week, it could be written as such:

Listing 10-1. Simple enum

```
enum Days { Sunday, Monday, Tuesday, Wednesday, Thursday, Friday, Saturday };
```

This `enum`, called `Days`, contains 7 constants starting with *Sunday* as value 0, *Monday* as 1, up to *Saturday* with the value 6. Creating an instance of this type is virtually identical to creating any other value type variable, except only a constant value from Days should ever be assigned to it. If nothing is assigned it will automatically be given the value 0, whether or not there is a constant that maps to 0. You should avoid assigning a numeric value directly to an enum variable. Instead, use the syntax: `<enum name>.<constant name>`

Listing 10-2. Creating an enum Variable

```
static void Main(string[] args)
{
  Days day = Days.Monday;
}
```

Notice that when you type the dot "." operator after Days, Visual Studio will present an alphabetical list of valid choices:

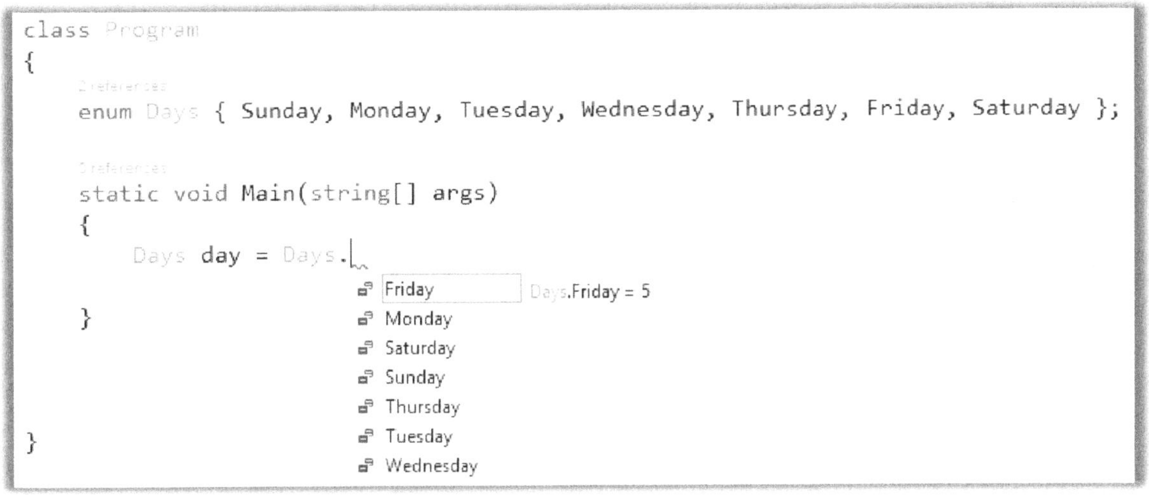

```
class Program
{
    enum Days { Sunday, Monday, Tuesday, Wednesday, Thursday, Friday, Saturday };

    static void Main(string[] args)
    {
        Days day = Days.
                      Friday      Days.Friday = 5
    }                 Monday
                      Saturday
                      Sunday
                      Thursday
}                     Tuesday
                      Wednesday
```

Figure 10-1. IntelliSense and enums

What about enumerations that require custom values, not a sequence starting from 0? In that case, define the values with assignment expressions as done in the following:

Listing 10-3. Defining enum with Custom Values

```
enum DeweyDecimalCategories
{
  GeneralWorks = 0,
  PhilosophyAndPsychology = 100,
  Religion = 200,
  SocialSciences = 300,
  Language = 400,
  PureScience = 500,
  Technology = 600,
  ArtsAndRecreation = 700,
  Literature = 800,
  HistoryAndGeography = 900
}
```

In this example, the first value is still 0; however, each value after this skips by 100. Also notice that in the Days enum example the numeric values are relatively arbitrary. I chose *Sunday* to be 0 but I could very well have defined *Monday* as 0. In the DeweyDecimalCategories example, the numeric values actually have special meanings in the library classification system, so the values are as significant as the constant names.

Since the default value for an enum is 0, it can be very useful to define a special constant with the value 0 to represent an "unknown" value. Therefore, when a variable of that enum is created the "unknown" value is automatically assigned to that variable if an explicit value is not supplied.

Listing 10-4. Enumeration with Explicit Default Value

```
enum MovieRatings
{
  Unknown = 0,
  G,    // General audiences
  PG,   // Parental guidance suggested
  PG13, // Parents strongly cautioned
  R,    // Restricted
  NC17, // No one 17 and under admitted
  UR    // Unrated
}
```

This enum contains a constant called *Unknown* to represent the value 0. When a variable of type MovieRatings is created it will automatically be assigned MovieRatings.*Unknown* if no value is explicitly supplied.

Enumerations Derived From Different Types

As mentioned earlier, an enum can be derived from types other than int. Since the legal base types are all integral types the usage of the enum is basically identical for all types. So, why bother? The most obvious reason to use a different base type is when int cannot represent the values necessary for your specific needs. Since an int cannot represent any value greater than

2,147,483,647, if your enum requires a larger value either a uint, long or ulong may be required as they can represent much higher values.

Listing 10-5. Enumeration Derived from Long

```
enum PlanetaryDistances : long
{
  Sun = 0,
  Mercury =   57909175,
  Venus =    108208930,
  Earth =    149597890,
  Mars =     227936640,
  Jupiter =  778412010,
  Saturn =  1426725400,
  Uranus =  2870972200,
  Neptune = 4498252900
}
```

This enum, which shows the distance of each planet from the Sun in kilometers, requires the long data type since the values of *Uranus* and *Neptune* fall outside the range of int. The *Sun* constant represents the default value for this enum which is 0 km from itself.

In reality, the PlanetaryDistance enum is not a great example, mostly because the values are so drastically different from one-another, with large gaps between them. While this is not necessarily an example of what not to do, it does tread very close to that territory.

Enumerations as Method Parameters

Once defined, an enum type can be used like any other value data type. As such, they can be used to create variables, as you have seen, and they can also be used as method parameters. Like other value types these parameters can be passed by value (default) or passed by reference (ref or out). Clearly, a programmer could use an int value as an input parameter and leave it up to the caller to select from a known list of constants, not defined in an enum, to pass as an argument. The problem is that ***any*** int could be passed in those circumstances, possibly leading to side effects in the code. Using an enum, the caller chooses from a list of values and no guess-work is involved.

Listing 10-6. Enumerations as Method Parameters

```
enum MathOps
{
  Unknown = 0,
  Add,
  Subtract,
  Multiply,
  Divide
}

static void Main(string[] args)
{
  double result = Calculate(2.5, MathOps.Multiply, 3.1);
  result = Calculate(10, MathOps.Subtract, 2.2);
}

static double Calculate(double num1, MathOps operation, double num2)
{
  switch (operation)
  {
    default:
    case MathOps.Unknown:
      return 0;
    case MathOps.Add:
      return num1 + num2;
    case MathOps.Subtract:
      return num1 - num2;
    case MathOps.Multiply:
      return num1 * num2;
    case MathOps.Divide:
      return num1 / num2;
  }
}
```

One item that should jump out at you in this example is how nicely the MathOps `enum` works with the `switch` statement. Since the values of an `enum` are really just plain old integers, the `enum` constants can be used directly in the `case` labels. This is also very much easier to read than if the numeric values were used instead. What has been accomplished here is the elimination of "magic numbers". Magic numbers are values that have special meaning but only within the context of a specific method or program. The value 1 was arbitrarily assigned to the *Add* constant, it could just as easily been 12345. To a human reading the code the word *Add* conveys a meaning and purpose, but the number 1 could literally mean anything depending on its usage.

Flags

Flags are a special type of `enum` where each constant value of the `enum` equates to a power of 2. This has the effect of making each constant equal to a single bit in the integral value. To fully understand this concept let's take a little detour and discuss bitwise operations.

Bitwise Operations

In computer science the smallest unit of memory in the binary system is a bit which can either represent 0 or 1 (off or on, respectively). A bit very much acts like a `bool`, but on a smaller scale since a `bool` requires 1 byte of memory which is actually 8 bits. A problem working with bits is that they are not individually addressable in C#. You can manipulate bits, but the smallest data type in C# is one byte of memory. Therefore, let's work with the `byte` data type and take a peek at its 8 bits.

A `byte`, as you may recall, can contain a value between 0 and 255. Each one of these 256 values is a unique combination of 0's and 1's in the byte's 8 bits. Bits are represented with the smallest bit value on the right and the greatest bit value on the left, where each bit is twice the value as the one to its right. The following table demonstrates the individual values of the bits in a `byte`:

Bit #	7	6	5	4	3	2	1	0
Value ($2^{bit\#}$)	2^7	2^6	2^5	2^4	2^3	2^2	2^1	2^0
	128	64	32	16	8	4	2	1

Notice that each bit is worth 2 raised to the power of the 0-based bit number. Therefore, to represent the value 73, the following bit pattern (or mask) is required:

Bit #	7	6	5	4	3	2	1	0
Mask	0	**1**	0	0	**1**	0	0	**1**
Value		64			8			1

This bit mask yields the following values: $2^6 + 2^3 + 2^0$, or 64 + 8 + 1 which equals 73. An interesting fact is that for a number to be odd the "0" bit must be set as it is the only power of 2 that yields an odd value.

When working at the bit level it is necessary to be able to determine if a bit (or set of bits) is on and to be able to flip bits on or off, like a light switch. This is done using some operators you are already familiar with when working with `bool`s: and, or, exclusive or and not. In addition, bit shifting operators "<<" and ">>" are frequently used. If multiple values are being manipulated at the same time, such as two `byte`s, only the corresponding bits in each `byte` are compared with each other. Here is an example using "&", but "|" and "^" work the same way:

Bit #	7	6	5	4	3	2	1	0
A	0	1	0	1	1	0	0	1
B	0	0	1	1	0	1	0	1
A & B	0	0	0	1	0	0	0	1

For the result of an "&" operation to be 1, both operands must be 1. This only occurs in bit positions 0 and 4, which is why the result is "00010001". "&", therefore, represents the **intersection** of bits between two bit masks.

Bitwise "|" works the exact same way as "&" but the result is the **union** of the bits in both bit masks. Exclusive or "^" produces a **non-overlapping union**, or the union without intersections. The following Venn diagrams illustrate these relationships where each circle (A & B) represents a different set of bits:

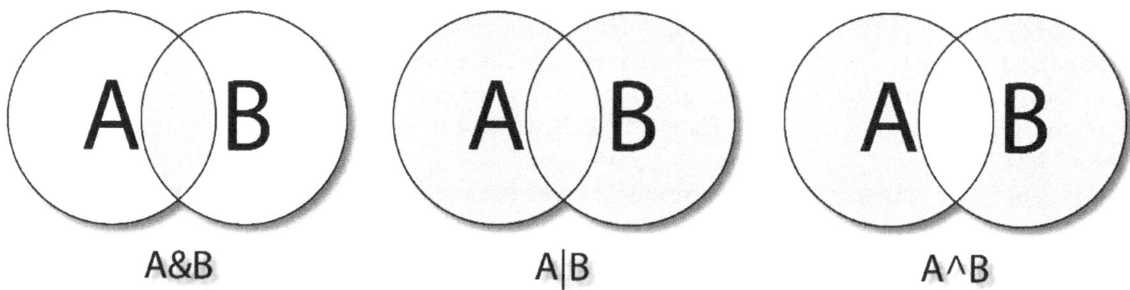

Figure 10-2. Relationship between Bitwise Operations

The "A&B" diagram demonstrates that the result of "&" is the set of bits both A and B share in common. The "A | B" diagram shows the result of " | " is the set of all bits from both A and B. "A^B" demonstrates the result of "^" is the union of only the distinct bits in both sets.

Table 10-1. Bitwise Operators

<table>
<tr><th>Bitwise Operator</th><th>Name</th><th>Purpose</th><th>Example</th></tr>
<tr><td>&</td><td>And</td><td>Compares two bits and returns 1 if both bits are 1, 0 otherwise. Works on single or multiple bits. For multiple bits, only bits in the same bit position are compared with each other. In the example, bit 0 is "1" for both bytes; therefore, the result is "1" because 1 & 1 = 1. However, in bit position 2 the operation is 1 & 0 which equals 0.</td><td>00011101
& 00110001
00010001</td></tr>
<tr><td>|</td><td>Or</td><td>Compares two bits and returns 1 if either bit is 1, 0 otherwise. Works on single or multiple bits. Again, only bits in the same bit position are compared with each other.</td><td>00011101
| 00110001
00111101</td></tr>
<tr><td>^</td><td>Exclusive Or</td><td>Compares two bits and returns 1 if either bit is 1, but not both, 0 otherwise. Works on single or multiple bits. Once again, only bits in the same bit position are compared.</td><td>00011101
^ 00110001
00101100</td></tr>
<tr><td>~</td><td>Not</td><td>Flips the value of a bit, from 0 to 1 or 1 to 0. Works on single or multiple bits.</td><td>~ 00110001
11001110</td></tr>
<tr><td><<</td><td>Left shift</td><td>Shifts the first operand left by the number of bits specified by its second operand (integer-style numbers only). Effectively multiplies left operand by 2^n.</td><td>00011101 << 2
= 01110100</td></tr>
<tr><td>>></td><td>Right shift</td><td>Shifts the first operand right by the number of bits specified by its second operand (integer-style numbers only). Effectively divides left operand by 2^n. Notice that the bit in position 0 is lost as it is shifted off the right edge.</td><td>00011101 >> 2
= 00000111</td></tr>
</table>

Back to Flags...

So, what did all of that have to do with enums? Remember, a flag is a constant of an enum where the value is a power of 2, and therefore, represents a bit. Now that we know what they are, what value do they provide regarding your code? By using flags, multiple values can be represented in a single variable, where each value is a bit. Therefore, a `byte` can represent 8 distinct values, a `short` can hold 16 values, an `int` has 32 and a `long` can represent 64. Consider the next `enum` example which represents the different styles of a font. Just like a font can have multiple states set simultaneously, like bold and italic, so can a variable of this `enum`.

Listing 10-7. Flags enum

```
[Flags]
enum FontStyles
{
  Normal = 0,
  Bold = 1,          // 2^0
  Italic = 2,        // 2^1
  Underline = 4,     // 2^2
  Strikethrough = 8  // 2^3
}

static void Main(string[] args)
{
  FontStyles style = FontStyles.Bold;
}
```

There's not much different about this `enum` compared to the others that we've created; however, there are two items worth noting. First, the `enum` is prefaced with something called an attribute, called [Flags] in this case. This actually does nothing to the compiled code except add a note in the assembly's metadata that says FontStyles is a flags `enum`. The `enum` itself will only be handled specially by code that specifically looks for that note in the metadata, like `string`.Format(). Second, each constant value is a power of 2. The *Normal* constant is not actually represented by any specific bit, rather it is the default value of the `enum` when no bits are on. If we wanted to add another constant to the list it would most likely have a value of 16. Although the `enum` is marked with the [Flags] attribute the compiler will allow non-power of 2 values since, as mentioned, that attribute does not affect the compilation of the code. However, doing so runs afoul of the intentions of that attribute so it is not recommended.

In Main(), a variable called *style* is created that is of the FontStyles type, but we don't do anything fancy with it other than set it to a value. The whole point of the flags `enum` is to combine and remove flags from the value, so that is what the next examples demonstrate. Assume that these examples all use the *style* variable.

Assigning a Single Flag

To assign a single bit to a flags `enum` variable, simply assign to it one of the `enum`'s constants.

```
style = FontStyles.Bold;
```

To change the value, do another assignment:

```
style = FontStyles.Italic;
```

Assigning Multiple Flags

To assign multiple flags simultaneously, use the "|" (or) operator to combine the flags:

```
style = FontStyles.Bold | FontStyles.Italic;
```

This code assigns both *Bold* and *Italics* to the *style* variable. Since the result of the "|" operation is assigned to *style* using "=", any previous value in *style* is replaced with this. Don't believe it? Here's what is going on bit-wise when this operation occurs. First, let's consider what the bit mask for FontStyles looks like:

Bit #	3	2	1	0
Name	Strikethrough	Underline	Italic	Bold
Value	$2^3 = 8$	$2^2 = 4$	$2^1 = 2$	$2^0 = 1$

Since we are only using the first 4 bits of a byte, this graph only shows those 4. The "|" operation described above (`FontStyles.Bold | FontStyles.Italic`) is actually doing this:

```
  0001  ← Bold
| 0010  ← Italic
  0011  ← Bold | Italic
```

What if we want to add a flag to an `enum` variable without overwriting the existing value? We still use the "|" operator but in conjunction with an assignment operator, "|=". So, assuming *style* is already *Bold | Italic*, adding *Underline* to the mask requires this operation:

```
style |= FontStyles.Underline;
```

If *Underline* was already part of the mask the previous line would have no effect since the "or" operation is the union of two sets. Since the *Underline* bit is already part of the set of bits in *style*, a union with *Underline* would yield the exact same value, no matter how many times it is performed.

Testing for a Flag

As you may have already guessed, since assigning a flag utilizes the "|" operator, testing for a flag utilizes the "&" operator. When preforming "&", the resulting bit is 1 only if both bits being compared are also 1. Therefore, you can use "&" between the mask you are testing (*style*) and the bit you wish to test, *Italic* for our example. If the result of the operation is the test bit, then that bit was set.

```
bool italicSet = (style & FontStyles.Italic) == FontStyles.Italic;
```

This one is a fair bit more complex than the operation for setting a bit. Let's look at the "&" calculation in more detail:

```
  0111  ← Bold | Italic | Underline
& 0010  ← Italic
  0010  ← Italic
```

This problem is much simpler when you approach it like this. If the *Italic* bit was not "on" in the top bit mask then the result would have been all 0's. However, since that particular bit is "on" in both bytes, the result is a 1.

The good news is that C# added a method to do this exact test without the use of "&". It is called "HasFlag()" and you call it on the mask you are testing. Here is how that previous line would be rewritten to use HasFlag():

```
bool italicSet = style.HasFlag(FontStyles.Italic);
```

This is much easier to read and understand. It is also one of those special methods that looks for the [Flags] attribute in the program's metadata mentioned earlier. We'll look at more `enum` methods in just a bit.

You can also use either technique to test for multiple bits simultaneously. Just "or" the bits together in a compound expression as such:

```
bool boldAndItalicSet = style.HasFlag(FontStyles.Bold | FontStyles.Italic);
```

Removing a Flag

Removing a flag from a bit mask actually requires two of the bitwise operators, "&" and "~". First, we use the "~" operator to create a mask of the flags we wish to keep turned on. If we want to turn off the *Underline* flag then you would use *~Underline* to create a bit mask with 1s for all bits except that one particular bit. Using "&" between the mask you wish to change and the *~Underline* mask will result in a new mask where all bits are unchanged except the one specific bit which will be 0, regardless of its original value. In code it would look like this:

```
style &= ~FontStyles.Underline;
```

A detailed look at the bits…

```
~Underline = ~0100 = 1011

  0111  ← Bold | Italic | Underline
& 1011  ← ~Underline
  0011  ← Bold | Italic
```

Toggling a Flag

Toggling a flag, or switching it from 0 to 1 or from 1 to 0, can be done several ways. The first way is to check if the flag is set using the HasFlag() method then turning on the bit if it is not set or turning it off if it is.

Listing 10-8. Toggling a Flag

```
// Toggle Italic
if (style.HasFlag(FontStyles.Italic))
{
  style &= ~FontStyles.Italic;
}
else
{
  style |= FontStyles.Italic;
}
// OR
style = style.HasFlag(FontStyles.Italic) ? style & ~FontStyles.Italic :
    style | FontStyles.Italic;
```

Yuck. Neither way is particularly desirable regarding readability or conciseness. The good news is that the "^" operator is designed to do just this. Remember, "exclusive or" yields a 1 only if exactly one of the bits being compared is also 1. So, if *style* starts with *Bold* | *Italic* | *Underline*, then using "^" with *Italic* gives us:

```
  0111  ← Bold | Italic | Underline
^ 0010  ← Italic
  0101  ← Bold | Underline
```

Doing it again, with *style* set to *Bold* | *Underline* yields:

```
  0111  ← Bold | Underline
^ 0010  ← Italic
  0111  ← Bold | Italic | Underline
```

That seemed simple, but what does the code look like?

```
style ^= FontStyles.Italic;
```

Yep, not bad at all. We knew that "^" had to be good for something!

Enumeration Methods

As you already saw with HasFlag(), `enums` have methods that can assist with their use. The following list contains the most useful methods, some of which are instance methods like HasFlag() that you call using an `enum` variable. The others are `static` and you call them using the "Enum." handle. Notice that it is a capital "E", not a lowercase "e". This is one of the few types that requires the use of the CTS name to call its static methods.

Table 10-2. Enumeration Members

Static*	Name	Description
✓	Format()	Formats the given enum value using the specified format string.
✓	GetName()	Gets the constant name for the given numeric value.
✓	GetNames()	Gets a list of all of the constant names in the given enum.
✓	GetUnderlyingType()	Determines the base type of the enum, typically System.Int32.
✓	GetValues()	Gets a list of all of the actual constants in the enum.
	HasFlag()	Determines if an enum bit mask contains the specified flag(s).
✓	IsDefined()	Determines if the given value (constant name or number) exists in the enum.
✓	Parse()	Parses the given string into a specific enum value.
	ToString()	Converts the enum to a string.
✓	TryParse()	Attempts to parse a given text string into an equivalent enum value.

We're only going to look at a few of these methods in detail, specifically the ones you will find useful in actual programming situations. In addition, HasFlag() was already covered in the previous sections so it will not be re-examined here.

GetName()

The GetName() method provides a quick mechanism for determining the name of a constant in an enum given its numeric value. This will work with [Flags] enums, but not composite flags (two or more flags or'd together). Example:

```
string name = Enum.GetName(typeof(FontStyles), 4);
```

This example would store the value "Underline" in the variable *name* since the constant *Underline* has the value 4 in the FontStyles enum in Listing 10-7. If the numeric value is not found the method returns null.

One aspect of this method that you may have not seen before is passing a Type as a parameter. The typeof operator returns a Type variable for the type provided as its argument. In this case it is the type name of the FontStyles enum. This technique is used for all of the static Enum methods.

GetNames()

This method returns an array of strings containing all of the constant names in an enum.

```
string[] allNames = Enum.GetNames(typeof(PlanetaryDistances));
```

This array can then be iterated through using a `foreach` or similar loop construct.

GetUnderlyingType()

This method returns a Type variable representing the base type of the `enum`. Unless otherwise specified, the underlying type is always System.Int32, the CTS name for `int`.

```
Type type = Enum.GetUnderlyingType(typeof(PlanetaryDistances));
```

GetValues()

Gets an array containing all of the constants defined in an `enum`. Unlike GetNames(), this method returns the actual constants defined in the `enum`. This means each item in the array contains both the name of the constant and its value. The following example calls GetValues() for the PlanetaryDistances `enum` defined in Listing 10-5.

Listing 10-9. Enum.GetValues()

```
Console.WriteLine("All Planet Values");
var allValues = Enum.GetValues(typeof(PlanetaryDistances));
foreach (var value in allValues)
{
  Console.WriteLine($"{value:G} = {value:D}");
}
```

```
All Planet Values
Sun = 0
Mercury = 57909175
Venus = 108208930
Earth = 149597890
Mars = 227936640
Jupiter = 778412010
Saturn = 1426725400
Uranus = 2870972200
Neptune = 4498252900
```

Figure 10-3. Enum.GetValues() Output

Did you notice the custom format codes used to display each value on line 5? The "G" format specifier will output the constant name while "D" is used to get the numeric value. This is a useful technique allowing you to work with the names or numbers as necessary.

IsDefined()

The IsDefined() method determines if the given `string` maps to a constant in an `enum`. The text comparison is case sensitive so the spelling must be exact. This method works with [Flags] `enums` only if composite flags (combined bits) are not used.

In the following example, *defined* is set to `false` since the spelling of "bold" does not match the text case shown in Listing 10-7.

```
bool defined = Enum.IsDefined(typeof(FontStyles), "bold");
```

This next example also returns false since the numeric value provided, 3, also does not exist explicitly in that `enum`:

```
bool defined = Enum.IsDefined(typeof(FontStyles), 3);
```

Parse() and TryParse()

These methods work very similarly to the Parse() and TryParse() methods of the built-in types, like `int` and `double`. Recall that Parse() will fail with an exception if parsing is not possible while TryParse() will return `false`. Since TryParse() avoids exception handling it is generally the more desirable of the two methods, for both execution speed and readability.

Parse() and TryParse() have the ability to do case-insensitive comparisons to the `enum` constant names and both are able to parse composite flag values (comma separated).

Listing 10-10. Enum.TryParse()

```
FontStyles fontStyle;
if (Enum.TryParse("Bold, Italic", true, out fontStyle))
{
  Console.WriteLine($"Parsed: {fontStyle:G} = {fontStyle:D}");
}
```

```
Parsed: Bold, Italic = 3
```

Figure 10-4. Enum.TryParse() Output

The three arguments on line 2 correspond to: the text being parsed, a `bool` flag indicating case-insensitive text comparison and the variable to contain the parsed value if successful, respectively.

ToString()

The ToString() method of an `enum` prints the name of the constant represented by the value. The overload of the method that accepts a format `string` can be used to change the output behavior. The two most commonly used format specifiers are "G" and "D" which have been demonstrated several times in the other method examples.

Casting Enumerations

When it is necessary to deal with an `enum` value as a number the standard casting operators can be used to convert the value. Since most `enum`s have a base type of `int`, the most common cast will be "`(int)`". However, ensure you are casting to the correct type to avoid unexpected overflow exceptions.

Once the `enum` value has been cast to a numeric value it is no longer equivalent to an `enum` constant value and thus no longer has a "name". To get it back to an `enum` value it either has to be cast back into the `enum` value, using "`(<enum name>)`" or converted using Enum.Parse() or Enum.TryParse(). Be aware that casting back to an `enum` with a value that doesn't exist in the `enum` will technically work but it won't actually map to a constant name.

Due to the fact that the `enum` constants are not just numeric values, direct comparisons between `enum` values and numeric values are not allowed. In those instances you will have to cast one of the values to the other's type, typically the `enum` to a numeric value. Assuming you have a variable called *fontStyle* which is an `enum` value the comparison may look something like:

```
if ((int)fontStyle == 2)
```

Enumeration Dos and Don'ts

Let's look at some of the guidelines regarding the use of `enum`s in your code.

Do:

- Use an `enum` to group like constants together into a common data structure.
- Define a default value that represents 0.
- Define constants within a flags `enum` as powers of two.
- Try to rely on the `enum` constant names in code rather than the numeric values as those can change.

Don't:

- Don't create "sentinel" values in the enum, such as *FirstValue* and *LastValue*, indicating the first and last constants in the list. Adding new values may adversely change the numeric components of these constants breaking future versions of the code.
- Don't create "placeholder" constants in an enum, such as *FutureUse1*.
- Don't use an enum for open sets of data (data that is intended to change frequently over time) like operating system versions.
- Try not to alter the value of an enum constant after code has been placed into production. It is entirely possible that parts of the application, like a database table, are tied to the enum using numeric values not the names. Instead, try to add new items at the end of the enum list using new numeric values.

10.2 struct

As programs start to get more complex it may be desirable to group variables together into a common entity. Consider a two-dimensional point that consists of an *x* and a *y* member. Not only do those variables have to be maintained separately, any time you wish to pass these values to a method, such a method for calculating distance between two points, each individual value would be required as a parameter:

Listing 10-11. Distance Between Points

```
static void Main(string[] args)
{
  double x1 = 2.3, y1 = 6.2;
  double x2 = 5.4, y2 = 1.7;
  double dist = PointDistance(x1, y1, x2, y2);
}

static double PointDistance(double x1, double y1, double x2, double y2)
{
  return Math.Sqrt(Math.Pow(x2 - x1, 2) + Math.Pow(y2 - y1, 2));
}
```

The only reason this code works is because *x1* is logically associated with *y1* and *x2* is associated with *y2*. However, that is only because we chose to pass those variables to the PointDistance() method in a particular order. We could just as easily called PointDistance () using:

```
double dist = PointDistance(x1, y2, x2, y1);
```

Now, the answer is fundamentally different. This demonstrates the difference between syntax and semantics. Syntactically, both calls are 100% valid as they will both produce a result without exception. However, semantics refers to the "meaning" of the code. We know logically that *x1* and *y1* belong together but there is nothing in the code that forces us to use them in that manner.

So, the meaning is implied but cannot be enforced. Wouldn't it be nice to find a way to associate *x1* and *y1* syntactically? Enter the struct…

First and foremost, a struct is a data structure that allows us to group values together into a single, logical entity. Since a struct is a data type, variables of its kind can be created just like an int or double, which can then be passed as a whole to methods. Here is a simple struct that groups two double variables together, comprising a logical point:

Listing 10-12. The Point struct

```
struct Point
{
  public double X;
  public double Y;
}
```

Notice that *X* and *Y* are declared with the public keyword. This is important because the default access modifier for variables of a struct is private which would deny access to the variables by anything accept other members of Point. The public keyword allows access to these members from external sources, such as from Main(). Also, these variables cannot be initialized like regular variables in their declarations. Instead, they will be given default values until they are overridden when a struct variable is created. The struct members, *X* and *Y*, can be accessed using the dot "." operator on a Point struct variable as follows:

Listing 10-13. Accessing the Point struct

```
Point point1;     // Create a variable of type Point called point1
point1.X = 2.3;   // Assign values to the fields of point1
point1.Y = 6.2;
Console.WriteLine($"Point1 = ({point1.X}, {point1.Y})");
```

The variable *point1* is an ***object*** of the type Point. Publicly accessible variables of an object, such as X and Y, are known as ***fields***. This terminology is standard for object-oriented programming and will be used for the remainder of the text. None of this should be all that new since we've been working with objects and their syntax all along, even though we skirted around the OOP terminology.

What about the PointDistance() method? How would that change if we no longer pass the ordinates as separate values but as Point objects instead? Here's what the new version, using Point, looks like:

Listing 10-14. PointDistance() Using Point Objects

```
static void Main(string[] args)
{
  Point point1;
  point1.X = 2.3;
  point1.Y = 6.2;
  Point point2;
  point2.X = 5.4;
  point2.Y = 1.7;
  dist = PointDistance(point1, point2);
}

static double PointDistance(Point pt1, Point pt2)
{
  return Math.Sqrt(Math.Pow(pt2.X - pt1.X, 2) + Math.Pow(pt2.Y - pt1.Y, 2));
}
```

In the end, both the method that accepts ordinates as individual values and the one that accepts aggregated Point objects perform the same operation and return the same results. What we did gain, however, is a better sense of the code's purpose. Points are now entities that group two ordinates together into a single coordinate, rather than having two separate values that require extra thought and care to ensure they are used in the correct manner. When done right, OOP can help organize and define entities and their usage in your programs. But, we're only a fraction of the way to a true object-oriented program. Filling in the field values one-at-a-time after object creation is a bit tedious. Let's look at a mechanism to optimize that part of the code.

10.3 struct Constructors

Parameterized Constructors

It is a requirement for `struct` objects that all fields must be set prior to using the objects for any purpose. However, it is incredibly monotonous and lengthy setting individual fields before you can use them. The good news is that `struct` types can define specialized methods which allow you to set all of the fields in a single call. These specialized methods are called constructors and you have used them before with the DateTime `struct`. Consider this call to create a DateTime object using a series of numbers to pre-populate its contents:

```
DateTime date = new DateTime(2010, 3, 12);
```

DateTime is a `struct` and this call uses the "`new`" keyword to trigger a call to one of its constructors. This particular overload of the constructor accepts three `int` values corresponding to the year, month and day values that define the *date* object. After this call the *date* object is ready to be used without any further field modifications. Likewise, the Point `struct` can be enhanced to support this type of construction.

Listing 10-15. Point Constructor

```
1  static void Main(string[] args)
2  {
3    Point pt = new Point(1.7, 2.4);
4  }
5
6  struct Point
7  {
8    public double X;
9    public double Y;
10
11   public Point(double x, double y)
12   {
13     X = x;
14     Y = y;
15   }
16 }
```

Note: Main() is actually part of the Program class, explaining the separator between it and the Point struct. Most programmers place classes and structs in separate files so this boundary makes even more sense in those instances.

Constructors (sometimes abbreviated as "ctor") are very much like methods except they have no return value and they always have the same name as the `struct` they are defined in. So, inside the Point `struct`, in addition to the fields, we now have a method called Point() that accepts two `double` parameters, *x* and *y*. The sole purpose of this method is to assign the contents of the parameters into the fields. Therefore, on lines 13 and 14, the parameter value *x* is assigned to the field *X* and *y* is assigned to *Y*. Once this method finishes executing a new Point object is fully initialized and ready to be used.

By the way, this is where a good naming convention comes in handy. Notice that the fields of Point are uppercase and the parameters of the constructor are lowercase. This prevents any conflict that would occur if both fields and parameters shared the same spelling and casing. It is not apparent here because the names in this example are only one character long, but fields are typically Pascal cased, like method names, while parameters are camel cased, just like variables. Later examples will demonstrate this more clearly. If both the field and parameter were called "*x*", then the assignment in the constructor would be "`x = x;`", or literally assigning the value of *x* to itself. Since the more locally-defined value takes precedence in cases like these, the "*x*" name would refer to the parameter and the field would be completely ignored. Moral of the story? Ensure the spelling or casing is distinct between fields and parameters!

There is no limit to the number of constructors your `struct` provides as long as the parameter list for each one is unique, just like standard overloaded methods. The only exception to this is that a constructor that accepts no parameters cannot be added to a `struct`.

Default Constructors

An interesting thing about `struct` entities is that they come with a built-in constructor, known as the default constructor. A default constructor accepts no parameters and is used to set all fields of the struct object to the default values of their respective types. Normally, any constructor call, including the default constructor, would use the "new" keyword to initialize an object, such as:

```
Point pt = new Point();
```

However, struct objects do not need to be initialized in this manner. In Listing 10-13, a Point object was created just by calling "Point pt;" and then setting all of the fields to some value. This is legal because all struct entities are value types, just like int. In fact, the default constructor is actually called behind-the-scenes immediately preceding the call to set the first field to a value. If the object was declared and the fields were never set to a value then the default constructor would never be called. All of this is moot if a constructor is explicitly called, but it is good to understand the behavior when constructors are not employed.

Another important note about the default constructor is that it is the only one you cannot define for your own structs. That is to say, the following statement is illegal in the Point struct:

```
public Point() { // initialize fields here }
```

The default constructor is supplied by the compiler and there is no provision to override that functionality. Several iterations of the C# language, including C# 6, almost included this capability but the use cases for adding this feature were far outweighed by the impact to existing code. This feature may eventually show up in the language but for the immediate future its inclusion is unlikely.

Copy Constructors

Another specialized constructor that can be defined in struct entities is called a copy constructor. This type of constructor typically accepts a single parameter that is the same type as the struct it is defined in. The whole purpose of the copy constructor is to provide a mechanism for creating a brand new object of a given type, copying the fields from another object. This process is also sometimes referred to as cloning. Here is an example of a copy constructor for the Point struct:

Listing 10-16. Copy Constructor

```
 1 static void Main(string[] args)
 2 {
 3   Point pt = new Point(1.7, 2.4);
 4   Point copy = new Point(pt);
 5   Console.WriteLine($"pt = ({pt.X}, {pt.Y})");
 6   Console.WriteLine($"copy = ({copy.X}, {copy.Y})");
 7 }
 8
 9 struct Point
10 {
11   public double X;
12   public double Y;
13
14   // Parameterized ctor
15   public Point(double x, double y)
16   {
17     X = x;
18     Y = y;
19   }
20
21   // Copy ctor
22   public Point(Point other)
23   {
24     X = other.X;
25     Y = other.Y;
26   }
27 }
```

```
pt = (1.7, 2.4)
copy = (1.7, 2.4)
```

Figure 10-5. Copy Constructor Output

First, let's focus on lines 22 - 26. It is clearly a constructor since the name of the method is the same as the `struct`. Furthermore, it is a copy constructor because it accepts a parameter of type Point which is also the same name as the `struct` it is defined within. The parameter is called *other* and the constructor will copy each of the fields from within that object into the fields of the object being constructed. Once the call is complete the object that triggered this constructor call with the "`new`" keyword will be virtually identical to the object that was passed into the copy constructor. Any change to *pt* or *copy* after line 4 in Main() will be completely contained to that particular object. This behavior is a direct result of the fields *X* and *Y* being value types. Remember, assignment of the value of one value type variable to another results in two completely separate variables that have identical values. That is exactly what is happening inside the copy constructor when the values of *other.X* and *other.Y* are copied into *X* and *Y* of the new object, respectively. This process would require some extra thought if *X* or *Y* were reference types; however, that practice is strongly discouraged when designing struct entities since they are really meant for value types only.

10.4 Instance Methods

We are getting closer and closer to using object-oriented programming in the manner that is intended. We know how to package variables together as the fields of a `struct`. Then, we learned how to create and use constructors to instantiate and initialize objects of our `struct` type. However, we have one lingering issue that is keeping us away from OOP nirvana. The PointDistance() method we defined is very "procedural" and really not OOP at all. Recall the definition of OOP given at the beginning of the chapter: "Programming is centered on objects that contain data and *methods to manipulate that data*". That last phrase was emphasized to show what we are still lacking in the Point `struct`. It does not contain methods to manipulate the data. PointDistance() would most definitely qualify but it is not actually part of Point. Rather, it depends on the programmer to pass two Point objects to it. We'll get to implementing the distance method in Point shortly, but let's start with a simpler method first.

In virtually all of the examples in this book results of methods are printed to the console window. This is almost exclusively done within the Main() method, usually after some calculation is performed. One facet of OOP is that objects should be able to perform their own operations without relying on external code. So, with that in mind, let's teach Point how to print itself to the console window. We know from Main() we could print the contents of a Point object with a command similar to the following, assuming an object of type Point called *pt*:

```
Console.WriteLine($"({pt.X}, {pt.Y})");
```

Let's start by defining the method in the Point `struct`. Normally, in procedural programming a method is named with a verb and sometimes a noun, like PrintPoint(). However, in OOP, methods typically only contain a verb, such as Print(). Here's the reason. If you create a method in a `struct`, it would be called using an object handle, such as "*pt*.Print()". Context is everything - the Print() method is being called on a specific Point object. So, if the method was called PrintPoint(), and is called using "*pt*.PrintPoint()", it is like saying "Point Print Point", which is redundant. Therefore, this method will just be called Print() since the "Point" part is implied.

What about parameters? Does Print() require anything to be passed to it? In this case, no. Because we are calling Print() within the context of a Point object the method will already have access to *X* and *Y* which is what we are trying to print. Here's what Point looks like with the added Print() method:

Listing 10-17. Point struct with Print()

```
struct Point
{
  public double X;
  public double Y;

  public Point(double x, double y)
  {
    X = x;
    Y = y;
  }

  public Point(Point other)
  {
    X = other.X;
    Y = other.Y;
  }

  public void Print()
  {
    Console.WriteLine($"({X}, {Y})");
  }
}
```

Since Print() is a member of Point, just like the constructors, it has direct access to the *X* and *Y* fields. And, just like the constructors, it is a specific *X* and *Y*, associated with the object the method was called on. Since the method is called using an instance (object) of type Point the method is called an "instance method". Here's an example of calling Print() from Main():

Listing 10-18. Calling Point.Print()

```
static void Main(string[] args)
{
  Point pt1 = new Point(3.4, 7.1);
  Point pt2 = new Point(1.9, 3.2);
  pt1.Print();
  pt2.Print();
}
```

```
(3.4, 7.1)
(1.9, 3.2)
```

Figure 10-6. Point.Print() Output

As you can see, when Print() is called it prints the *X* and *Y* associated with the specific Point object it is called on. Since *pt1* is created with the values of *X* and *Y* as 3.4 and 7.1, respectively, those are the values used when Print() is called.

Now, let's move onto a trickier problem – the PointDistance() method. We could follow the same exact pattern as the Print() method except for one problem – the PointDistance() method requires two Point objects. Remember, when a method is called on an instance of Point that method has direct access to the fields of that particular instance. So, that would account for one of the objects needed for the PointDistance() method. What about the other? That will have to be a parameter that is passed to the method. Also, since this method is being called within the context of a Point object, let's rename the method Distance().

Listing 10-19. Point.Distance()

```
struct Point
{
  public double X;
  public double Y;

  // Other methods omitted for brevity

  public double Distance(Point other)
  {
    return Math.Sqrt(Math.Pow(other.X - X, 2) + Math.Pow(other.Y - Y, 2));
  }
}
```

Compare this to the procedural version of PointDistance():

Listing 10-20. Original PointDistance() Method

```
static double PointDistance(Point pt1, Point pt2)
{
  return Math.Sqrt(Math.Pow(pt2.X - pt1.X, 2) + Math.Pow(pt2.Y - pt1.Y, 2));
}
```

Fundamentally, the calculations are the same. The biggest difference is that PointDistance() requires two Point parameters, *pt1* and *pt2*, while Distance() has only one called *other*. In the Distance() method, *other* takes the place of *pt2*, but *pt1* is replaced by the instance fields *X* and *Y* of the Point object that the method is called upon. Let's see what this would actually look like when called.

Listing 10-21. Calling Point.Distance()

```
static void Main(string[] args)
{
  Point pt1 = new Point(3.4, 7.1);
  Point pt2 = new Point(1.9, 3.2);
  double distance = pt1.Distance(pt2);
  Console.WriteLine($"The distance between pt1 and pt2 is {distance:0.00}");
}
```

```
The distance between pt1 and pt2 is 4.18
```

Figure 10-7. Point.Distance() Output

Since *pt1* is the object that Distance() is called upon, *X* inside the method is 3.4 and *Y* is 7.1. Also, *pt2* is the argument passed to the *other* parameter, therefore, *other.X* is 1.9 and *other.Y* is 3.2.

The whole concept of context is one of the trickiest parts of object-oriented programming to grasp. Most people understand that the fields of a `struct` instance belong to a specific variable of that `struct` type, as if it were a bag holding the items. Another instance is another bag with distinct items. However, once methods are thrown into the mix, people tend to scratch their heads in bewilderment. It really is not that complicated if you can remember that calling a method using a specific object means that method has direct access to that specific object's fields and no other object's fields. If another object's fields are required by that method then they must be passed as arguments to the method, as was done in Distance().

10.5 Static Methods

Besides instance methods, a `struct` can also define `static` methods. A `static` method does not require an instance of the `struct` to call it upon. Although this topic is being presented as a brand new concept this is what you worked with for the entirety of the book up until this chapter. Consider Console.WriteLine(), a method we've used hundreds of times before. Notice that the WriteLine() method is being called using the type name "Console" as the handle and not an object or variable. What this means is that the WriteLine() method does not belong to any given instance of Console. Instead, it belongs to the `struct` itself. In fact, were we to add a `static` method to our Point `struct`, that method would not have access to the *X* and *Y* fields at all. Remember, *X* and *Y* belong to a specific instance of a Point and `static` methods belong to no instance. Think of it this way - if you have 20 Point objects and called a `static` method on Point, which of the 20 instances would *X* and *Y* refer to in that method? Better yet, what if you didn't create any Point objects? The `static` method would still be valid to call, just like Console.WriteLine(). After all, do you remember ever creating a Console object? I hope you answered no to that since it is not even allowed…

Let's create a `static` method to determine the quadrant a Point object is in. Instead of making it an instance method (which we very well could) let's define it as `static`. Because it is `static`, the method will not have an object context to work with; therefore, we will need to pass a Point object into the method for it to operate correctly. As an added bonus, let's use an `enum` to define the location on the Cartesian plane that will act as the return value from the method.

Listing 10-22. Static Method

```
struct Point
{
  public enum PointLocation
  {
    Unknown, Origin, XAxis, YAxis, QuadrantI, QuadrantII, QuadrantIII, QuadrantIV
  }

  public double X;
  public double Y;

  // Other methods omitted for brevity

  public static PointLocation GetLocation(Point pt)
  {
    PointLocation result = PointLocation.Unknown;
    if (pt.X == 0 && pt.Y == 0)
    {
      result = PointLocation.Origin;
    }
    else if (pt.X == 0)
    {
      result = PointLocation.YAxis;
    }
    else if (pt.Y == 0)
    {
      result = PointLocation.XAxis;
    }
    else if (pt.X > 0)
    {
      result = (pt.Y > 0) ? PointLocation.QuadrantI : PointLocation.QuadrantIV;
    }
    else if (pt.X < 0)
    {
      result = (pt.Y > 0) ? PointLocation.QuadrantII : PointLocation.QuadrantIII;
    }
    return result;
  }
}

static void Main(string[] args)
{
  Point pt = new Point(2.5, -8.1);
  Point.PointLocation loc = Point.GetLocation(pt);
  Console.WriteLine($"The point ({pt.X}, {pt.Y}) is located at: {loc}");

  pt = new Point(-7.1, 0);
  loc = Point.GetLocation(pt);
  Console.WriteLine($"The point ({pt.X}, {pt.Y}) is located at: {loc}");
}
```

```
The point (2.5, -8.1) is located at: QuadrantIV
The point (-7.1, 0) is located at: XAxis
```

Figure 10-8. Static Method Output

An interesting twist in this example is that the PointLocation `enum` is defined within the Point `struct` itself and not in the `namespace` directly. What this means is that to create a variable of this type from Main(), or anywhere not inside Point, you must prefix the type name with the parent `struct`'s name and a dot operator: "Point.PointLocation". Notice that this technique is employed on line 43 in the above example when creating the *loc* variable. However, on line 15, inside the GetLocation() method, the *result* variable does not require that prefix. You could use the "Point." handle without harm, but since the method is defined within the Point `struct`, just as the `enum` is, PointLocation is visible and usable at that scope without the explicit need of the prefix.

10.6 Immutability

While it seems straight-forward that the fields of a `struct` can be changed at-will there are good reasons not to do so. Remember, `struct` objects are value types and as such are governed by the same rules that govern all value types. When a value type object is passed to a method a copy of that object is actually passed, not the object itself. Of course, you could mark the method parameter "`ref`" to make the intentions of the method clear – it may change the original value. However, the problems of mutable `struct`s go much deeper than this. Let's look at what happens when Point objects are placed in an array.

Listing 10-23. Structures in an Array

```
1 Point[] points = new Point[10];
2 points[0] = new Point(3, 4);
3 points[0].X++;
4 points[0].Print();
5 Point pt = points[0];
6 pt.X = 8;
7 pt.Print();
8 points[0].Print();
```

This code creates an array of 10 Point elements, called *points*, and populates the first item with the values 3 and 4 for *X* and *Y*, respectively. Then, on line 3, the value of the *X* ordinate of the *points*[0] element is augmented. The output of line 4 predictably is "`(4, 4)`". Next, the first point is retrieved into a Point variable called *pt* and its *X* field is changed to 8. Again, this value is printed on line 7 and the output is "`(8, 4)`". However, when *points*[0] is printed once again, the output remains "`(4, 4)`". Why is that? Again, it is due to the fact that a `struct` is a value type and the code on line 5 is performing an assignment from the first element in the array to the *pt* variable. Since all value assignments make a copy of the source value prior to assignment, the variable *pt* actually represents a new Point that is physically disconnected from the original. The difference in behavior on line 3 is because it directly manipulates the object's *X* field, not a copy.

Many programmers have been caught off-guard due to these behavioral differences. It gets even more interesting with nested struct values inside class objects, but that does not need to be addressed here.

Now, if we treat all struct values as immutable and never make a change to the objects once created these problems can be avoided. In other words, once a struct value has been created it represents a specific value, or set of values, and that is what makes that object unique. Instead of changing a field in the struct, create a new one with the new values. But, since the fields of a struct are meant to be declared public, is there a syntactic mechanism to prevent the values from changing once the object is created? The answer is "yes", fields can be marked "readonly".

readonly Fields

A field marked with readonly works like any other field except that once the constructor of the object has completed execution it can no longer be modified. However, these fields can still be read from until the object is destroyed. The readonly keyword is placed between the field's access modifier and its type, as in the following:

```
public readonly int Value;
```

To create a struct object that contains readonly fields, a parameterized constructor must be used as it is the only code that has an opportunity to change the value. Otherwise, the field will remain its default value for the life of the object. The following code demonstrates a point structure that contains readonly fields.

Listing 10-24. ImmutablePoint

```
struct ImmutablePoint
{
    public readonly double X;
    public readonly double Y;

    public ImmutablePoint(double x, double y)
    {
        X = x;
        Y = y;
    }
}

ImmutablePoint pt1;
// pt1.X = 2.1;  // Not legal!
// pt1.Y = 5.4;

ImmutablePoint pt2 = new ImmutablePoint(2.1, 5.4);
// pt2.X = 8;  // Also not legal

Console.WriteLine($"({pt2.X}, {pt2.Y})");
```

In programs that require extreme performance, like games or 3D simulations, modifying `struct` fields can be faster than repeated creation of new `struct` objects. Therefore, although it is a recommendation that `struct` fields should be immutable, it is not a requirement and there are legitimate uses for mutable `struct` objects.

10.7 Rules and Guidelines for struct Types

We've covered many different aspect of `struct` types so it would be good to have a review of the rules involved when creating and using them in your code.

- A `struct` is a data structure that contains a set of related data (fields) and the methods to manipulate that data.
  - A method that does not operate on the contained data or does not logically belong in the `struct` should not be part of the `struct` definition or at least be made `private` if its functionality is required by other methods of the `struct`.
- A `struct`'s name must follow the same rules as variables and methods:
  - Cannot use a reserved keyword.
  - Must start with an alphabetical letter.
  - Every additional character must be non-whitespace, alphanumeric or underscore.
  - Should use Pascal casing rules.
  - Should be a noun as it typically represents a "thing".
- A `struct` must be defined within a `namespace`, another `struct` or a `class`.
- A `struct` object is a value type and as such it is allocated in the stack
  - The memory consumption of the fields of a struct should optimally be limited to 16 bytes. Example: 2 `double` values or 4 `int` values (methods have no impact on memory footprint).
  - Fields should be limited to value types to avoid involving the heap. If heap/reference data is required, consider a `class` instead.
  - `struct`s should be small, lightweight, short-lived entities.
- A `struct` cannot implement a custom default (parameterless) constructor which is automatically provided by the compiler.
  - Any custom constructor must ensure all fields are properly initialized whether or not appropriate arguments are passed to it.
- A `struct` object can be created using a constructor or by declaring a variable of that type and setting all field values.
- Fields cannot be initialized in their declarations – in other words they must remain the default value for their type.
- Fields should be marked `public` unless explicitly required to be private.
- Once set, values of a `struct` object's fields typically should not be modified.
  - There is no technical restriction preventing modification but the intended usage pattern for a `struct` is to store immutable data.
  - To enforce immutability, mark fields as `readonly`.

- A `struct` should typically be defined within its own file, using a filename with the pattern "<struct name>.cs". It leads to code that is more manageable, especially in multi-developer environments.

10.8 Access Modifiers

Several times we have encountered the `public` and `private` keywords but their significance has been glossed over. As you may have already gathered, these keywords govern the accessibility of the items that they modify. In the case of `public`, access is granted to anything that can see the object that contains the member marked with that modifier. With `private`, however, only the `struct` (or `class`) where the item is defined can manipulate the member. There are several other access modifiers which you will encounter, but you will not use them until you create `class` derivatives or libraries.

Table 10-3. Access Modifiers

Name	Description
`public`	The most permissive access level. No access restrictions are placed on the member.
`private`	The least permissive access level. These members are accessible only within the `class` or the `struct` in which they are declared.
`protected`	Same access level as `private` except the members are also accessible from derivative `class` types.
`internal`	These items can only be accessed by other types in the same assembly.
`protected internal`	Items marked with this access modifier are only accessible by other types in the same assembly or by `class` types derived from the `class` that owns the member.

As you can see, the last three items in the list don't make much sence at this point, but in time their usage will become apparent.

10.9 Summary

Enumerations provide a mechanism for grouping like constants together into a common, named data structure. By default, all `enum` constants are type `int`, but they can be any other integral data type. When used as a method parameter, `enum`s utilize IntelliSense to limit the input arguments to the legal list of values. A special type of `enum`, called a "flags" `enum`, is designed to work with constants that are powers of 2. This allows multiple constants to be set simultaneously in a single `enum` value. Using enumerations makes code easier to read and can help eliminate certain types of code irregularities (a.k.a. bugs).

The `struct` data structure is your first foray into the creation of complex data types. With a `struct` you can group variables (fields) together into a single entity which eliminates a lot of clutter when individual variables are used instead. It also makes passing these values to methods much simpler and concise. A `struct` can contain constructors to initialize objects and methods to manipulate the data of those objects. Methods of a `struct` can be instance methods (requires an object to call) or `static` methods (called without an object reference).

Fields and methods of a `struct` are called members as they "belong" to the `struct`. Members of a `struct` are typically marked public so they can be accessed via an object instance. Types defined using `struct` should be lightweight, short-lived and contain value type fields as they are managed in the CLR's stack.

In this chapter you got a taste for object-oriented programming. We are not done with this topic by a long shot as we still need to discuss `class` types. However, what you started to learn is the concept of working with objects first, then methods second. This concept will be continued in the next topics.

11

11. Classes

As you learned in the previous chapter, object-oriented programming techniques are a very powerful tool for creating multi-field entities that possess methods to calculate values based on those fields. The `struct` user-defined type is only one part of the puzzle. Another user-defined type, called a `class`, represents the largest piece of this puzzle. Because `struct` and `class` fill much the same role you will notice many similarities between the two. However, the differences are what make the `class` type a critical component of OOP.

11.1 class vs. struct

Classes have virtually all the same capabilities of a `struct`. The biggest difference between the two is that a `class` is a reference type and, therefore, stores instance data in the heap rather than on the stack. Objects of a `struct` type are immediately cleaned out of the stack as soon as they "fall out of scope". Class objects, which store references to the heap in the stack, will also be cleared off of the stack when they fall out of scope, but the reference data in the heap remains until the CLR garbage collector determines it is the best time to reclaim the memory. We're not going to get into garbage collection at this time as it is a fairly advanced topic. Just be aware that `class` objects may stick around longer than you realize when you are done using them.

Besides the value and reference type issue what else is different between `struct` and `class`? Actually quite a bit. Here's a quick list of differences between the two:

- `class` objects are reference types and have a default value of `null`
- Since `class` objects already consume data in the heap there is already a performance hit due to memory reference lookups so reference type members are acceptable. Objects of type `struct` should contain only value types (suggestion, not a rule).
- Since `class` objects utilize the heap there is no suggested upper-bound limit on memory usage while `struct` objects should consume 16 bytes or less (suggestion, not a rule).
- Instances of type `struct` consume only the memory required to store its fields. `class` instances consume a small extra amount of memory due to the entries in the stack and the heap (overhead).
- `class` objects must be created using a constructor but `struct` objects can use value type initialization (declare a variable and assign all fields).
- A `struct` field definition cannot include a default value assignment but it can in a `class`.

- A class can implement a custom default constructor, a struct cannot.
- A class can define a finalizer (destructor), but not a struct.
- A class can extend the definition of another class (inheritance) but structs cannot.
- A struct object is generally intended to be immutable (field state remains unchanged) while class objects are not held to that standard (suggestion, not a rule).
- Assignment of a struct object into another using "=" creates a second copy of the source object's stack data in the destination object's stack location (value copy). The two objects have independent copies of the same data, just like assigning one int value to another int. The same assignment operation on a class object copies the reference of the source object into the second object's stack location, linking both variables to the exact same heap data (reference copy). Therefore, any change to the state of one object is immediately reflected in the other since they both point to the same data.

That's a lot of differences for two things that fundamentally solve the same set of problems. However, most of the differences revolve directly around the fact that one is a value type and the other is a reference type. Keeping that fact in mind will help you decide which type is the best for your applications.

In reality, unless you do a lot of scientific, mathematical or game programming with things like vectors and points, most of your user-defined types will be classes. Structs are really meant for small sets of data that are short-lived in your programs. For that reason, most business applications will likely have a class:struct ratio of 50:1 or higher.

11.2 Modeling a class

The syntax of a class is so similar to a struct that the biggest difference you'll initially notice is just the keyword change from struct to class. Just like a struct, a class can either be defined within a namespace or another class. Also, for clarity and maintainability, a class should be defined within its own file, using the filename "<class name>.cs". Instead of duplicating the Point example which is ideal for demonstrating a struct, let's use a more appropriate example for our first class. Since classes, like structs, typically model a "thing", we'll model something everyone should understand - a Person.

Before you actually write any code it is always a good idea to design what it is you intend to write. The Point example was relatively trivial, but a Person class will be a bit trickier, but not because the syntax is more complicated. When you start working with complex types you have to consider the context in which the type will be used. Well, a person is a person no matter what the context, right? Wrong. Consider two separate industries that may wish to track person data, such as a school and a doctor's office. In the context of the school the important attributes of a person may be:

- Identification number (school ID)
- First name
- Last name

- Date of birth (DOB)
- Gender
- Grade level
- Grade point average (GPA)

However, in the doctor's office the attributes required may be a bit different:

- Identification number (Social security number)
- First name
- Last name
- Date of birth (DOB)
- Gender
- Height
- Weight

Clearly, both examples could easily have many more attributes each, but this subset will still help drive the idea home that the same conceptual thing may have completely different meanings depending on the context in which they are defined. Rather than pick either of these industries for our example we'll start smaller and define a person to contain the following information:

- Identification number
- First name
- Last name
- Date of birth (DOB)
- Gender

Actually, there is a much better way to show a `class`'s makeup - a UML (Unified Modeling Language) class diagram. Here's what our Person `class` looks like in a UML class diagram:

Table 11-1. Person UML Class Diagram

	Person
+	ID : `long`
+	FirstName : `string`
+	LastName: `string`
+	DOB : DateTime
+	Gender : Genders (`enum`)
+	Person()
+	Person(id : `long`, firstName : `string`, lastName : `string`, dob : DateTime, gender : Genders)

There are three sections in this diagram, the entity name, the attributes (fields) of the entity and the entity's operations (methods). In the left margin next to each member there is a "+" symbol that indicates the item associated with the symbol is publicly accessible. The list of possible symbols are:

Table 11-2. UML Member Accessibility Levels

Symbol	Accessibility/Visibility Level
+	Public
#	Protected
-	Private
~	Package (internal)
/	Derived (can be combined with the other modifiers)

When you are ready to add a `class` to a project, click on the "Project" menu followed by "Add Class..." The "Add New Item" dialog will be displayed with the Class template item already selected. In the "Name" textbox at the bottom of the window, enter the name of the `class` you wish to add. In our case it will be "Person.cs". Don't worry if you forget the ".cs" extension as it will automatically be added if necessary.

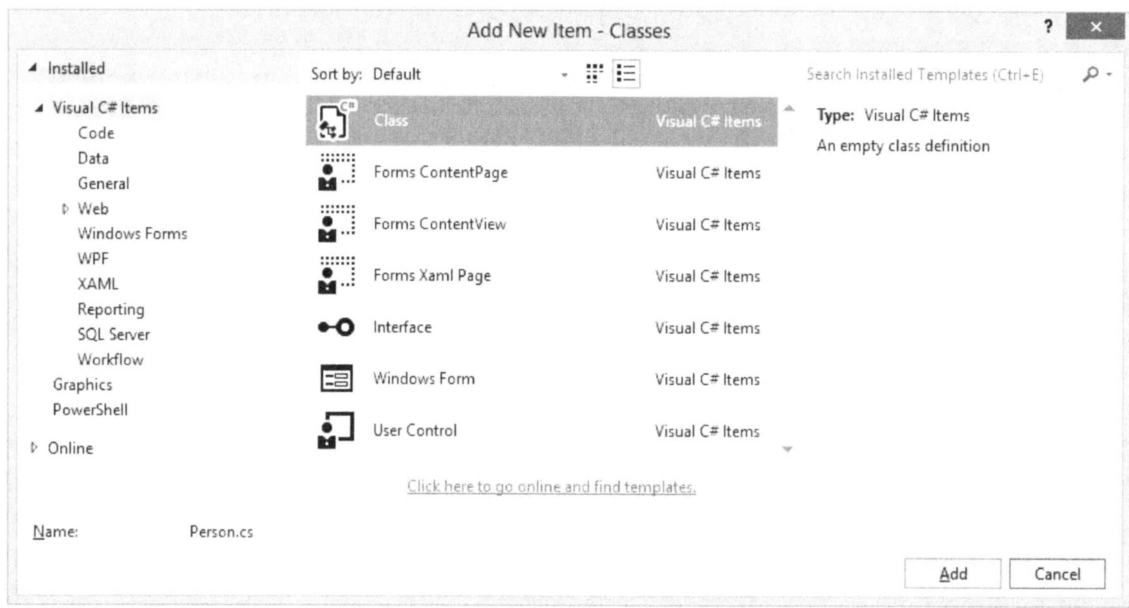

Figure 11-1. "Add New Item" Dialog

In the Solution Explorer tool window, "Person.cs" will be added to your project at the same level as "Program.cs". Double-clicking on the item in Solution Explorer will open the file for editing. This is also the correct way to add a struct to your project as there is no dedicated template for that data type. Just make sure to change the `class` keyword to `struct` in the text editor once the file is created.

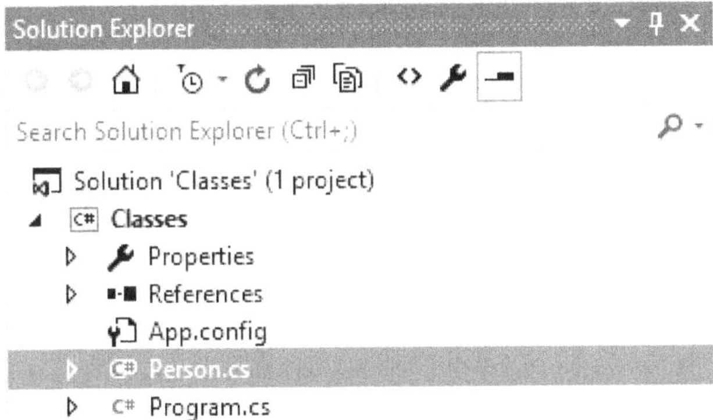

Figure 11-2. New Class in Solution Explorer

The next step is to add the code described in the UML diagram. Because we also have a Genders enum to define for the *Gender* field, that will also be added to this class. If we felt we might use the Genders enum in other types then it would be best to define it outside the class, directly in a namespace.

Listing 11-1. Person Class Definition

```
public class Person
{
  public enum Genders { Unknown, Male, Female };

  public long ID = 0;
  public string FirstName = string.Empty;
  public string LastName = string.Empty;
  public DateTime DOB = DateTime.MinValue;
  public Genders Gender = Genders.Unknown;

  public Person()
  {
  }

  public Person(long id, string firstName, string lastName, DateTime dob, Genders gender)
  {
    ID = id;
    FirstName = firstName;
    LastName = lastName;
    DOB = dob;
    Gender = gender;
  }
}
```

In reality, the only two major differences between this code and a struct with similar fields is the inclusion of a parameterless constructor and the default values assigned to the fields. For your information, those fields are assigned their details prior to the execution of any constructor.

As a result, the default constructor, in this example, has nothing to do other than exist. We'll discuss why we included the default constructor in the next section. Also notice that the `class` is marked with the `public` access modifier. This is not critical at this stage as all of our projects contain only one namespace within one assembly. However, once you start routinely placing classes and structs within libraries it becomes important to include this access modifier so consumers of the libraries can actually use them.

How about creating instances of Person? Again, it is going to be pretty much the same as creating a `struct` instance via a constructor.

Listing 11-2. Creating and Using Person Objects

```
1  static void Main(string[] args)
2  {
3    Person p1 = new Person(123456789, "John", "Smith", DateTime.Parse("5/6/1978"), Person.Genders.Male);
4
5    Console.WriteLine($"{p1.ID:000-00-0000} {p1.LastName,-15} {p1.FirstName,-10} {p1.DOB:yyyy-MM-dd} {p1.Gender}");
6    p1.FirstName = "Bill";
7    p1.ID = 987654321;
8    Console.WriteLine($"{p1.ID:000-00-0000} {p1.LastName,-15} {p1.FirstName,-10} {p1.DOB:yyyy-MM-dd} {p1.Gender}");
9
10   Person p2 = new Person(111223333, "Jill", "Jones", DateTime.Parse("2/3/1945"), Person.Genders.Female);
11   Console.WriteLine($"{p2.ID:000-00-0000} {p2.LastName,-15} {p2.FirstName,-10} {p2.DOB:yyyy-MM-dd} {p2.Gender}");
12 }
```

First of all, don't panic about the formatting of the code above. Due to the length of the interpolation `strings` there are a lot of line continuations. So, line 5 continues on to the next line of text ***without*** a carriage return. If there was a carriage return in the middle of the interpolation `string` the compiler would not like it.

A Person object, *p1*, is created on line 3, its contexts output to the console on line 5 and its fields modified on lines 6 and 7 before being output again on line 8. Modifying fields like this is something that can be done with a `struct` object as well, but they are typically treated as immutable. The second object, *p2*, is created on line 10 and also output to the console.

```
123-45-6789 Smith           John       1978-05-06 Male
987-65-4321 Smith           Bill       1978-05-06 Male
111-22-3333 Jones           Jill       1945-02-03 Female
```

Figure 11-3. Person Output

The lengthy Console.WriteLine() statements pay off since the Person objects output line up in a tabular fashion. It really is beneficial to use these formatting techniques in your code, especially for outputting lists of similar data such as this.

Abstraction

The process of designing a `class` to model an entity is known as abstraction. Identifying the required fields (attributes) and methods (actions) that allow the outside world to interact with the object is the most critical component of abstraction. We are trying to define the essence of the thing being modeled, only providing access to the data and methods pertinent for someone trying to work with that entity. We are also trying to remove complexity from the calling/client code and place it inside the `class`, where it belongs. For instance, if a `class` object models a table in a database, at some point it is likely that a `class` object will be created from data stored in the database and another object's data will be saved to the database. Instead of requiring the client code figure out how to write and read these objects to and from the database, the `class` should possess Save() and Load() methods to handle these operations. Therefore, the details of the operations are *abstracted* from the caller. All they have to do is call the methods and let them do the work.

Abstraction is one of the terms interviewers love to ask potential employees to define. Instead of regurgitating the computer science definition (which I didn't bother to include because it is long-winded) just explain it this way... Abstraction is the process of designing a class so that only pertinent fields and methods are visible to a consumer of the class. The details of how the methods operate is abstracted, or hidden, from the user. Abstraction is focusing on the "what", not the "how". I also try to remind people that it is not the definition that matters but whether or not you can implement the concept using the appropriate code.

11.3 Constructors and Destructors (Finalizers)

Constructors in `class` types are virtually identical to those in `struct` types with one major distinction – a `class` can define a custom, default constructor. Just as in a `struct`, if no constructor is supplied in `class`, the compiler will automatically provide the default constructor. Recall, the default constructor is the one that accepts no parameters. Regardless of which constructor is called when creating a `class` object, all fields are initialized prior to its execution. Therefore, it is important to assign values to your fields where they are defined, otherwise they will retain their default values, such as `null`.

A class can supply as many constructors as required as long as each one has a unique parameter list. Something interesting happens as soon as a `class` defines any constructor – the default constructor supplied by the compiler disappears. This is why the default constructor is explicitly defined in Listing 11-1. If the default constructor was not explicitly defined, then there would no longer be a way to create a Person object without arguments since another parameterized constructor was supplied in the `class` definition. In the example, the default constructor was not actually called, so it could have been left off without impact. In fact, that may be the case for types you design where you require all new objects to be created with appropriate parameters. The need for parameterless, default constructors becomes much more important when working with inheritance and serialization, so it may be best to get into the habit of including them in your designs now.

Constructor Chaining

One of the goals of good programming is to reduce repetitious code. We saw how methods allow us to encapsulate certain functionality so it is not repeated inline throughout a program. Since the purpose of a constructor is to get an object into a "running state", having multiple constructors in a single class may lead to code repetition because many of the constructors actually end up doing the same thing, but with different inputs. Constructors can employ a neat trick to eliminate the code repetition: constructor chaining.

Constructor chaining is the process of calling one constructor from another to facilitate the initialization of an object. Consider a `class` with the following diagram:

Point3D
+ X : `double` + Y : `double` + Z : `double`
+ Point3D() + Point3D(x : `double`, y : `double`) + Point3D(x : `double`, y : `double`, z : `double`) + Point3D(other : Point3D)

This `class` represents a point in 3D space and has three ordinates, *X*, *Y* and *Z*, to represent the point's position. There are four constructors to create and initialize the point, one default and three parameterized. Here's a first stab at the code for this `class`:

Listing 11-3. Point3D Without Constructor Chaining

```
public class Point3D
{
  public double X, Y, Z;

  public Point3D()
  {
    X = 0;
    Y = 0;
    Z = 0;
  }

  public Point3D(double x, double y)
  {
    X = x;
    Y = y;
    Z = 0;
  }

  public Point3D(Point3D other)
  {
    X = other.X;
    Y = other.Y;
    Z = other.Z;
  }

  public Point3D(double x, double y, double z)
  {
    X = x;
    Y = y;
    Z = z;
  }
}
```

Although there is nothing technically wrong with this code, it is far from optimal. One thing that should pop out at you is that the constructors are all essentially doing the exact same thing, assigning values to *X*, *Y* and *Z*, albeit with different values. One big problem with this approach is that each constructor has to be thoroughly tested to ensure that each initialization path yields a viable and consistent object once complete. One small logic error could lead to critical bugs that might go undetected, especially if it is in a code path that is not frequently executed. To get around this problem all initialization logic can be constrained to one of the constructors and the other three constructors will utilize it to do the majority of its initialization work. The trick is knowing how to call one constructor from another and which constructor is best for containing the core initialization logic.

A special keyword, `this`, has many meanings in object-oriented programming, one of which is to call another constructor in the `class`. To implement a chained constructor call, use the following syntax:

```
<class name>(<parameters>) : this (<arguments>) { // constructor body }
```

The first part of the syntax, before the ":" is a standard constructor signature. Before the constructor body (the code between { and }), call the other constructor using the keyword "this" as the method name. Any arguments you wish to pass to the other constructor are placed inside the parentheses just like a regular method call. It is important that the argument list supplied actually maps to another constructor's parameter list as the compiler will not allow constructors to call themselves or a constructor that doesn't exist. You can utilize the parameters of the initially called constructor as arguments to the chained constructor. The call to the other constructor always precedes the execution of the constructor's body that is making the call, so whatever logic is performed in the chained constructor will have been completed prior to execution of the initially called constructor.

It is possible to chain multiple constructors together by having the first chained constructor call yet another constructor. This practice should be minimized as it makes reading and debugging code a bit trickier. So, which constructor should be the target of chaining? It is recommended that the constructor that accepts the most parameters be the chaining target for the other constructors as it typically has the most data to work with. For the Point3D class, the logical choice for the chaining target is the constructor that accepts three double parameters as it is the only one that is provided enough information to set all fields to appropriate values.

Listing 11-4. Point3D with Chained Constructors

```
public class Point3D
{
  public double X, Y, Z;

  public Point3D() : this(0, 0, 0)
  {
  }

  public Point3D(double x, double y) : this (x, y, 0)
  {
  }

  public Point3D(Point3D other) : this (other.X, other.Y, other.Z)
  {
  }

  public Point3D(double x, double y, double z)
  {
    X = x;
    Y = y;
    Z = z;
  }
}
```

Notice how empty most of the constructor bodies are, all of the work having been delegated to the last constructor - even the copy constructor. It is not always this clean but the majority of the initialization logic should be constrained to one constructor.

To call the first constructor, the following code must be invoked from somewhere else in the project:

```
Point3D point = new Point3D();
```

The first constructor is invoking the "`this`" call with three 0 values. This signifies that the final constructor is called passing all 0's as the arguments for the *x*, *y* and *z* parameters – 0 being a good default value for an ordinate. Then, the fields are set to their corresponding parameter values and control is returned to the first constructor. Since the body of this constructor is empty control is immediately returned to the code that called the Point3D constructor.

The second constructor works very much the same way as the first except this constructor requires an *x* and *y* value be passed as arguments.

```
Point3D point = new Point3D(3.1, 5.2);
```

Instead of passing three 0's to the chained constructor, this time the arguments are *x*, *y* and 0, or 3.1, 5.2 and 0. Therefore, after the chained constructor is finished executing, *X* will equal 3.1, *Y* will be 5.2 and *Z* will be set to 0.

The third constructor is a copy constructor which requires a Point3D object as the argument passed to it.

```
Point3D point2 = new Point3D(point);
```

To call the fourth constructor from this constructor the individual elements of the *other* parameter must be extracted and passed using their corresponding arguments. That is done with the following command:

```
this(other.X, other.Y, other.Z)
```

Be forewarned – if *other* is `null` a NullReferenceException will be thrown when *other.X* is evaluated. You can change the command to use null-conditional operators to force a default value, like 0, to be passed instead of allowing the exception to be thrown as such:

```
this(other?.X ?? 0, other?.Y ?? 0, other?.Z ?? 0)
```

Now, if *other* is `null`, the "`?.`" operator will return `null`, forcing the "`??`" operator to choose 0. If *other* is not `null`, then the new object's *X*, *Y* and *Z* fields will be set to the same values as in *other*.

The final constructor can still be called to create an object directly from code.

```
Point3D point = new Point3D(3.1, 5.2, 7.8);
```

Since the core logic already exists within this constructor there is no need to employ chaining. Once complete, *point* will contain 3.1, 5.2 and 7.8 for the *X*, *Y* and *Z* fields, respectively.

If you are not a fan of the constructor chaining syntax but would still like to take advantage of a single method for initialization logic you can use the initialization method technique instead.

Basically, a single, private method will exist within Point3D that will perform the exact same duties as the fourth constructor in the chaining example. Each constructor body will then execute this method as their first line of code. One of the benefits of this technique is the ability to check for null parameters with an if statement instead of employing the null-condition and null-coalescing operators.

Listing 11-5. Constructor Initialization Method

```
public class Point3DX
{
  public double X, Y, Z;

  public Point3DX()
  {
    Init(0, 0, 0);
  }

  public Point3DX(double x, double y)
  {
    Init(x, y, 0);
  }

  public Point3DX(double x, double y, double z)
  {
    Init(x, y, z);
  }

  public Point3DX(Point3D other)
  {
    if (other != null)
    {
      Init(other.X, other.Y, other.Z);
    }
    else
    {
      Init(0, 0, 0);
    }
  }

  private void Init(double x, double y, double z)
  {
    X = x;
    Y = y;
    Z = z;
  }
}
```

As you can see, each constructor calls Init(), but the copy constructor first tests to make sure the *other* parameter is not null before accessing its members.

Destructors/Finalizers

A destructor, actually known as a finalizer in C#, is a method that is called when the object is being cleared from memory. As the name implies, it is the final method called in a `class` object when it is no longer needed. This special method is not actually needed by most classes but it is useful when the class object allocates some reference variables that need special attention prior to destruction. Unlike constructors, the finalizer cannot be called directly by code, instead it is called when the CLR garbage collector is about to remove the reference from the heap. The syntax for a finalizer is:

```
~<class name>() { // Finalizer body }
```

Unlike constructors, there is no access modifier for the finalizer. Also, unlike constructors, there can be only one finalizer.

Since finalizers are executed non-deterministically and from a separate thread of execution, their usefulness at this juncture is very limited.

11.4 Encapsulation

Encapsulation is one of the big buzzwords related to object-oriented programming. However, don't let the big word scare you off. While abstraction is the process of designing a `class` and hiding implementation details from a consumer of the `class`, encapsulation focuses on the details of implementing the code to accomplish the abstraction. When fields are added to a class, the class acts as a "capsule" containing the data, hence the word encapsulation. However, there is more to it than simply adding public fields to a `class`. Proper encapsulation also protects the integrity of a `class` object, preventing the object from being placed in an invalid state. Consider a `class` called RangeValue with the following design:

RangeValue
+ MinValue : int = 0
+ MaxValue : int = 100
+ Value : int = 0
+ RangeValue ()
+ RangeValue (minValue : int, maxValue : int, value : int)

The intent of this `class` is to store a value (*Value*) that must fall between two other values, *MinValue* and *MaxValue*, inclusively. Notice that the fields are all given default values and that *Value* is between *MinValue* and *MaxValue* to begin with. It is trivial to ensure that the values passed into the parameterized constructor are legal and obey the business logic with an `if` statement. However, a problem can arise immediately after the object is constructed since the fields of the object can be manipulated externally with no way to prevent illegal values. For example, consider creating an object of type RangeValue using the default constructor:

```
RangeValue rangeVal = new RangeValue();
```

Initially, *rangeVal.MinValue* is 0, *rangeVal.MaxVal* is 100 and *rangeVal.Value* is 0. What happens when the next line is executed?

```
rangeVal.Value = 200;
```

Whoops! Now, *rangeVal.Value* is out of its defined legal range and there was nothing the RangeValue class could do to stop it as it is currently written. What would happen if we changed the design of the class to the following?

RangeValue
- MinValue : int = 0 - MaxValue : int = 100 - Value : int = 0
+ RangeValue () + RangeValue (minValue : int, maxValue : int, value : int)

Now, all of the fields are marked with the private access modifier. This would still allow the constructors to be called, since they are public, but the fields can no longer be accessed from code outside of the RangeValue class. This definitely protects the data, but now it also completely hides the data from the outside world. What if we used methods to access the fields?

Encapsulation Using Accessors and Mutators

RangeValue
- MinValue : int = 0 - MaxValue : int = 100 - Value : int = 0
+ RangeValue () + RangeValue (minValue : int, maxValue : int, value : int) + GetMinValue() : int + SetMinValue(minValue : int) + GetMaxValue() : int + SetMaxValue(maxValue : int) + GetValue() : int + SetValue(value : int)

Now, instead of having direct access to the field data, they can only be accessed via the appropriate Get and Set methods. Since we are allowed to place logic like if statements within methods we can now protect our data from storing invalid values. A method whose primary purpose is to return a value representing a field is called an ***accessor*** or, more informally, a ***getter***. Likewise, any method whose sole purpose is to set the value of a field is called a ***mutator*** or a ***setter***. Here is what this code looks like fully implemented in C#:

Listing 11-6. RangeValue Class

```
public class RangeValue
{
  private int MinValue = 0;
  private int MaxValue = 100;
  private int Value = 0;

  public RangeValue()
  {
  }

  public RangeValue(int minValue, int maxValue, int value)
  {
    if (value >= minValue && value <= maxValue)
    {
      MinValue = minValue;
      MaxValue = maxValue;
      Value = value;
    }
    else
    {
      throw new ArgumentOutOfRangeException("value",
"Rule: minValue <= value <= maxValue");
    }
  }

  public int GetMinValue()
  {
    return MinValue;
  }

  public void SetMinValue(int minValue)
  {
    if (minValue <= Value && minValue <= MaxValue)
    {
      MinValue = minValue;
    }
    else
    {
      throw new ArgumentOutOfRangeException("minValue",
"Rule: minValue <= value <= maxValue");
    }
  }

  public int GetMaxValue()
  {
    return MaxValue;
  }

  public void SetMaxValue(int maxValue)
  {
    if (maxValue >= Value && maxValue >= MinValue)
```

```
    {
      MaxValue = maxValue;
    }
    else
    {
        throw new ArgumentOutOfRangeException("maxValue",
"Rule: minValue <= value <= maxValue");
    }
  }

  public int GetValue()
  {
    return Value;
  }

  public void SetValue(int value)
  {
    if (value >= MinValue && value <= MaxValue)
    {
      Value = value;
    }
    else
    {
      throw new ArgumentOutOfRangeException("value",
"Rule: minValue <= value <= maxValue");
    }
  }
}
```

Those accessors and mutators sure do add a lot of extra code! Sometimes, that is the price to pay for robust programs.

Here's some code to drive this `class` – pay particular attention to the `try` block since we are going to trigger an exception on line 6.

Listing 11-7. Testing RangeValue

```
 1 try
 2 {
 3   RangeValue range = new RangeValue(0, 100, 50);
 4   range.SetValue(75);  // Fine
 5   Console.WriteLine(
   $"[{range.GetMinValue()}..{range.GetValue()}..{range.GetMaxValue()}]");
 6   range.SetMaxValue(50);  // Not valid since Value is now 75!
 7 }
 8 catch(ArgumentOutOfRangeException ex)
 9 {
10   Console.WriteLine($"Error: {ex.Message}");
11 }
```

The *range* object is initialized on line 3 with *MinValue* set to 0, *MaxValue* set to 100 and *Value* set to 50. To set the *Value* field of *range* the SetValue() method must be called on that object. This is done with the value 75 on the next line. The values for all three fields are displayed using Console.WriteLine() and the three "Get" methods on line 5. Next, using the *range* object's SetMaxValue() method we are triggering an exception since 50 is not greater than or equal to 75, a violation of the defined business logic.

We have successfully encapsulated our data; however, it comes with the loss of simple field-access calls as they were replaced by methods. Wouldn't it be nice if we could have our cake and eat it too? In other words, can we have the simplicity of field-access calls with the ability to protect the field data? C# provides just the thing – properties!

Properties

Properties are specialized methods that encapsulate fields providing read or write access (or both) to fields without compromising security. Also, properties use field-access syntax to access these specialized methods. A property is typically bound to a single "backing" field (a `private` field that represents either some or all of the state of a `class`); however, properties can be bound to multiple fields or none. We'll look at those specialty properties a bit later. In a nutshell, properties are the backbone for the implementation of business logic in a `class`.

The property syntax takes some time to get used to. But, before we can look at the syntax we need to make some modifications to the way we name our fields. Properties, to the outside world, look and behave like fields even though they are actually methods in disguise. Because of this we want the property names to stand in for the field names that were directly accessed before. The caller will treat these properties as if they are the fields themselves. So, if the properties will uses the names that the fields used to have, how shall we rename the fields so there is no conflict? There are several schools of thought on this topic, all of which have various levels of support in the industry. Here, we'll look at the three most common conventions for naming `private` backing fields.

- Camel-casing: Many programmers like to name their backing fields the same way they would name any variable, using camel-casing.
  - Pros: Camel-casing ensures all of your fields, local variables and parameters all share the same naming convention.
  - Cons: No way to determine the scope of a field based on the name alone. When the fields were Pascal-cased they were the only variables with that convention. Also, there is a higher degree of probability that a field name will conflict with a local variable or parameter requiring the use of "`this.`" to disambiguate.
- Leading or trailing "_": This is kind of a hold-over from C++ where a private, class-level variable (field) would either start or end with an underscore. The rest of the name would either be camel-cased or Pascal-cased.
  - Pros: The underscore is a dead give-away that the name has special meaning, in this case class-level scope. There is no real chance for naming conflicts with local variables or parameters since they typically won't contain underscores. If the fields are prefixed with "_" then all of them will be grouped together in IntelliSense.

    - Cons: It looks weird. C# names typically don't have symbols in them. Even constants, which used to follow the old C naming standard of all upper-case with underscores separating words, have migrated to camel-casing. The good news is that these details are abstracted from consumers of the `class` as they cannot work with `private` fields.
- Leading "m_" prefix: This is a common technique in an old naming convention called "Hungarian notation". The "m_" stands for private member. The rest of the name would either be camel-cased or Pascal-cased.
    - Pros: Like "_", this prefix clearly identifies the scope of the variable. It was commonly used in C++ and Visual Basic prior to .NET and still can be found in circulation today.
    - Cons: Hungarian notation in all forms has essentially been abandoned by most programmers.

In this text we will use the leading "_" prefix with the remaining text Pascal-cased to identify fields. This is done for one primary reason – to eliminate the need for "`this.`" in your code.

This topic is practically a religious issue to some programmers. Some people are so stubborn and set in their ways that they refuse to accept the merits of other conventions. I have known people who quit a job because the company standards and conventions didn't line up with theirs. For your information, I have used all three conventions since .NET was released in 2002. As of right now I gravitate toward leading "_", but that may change by the next edition of this book. Whatever style you decide to use in your own code, just be consistent. Nothing is more frustrating than having to maintain code that has multiple naming conventions.

Now that we have worked out what fields will look like, let's get back to property syntax. A property can consist of two sections: a `get` accessor and a `set` mutator. If a read-only property is desired, the mutator can be omitted. Likewise, if a write-only property is desired, then the accessor can be left off. The syntax of a property in its simplest form looks like this:

```
<access> <type> <Name>
{
   get
   {
      return <backing field>;
   }
   [<access>] set
   {
      <backing field> = value;
   }
}
```

The `<access>` modifier at the leading edge of the property governs both the accessor and the mutator. If both accessor and mutator are defined in the property, then the mutator can define its own access modifier as shown by the optional `[<access>]` prior to `set`. This would provide the ability to have a `public` accessor but a `private` mutator.

`<type>` represents the datatype that this property encapsulates and it is almost always the same as the backing field.

The `<Name>` of the property should be Pascal-cased and should be descriptive to the consumers of the `class`.

The `get` block (accessor) represents the code that is executed when the property is used as an "rvalue" or read operation, such as when the property is on the right-hand side of the "=" operator. The block must always end with a `return` statement or a thrown exception. Unless some transformation of the data is required, the accessor typically only contains one line of code, the returning of the backing field.

The `set` block (mutator) represents the code that is executed when the property is used as an "lvalue" or write operation, such as when the property is on the left-hand side of the "=" operator. A special keyword, `value`, represents the value passed to the mutator, not unlike a parameter that has a special name. A mutator that does not require validation of the incoming `value` can simply assign `value` to the backing field.

The following code demonstrates the RangeValue `class` using properties instead of dedicated accessor and mutator methods.

Listing 11-8. RangeValue Using Properties

```
public class RangeValue
{
  private int _MinValue = 0;
  private int _MaxValue = 100;
  private int _Value = 0;

  public int MinValue
  {
    get
    {
      return _MinValue;
    }
    set
    {
      if (value <= Value && value <= MaxValue)
      {
        _MinValue = value;
      }
      else
      {
        throw new ArgumentOutOfRangeException("MinValue",
"Rule: MinValue <= Value <= MaxValue");
      }
    }
  }

  public int MaxValue
  {
    get
    {
      return _MaxValue;
    }
    set
    {
      if (value >= Value && value >= MinValue)
      {
        _MaxValue = value;
      }
      else
      {
        throw new ArgumentOutOfRangeException("MaxValue",
"Rule: MinValue <= Value <= MaxValue");
      }
    }
  }

```

```
  public int Value
  {
    get
    {
      return _Value;
    }
    set
    {
      if (value >= MinValue && value <= MaxValue)
      {
        _Value = value;
      }
      else
      {
        throw new ArgumentOutOfRangeException("Value",
"Rule: MinValue <= Value <= MaxValue");
      }
    }
  }

  public RangeValue()
  {
  }

  public RangeValue(int minValue, int maxValue, int value)
  {
    if (value >= minValue && value <= maxValue)
    {
      _MinValue = minValue;
      _MaxValue = maxValue;
      _Value = value;
    }
    else
    {
      throw new ArgumentOutOfRangeException("value",
"Rule: minValue <= value <= maxValue");
    }
  }
}
```

Listing 11-9. Testing RangeValue Using Properties

```
try
{
  RangeValue range = new RangeValue(0, 100, 50);
  range.Value = 75;  // Fine
  Console.WriteLine($"[{range.MinValue}..{range.Value}..{range.MaxValue}]");
  range.MaxValue = 50;  // Not valid since Value is now 75!
}
catch (ArgumentOutOfRangeException ex)
{
  Console.WriteLine($"Error: {ex.Message}");
}
```

A real short answer for why properties are used instead of methods is "because that's just how encapsulation is done in .NET", but there really are legitimate reasons. Using properties clearly doesn't provide shorter code than methods, so that is not one of the reasons to migrate to properties. Field-access syntax, however, is one advantage, making it seem like the code is accessing variables when it actually is executing methods. To many programmers, using the properties feels more natural than calling methods to manipulate the state of an object. The statement on line 4 is definitely calling the `set` mutator of the *Value* property of the *range* object, not assigning a value directly to a field. Remember, there is no longer a field called *Value*, so the call must be handled by the *Value* mutator. Reading the values using the accessors on line 5 also makes it look like the code is directly accessing *range*'s state. In fact, the compiler does create individual methods for the property accessors and mutators, but C# adds syntactic sugar to make property calls look and feel more like accessing fields.

Beyond the simpler field-access syntax, another main reason for using properties instead of Get/Set methods is that data binding in C# and Visual Studio is done via properties, not methods. The Properties window in Visual Studio works strictly with properties for getting and setting the state of an object. Technologies like Entity Framework, serialization and LINQ are all natively designed to interact with properties, not fields or methods. Methods also typically indicate an action, which is why they tend to have verbs in their names. Properties, however, are typically wrappers for data so this syntax also keeps them semantically separate from the object's actions. One last reason is that modifying field definitions breaks something called "binary compatibility" requiring that any other code linked to that `class` be recompiled after any change. Properties do not have the same effect since, even though they represent a `class`'s state, they are really just methods.

Now that the business logic to maintain consistency is contained in the properties, those should be accessed virtually everywhere instead of the fields, including from within the `class` where the properties are defined. Then, only the property that encapsulates a field should utilize that field. This helps guarantee that the state of the object will not be placed in an abnormal state since the business logic is utilized from every possible code execution path.

The constructors of a `class` should also typically only modify the fields through the properties as well, except when it is absolutely necessary to bypass the logic defined within them. Listing 11-8 actually demonstrates this in the second constructor starting on line 72. Notice that the fields are modified directly rather than utilizing the mutators, which violates the previous recommendation. This is because all three values must be evaluated simultaneously. Consider creating a RangeValue object with the arguments for *minValue*, *maxValue* and *value* set to 1000, 2000 and 1500, respectively. The values are legal since 1500 is between 1000 and 2000. However, if an attempt is made to set *MinValue* to 1000 when *MaxValue* is still 100, the logic in the property will fail and throw an exception. You might consider setting *MaxValue* first to eliminate the problem. But, if the constructor is called with the values -1000, -100 and -500, the same problem will occur but with *MaxValue* triggering the failure. So, the easiest solution is to bypass the properties and set the fields directly. Although this is a good example as to when bypassing the property logic is useful, it should be done as infrequently as possible.

Creating Properties Using Visual Studio

One of the pains of creating properties, especially for beginners to the syntax, is remembering how to write them properly. The good news is that Visual Studio can do most of the grunt work. Consider a simplified version of the Person class that was introduced earlier in the chapter. The fields of Person may look like this:

Listing 11-10. Person class Fields

```
public class Person
{
  private long _ID = 0;
  private string _FirstName = string.Empty;
  private string _LastName = string.Empty;
  private DateTime _DOB = DateTime.MinValue;
}
```

By right-clicking one of the fields you can select "Quick Actions…" followed by "Encapsulate field". This will generate the property code for that field below your field list, assuming you group your fields in the same location as demonstrated in the example. If you prefer using keyboard short-cuts, and you are using the C# Visual Studio settings, you could type Ctrl+R, E (for refactor, encapsulate field). In fact, the context menu for this operation in earlier versions of Visual Studio was called "Refactor" not "Quick Actions…". Alternatively, you can select all of the fields simultaneously and perform the same action which will generate all of the properties in one quick operation. All that is left to do is add any additional logic in the accessors and mutators as required by the business logic of your application. Yet another clear demonstration of the power of a real IDE instead of a simple text editor…

Automatic Properties

Sometimes the fields of a class may not require any logic or bounds checking and the properties used to encapsulate them are present only to assign and return the field's value. In this case it may be very tempting to bypass the property altogether and revert back to a field. Due to the reason mentioned previously, such as data binding and binary compatibility, please do not succumb to this temptation. Instead, consider using something called an automatic property, or auto-prop for short.

An automatic property completely does away with the need for a backing field as one will be created by the compiler when the code is compiled. Your code will not have any knowledge or access to this auto-generated backing field so it must interact exclusively with the property. The syntax for a basic auto-prop is:

```
<access> <type> <Name> { get; set; }
```

Assuming a Person class requires a *MiddleName* value, it could be implemented with the following code:

```
public string MiddleName { get; set; }
```

Since an automatic property does not allow custom logic in either the accessor or mutator this property will truly behave as if it were simply a field. If, later in the development cycle, it is determined that custom logic is required, then a backing field can be added to the class and this property can be exchanged with a regular property without any threat to backwards compatibility.

What about default values for automatic properties? The good news is that C# 6.0 and higher support default value assignments without requiring explicit assignments in the constructors using automatic property initializers. The syntax remains mostly the same, with the exception of the assignment of the default value and a semicolon.

```
<access> <type> <Name> { get; set; } = <default value>;
```

The default value can be a constant, literal or a static value. So, if the *MiddleName* property should not be null by default it could be changed to the following:

```
public string MiddleName { get; set; } = string.Empty;
```

What if the requirements state that the *MiddleName* property can never be changed by code outside of the Person class? In this case the mutuator (set) statement can be set to a different access modifier, like private, as such:

```
public string MiddleName { get; private set; } = string.Empty;
```

Now, the *MiddleName* property can be accessed for reading purposes from anywhere in the code, but the mutator is strictly off-limits to any code outside of the Person class.

What if you wish to restrict access to the mutator everywhere, including from within the Person class as well? Then, you can completely remove the set keyword, and thus the mutator. So, once the constructor of the class has completed executing the value can no longer be changed.

```
public string MiddleName { get; } = string.Empty;
```

The value of *MiddleName* must either be set using an automatic property initializer or must be set in one of the constructors. In essence, this technique works very much like a field with the "readonly" modifier applied to it, making it immutable.

Typically, a class will contain a mix of traditional properties and automatic properties, using traditional properties when custom logic is required and auto-props when they need to behave like fields. The following code demonstrates how they work side-by-side. Also, notice the use of code regions (#region and #endregion) to group similar code together.

Listing 11-11. Properties and Automatic Properties

```
public class Person
{
  #region Fields
  private string _FirstName = string.Empty;
  private string _LastName = string.Empty;
  private DateTime _DOB = DateTime.MinValue;
  #endregion Fields

  #region Properties
  // Auto-properties
  public ulong ID { get; } = 0;
  public string MiddleName { get; set; } = string.Empty;

  // Traditional properties
  public string FirstName
  {
    get { return _FirstName; }
    set
    {
      _FirstName = ValidateStringNonEmpty(value, "FirstName");
    }
  }

  public string LastName
  {
    get { return _LastName;   }
    set
    {
      _LastName = ValidateStringNonEmpty(value, "LastName");
    }
  }

  public DateTime DOB
  {
    get { return _DOB; }
    set
    {
      if (value <= DateTime.Now)
      {
        _DOB = value;
      }
      else
      {
        throw new Exception("DOB cannot be a future date.");
      }
    }
  }
  #endregion Properties
```

```
  #region Constructors
  public Person(ulong id, string lastName, string firstName, string middleName, DateTime dob)
  {
    ID = id;
    LastName = lastName;
    FirstName = firstName;
    MiddleName = middleName;
    DOB = dob;
  }
  #endregion Constructors

  #region Methods
  private static string ValidateStringNonEmpty(string value, string propName)
  {
    if (!string.IsNullOrEmpty(value))
    {
      return value;
    }
    throw new ArgumentNullException("value", $"{propName} cannot be empty");
  }
  #endregion Methods
}
```

First, notice that the *ID* and *MiddleName* properties are auto-props and that *ID* is further restricted as an immutable value since only get is defined. In fact, other than the default value 0 that is assigned in its initializer, the only time *ID* can be modified is in the constructor. Here's what Visual Studio shows if an attempt is made to modify *ID* on a Person object:

```
Person p = new Person(123456789, "John", "Doe", "Q", new DateTime(1960, 11, 12));
p.ID = 5;
```

ulong Person.ID { get; }

Property or indexer 'Person.ID' cannot be assigned to -- it is read only

Figure 11-4. Attempt to Change Read-only Auto Property Value

A method called ValidateStringNonEmpty() was created to provide a common method for the *FirstName* and *LastName* mutators to validate their incoming *value* parameter. This eliminates duplicate statements and simplifies the code. If the *value* parameter is non-empty then this method simply returns the value and it is assigned to the appropriate field. Otherwise, an exception is thrown using the second parameter, *propName*, as part of the exception's message.

The DOB property does not allow birthdays in the future, so if a future date is passed to this property an exception is thrown. Since there is only one property that requires this logic, a separate method was not created to do the validation. Sometimes, adding extra methods to encapsulate logic, a form of refactoring, is not warranted if the resulting changes do not enhance the reliability or readability of the code.

Non-Encapsulating Properties

Although it is most common for a property encapsulate a particular field, it is not always necessary. In fact, a property may govern many fields simultaneously or none at all. Consider a Fraction class with the following design:

Fraction
- _Numerator : int = 0
- _Denominator : int = 0
+ Fraction (numerator : int, denominator : int)
+ get_Numerator () : int
+ set_Numerator (value : int)
+ get_Denominator () : int
+ set_Denominator (value : int)
+ get_Mixed () : string

Remember, properties are really methods in the code; therefore, they are typically modeled in UML as separate "get_" and "set_" methods. With that knowledge, it is clear that there are *Numerator* and *Denominator* properties governing the *_Numerator* and *_Denominator* fields, respectively. But, there is one extra read-only property hanging out at the end, called *Mixed*. In this case, the *Mixed* property, which only has a `get` accessor, is used to return the fraction in mixed fraction form. So, if *Numerator* contains 5 and *Denominator* contains 4, *Mixed* should return "`1 1/4`". Sometimes, a property such as this is also known as a "helper" property.

Another helper property could be a *FullName* property that creates a formatted `string` containing the values of the *FirstName*, *MiddleName* and *LastName* properties of a Person `class` object.

Properties and structs

Since the `class` and `struct` types are so closely related you may be wondering if properties can be used within `struct` types as well. The short answer is yes, they can be used in very much the exact same manner in `struct`s. However, there are some caveats which you should be aware of prior to changing all of your `struct` types to use properties instead of `public` fields.

- The constructor of a `struct` requires all fields to assigned to prior to completion. In a `class` constructor it is recommended to utilize the properties to assign initial values for the backing fields. So, to follow the same pattern in a `struct` constructor, the fields would first need to be assigned "dummy" values prior to calling the mutators.
- The `struct` type is designed to be lightweight and fast. Properties are almost always slower to access than fields since they are actually methods.
- `struct` types are typically intended to be immutable making the inclusion of a custom mutator encapsulating a field unnecessary.

11.5 Static Members, Instance Members and "this"

Just like with `struct`s, members of a `class` can be instance members or `static` members. Instance members belong to a specific instance of a `class` while `static` members belong to the `class` itself. In fact, each `static` field in a `class` (or `struct`) is created in memory only once but each instance field has memory allocated for each object created.

From within an instance member of a `class`, any other member of the `class`, `static` or instance, can be accessed via that member's name without any handle (prefix). However, inside a `static` member, only other `static` members can be accessed directly – instance members are completely off-limits. The reason for this is "instance ambiguity" from within a `static` member. Since there is only one memory space for all `static` members, there is no confusion as to which memory location is being accessed regardless of whether the call is being made from an instance or `static` member. However, since there can be many instances of a `class` (or none) there is no way for a `static` member to know which one to access.

Externally, all `static` members of a `class` are accessed via a handle, or prefix, using the `class`'s name followed by a dot "`.`" operator, then the member's name. Instance members can only be accessed via an instance, or variable, of the `class` type. It is not legal to access a `static` member via an instance handle nor is it legal to access an instance member via the `class` handle. The following code contains a "dummy" `class` that demonstrates the scope and visibility of instance and `static` members.

Listing 11-12. Static and Instance Members

```
public class TestClass
{
  public static int StaticNum1 = 0;
  public static int StaticNum2 = 0;
  public int InstanceNum1 = 0;
  public int InstanceNum2 = 0;

  public static void StaticMethod1()
  {
    // Only the following can be accessed here:
    StaticNum1++;
    StaticNum2++;
    StaticMethod2();
  }

  public static void StaticMethod2() { /* No-op */ }

  public void InstanceMethod1()
  {
    // The following can be accessed here:
    StaticNum1++;
    StaticNum2++;
    StaticMethod1();
    StaticMethod2();
    InstanceNum1++;
    InstanceNum2++;
    InstanceMethod2();
  }

  public void InstanceMethod2() { /* No-op */ }
}

```

```
static void Main(string[] args)
{
  TestClass.StaticNum1++;
  TestClass.StaticNum2++;
  TestClass.StaticMethod1();
  TestClass.StaticMethod2();

  TestClass test = new TestClass();
  test.InstanceNum1++;
  test.InstanceNum2++;
  test.InstanceMethod1();
  test.InstanceMethod2();
}
```

As this code demonstrates, `static` members can only access other `static` members. Instance members, on the other hand, can access all members regardless of their instancing type. Externally, from Main(), the `static` members can only be called using the "TestClass." handle. The instance members require a variable of type TestClass to access them.

What happens when there is a naming conflict in the `class` such that a field is hidden by a variable or parameter using the same name as the field? If the hidden field is `static` then the method could access that field using the `class`'s name as a handle. In essence, the `class` name handle forces the compiler to look at the `class`-level scope instead of the local scope to find the field. When the hidden field is an instance field, however, the `class` name cannot be used as a handle to access it. Instead, there is a special keyword, "`this`", which can be used as a handle to access instance members. Just as the `class` name handle forces the compiler to search the class-level scope to find the `static` field, "`this.`" tells the compiler to search the `class`-level scope for an instance field of that name.

Listing 11-13. Disambiguating Member Access

```
public class Ambiguous
{
  private static int number1 = 0;
  private int number2 = 0;

  public void TestMethod(int number1)
  {
    int number2 = 0;

    // This modifies the parameter, number1:
    number1++;
    // This modifies the local variable, number2:
    number2++;
    // This modifies the static field, number1:
    Ambiguous.number1++;
    // This modifies the instance field, number2:
    this.number2++;
  }
}
```

If there is no conflict between the names of local variables and `class` fields then the use of these handles is superfluous. Some programmers prefer to always use handles as it shows the scope of the items being called without having to determine their scope by finding the items' declarations. Some programmers will use the handles only when necessary to disambiguate between items with the same names in different scopes. Like all other programming style guidelines, just be consistent.

11.6 Static Classes

One of the features missing from C# that many programmers miss when moving from another language is the concept of global methods and variables. It surely can be convenient to have data and methods accessible and shared by all of the code in a project. The good news is there is a way to emulate this capability using a `static class`.

Recall that `static` members are stored in memory only once regardless of how many instances of that type are created. That implies that any code in a project that can see the `class` with the static member can access that member as well (assuming the access modifier on that member permits it). We can take this concept one step further and ensure that all members of that class are marked static. With all members static, there is never any reason to create an instance of that class, so C# allows us to mark the entire class as static. It should come as no surprise that the Console class, which we've used practically from the beginning, is a static class. There is no way to create an instance of Console due to its static nature. Don't believe me? Type this code in one of your Main() methods and see what happens, I'll wait:

```
Console console = new Console();
```

Most likely the compiler gave you two errors:

- Cannot declare a variable of static type 'Console'
- Cannot create an instance of the static class 'Console'

So, the only way to use Console is to access its members using "Console." when its services are required. Console is comprised of several methods and properties, but no public fields. It is common for classes to have only public properties, encapsulating its private fields - even static classes.

Let's use what we know to create a static class that can be used to store values and methods of a mathematical nature.

Listing 11-14. Static Class

```
public static class GlobalMath
{
  #region Fields and Constants
  public const double PI = 3.14159265358979;
  public const double E = 2.718281828459;

  private static List<double> _SampleData;
  #endregion Fields and Constants

  #region Properties
  public static List<double> SampleData
  {
    get { return _SampleData; }
    set
    {
      if (value != null)
      {
        _SampleData = value;
      }
      else
      {
        throw new ArgumentNullException();
      }
    }
  }
  #endregion Properties

  #region Constructors
  static GlobalMath()
  {
    SampleData = new List<double>();
  }
  #endregion Constructors

  #region Methods
  public static void AddSamples(params double[] values)
  {
    SampleData.AddRange(values);
  }

  public static double GetAverage()
  {
    return SampleData.Average();
  }

```

```
  public static double GetMedian()
  {
    var sorted = new List<double>(SampleData);
    sorted.Sort();
    if (sorted.Count > 0)
    {
      return sorted[sorted.Count / 2];
    }
    return 0;
  }

  public static double Logarithm(double value, double logBase = E)
  {
    return Math.Log(value) / Math.Log(logBase);
  }

  public static double CircleArea(double radius)
  {
    return PI * radius * radius;
  }
  #endregion Methods
}
```

Listing 11-15. Testing GlobalMath Class

```
static void Main(string[] args)
{
  double log = GlobalMath.Logarithm(128, 2);
  double area = GlobalMath.CircleArea(10.5);

  GlobalMath.AddSamples(2.1, 3.5, 3.5, 6.8, 1.4, 5.2, 4.2);
  double average = GlobalMath.GetAverage();
  double median = GlobalMath.GetMedian();
}
```

All of the items in GlobalMath are either `static` or `const`. Because of their singular nature, `const` values are treated as `static` by the compiler so there is no compiler error. The *PI* and *E* constants are straight-forward; and, because they are declared `public` they can be used in other parts of the program as needed. The Logartihm() and CircleArea() methods are also fairly obvious in their implementations, although the logarithm logic is a bit complicated. However, this is a C# class not a math class, so just assume the method does what it should. Finally, we have the statistics members: *StaticData*, AddSamples(), GetAverage() and GetMedian(). Each of these statistical methods works with the *SampleData* list which is the property that encapsulates the *_SampleData* field. Data can be added to the list using AddSamples() which accepts an unlimited number of doubles due to its use of a parameter array. Alternatively, items could be added directly to GlobalMath.*SampleData* as follows:

```
GlobalMath.SampleData.Add(3.45);
```

Another new concept in this example is GlobalMath's constructor. Notice that is also marked `static` like all the other methods in the `class`. Wait, what?!? If we cannot create an instance of GlobalMath, how in the world can there be any need for a constructor? This is a special constructor, known unsurprisingly as a `static` constructor. This constructor is automatically called when the first request is made to GlobalMath, which is on line 3 of Main() in the example. As demonstrated, this is the perfect place to initialize fields (via properties, of course) and get the `class` ready for use. Since there is no way to call it directly, this constructor is also assumed to be parameterless.

In C#, we don't have global variables, but we do have `static` classes. The nice thing about C#'s approach is that the global data and methods can be grouped together logically by their usage. So, if an application requires global data to keep track of orders, they would definitely not belong in GlobalMath, but in another `class`, maybe GlobalOrders. By the way, the "Global" prefix is not a requirement or a standard but it does clearly identify its purpose to users.

11.7 Indexer Properties

An indexer is a special type of property to access data in an object using an index that identifies a specific item. Indexers are most commonly associated with array and collection types, such as List<T>. The index value is typically of type `int`, corresponding to the item's 0-based position in the list. However, any data type can be used as an index value and can represent something other than the item's location. Essentially, the index represents a unique key to an element in the collection data. Consider a collection of person objects where it is necessary to retrieve a specific item from the collection by a person's identification number or their last name. In this case, there would be two indexers, one that accesses elements by `int` and the other by `string`.

An indexer is accessed on an object by using the "`[<index>]`" operator, where `<index>` is the index of the element being sought. Indexers, like regular properties, can be designed to support both read and write operations, or just one of the operations, depending on requirements. The name of an indexer property is always "`this`", representing yet another use of that keyword. Typically, a `class` that possesses an indexer contains a collection of some type and the indexer is used to find elements in that collection. The following is the formal syntax for an indexer property:

```
<access> <item type> this[<index type> index]
{
   get
   {
      // Returns the item with index of index
   }
   [<access>] set
   {
      // Assigns value to the element with index of index
   }
}
```

Much of the syntax of an indexer is similar to that of a standard property.

The <access> modifier applies to both the accessor and mutator, but the mutator can override this setting with its own, optional <access> modifier just prior to the set keyword.

<item type> represents the type of element in the collection being retrieved or assigned.

All indexers must be named "this" as mentioned previously.

Inside the mandatory square brackets is the data type for the index used to identify an element in the collection (<index type>). The name of the index parameter is *index* in this example but it can be whatever name makes the most sense for the indexer.

The accessor (get block) is responsible for finding an item represented by *index* and returning that value. In the event that no item can be found matching *index* then an exception, typically an IndexOutOfRangeException should be thrown.

The mutator (set block) is responsible for finding the item in the collection with the given *index* value. For your information, both the accessor and mutator use the same index parameter name. Then, the mutator assigns value to the location specified by *index*. In the event that the element associated with *index* is not found, it is up to the programmer to decide if that warrants throwing an exception or adding a new item with that *index* and value.

Like any code that accesses items in a collection, care must be taken to avoid accessing elements outside the bounds of the collection. This is most important when emulating the standard indexer of ordered collections, like arrays and List<T>. If the caller requests an item with an invalid index it is up to you to decide if you want to throw your own exception or just let the CLR do it when the code attempts to retrieve the item. Since the most logical exception to throw would be an IndexOutOfRangeException you might as well just let the CLR do it for you as that will be the exception it throws. Alternatively, you can also be proactive and detect these indexing errors and perform some other code that doesn't require exceptions, such as returning null from the accessor.

The following example, Listing 11-16, creates a simple data class called Person which contains three automatic properties and a single constructor. Another class, called PersonList, contains a field called *_People* that is of type List<Person>. Rather than directly expose this collection using a property, two indexers manage access to its data. The first indexer simply wraps the default indexer supplied by List<Person>, using the *index* parameter and value to make indexer calls into *_People*. The second indexer is far more involved as it accepts an index of type string called *lastName*. As it implies, the accessor and mutator will search for a Person element that shares the same *LastName* property value as *lastName*. In the event that the accessor cannot find a matching element it will throw an exception. The mutator will not throw an exception if the item is not found, instead it adds value as a new item in the list.

Did you catch the downside to this logic? Due to the way the second indexer's mutator searches for and adds items, only one person with a given last name can exist at any one time in the list. Clearly not production-worthy, but it does walk you through the logic of finding an item in a collection by using something other than its position.

Listing 11-16. Indexer Demo

```
public class Person
{
  public long ID { get; set; }
  public string LastName{ get; set; }
  public string FirstName { get; set; }

  public Person(long id, string lastName, string firstName)
  {
    ID = id;
    LastName = lastName;
    FirstName = firstName;
  }
}

public class PersonList
{
  private List<Person> _People = new List<Person>();

  // Access items in _People by position. Mimic default indexer of _People.
  public Person this[int index]
  {
    get
    {
      return _People[index];
    }
    set
    {
      _People[index] = value;
    }
  }

  // Access items in _People by last name.
  public Person this[string lastName]
  {
    get
    {
      // Find and return the item
      foreach (Person p in _People)
      {
        if (p.LastName == lastName)
        {
          return p;
        }
      }
      throw new ArgumentOutOfRangeException();
    }
    set
    {
      // Find location of the item
      int index = -1;
      for (int i = 0; i < _People.Count; ++i)
```

```
      {
        if (_People[i].LastName == lastName)
        {
          index = i;
          break;
        }
      }
      if (index != -1)
      {
        // Found item in list, replace it with value
        _People[index] = value;
      }
      else
      {
        // Item not found, add a new one
        _People.Add(value);
      }
    }
  }

  public void Print()
  {
    Console.WriteLine($"======== People: {_People.Count} ========");
    foreach (Person p in _People)
    {
      Console.WriteLine($"{p.ID:000-00-0000} {p.LastName,-15} {p.FirstName,-10}");
    }
    Console.WriteLine();
  }
}
```

Listing 11-17. Testing PersonList

```
static void Main(string[] args)
{
  PersonList people = new PersonList();
  Person p = new Person(123456789, "Doe", "Jane");
  people["Doe"] = p;
  people.Print();
  p = new Person(654987321, "Deer", "Bill");
  people["Deer"] = p;
  people.Print();
  p = new Person(564323154, "Doe", "John");
  people["Doe"] = p;
  people.Print();
  p = people["Doe"];
  p = people[0];
  Console.WriteLine($"p: {p.ID:000-00-0000} {p.LastName,-15} {p.FirstName,-10}");
  Console.WriteLine($"p: {p.ID:000-00-0000} {p.LastName,-15} {p.FirstName,-10}");
}
```

```
======== People: 1 ========
123-45-6789 Doe          Jane

======== People: 2 ========
123-45-6789 Doe          Jane
654-98-7321 Deer         Bill

======== People: 2 ========
564-32-3154 Doe          John
654-98-7321 Deer         Bill

p: 564-32-3154 Doe          John
p: 564-32-3154 Doe          John
```

Figure 11-5. PersonList Test Output

In the test driver, three Person objects are added to the PersonList object *people* by using the indexer that accepts a `string`. The call on line 11 forces the original object with the *LastName* of "Doe" out of the list in favor for the new item. The output demonstrates that change. The accessors for two indexers are demonstrated on the last lines of the test.

11.8 Object Initializer

Occasionally you'll come across a `class` that has only a parameterless constructor but the `class` also contains many properties to initialize. The following `class` demonstrates this scenario:

Listing 11-18. Class without Parameterized Constructor

```
public class Person
{
  public long ID { get; set; }
  public string LastName{ get; set; }
  public string FirstName { get; set; }
}
```

A Person object can be created an initialized with the following code:

Listing 11-19. Creating and Initializing a Person Object

```
Person p = new Person();
p.ID = 123456789;
p.LastName = "Doe";
p.FirstName = "John";
```

There is absolutely nothing wrong with this code; however, it is treated as 4 separate statements. If there was a constructor that accepted all the parameters required to initialize the `class` completely that would only be 1 statement. Again, this is not a serious problem, unless you wanted to create the object and use it in the same statement, such as passing the object to a function. C# provides a specialized constructor initialization scheme that can reduce the code in Listing 11-19 to 1 statement.

Listing 11-20. Object Initializer Example

```
Person p = new Person
{
  ID = 123456789,
  LastName = "Doe",
  FirstName = "John"
};
```

The default Person constructor is called, but the parenthesis are omitted. Instead, a code block with curly braces is opened. Inside this block the properties of *p* are assigned, but notice the "`p.`" handle is not required as the context of this code block is the *p* object itself. Not all properties require assignment and each property can be assigned to only once. Which properties the code elects to initialize, and the order, is entirely dependent on the business rules of the `class`. Also, the individual assignments are separated by commas, not semicolons.

If the default constructor is not supplied by the `class`, this technique can still be applied to any parameterized constructor as well. If Person contained this additional constructor:

Listing 11-21. Parameterized Person Constructor

```
public Person(long id)
{
  ID = id;
}
```

then an object could be initialized using the following:

Listing 11-22. Object Initializer Using Parameterized Constructor

```
Person p2 = new Person(123456789)
{
  LastName = "Doe",
  FirstName = "Jane"
};
```

So, why would we elect to use this style of constructor? Functional programming techniques require object initializers, but that's a bit beyond the level of complexity we're going to address here. However, there are other very practical uses of object initializers, such as populating a list. If you wanted to create a List<Person> and populate that list in a single statement, object initializers are the easiest way to accomplish that goal:

Listing 11-23. Creating and Populating a List in One Statement

```
List<Person> people = new List<Person>()
{
  new Person { ID = 123, LastName = "Doe", FirstName = "John" },
  new Person { ID = 456, LastName = "Doe", FirstName = "Jane" },
  new Person { ID = 789, LastName = "Smith", FirstName = "Bill" }
};
```

11.9 Namespaces and the using Clause

The `namespace` keyword is ubiquitous in all C# programs. All `class`, `struct` and `enum` types must belong to a `namespace` for compilation to succeed. But, what exactly is a `namespace`? A `namespace` is used to organize types into named units. By default, the `namespace` name for a new type in a project will be the project's name. So, if you have a project called "HelloWorld", all C# files created in that project will have the following `namespace` declaration, with some `class`, `struct` or `enum` defined within:

Listing 11-24. namespace Declaration

```
namespace HelloWorld
{
  class Program
  {
    static void Main(string[] args)
    {
      Console.WriteLine("Hello world!");
    }
  }
}
```

Therefore, the fully qualified name for the Program `class` is actually HelloWorld.Program. You typically never use the fully qualified name since all of the other types in the project will be part of the same `namespace` making the "`<namespace>.`" handle superfluous.

So, why is this `namespace` step necessary? Let's say Microsoft also created a `class` called Program somewhere in the BCL. How could you possibly tell them apart? That's what the `namespace` is for. It is likely that a BCL type would be in the System `namespace`, or some descendant of System, like System.Collections. Therefore, Microsoft's type would have the fully qualified name System.Program, whereas yours might be HelloWorld.Program. In a way, a `namespace` acts like a folder and the types defined within the `namespace` are papers in that folder. Again, it all comes back to organization.

What if you wanted to change the default `namespace` for newly added types? Click on the "Project" menu followed by "<Project Name> Properties…". In the Application tab, there is a "Default namespace:" textbox that indicates the `namespace` to use when adding a new file to the project.

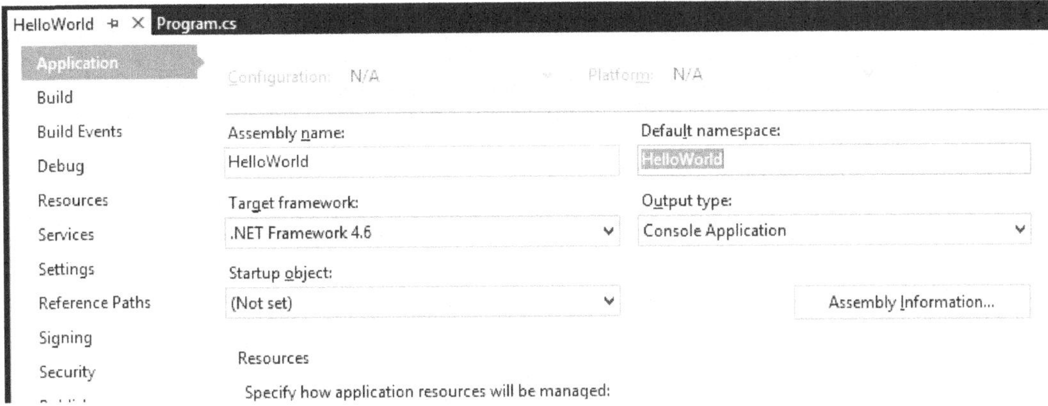

Figure 11-6. Changing the Default Namespace

Changing this value has no effect on existing files in the project, but any new C# code file will use the `namespace` indicated in that field.

Nested Folders and Namespaces

As you may recall, the Solution Explorer in Visual Studio displays the physical layout of solutions and projects. Typically, a solution (*.sln file) belongs to the parent folder and all projects (*.csproj files) belong to subfolders inside the parent. If the solution contains only one project then it is also common to see both the solution and project coresident in the same folder. Inside each project folder it is also possible to create subfolders to help organize code. For instance, if the project contains files pertaining to the user interface, business logic and data storage, it may be appropriate to segregate the files logically into different folders. So, the project may look like this in Solution Explorer:

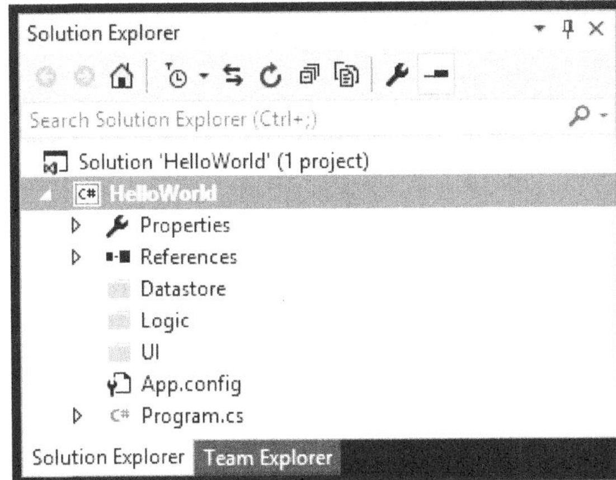

Figure 11-7. Solution Explorer Folders

Note: Folders can be added to a project by right-clicking on the project name and selecting "Add" followed by "New Folder".

So, what happens when a `class` is added to one of the new folders? By right-clicking on the "UI" folder and selecting "Add" then "Class", then typing in "TestClass" for the `class` name, the following file is generated:

Listing 11-25. Adding a class to a Subfolder

```
using System;
using System.Collections.Generic;
using System.Linq;
using System.Text;
using System.Threading.Tasks;

namespace HelloWorld.UI
{
  class TestClass
  {
  }
}
```

Notice anything peculiar about the `namespace`? Automatically, ".UI" was appended to its name, which corresponds to the folder where the file resides. As you can probably guess, any additional subfolders would yield additional dot separators and subfolder names. Therefore, the fully qualified name for TestClass is actually HelloWorld.UI.TestClass. Of course, if you prefer to have the `namespace` not include the folder name you can always manually change it.

The using Clause

The previous example actually presents somewhat of a problem if you attempt to use TestClass from within Program's Main() method:

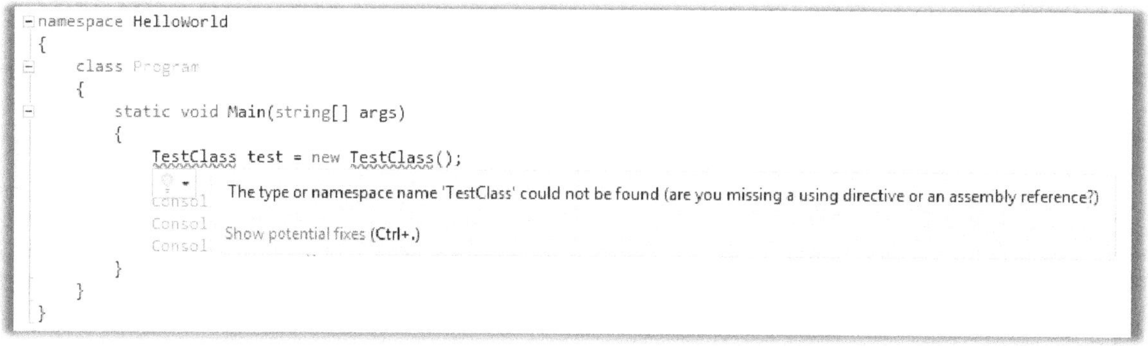

```
namespace HelloWorld
{
    class Program
    {
        static void Main(string[] args)
        {
            TestClass test = new TestClass();
            Consol   The type or namespace name 'TestClass' could not be found (are you missing a using directive or an assembly reference?)
            Consol   Show potential fixes (Ctrl+.)
            Consol
        }
    }
}
```

Figure 11-8. Error Using Class in Different Namespace

IntelliSense is warning us that TestClass cannot be found. Why is this? Remember, Program is contained within the HelloWorld namespace, but TestClass is contained within HelloWorld.UI. Any code within Main() can only "see" the types declared within the local namespace, HelloWorld. You could use the fully qualified name instead, such as:

```
HelloWorld.UI.TestClass test = new HelloWorld.UI.TestClass();
```

However, there is a much simpler mechanism for dealing with namespaces that will save a lot of typing: the using clause. A using clause, also known as a using directive, gives the compiler a hint where to look for type names when compiling. So, instead of prepending the namespace to each reference of TestClass in Program, a single using clause can be added at the top of the file and the compiler will be abe to find TestClass whenever the name is encountered.

Listing 11-26. Adding a using Clause

```
using HelloWorld.UI;
using System;

namespace HelloWorld
{
  class Program
  {
    static void Main(string[] args)
    {
      TestClass test = new TestClass();
      Console.WriteLine("Hello World!");
      Console.Write("Press <ENTER> to quit...");
      Console.ReadLine();
    }
  }
}
```

By the way, starting with the code shown in Figure 11-8, you can have Visual Studio add the using clause for you. On one of the TestClass names with the red underscore, right-click and select "Quick Actions..." then select "using HelloWorld.UI;". Alternatively, you can type Ctrl+. while the cursor is on one of the "TestClass" names to bring up the Quick Actions menu list.

Namespace Collisions and Aliases

What happens if the code contains two using clauses identifying two namespaces and each of these namespaces contains a class called TestClass. IntelliSense will once again complain, but this time because the name "TestClass" is ambiguous. So, assuming there is a class called TestClass in the Logic folder and there is a using clause for both HelloWorld.UI and HelloWorld.Logic, then there is no way to create a TestClass object in Main() without first giving the compiler more information so it knows which one to pick. We could, of course, revert to using fully qualified names, but there is a much simpler way out of this problem - use an alias to identify one or both of the offending using clauses.

Listing 11-27. Namespace Aliases

```
using hwui = HelloWorld.UI;
using hwl = HelloWorld.Logic;
using System;

namespace HelloWorld
{
  class Program
  {
    static void Main(string[] args)
    {
      hwl.TestClass test = new hwl.TestClass();
    }
  }
}
```

Now, whenever you need to reference TestClass from HelloWorld.UI you can use the prefix "hwui.". Likewise, the "hwl." prefix is used to reference TestClass contained within HelloWorld.Logic. The names given to each alias are completely at your discretion. In this case they were assembled from the first letter of each word in the namespace name. Yes, you must still use a prefix to access the types, but "hwl." is far shorter than "HelloWorld.Logic.".

Static Classes, Enums and the using static Clause

In C# 6, a new feature was added to the language to simplify the use of `static class` members and `enum` values. By placing the `namespace` AND the `static class` or `enum` name in a `using static` clause the members of those entities can be accessed without a prefix. Assume there is an `enum` with the following definition in the project within the HelloWorld `namespace`:

Listing 11-28. Enum Definition

```
[Flags]
public enum FontStyles
{
  Normal = 0, Bold = 1, Italics = 2, Underline = 4
}
```

Then, normally, to use a value from this `enum` would require the "FontStyles." prefix, such as:

```
FontStyles fs = FontStyles.Bold;
```

However, by adding the following `using` clause to the top of the file where you wish to use FontStyles, the use of the prefix becomes unnecessary:

```
using static HelloWorld.FontStyles;
```

Now, the statement assigning a value to *fs* can be rewritten as:

```
FontStyles fs = Bold;
```

Notice the use of the "`static`" keyword after `using`. This simply informs the compiler that the item is not a namespace but a `static class` or `enum`. So, if you wanted to do the same trick with a `static class` such as Console, you could add the following `using` clause:

```
using static System.Console;
```

Now, a call to Console.WriteLine() can be made without the "Console." prefix, such as:

```
WriteLine(fs);
```

Care should be taken when using this technique because while it makes the code more compact it can hide some of the meaning that is conveyed when the prefixes are present.

I love the "`using static`" clause, especially for things like `enums`, the System.Math and System.Console classes. However, I try to limit my use of this clause when working with my own custom types as their names and usage are not as obvious as the core BCL types. Within this book and examples, I refrain from using this technique as much as possible to limit confusion.

11.10 Summary

The `class` and `struct` types together form the backbone of object-oriented programing in C#. A `struct` is a lightweight value type, while a `class` is a more versatile reference type which allows for larger objects. Both types are designed to represent an abstract concept that contains like data and the methods to manipulate that data. Only members that logically belong to a type (fields, properties and methods) should actually be a part of that type.

Properties provide a mechanism to encapsulate the fields of a `class`. Accessors, represented by the `get` block of a property, provide read access to the `class` fields while mutators, represented by the `set` block of a property, provide write access to the fields. These specialized methods are accessed like fields but allow more granular control over the soundness of the values based on the business logic defined for the `class`. Properties are the projection of business logic in a `class`. Properties can also be used to encapsulate multiple fields or no fields at all.

Classes can contain instance and `static` members. Each `class` instance (a.k.a. object or variable) allocates memory for each instance field it possesses. The set of fields for an instance is unique to that instance and represents a single entity. The `static` members, on the other hand, do not belong to any instance of a `class`. Instead, they belong directly to the `class` itself. Due to this behavior, only one copy of each `static` field is ever contained in memory. Instance members are always accessed externally by using the instance object's handle while the `static` members are accessed via the `class` name's handle. A `class` can be marked `static` to provide global variable emulation.

Indexers are specialized properties that provide access to collection data within a `class`. Indexers can be defined to use not only the `int` position of elements in the data like arrays but any other data type that represents a unique key for elements in the collection.

Object initializer syntax provides an alternate mechanism for creating objects in a single statement when an appropriate constructor is not available. This technique is invaluable when using advanced functional programming techniques which are a bit advanced to be discussed at this point.

Finally, `namespace`s help organize code into logical "folders" preventing conflict with similarly named types in other `namespace`s. By default, `namespace`s are named after the project they are contained within, and files nested within subfolders will adopt the subfolder names as part of the `namespace` name. The `using` clause simplifies the use of types contained within a `namespace` so the fully qualified name of a type does not need to be present in code whenever a type is used.

Looking Ahead...

The concepts reviewed up to this point represent the foundation of programming with C#. Mastering these concepts is an essential step on the way to becoming a competent programmer. Future topics, such as inheritance, polymorphism, generics and multi-threaded programming, all build upon these concepts so take the time to review this material before moving forward. The trickiest part of programming is taking what you have learned and applying it to real-world problems.

Index

#

A

B

C

D

E

Made in the USA
Middletown, DE
25 September 2023